Women's Drug Use in Everyday Life

Emma Eleonorasdotter

Women's Drug Use in Everyday Life

palgrave
macmillan

Emma Eleonorasdotter
Humanistiska och teologiska fakulteterna
Lund University
Lund, Sweden

ISBN 978-3-031-46056-2   ISBN 978-3-031-46057-9   (eBook)
https://doi.org/10.1007/978-3-031-46057-9

Cover illustration: © Ekaterina Litvinova/Alamy Stock Photo

This Palgrave Macmillan imprint is published by the registered company Springer Nature Switzerland AG
The registered company address is: Gewerbestrasse 11, 6330 Cham, Switzerland

Paper in this product is recyclable.

To Cindy and Rita

Acknowledgements

First of all, I would like to thank the twelve brave women who shared their experiences with me. I strongly believe that many of your stories reveal important aspects of drug use that have not been studied before. Thank you for giving me this opportunity.

I would also like to thank my dear colleagues, most of all my previous supervisors Gabriella Nilsson and Karin Salomonsson, for making this study possible and for all the hours of reading, commenting and discussing my dissertation that have led to this book. The commitment you have shown has been an honour to experience. I also want to thank you Gabriella and Måns Weimarck for the problem solving that was crucial to the success of the book. Thanks also to the entire Department of Ethnology for all the inspiring conversations and seminars, and in the consumption node as well. A big thank you to Susanne Lundin and Lars-Eric Jönsson for your valuable readings and comments. To Rachel Irwin, Jessica Enevold, Jonas Bornsäter, Cecilia Andersson, Andréa Wiszmeg, Josefine Löndorf Sarkez-Knudsen, Talieh Mirsalehi, Helena Larsson, Anna Burstedt, Kasia Herd, Billy Jones, Simon Halberg, Jakob Löfgren, Raquel Garcia Plaza and Alma Aspeborg, I also direct a very warm thank you, for all your collegiality and support. Thank you Signe Bremer for your readings and your thoughtful and always power-sensitive input, and a massive thank you Evelina Liliequist for helpful reading at the last minute! Ellen Sunesson, thank you for our queer conversations, for wine and laughter and inspiration. Thank you Johan Edman, Michelle Addison and Elizabeth Ettorre for your works, and for readings and valuable comments, they meant a lot. Thank you Karin Westerberg for your brilliant contributions on all sorts of issues, not least in chemistry but also everything else. Thank you Julius von Wright for your help and input. Thank you Daniel Svensson at the National Board of Health and Welfare for quick responses and encouraging and engaging conversations. Thank you Niklas Eklund at Brukarföreningen in Stockholm for your commitment and generous, lightning-fast, tireless approach to drug issues at all levels. Thank you Johanna Ingemarsson for friendship and recurring input regarding legal issues and to Olle for your ability to make deciphering numbers and statistics a pleasure. I also want to direct a big thank you to all the librarians at LU and elsewhere who helped this project all the way through.

I'd like to thank my editor Josie Taylor at Palgrave for support and Liz Sourbut for rapid proofreading during the summer. I am also grateful to Anette Skårner, Malin Gunnarsson, Tuulia Lerkkanen, Aida Paridad, Maria Nordstedt, Björn Johnson, Elín Björk and Kristin Rotin, for inviting me to come and talk about my project and all the inspiration it has given me.

Thank you Professor Fiona Measham and Dr. Karenza Moore for your brilliant and inspiring work and for welcoming me to take part in the Loop, study your research in situ and discuss my topics of interest. The visit to Manchester was absolutely crucial for how my project evolved. Thank you Anders, Anna-Majje and Mantis for always trying to simplify and support! I can become overwhelmed by gratitude when I think of you. Thank you Lisa Svensson for all the dinners and trips, conversations and plans. Thank you Johanna Gustavsson for all the inspiration you've given me. Thanks also to Dorota, Ida, Nopa, Lisa P, Rodrigo, Lovisa, Linda, Mirre, Sofia, Paola, Blasi, Annalisa, Suus, Emmy and all of you who make life worth living.

Thank you Mana editorial team for always being a source of strength and smart thoughts and a counterforce to hopelessness. Thank you Sarah Katarina Hirani for your friendship, genius and the most beautiful illustrations. Thank you Pål Brunnström for being such a rock! For all the conversations and laughter and, yes, everything.

Paula Mulinari and Maja Sager, what would I have done without you?! All the fun, all the readings and just knowing there are two people who always make me feel there are things we have to do and that it will be great to do them. Your thoughts are the best gifts.

Lova, my teenage freedom fighter, I am again so grateful for the time you've given me to write, even though this meant I broke my promise and continued to be unbearably boring a lot of the time. I don't think you will like this book either, but I felt I had to do it. I love you so much and I am so proud to be your mum. Penny, my warmest thank you for being there with all your love and support and helpfulness. And thank you Puk and Ossian for being reminders of what is most important in life.

Contents

Part I

Contextualising the Women and the Drugs

1

Introduction

Over the past two decades, female drug users have moved from their "mad, sad or bad" marginal status, as addicts and substance abusers, out of control and/or needing control, to being mainstream consumers in society. (Measham 2002, p. 344)

In 2015, when I was a recently admitted doctoral student in ethnology at Lund University, Sweden, reading these words in English criminologist Fiona Measham's article "Doing gender – doing drugs" was puzzling. Thirteen years after they were written, I could not think of any instance of having heard or read in any public, Swedish context of women who use drugs who were not mad, sad or bad, or all of these at once. Neither had Katy, who is interviewed in this book, who says about cannabis:

[...] we'd all been taught how those things worked: a gateway to harder drugs and once you start, well, you'll end up on the streets. Or admitted to a psych ward.[1]

---

[1] All quotes in Swedish have been translated by me.

© The Author(s) 2024
E. Eleonorasdotter, *Women's Drug Use in Everyday Life*,
https://doi.org/10.1007/978-3-031-46057-9_1

While the normalisation of illegal drug use can be questioned (Duff 2020), the predictions that Katy describes are not necessarily accurate. Drugs are used by otherwise mainstream consumers as well as by non-mainstream consumers, and most of this use can be described as recreational (Schlag 2020). Cannabis legislation is "softening" around the world and research on psychedelics and other drugs previously understood as club drugs is thriving, which has positioned them in a different light (Heal et al. 2023). At the same time, drugs in the form of medicines are prescribed in continuously increasing quantities (OECD iLibrary 2021). The problems that can be related to drugs, in terms of madness, sadness and badness, are thus only one aspect of the role that they play in the world, including contemporary Sweden. Still, there is very little Swedish research on the everyday use of drugs. Who are the women who take the risk of dealing with stigmatised, mind-altering substances in a country that is striving to become drug-free (Regeringens skrivelse 2015/16:86)?

Measham finishes her article on the socio-cultural context of gender and drug use with the following words:

> Moving beyond the oppression/victimization–liberation/emancipation polarization, we can see that the multifaceted nature of [...] drugs cultures reflects the complexities of [...] accomplished femininities for female drug users: as "club babes", mothers, professionals, "good girls," "badass" street-wise women, and so forth. Thus for women, "doing gender" through "doing drugs" allows the possibility of both constructing and challenging traditional and nontraditional notions of femininity. (ibid., pp. 363–364)

How Measham exemplifies the complexity of femininity in multifaceted "drugs cultures" as represented by "'club babes', mothers, professionals, 'good girls', 'badass' street-wise women, and so forth" runs counter to stereotypes of drug-using women as miserable and crazy. Instead, it makes up a varying and unpredictable collection of everyday women "doing gender" through the ever-more-common act of using drugs. If approached with such openness to the possibilities of interpretation, as Measham's account shows, women who use drugs can be more than objects of research, they can also provide a window into contemporary living conditions and an understanding of the interplay between gender and mind-altering practices. In this book, twelve Swedish women's accounts of their drug use in everyday life—from parties to the city streets, at work and in the home—are investigated and given the spotlight. Their use of drugs is explored from an intersectional,[2] ethnological and queer phenomenological perspective, with particular attention being paid to gender and class. The meaning of contemporary drug use has a history that has shaped how drug use is understood in relation to different bodies and different societal positions. This book pays attention to that background (Part I) as well as to the current experiences of the interviewed women (Part II).

The discipline of ethnology studies the human as a cultural being, with a specific interest in local, meaning-making practices and how cultural meanings change over time. As will be explored in more detail in the next chapter, both drug use and the idea of the user of drugs have undergone fascinating changes in meaning over the last 75 years in Sweden (Tham 2021). Up until the mid-twentieth century, a person who used drugs was mainly understood as a low-key morphinist, representative of the middle class and probably a doctor. Any problems in dealing with the drugs were considered to be individual (Edman and Olsson 2014; Björkman 2002). In conjunction with the popularity and spread of amphetamine use in Sweden during the 1950s and 1960s, the image of the person who uses drugs transformed into that of a troublesome, criminal and/or bohemian amphetamine user. Rather quickly, this abuser of drugs, the *knarkare*,[3] developed into representing a major threat to society. They were a representative of a social problem that did not differentiate between what and how various illicit drugs were used, and was subject to the criminal law on drugs that was enacted in 1968 (Edman and Olsson 2014; Linton 2015). To counter the threat to society, Sweden employed strict policies

---

[2] An intersectional approach acknowledges how various forms of inequality operate together. It was coined by scholar of law and black feminism Kimberle Crenshaw (1989), in an article discussing the intersections of gender and race. The concept has thereafter inspired a vast body of literature on structural and systemic questions about all kinds of discrimination and inequality.

[3] Swedish word for a person who uses drugs, see Chapters 3 and 4.

and laws against drugs, and formulated a vision of a drug-free society, which is still an official political goal (Regeringens skrivelse 2015/16:86). Sweden is one of the few countries in the world in which the law criminalises the use of illicit drugs, and after prison sentences were included in the scale of possible sentences in 1993, the police were empowered to investigate bodily fluids based on the suspicion that drugs have been used. This is a practice that leads to several thousands of samples being tested every year, up to half of which show negative results (young people more commonly test negative than older people), and the practice has been criticised as intrusive (BRÅ 2018; Gynnå Oguz 2017).

Despite the relatively low numbers of people who are recognised as people who use drugs in Sweden, the idea of the *knarkare* has had a noticeable cultural and political impact on Swedish society (Linton 2015). This invites studies of meaning-making in relation to the person who uses drugs as a cultural being, from both an emic and an etic perspective. This is true for drugs and the people who use drugs in general, but the complexity of femininity highlighted by Measham, where oppression, victimisation, liberation and emancipation are all relevant topics in relation to the meaning of women's drug use, means that women who use drugs are in specifically interesting positions from a feminist point of view. The connotations of drug use connecting it to revolt, immorality, criminality, promiscuity and carelessness contrast with the classic feminine ideals of compliance, morality, obedience to the law, prudence and care just as much as they contrast with oppression and victimisation. On the other hand, addiction, understood as to be a slave to one's habits, and the vulnerable female positions that addiction to drugs connotes is the opposite of what feminism strives for. Considering this tension, why are people who use drugs not central figures in ethnological studies, and why are women who use drugs not central to feminist studies (Travis 2019; Chang 2020)?

One reason why people who use drugs can be missed by research that is focused on the human as a cultural being is the dehumanisation to which restrictive and stigmatising laws lead. Opioid replacement treatments, for example, have been strongly opposed, despite the knowledge that untreated opioid addiction often leads to death (Kakko 2017; Johnson 2005). The political struggles regarding syringe exchanges have been bitter and prolonged (e.g. Antoniusson et al. 2005) and, until a change in the law in 2017, they were very restrictive (Karlsson et al. 2020). Overdose prevention through Naloxone is another life-saving measure that has met with resistance (Eklund 2017). In short, it has been particularly dangerous to use drugs in Sweden because there has been no consensus that people who use them should be kept alive.

A number of researchers have criticised the reluctance to implement life-saving and harm-reducing measures (e.g. Heilig 2017; Richert 2017; Kakko 2011; Johnson 2005), and the high rates of casualties related to drug use have been used as an argument to revise policies (Ekendahl 2009). This has eventually led to an increasing focus on harm reduction, but at the same time political proposals continue in the direction of increases in penalties (Regeringens proposition 2022/23:53) and, according to historian Johan Edman (2021), not much has changed politically in the last 50 years.

This book has been written to counter the view of the woman who uses drugs as dehumanised by her drug use. It is a study of Swedish women who use drugs, considered as cultural beings, based on the notion that "women who use drugs are people", as an anonymous narcofeminist[4] activist puts it in an interview published in the Sociological Review (Bessonova et al. 2023, p. 755). This means a focus on how drugs and people who use drugs are entangled with social and intersectional factors such as class, gender and race. As we shall see, it is these factors, rather than the substances' pharmacological properties, that make the difference between a *"knarkare"* [Swedish, derogatory term for people who use drugs] and a "party girl", and are decisive in whether a drug will have the ability to add to artistic reputation or devalue human dignity.

---

[4] Narcofeminism is a movement founded by activists from Central Asia and Eastern Europe, and the term was coined in 2018. It is centered on the acknowledgement that resistance against repression and violence towards women who use drugs are feminist issues. It invites all women and relies on an intersectional analysis of power (Dennis et al. 2023).

1.1   Representations

When it comes to women who use drugs in Sweden, two distinguishable, polarised representations emerge, both in the media and in research. These end up being positioned to either side of the large majority of people who use drugs, who constitute an invisible grey zone in the space between (Rödner et al. 2007, p. 47). One representation is of celebrated artists, who actually do sometimes describe their use openly, without necessarily being marked as predominantly mad, sad or bad, but rather as extraordinary. Authors Agnes von Krusenstjerna (1894–1940) and Birgitta Stenberg (1932–2014) and contemporary pop star Tove Lo are examples of openness about drug use in this group. Their drug use is known, but they describe it, and it is described by others, as an interesting feature of otherwise elevated and respected lives. Agnes von Krusenstjerna is described in the historian of ideas Karin Johannisson's book *The Wounded Diva* (2015)[5] as consistently using morphine and other drugs in large quantities. "She sniffs ether, injects morphine, pumps in sleeping pills and tranquilizers. She is an upper-class woman in decline" writes Johannisson (ibid., p. 216). For page after page, she describes how von Krusenstjerna craves and acquires different types of drugs, especially morphine. Yet the detailed narrative is about her eventful life, her health and her prose. The use of drugs remains a side issue, both in Johannisson's book and in the general knowledge about von Krusenstjerna. As for Tove Lo, her most famous song is called *Stay High* (2014). It is a remix of the song *Habits* (2013), and is about how Lo has to stay constantly high, i.e. under the influence of drugs, to cope with being abandoned. In an interview, she said: "In Sweden, when you sing about drugs and numbing the pain, many people take offense and think it's irresponsible. But I'm not going to take that responsibility. I sing about my life, it's as simple as that" (Fahl 2014, n.p.). Tove Lo's life is thus affected by drugs, and this is a starting point she does not seek to hide. Major successes, both in Sweden and abroad, continue to mark the path of her career.

---

[5] *Den sårade divan* (2015).

For people in this group, drugs seem to function as integral parts of an experimental and luxurious lifestyle. Use may be perceived as "irresponsible" and the women may end up "in decline", but the choice to consume drugs does not take over their identities. Rather, it contributes to a class-anchored, individual complexity (cf. Skeggs 2004, pp. 56f.).

The second portrayal, about which there is much more research but which more rarely appears in the media other than as a stereotype, is the drug-abusing[6] woman (cf. Lander 2003). She is vulnerable, often a prostitute, often homeless and almost always mentally unstable. She is identified as a person at the bottom of society (cf. Campbell 2000, pp. 198f.; Mattsson 2005, pp. 78ff.). Swedish ethnographic studies have been conducted by ethnologist Annette Rosengren (2003) and criminologist Ingrid Lander (2003), both of whom placed great emphasis on depicting the women as individuals far beyond their identities as drug abusers. But in the absence of research that makes drug use visible in different social strata, these works still contribute to the image of women who use drugs as being at the bottom, or in Lander's words: women who have been dealt "the worst cards" (2003, pp. 31, 38 and 48; cf. Campbell 2000; Rosenbaum 1997).

In a study from 2005, sociologist Tina Mattsson has shown that the women she studied who were taken into care because of drug use were considered to have lost their femininity, perhaps even never having had it. The institution did not offer any activities other than (once in a while) the development of femininity, such as aerobics and beauty treatments, which she describes as being based on a middle-class ideal (pp. 185ff.). All the interviewees in the studies referred to above are described as drug users, but the type of use referred to is frequent and problematic use, i.e. use that is commonly described as drug addiction. But drug use occurs in all social classes (CAN 2021; BRÅ 2018; Wierup and de la Reguera 2010) and does not necessarily lead to addiction (Heilig 2015, pp. 29ff.; Richert 2014, pp. 33ff.). My view is therefore that the use of drugs in

---

[6] All illegal drug use has historically been described as abuse in Sweden (Olsson 1994, p. 5), and the term is still frequently used in both drug research and official documents. The term is avoided in this book except when it refers to a social construction, as in the discussion above. This is because its meaning is unclear and it has been criticised for being derogatory, not least from a medical perspective (see, e.g., Franck and Nylander 2011, pp. 12f.).

Sweden, that is, the use of usually very small and hidden quantities of substances that circulate at all levels of society, must be studied with a broad and mobile searchlight (Daun 2003; cf. the concept of "situated knowledge" explained below under "A power-sensitive approach", Haraway 1988) that is able to disregard the polarised stereotypes. Some bodies risk being constructed as linked to drugs through class-related conditions and cultural perceptions, while drugs themselves are located in many other places. What is the relationship between gender, class and drug use from different social positions?

There is a mystique around drugs that leads to the subject becoming loaded with connotations of danger, immorality and depravity. A person who uses drugs is by definition not only human. It is someone who has ingested psychoactive[7] substances that affect their thoughts, feelings, actions and decisions. Yet such substances are acceptable ingredients in completely normative contexts. Prescription medication treatments, medical care in hospitals, birthdays and wedding parties are examples of circumstances where substances such as amphetamines, opioids or alcohol can be used without being perceived as problematic. Thus, the concepts of drugs and drug use cannot be equated with the use of specific substances, but are given meaning through the cultural significance of

---

[7] The term psychoactive substance is used in this book to broaden the concept of drugs, as the latter has connotations of illegal psychoactive substances. The term *drug* is used when the cultural significance in a certain context is in the foreground, while *psychoactive substance* primarily refers to its effect. In this book, the term psychoactive substance includes both illicit drugs and substances found in medicines and alcohol. It also includes a number of substances that usually produce a weak psychoactive effect, such as nicotine, caffeine and sugar. This last group is important for background because it shows how the boundaries between drugs and non-drugs are blurred, but is less important for the study itself, which focuses on the concept of drugs, including the connotations the concept carries at any given time. In this book, the term drug is used to denote a cultural understanding of an object, that is, something that has been bought, used or experienced as a drug. Such a drug may in some cases be completely devoid of psychoactive substances (Measham 2019). However, drugs are assumed to contain psychoactive substances and are always discussed on the basis of this understanding. Another complicating factor is that medicines classified as narcotics become illegal drugs when used in ways other than as prescribed by a doctor. Moreover, even when used as prescribed, such medicines are in some cases perceived as drugs. The concepts are therefore intertwined. Furthermore, the term *substance* is sometimes used to refer to individual ingredients of a preparation, and the term *psychoactive preparations* when I want to highlight objects that include psychoactive substances, such as coffee, ecstasy or SSRI medicines.

how certain substances are used in certain contexts, relying on myths of "good and bad drugs" (Boyd 2004, p. 8).

These differences in meaning become even more evident from a class perspective. Substances, as well as the bodies that have ingested them, take on different meanings depending on whether they are consumed in low- or high-class situations—and this applies to drugs of all kinds (Olsson 1994; Björkman 2002; Bancroft 2009; Berridge 2013, p. 79; Edman 2019; Farber 2022). Class differences are particularly pronounced when it comes to women's use of such substances (Berridge 2013; Boyd 2004; Sigfridsson 2005; Wiklund and Damberg 2015). The concept of the whore as an image of the fallen woman is always close at hand when danger, immorality and depravity are linked to women (Frykman 1977; Johannisson 1995; Lennartsson 2019), but the differences between how two women's drug-affected bodies are perceived in a social context can be diametrically opposed, as I have illustrated above.

Part of the mystery of drugs is that one of the most obvious reasons for their use—pleasure[8]—is rarely discussed but is readily portrayed in films, books, song lyrics and magazines. This creates a discrepancy with information and news reports that focus on problems. In research that has focused on the lives of women who use drugs, the analysis usually returns to the original reason for why they started using drugs, which can be that they refused to accept a restrictive female role, and that drug use was a conscious choice, despite its accompanying difficulties (Lander 2003; Laanemets 2002, pp. 250ff.; Friedman and Alicea 1995; Du Rose 2017). One possible reading of these women's drug use can thus be one of agency exercised through a pleasure-filled revolt against oppressive expectations of the performance of femininity. It is thus a kind of class and gender rebellion. How drug-using women in different societal

---

[8] The reasons for using drugs can be many, and they overlap. Sociologist Mats Hilte lists the following possible motives: self-exploration, establishing an identity, altering mood, treating illness, escaping boredom or powerlessness, enhancing social interaction, amplifying experiences and pleasure, stimulating artistic creativity and performance, following peer pressure, rebelling and altering subjective experiences of time (2019, p. 112). But whether the primary motive is pleasure or not, pleasurable feelings induced by chemical changes in the body are central to the cultural meaning of drug use (see, e.g., Race 2009). This may go wrong, and drugs may instead induce discomfort, but pleasure is woven into the fundamental meaning of drugs.

positions orientate in relation to cultural perceptions, drugs as objects and stigma is an area of research that offers insights into gender and class orders, as well as a deeper understanding of the role of drugs in society.

1.2   Drugs in Everyday Life

Representations of women who use drugs, as expressed, for example, in the media, research, popular culture and national politics, seem to be directed towards two extremes, as I have described above. There are stories about the vulnerable woman at the bottom of the heap, or the eccentric star. Nevertheless, the statistics reveal something else: the vast majority of women who use drugs cannot be placed at either of these extremes. Instead, most are positioned along the spectrum in between (UNODC 2015; Statens Folkhälsoinstitut 2010, p. 75). In other words, drug use takes place in the middle of Swedish society, as well as on the margins. This book examines how women incorporate drug use into their everyday lives. How does drug use coexist with studies, professional life, children, partners and friendships? What significance do gender and class have for how drugs are used, problematised or legitimised? What drug use is possible and what does it do to women's life content, choices and conditions? To answer these questions, I focus on time, space and movement, with the intention of analysing how the acquisition, use and concealment of drugs become practices that have significance for the women in terms of gender and class.

Contradictions and taboos surround drug use, especially women's use of drugs. Why does Swedish society seem to be simultaneously obsessed with and dismissive of psychoactive substances and the bodies that ingest them (cf. Edman 2019)? Some use is visible everywhere, while other use, even of substances associated with less serious risks or illness, is associated with stigma and/or high penalties. In this way, drugs act as tools that create order, but it is a strange and disorderly order. The rules are different in different countries, but in Sweden, where attitudes towards illegal drugs are generally harsh, heavy drinking at certain places and times is an expected and encouraged feature of the street scene. The unrestrained intoxication of some bodies is thus given space in public places, while other bodies can only become intoxicated illegally in secret, and the slightest sign of improper influence is monitored. The subject is surrounded by complex cultural attitudes and boundaries that still surprise me after eight years of research, linked to dirt and cleanliness, order and disorder, sickness and health, morality and immorality.

Identifying as a woman is a starting point that is already closer to the negative category of the dichotomies listed above. Women's constant exposure to being associated with immorality, dirt and disease is linked to the risk of coming too close to the whore stigma (Lennartsson 2019). Feminist scholarship has delved into the mechanisms that place women in classed, confined spaces, where careless movements always threaten to lead to moral condemnation (Johannisson 2015; Skeggs 1998; Irigaray 1985). Idealised femininity is therefore about a constant striving towards order, purity, morality and cleanliness. How women approach—and do—illegal drug use are therefore questions that serve as gateways (cf. e.g. Löfgren and Ehn 2010, p. 78) to broader feminist questions about agency, desire, health and physicality.

Statistics show that the use of illegal drugs is increasing. The Central Association for Alcohol and Drug Information (CAN 2019, p. 5) states that, despite difficulties in producing reliable figures, the available data for the period 2014–2019 indicates that problematic drug use in Sweden is at historically high levels. Resold medicines are one of the groups of preparations that have increased the most, according to seizure statistics (ibid., p. 12) and are now the most commonly used drug group (ibid., p. 18) and the second most commonly seized, after cannabis. This makes discussions about what drugs are, and possible approaches to them, urgent. I have asked myself what feminist approaches to drugs can be and how alcohol, illegal drugs and narcotics relate to issues such as liberation, pleasure, risk, neoliberal society, violence and norms. In every possible answer, there are contradictions, which are not diminished by the wide variety of effects that different drugs can have. On the one hand, there are risks; on the other hand, there are opportunities. These thoughts have led to this study.

With this book, I want to contribute to a political and scientific awareness of the drugs that are all around us and within us, what we do with them and what they do to us, by looking at how the women in Sweden who participate in this study relate to their use of drugs.

1.3   The Women Participants

The study[9] is based on interviews with twelve women. They are all Swedish citizens, but four of them were born in other countries, three of whom came to Sweden as small children, while the fourth arrived as a young person. Two had been living abroad for some years at the time of the interviews. All of them can be perceived as white Swedes, and I believe—but did not ask—that all of them would describe themselves as such in situations where such identification is requested (although in a couple of cases the nationality of the country of birth might also be mentioned). These twelve women were the first to answer my call, and the selection does not mean to imply that all women are white. Instead, they speak from specific positions organised by race. Whiteness is a privilege based on a racialisation "invented" by science, which on the one hand constructs a notion that it is actually about the characteristics of individuals and groups, and on the other hand makes spaces comfortable and obvious for white people but uncomfortable and inaccessible for others (Ahmed 2007). Whiteness, feminist scholar Sara Ahmed writes, can be partly understood as an inherited, implicit knowledge of where things are and how they can be used (ibid., p. 155). The movements of the body are thus structured by race. Furthermore, whiteness is "a category of experience that disappears as a category through experience, and [...] this disappearance makes whiteness 'worldly'" (ibid., p. 150).[10] Although this book focuses on gender and class, the women's performance of whiteness and conditions of whiteness shaped their experiences of drug use, both in Sweden and abroad, profoundly. However, one or more of the women could perhaps perceive themselves as "not

---

[9] Approved by the Swedish Ethical Review Authority [Etikprövningsmyndigheten] 10 August 2016.

[10] This explanation of whiteness has parallels with the concept of habitus and the middle class in Bourdieu and Skeggs' interpretations. See further under the heading "Respectability and value".

quite white",[11] that is, not fully experiencing themselves as completely white and/or always being accepted as white. Race is an incredibly strong, structuralising factor in terms of how handling drugs is perceived and met (Farber 2022), and, as a consequence, the interviewees were usually using drugs under very different conditions than if they had been perceived as non-white women.

So, what is a woman? In my study, gender is understood as a set of social constructions situated in context (West and Zimmerman 1987), both subjectively and by the environment, working in dialogue. Since a person's categorisation as a woman also includes the environment's interpretations and reactions, people who enact femininity have experiences that can be similar to those of other women and differ from those of other gender categories. The reason why I chose to target people who identified as women was partly because, as I have described earlier, I have a feminist interest in how women's drug use might contest or align with classic ideals of femininity. But I was also interested in norm-breaking through drug use from positions that already do not conform to the expected male user of drugs (Campbell and Ettorre 2011). Therefore, I regretted not having been more clearly open in the invitation to the study, as any gender-queer person would have made relevant and valuable contributions. Non-binary gender identifications are invisible in the statistics and in most of the drug research that I have used, both quantitative and qualitative, and the contributions of such individuals would have contested the invisibility-making that is inherent in relying on invisibility-making statistics (cf. Buxton et al. 2020). However, despite an invitation directed at women, luckily it did not only attract women who follow straight lines of womanhood. At least four of the interviewees identify as lesbian or queer, one of whom has undergone gender-affirming treatment.[12]

---

[11] The term is used to capture how certain groups of people, such as the working class or people from poor countries, are not perceived as white despite their light skin colour. See, for example, Jamil Khoury and Stephen Combs' documentary *Not Quite White: Arabs, Slavs, and the Contours of Contested Whiteness* (2012) for an accessible introduction.

[12] Gender-affirming or gender-confirming treatment can include hormones, surgery and voice training, and is used by people who want to change their body and/or legal gender.

The interviewees

Here, the participants are briefly presented, each with a fictitious name, approximate age, occupation and current consumption habits in terms of drugs, medicines and alcohol, according to their own statements.

> **Agnes**, aged 25, psychologist: Uses amphetamines and the amphetamine-like drug mephedrone (4-methylmethcathinone) as well as MDMA/ecstasy at parties. Smokes cannabis. Self-reportedly drinks a lot of alcohol.
>
> **Nanne**, aged 65, retired, former journalist. Uses cannabis oil, so-called CBD oil. Receives opioid drugs on prescription for her pain conditions. Often drinks wine.
>
> **Boel**, in her 30s, works as a public-relations officer. Prefers to use hallucinogenic drugs such as LSD and MDMA. Also uses cocaine, amphetamines and poppers when the opportunity arises. Micro-doses MDMA during stressful periods at work. Claims to drink a lot of alcohol and to be a "funny alcoholic".
>
> **Katy**, in her 40s, consultant in an architectural office. Uses cocaine on select occasions. Smokes cannabis. Drinks alcohol sparingly.
>
> **Madelene**, aged 35, senior software analyst at an IT company. Uses a variety of prescription drugs, mainly Xanax, Oxynorm and Klonopin, for anxiety and pleasure. Injects heroin a couple of times a month. Does not drink alcohol.
>
> **Dora**, aged 25, is a student. Smokes cannabis a few times a year. Drinks alcohol almost daily but not very much at a time when there is no party.
>
> **Carolina**, aged 35, musician. Used amphetamines daily for eight years but has stopped and only uses Clomipramine for depression and OCD. Does not drink alcohol.
>
> **Thea**, aged 35, visual artist. Uses mainly hallucinogens such as psilocybin mushrooms and LSD, but on occasion also amphetamines, MDMA, cocaine and cannabis. Has undergone an extended period of illness that has caused a lot of physical pain and felt that she was in too poor a condition to use a lot of drugs or alcohol during the

interview period, but does so on occasion. Occasionally uses opioid painkillers, both illegally purchased and prescribed.

Pernilla, in her 40s, works for a book publisher. Prefers to use cocaine, but due to its high price in Sweden cannot do so very often. Sometimes uses amphetamines at parties. Smokes marijuana (cannabis). Likes to drink alcohol.

Angela, aged 45, paints, receives sickness benefit. Uses the drugs Elvanse for depression and as part of treatment for ADHD, Lyrica for anxiety, and amphetamines and MDMA at parties. States that she drinks quite a lot of wine at times.

Hanna, aged 50, receives financial assistance, shoplifts food and clothes, sells sex from time to time. Injects heroin daily. Uses drugs such as benzodiazepines when they come her way. Basically does not drink alcohol.

Filippa, aged 25, psychology student. Uses cannabis and psilocybin mushrooms. Likes to drink alcohol.

Filippa subsequently asked to be further anonymised, which means that I only use statements from her when the interview responses are in line with those of others. Sentences such as "several interviewees believe that …" may thus be partly based on Filippa's interview answers, but otherwise her statements have been omitted. We agreed on this because she was worried about being revealed in some way, for example through a personal way of expressing herself.

Other interviewees' information that is not relevant to the study has in some cases been changed to reinforce anonymity, which has been specifically important to consider in this study, where the interviewees have a lot to lose if their participation were to be revealed, such as jobs, reputations, children and so on (Waters 2015).

1.4   A Power-Sensitive Approach

Asking about everyday experiences and starting from there, in line with Sara Ahmed's queer phenomenology, with a focus on direction, emotions and objects but without ignoring political and social conditions, is not only useful as a theoretical perspective (to which I will return below) but also as a method. I see this method as close to what Donna Haraway (1988) describes as the pursuit of "situated knowledge", which is based on a multi-positioned, power-sensitive conversation with the environment. Skeggs writes about the importance of the research perspective with reference to Haraway's concept:

> knowledge is always a matter of positioning. It is the space from which we speak, the political, disciplinary and social inheritances that we travel through, which leave traces and marks upon us, enabling us to see some things and be blind to others. This is, of course, tautological, because it is our social positioning and categorisation (of which class is one) that enables our only ever partial perception. (Skeggs 2004, p. 45)

Having a place, the academy, from which we can speak is, on the one hand, a privilege that allows some perspectives to be heard and seen far more than others. On the other hand, as I read Skeggs and Haraway, positioning implies a feminist responsibility to widen the field of vision by not failing to point out what we see, even if few others seem to see the same thing. Haraway writes:

> Rational knowledge is a process of ongoing critical interpretation among "fields" of interpreters and decoders. Rational knowledge is a power sensitive conversation. (1988, p. 590)

For the science produced to be rational, Haraway argues that many perspectives are needed. In the case of drug-use issues, representation is currently virtually impossible, especially in Sweden, where being under the influence of drugs is a punishable offence. Illegality, stigma and perceptions of unreliability mean that people who use drugs are rarely heard. Elizabeth Ettorre writes:

> Even within the women's movement, women's drug use was considered as emblematic failure of gendered performativity [...] Drug-using women were seen as "failures" as women. As Campbell [...] has argued, drug using women are not epistemologically credible; they continue to be

constructed as willfully wayward women who are morally corrupt and "deviant" in socially unacceptable ways. (2015, p. 795)

Women who use drugs are thus impossible subjects, both as people who use drugs and as women. Despite the fact that women who use drugs are not perceived as exempt from men's violence, sexism or harassment, Ettorre argues that even feminist movements are exclusionary. In Sweden, where drug-related mortality is described as more than four times the European average (EMCDDA 2021, p. 8), but where gender-equality issues are prioritised, it may seem strange that the voices of women who use drugs are not heard. However, the laws targeting personal use effectively place the drug-affected voice outside the public debate. This project has been about collecting material from such positions and building the text in dialogue with previous and contemporary research, as well as with the interviewees.

1.5   The Interviews

In order to reach people who use drugs who were not to be found in institutions, I sent an invitation mail to people I knew, encouraging them to pass it forwards to potential participants. I also spread the word at conferences and talks. After receiving expressions of interest in participating from the women presented above, I conducted semi-structured in-depth interviews with each of them, in locations chosen by them, preferably at home or in a café. In some cases, subsequent email, messenger and WhatsApp communication has also become part of the material. Six of the women also participated in go-along interviews, in places that they considered to be important to them in relation to their use of drugs.

During the collection of my interview material, the balance of power created by the topic between researchers and people who use drugs has been a relevant issue. I have tried to address it primarily through a straightforward and respectful approach and by acting and asking questions in a way that, as far as possible, does not resemble the language of an authority (Nairn et al. 2005). Ethnologist Signe Bremer describes interview material as collected versions of a social reality, a product of an interpersonal encounter (2011a, p. 196). This highlights the researcher's own role in the interview situation and makes visible that other researchers would have collected at least partially different material from the same interview situation. This returns us to Skeggs' words that knowledge is always a question of positioning and that this position allows us to see some things but leaves us blind to others (2004, p. 45). But it also applies to the interviewee him/herself and the specific perspective that he or she contributes.

Traditional methodological texts that specifically deal with interviewing people who use drugs commonly describe encounters with excluded people, where the power relationship between interviewer and interviewee becomes conspicuous. Anthropologist Trond Grønnestad and researcher in social work Philip Lalander write for example:

> When a person who is labelled as outsider, for example a narcotic user, meets people who are "normal", he or she may try to hide the stigma in order to "pass" as a normal person. The objective is then to avoid being labelled and seen as inferior in the encounter and in the gaze of the other. If that is difficult, if the stigma is easily discovered, for example, through a worn appearance, an individual may experience the encounter as uncomfortable, an occasion of inferiority (Garfinkel 1967).[13] (Grønnestad and Lalander 2015, p. 168)

Most of the interviewees whom I met are in completely different positions from the "outsiders" described above. Several are clearly proud of their careers and life choices and highlighted these, with or without the intention of overshadowing their stigmatising drug use. As a result, I could sometimes feel that I was "studying upwards" (Nader 1972), while the interviewees, like the "outsiders" described in the quote, often related to notions of normality as the antithesis of drug use in different

---

[13] In this quote, people who use drugs are contrasted with "normal" people. The quotation marks show that the researchers do not reproduce the concept of normal without reflection, but they do leave it uncommented, which nevertheless suggests an image of their own starting point as neutral. I question the use of quotation marks around a word that signals an objective research approach, since "the god-trick", in the words of Donna Haraway (1988), i.e. the idea that the starting point can be objective, is thus reproduced without changing significantly.

ways. This can be described as a third presence, or sometimes rather a "questioning ghost" (Pripp 2011, p. 69), who is silently questioning the interviewees based on expected negative perceptions. In situations where I felt that such a questioning ghost began to take over, or in some other way the interview took a turn away from the purpose of the study, I turned to the interview guide and changed the topic to something that I hoped would be inspiring rather than threatening.

The go-along interviews were conducted by me taking walks together with the women to places that, for various reasons, they associated with drug use. The point of the method is to evoke associations, memories and feelings and thus generate an in-depth narrative that is difficult to access in a traditional interview situation (Kusenbach 2003). Sociologist Margarethe Kusenbach describes the go-along method as a phenomeno-logically based method that aims to bring together the different strengths of the observation and interview methods. This, she argues, makes the go-along method better suited to capturing two key aspects of lived experience: its constitutive role and the transcendent significance of the physical environment (ibid., p. 458). She argues that methods that can take into account movement through the environment are a necessary step in conducting phenomenological ethnography that considers how experiences change in relation to place. They allowed me to follow the interviewees' directions and to see how they oriented themselves and at the same time reasoned about memories that emerged in relation to the places. Experiences of disorientation often became significant (cf. Ahmed 2006a, pp. 157ff.) during the go-alongs as important and thoroughly described processes. I believe that these experiences would not have been mentioned at all, or would have been talked about in other ways, in a seated interview situation. During the go-alongs, scenarios that were confusing and/or contradictory for the interviewee could be recounted in detail, based on their memories of emotions that arose at the site, and I believe that summary accounts of the same events could have given different impressions (cf. Kusenbach 2003, pp. 472ff.).

1.6   A Queer Phenomenological Approach to Drug Use

In this book, Sara Ahmed's queer phenomenology (2006a, 2006b) serves as the main theoretical approach.

Phenomenological perspectives on the body, space and objects, as developed by, for example, the philosophers Martin Heidegger (1962/1927), Simone de Beauvoir (2004/1949), Maurice Merleau-Ponty (1968, 2010) and Sara Ahmed (2006a, 2006b), can be used as valuable ethnological tools to explore ethnographic material as lived, bodily experiences, and for understanding directions and movements of consciousness in space (see, e.g., Hansson 2007; Bremer 2011b; Göransson 2012).

> Phenomenology emphasizes the importance of lived experience, the intentionality of consciousness, the significance of nearness or what is ready to hand, and the role of repeated and habitual actions in shaping bodies and worlds. (Ahmed 2006b, p. 544)

What is close and what movements are repeated, writes Ahmed, is significant for how bodies and worlds take shape. Furthermore, consciousness is always assumed to be directed towards objects and is therefore always worldly, situated and embodied (ibid.). Phenomenology thus focuses on how bodies and objects (all kinds of objects, including drugs) are positioned in the world, and how bodies and objects take up that position together, how they approach, and distance themselves from, each other. How then do bodies, objects and places in proximity to each other take shape when drugs are one of the objects?

Heidegger describes how, when used, objects can disappear from the consciousness and become extensions of the body (1962/1927). Frykman exemplifies such a change in the relationship between body, mind and object as the difference between thinking about an object and thinking with the object (2006). He uses the example of a car. When a driver makes their way along a road with a country house in sight, past other road users and with rowdy children in the back seat, the car is an object through which the driver experiences the world, rather than something they think about in terms of what it represents (ibid., pp. 66ff.). In the context of drug use, this phenomenological starting point is complicated. Drugs come much closer to bodies than a car can. They are objects in the world that can be moved and thought about, but their purpose for the person who uses them is to be introduced into the body and dissolved in bodily fluids, which leads to bodily changes (cf. Hansson 2007). The drug thus temporarily becomes the body in a physical sense. The unification between the body and the drug in turn affects the direction of the consciousness. Once the drug has been ingested, the person who used it *must* think with the drug, even while thinking about the drug, until its effects have ceased. The living body is thus altered in a distinctive way that distinguishes the use of drugs and medicines from most other uses of objects.

Moreover, since the 1960s, the type of object that drugs constitute has been associated with strong cultural charges of danger and threat (Edman 2019). Drugs can therefore induce experiences of disorientation both through their pharmacological properties when used and as stigmatised and criminalised objects that are consequently socially risky to approach at all. To analyse the use of such a type of object, phenomenology must focus on these disorienting experiences, their meanings and also on the conditions surrounding drug use as an act. Ahmed writes that phenomenology has to be queer in order to understand how disorientation can be a meaningful starting point. Rather than quickly moving on from disoriented queer moments—which can be experienced as unpleasant and as preventing the possibility of action (2006a, pp. 66, 159)—she writes that a queer phenomenology can orient itself differently in relation to them. She argues:

> A queer phenomenology might find what is queer within phenomenology and use that queerness to make some rather different points. Phenomenology, after all, is full of queer moments, moments of disorientation. (2006b, p. 544)

Considered as significant focal points, Ahmed thus means that theoretical disorientations can open up other insights than oriented starting points, when things are in their expected places, so to speak. But experiences of disorientation can also be about the researcher's bodily starting point. Ahmed gives the example of the female philosopher, who deviates from the male norm.

> bodies can take up spaces that do not extend their shape, which can in turn work to "reorientate" bodies and space. [...] there are women philosophers, and [...] they still cause trouble as "bodies out of place" in the "home" of philosophy [...] So what happens when the woman philosopher takes up her pen? What happens when the study is not reproduced as a masculine domain by the collective repetition of such moments of deviation? (2006a, p. 61)

As a woman, turning towards philosophy and taking up a pen to write is to orientate oneself in an unexpected way and can lead to experiences of disorientation. But in order to do what was intended, to write, Ahmed argues, is to tread a new path that becomes more accessible as spaces, objects and bodies take shape from each other. New paths are trodden by the female philosopher who insists on writing, which, Ahmed points out, can involve a different, feminist approach to where the attention should be directed (ibid., pp. 61ff.). In this way, queer phenomenology becomes a political phenomenology, in line with, for example, critical cultural theory, feminist theory and postcolonial theory, all of which are interested in exploring the creation and maintenance of power.

Unlike Ahmed's primary work, this book is based on fieldwork and the contributions of interviewees. The queer phenomenology developed by Ahmed therefore takes on additional dimensions. Following in Ahmed's footsteps and thinking in line with her theory turns me into the female researcher who picks up a pen and seeks to orient herself, not primarily as a philosopher but as a feminist and ethnologist in a field researched predominantly by male drug researchers and ethnologists who rarely research drugs. Thus, what is noticed is not always the same as what has been noticed before. To a certain extent, this path has been trodden by other feminists, but to the extent that it has been followed by ethnologists, it is different ways of thinking than those common in drug research that have inspired them. The quest for reorientation has therefore often been overriding. But what is noticed is based on fieldwork, i.e. what the interviewees, the women who use drugs, have noticed. The queer phenomenology is therefore partly performed by them—for example, they remain in the memory of the disoriented moments together with me and formulate the material I have to work with. This creates a link between the field and the desk, to which I want to draw attention, particularly because the reproduction of deviance in research on women who use drugs is a problem that researchers have struggled to resolve (Campbell 2000). There are interesting similarities between philosophers, other researchers and people who use drugs. Drugs are not alone in their ability to alter consciousness and intentions. Disorientation and orientation as analytical concepts serve as a bridge between the orientation of the interviewees (after all, what is participation in an interview about drug use, other than an attempt to concretise disorientation, orientation, intentional directions and the conditions for them?) and my own efforts to orient myself analytically through the material in the form of text production.

The influence of drugs has inevitable links with disorientation, through drug effects and illegality, which in turn implies drug-related orientations—the striving for or the obviousness of feeling oriented. Paying attention to experiences of orientation and disorientation in studies of direction, movement and their conditions in relation to the environment can shed light on power relations and opportunities for action.

Such attention is directed towards what the interviewees have noticed, as well as what the researcher sees and how directions are taken from there. People who use drugs turn to drugs just as philosophers turn to their desks to become philosophers (Ahmed 2006a, pp. 52, 55). It is through drug use that the women become people who use drugs, and this, perhaps with even greater intensity than women writing philosophy, can produce experiences of being "out of place", since drug use, unlike philosophy, is prohibited by law. (These are relationships that have changed over time, but in opposite directions. Philosophical institutions in Sweden were opened to women in 1873 and the penal code for drugs was established, as previously stated, in 1968.) Thus, perhaps what happens during thinking and under the influence of drugs is not as different as it might first appear? Both states refer to different forms of mind alteration—consciousness can change and disorientation can occur—from which new orientations take place. People who use drugs may feel that the world is against them. It can also be an uncomfortable experience to write about a taboo subject, allowing research and empirical material to lead the way, when this is not in line with heavily morally charged cultural beliefs. I have often been angry, scared and lost (cf. Ettorre 2017). Ahmed writes:

> disorientation happens when the ground no longer supports an action. We lose ground, we lose our sense of how we stand; we might even lose our standing. (2006a, p. 170)

To make things queer is to disrupt the order of things, Ahmed writes (ibid., p. 161), and it entails a deviation that is not always comfortable, but can be a prerequisite for seeing new patterns (ibid., p. 171). A central idea throughout this book is therefore to keep this relationship in mind. Orientation takes place from the point where consciousness of the body is located, and directions are determined from there (2006b, p. 544). This is an ever-changing process, whether the mind/body is influenced by philosophy (and other research), drugs or something else, and new directions take shape in the constant pursuit of orientation through temporary, prolonged, uncertain, shifting states of disorientation. What I perceive as the queer in queer phenomenology, with parallels to the risks faced by both researchers and people who use drugs, is a view of disorientation, including the feelings to which it can give rise—of uncertainty, anxiety and many more—as a starting point for possibilities of renewal that may not cease to be uncomfortable. Interviewing people who use drugs is thus a queer encounter between different processes of orientation, disorientation and reorientation, and between subjects who sometimes claim "I can", even though the starting point does not seem to be in line with the environment (2006a, p. 159).

1.7   Power Relations

Ahmed's works often focuses on gender, sexuality and race. They have a clear political orientation and these focus areas make it clear why uncomfortable feelings of not belonging are important starting points in Ahmed's analyses. When she writes "queer", the analytical examples are often about non-heterosexual relationships. Drug use has some similarities with sexuality, as both often involve curiosity, pleasure-seeking and desire that directs bodies, making them follow "desire lines" (2006a, p. 19), and can lead to social consequences, such as categorisation and identification. Both sexuality and drug use can also manifest as love relationships (Shulgin and Shulgin 2019; Svensson 1996; Lander 2003, p. 180). But is it really okay to transfer theory designed to illuminate racist, misogynist and heteronormative structures to analyse something that may seem as banal and temporary as the use of drugs?

As previous research has shown, drug use does not have to be banal or temporary, but can have a crucial impact on how people are valued, and their ability to move around in the world (e.g. Boyd 2004; Campbell and Ettorre 2011; Du Rose 2015). But even the most banal drug use occurs, as we will see in the empirical chapters, in relation to risks of changes in value. Such changes do not occur in a vacuum but are in turn linked to other power relations, as queer phenomenology makes visible. But I have also wondered whether there is a risk of undermining the concept of queer when it is used in research that does not focus on sexuality.

Ahmed uses the word queer both in the sense of the expression of something strange or deviant and in the sense of non-straight sexuality or non-heterosexual (2006b, p. 565). She writes that she thinks it is important to emphasise both of these meanings so that the concept retains its full breadth with a common historical origin, without the meanings being reducible to each other. She writes:

> This means recalling what makes specific sexualities describable as queer in the first place: that is, that they are seen as odd, bent, twisted. The root of the word queer is from the Greek for cross, oblique, adverse. The word might allow us to 'twist' between sexual and social registers, without flattening them or reducing them to a single line. Although we risk losing

the specificity of queer as a commitment to a life of sexual deviation, we would also sustain the significance of deviation in what makes queer lives queer. (ibid., p. 565)

The significance of the odd, bent and twisted, rooted in spatial meanings such as cross and adverse, allows the concept of queer to twist, according to Ahmed. It does not need to be straightened out but can retain both its sexual and its social dimensions, which she points out is fundamental to why queer lives are queer. At the same time, she sees a risk that such use could cause the concept to lose its sexual meaning. The direction of desire, in the case of drug use a direction towards psychoactive substances, could be interpreted as interesting for a semi-queer phenomenology. The use is not necessarily either queer (deviant) or queer (sexuality). Can an activity such as drug use be analysed within this tradition of ideas without detaching it from its association with sexually deviant lives?

It can also be argued that sexuality is based on a technical-biological bodily starting point, which is highlighted particularly clearly by postmodern transsexuality. The philosopher Paul B. Preciado, who himself uses testosterone, describes the use of pharmacological preparations as an integral, non-natural part of being human in the postmodern world (2013, p. 35). The picture he paints when describing the extent of the global industries behind technological inventions intended to change the body and consciousness, such as medicines, prostheses, sex aids and drugs, depicts the human living in that world as a cyborg. This is in reference to Donna Haraway's concept of the human being as a fusion of body and technology (Haraway 1991). Preciado argues that Judith Butler's analysis of gender as performative acts that produce the subjects they claim to describe has now been pushed even further into the body. Nowadays, he argues, even organs, cells, bodily fluids, chromosomes and genes are about performative production (2013, p. 110). If we are all cyborgs living as techno-biological beings, such subjectivity is not queer per se, but Preciado argues that the strategic use of technological possibilities can implode the dichotomous divisions between men and women, hetero- and homosexuality and so on. On the other hand, technological solutions can also be used to reinforce these very dichotomies. Whether psychoactive drugs queer sexuality therefore becomes a subjective, or at least contextual, issue, which is also related to class and opportunities for performativity (cf. Skeggs 2004, p. 67). However, in this book, the concept of queer is primarily used to analyse dichotomies and norms that are bent, crossed and resisted, and it is not my intention to hollow out the important meaning of non-straight sexualities as queer, but rather to elaborate on the potentials of queerness.

1.8   The Concepts of Lines and Orientation

The concept of lines is important in this book. It is used in a way that emphasises its starting point, the body: where the body is located and the perspectives that are made possible from there. I perceive experiences of being oriented and from there pointing out a direction, being in line with a direction or, conversely, not being in line and experiencing disorientation, as complex and sometimes contradictory, everyday and constantly changing experiences. Ahmed makes normative lines visible as "straight lines". This has a double meaning: both as "thick" and persistent lines that have been followed by many and as straight lines not designed for queer people (2006b, pp. 554ff.). She argues that following "straight lines" can be rewarding (2006a, p. 179; 2010, p. 115). At the same time, people can avoid following normative lines, for example by fighting against racism or living their life as a queer person. Both normative and non-normative lines can thus provide experiences of being oriented and, depending on the context, the line can be about either following or staking out. The use of drugs can in itself be a deviation from a thick, straight and normative line. However, using them can also be about following such a line, for example when controlled drugs are prescribed. According to phenomenology, orienting oneself in a certain direction and moving in that direction is an intentional act. But intentions change along the path, and the use of drugs can change intentions in an instant, and it is therefore specifically interesting to theorise phenomenologically. How are lines affected by the use of drugs?

Ahmed describes the intention to direct oneself and approach something as being linked to desires and to points along the lines that are being followed. For example, getting married and having children are points along a normative line (2010, p. 91). Lines therefore take the form of conceptions of long lines, such as a "straight line", an expected line where the goal is happiness and many points are visible from afar. But lines can also be deviant, winding, uncertain, diffuse or interrupted. In empirical material, a winding line can look short, like a sudden detour without any thought for the future, towards something that has appeared in the field of vision—for example a decision to try heroin—as an effect of being oriented in that direction (2006a, pp. 15, 27). Such a line can turn out to run parallel with longer lines, maybe a childhood decision to try all drugs and become someone who did. However, from the point of trying, the line can also develop in new directions. The visual field changes as the body moves, from a certain point the world unfolds in a different way than it did before that point had been reached (ibid., pp. 28ff.). From the body's here and now, further orientation takes place, and this is always shaped by factors such as gender and class. Ahmed writes:

> Orientations are about how we begin, how we proceed from here. [...] The starting point for orientation is the point from which the world unfolds: the here of the body and the where of its dwelling. (2006b, p. 545)

This is a central starting point for this book's focus on the use of drugs. Orientation is based on a situated body and drug use changes the vantage point, the body's experience of how the world develops. This can be significant both for further orientation and for how lines are followed and what appears in the field of vision. But the body's starting point is also situated. Where it lives or is usually located, its historical and current social and material contexts shape how the lines are drawn.

1.9   Respectability and Value

Phenomenology's starting point in the body is complemented by queer phenomenology's focus on the power relations and material conditions that surround that body. The perspective is thus broadened by being queered. As it has been necessary to understand how ethnographic material can be analysed in relation to class, the queer phenomenology in this book is further broadened and queered by many other theoretical inputs, the most significant being sociologist Beverley Skeggs' (1998, 2004) theory of class.

Skeggs has conducted a number of ethnographic studies with a primary focus on class. She describes class categorisations as the middle class's effort to construct itself as the moral, modern, knowledgeable, clean and reliable social group. But, for these values to mean anything, a counterpart is needed, a class whose members are defined from the perspective of the middle class as failing on every point (cf. 2004, p. 6). She writes:

> What we read as objective class divisions are produced and maintained by the middle-class in the minutiae of everyday practice, as judgements of culture are put into effect. Any judgement of the working-class as negative (waste, excess, vulgar, unmodern, authentic, etc.) is an attempt by the middle-class to accrue value. This is what the representations of the working-class should be seen to be about; they have absolutely nothing to do with the working-class themselves, but are about the middle-class creating value for themselves in a myriad of ways, through distance, denigration and disgust as well as appropriation and affect of attribution. (2004, p. 118)

Skeggs' definition can thus be interpreted as meaning that the descriptor "working class" is rather about the constant work to constitute the middle class, without any payment. On the contrary, the working class is put into positions from which it is difficult to accumulate capital. Being in a vulnerable social position is a concrete, lived experience with very tangible consequences (Skeggs 2011, p. 503), but the concept of class is not inherent in either people or things. It is intended to raise the analysis of lived experiences to an abstract level, where questions can be asked about how class constructions operate.

Skeggs describes class as closely linked to respectability and thus morality. A person who lacks respectability has low social value and weak legitimacy (1998, p. 3), which can be transferred to the meaning of low class. Instead, she shows that having respectability and morality is an inherent part of how the middle class has been constructed historically. She writes:

> Respectability embodies moral authority: those who are respectable have it, those who are not do not. But only some groups were considered to be capable of being moral, others were seen to be in need of control. (1998, p. 3)

According to Skeggs, this relationship has continued unabated and permeates society at all levels. She states that, among other things, this means that the middle class is attributed individuality, a unique way of being, unlike the working class. Managing individuality through choice, Skeggs argues, is a coercive, capitalist norm for the middle class that aims to increase the value of the self (2004, p. 140). These choices are thus made from a class position with access to cultural, moral capital. She writes:

> Using culture as a resource is one of the ways morality is coded into social relations and institutionalized through property relations, most obviously institutionalized through law. Morality is always present in the 'social contract', through the ways we know and relate to others in civil society. (ibid., p. 174)

However, expressing the complex self requires access to exciting cultural expressions which, paradoxically, are often appropriated from the working-class community (ibid., p. 105). What is taken and managed, however, is not the same as that which was held, and the change is determined by the relationship (ibid., p. 12). Applying such an analysis—in which moral authority is attributed to some groups in society while others lack it—to the subject of this book means that the act of drug use per se is loosened from moral judgements. It indicates a fluid valuation of drugs if the morality of an action is determined by the class-based morality of the actor. The drug then takes on different meanings depending on who is handling it. Several drug researchers have pointed this out with regard to opium, amphetamines and tobacco, for example, all of which have made downward class journeys to the same extent as they have become popular with the working class (Berg 2016; Edman and Olsson 2014; Berridge 2013). At the same time, socially vulnerable people who use drugs, as described above, have just as rapidly been formulated as constituting a societal problem, even as being "public enemy number one" (see, e.g., Nelson 2021). A number of researchers (see Chapter 2) have argued that ideological positions—which have been aimed, not at helping people who use drugs but at disciplining them, although often lacking the resources to do so (Lander 2003, pp. 259f., 301)—have caused a large number of unnecessary deaths. How do people become so worthless?

Conceptions of certain social groups as threats to the nation have a long history. Post-colonial scholar Anne McClintock links the emergence of the class concept to imperialist and racist ideas (see also Johannisson 1995, p. 81) about "degenerate classes":

> The degenerate classes, defined as departures from the normal human type, were as necessary to the self-definition of the middle class as the idea of degeneration was to the idea of progress, for the distance along the path of progress traveled by some portions of humanity could be measured only by the distance others lagged behind. [...] Normality thus emerged as a product of deviance, and the baroque invention of clusters of degenerate types highlighted the boundaries of the normal. (McClintock 1995, p. 46)

Thus, according to McClintock, degeneracy, a term used to define those classes considered non-normal, was necessary for notions of social progress. This brought together notions that gave rise to middle-class racial categorisations and their view of the non-respectable working class (which differed from the respectable working class, who could and would work, see ibid., footnote 56, p. 401) into a common image of "dangerous classes". Such notions, Skeggs argues, take on a tautological character, placing people in positions that in turn affect their access to cultural and economic resources (1998, p. 5). The notion of the working class as a mass of non-individuals who are pathologised and alienated, she argues, is still very much at work in both academic and popular representations (1998, p. 3, see also 2004, pp. 173ff.). Skeggs gives the example of descriptions of "welfare mothers" or "crack babies" in the USA and shows how these are based on historical thought constructions that give the concepts their meaning (1998, p. 3). She writes that the damage and wounds inflicted upon those who are not recognised as human beings are not recognised either (2004, p. 184).

The picture of successful women's individualised use of drugs, in contrast to their use by vulnerable, anonymous people, which I drew at the beginning, can be interpreted from a historical perspective as rendering the drug use of the working class dangerous and pathological but expected, as the group is already considered degenerate. The use of drugs by successful women becomes part of their complex individual selves. But isn't drug use generally pathologised, albeit in different ways for different social groups? In her book *The Dark Continent*[14] (1995), the historian of ideas Karin Johannisson describes how women from both the upper and lower classes were considered malfunctioning in the nineteenth century. The upper-class woman, she writes, was weak, fragile and sickly, while the lower-class woman was strong, dangerous and contagious (ibid., p. 14). However, the weak body was not a defect but a mark of nobility. It was highly valued as imbued with soul, while strong and capable bodies were good only for work (ibid., p. 81). She writes:

> Through a kind of collective projection, the underclass took on the physicality – dirt, smell, sound, and sexuality – that the bourgeoisie had sorted out from its own culture through long processes of disciplining. The underclass became the carrier of the forbidden impulses. It was identified with the lower and more primitive, a residual product of past stages of development: it drank, slurped and copulated unconcerned with the progress of civilization. (Johannisson, 1995, p. 81)

---

14 *Den mörka kontinenten* (1995).

The dirty, impulse-driven physicality of the lower class, even though—or indeed because—it was strong and fit for work, thus became a sign of degeneration, which was contrasted with a weak, civilised body. However, the view of the upper-class woman's morbidity changed and in the twentieth century began to be regarded as a problem (ibid., p. 92). Weak women could not give birth to strong children. The view of middle-class women's health swung instead towards notions of moral responsibility to take care of oneself. This has similarities with how the modern individual in the consumer society is expected to invest in her own health (cf. Lupton, 2012, chapter 2, pp. 13ff.), and who makes herself valuable by making choices through consumption (Skeggs 2004, pp. 56ff.). These choices, which are required and made, demonstrate morality, but now they also need to show individuality, which according to Skeggs is achieved through performative reflexivity. She describes the contradiction between demands for a sense of moral duty and hedonistic consumption that renders individuality an ethical problem, inherent in the premises of capitalism, which is overcome by the ability to demand recognition of one's pain (2004, p. 184). How the actual performance of individuality is achieved thus constitutes both morality and other components of a valuable self (ibid., pp. 56ff., see also pp. 119ff.).

Whether performative individuality is performed at all, and how it is valued, is related to the resources available. Skeggs uses French sociologist Pierre Bourdieu's conceptual apparatus to theorise middle-class capital. Four forms of class-defining capital serve as the basis for his concept of class: economic capital (which is about money), cultural capital (which includes institutionalised capital such as education, objectified capital in the form of cultural affiliations, and embodied capital such as habitus[15]), social capital (that is, a person's social network) and symbolic capital (Bourdieu 2010). In simple terms, his class theory means that the first three forms of capital are anchored in concrete assets. However, none of these assets functions as a status-enhancing class definition in all contexts. They must be recognised by the environment as class markers in order to become symbolic. On the basis of this type of capital, valuable selves

---

[15] Habitus refers to the bodily incorporation of cultural capital. This consists of habits, tastes, knowledge and dispositions shaped by different experiences.

can thus be expressed. But one problem is that, according to Bourdieu's theory, being working class is defined as lack, and it becomes difficult to analyse values that do not fit into middle-class capital metaphors.

Some time after Skeggs' book *Becoming Respectable: Constructions of Class and Gender* (1998) was published, she realised that respectability was really about value (2012, p. 69). What the women in her study were constantly fighting for was to establish and maintain their value, she writes. But Bourdieu's capital metaphors are not sufficient to theorise the value of the working class, i.e. a social group constituted as scarcity (Skeggs 2011, pp. 501ff.). His metaphors are about values that are regarded as valuable according to the capitalist logic of the middle class, i.e. as market values. Instead, Skeggs argues that we need an analysis that allows us to see personal values, which the bourgeois gaze does not perceive (2011, p. 496), such as integrity, care and love (ibid., p. 504). In this book, I have thus strived to move beyond the capital metaphors. However, to do so in an academic text from an academic position integrated into the perspectives that underlie the entire academic conceptual apparatus is difficult, but aided by the use of a power-sensitive approach, aiming to view the world as it unfolds from the bodily positions of the interviewees. However, the analysis reveals spaces for value beyond the metaphors of capital, rather than a new conceptual apparatus for value. A new language for these spaces is needed.

1.10 Disposition

I want to emphasise that drug use linked to gender and class could be researched in countless ways. This is true of all research subjects, but in this book, which sheds light on the subject from many angles, it is important to emphasise that the study is not an attempt to get a grip on drug use as a whole. The themes that have emerged are about interesting issues that came to light from a queer phenomenological perspective that makes class and gender visible.

Drugs are a topic that evokes strong emotions. Talking about drugs makes people stop in their tracks and raise their eyebrows. At the same time, it is a subject about which few people have in-depth knowledge.

This combination of strong emotions and vague understandings of the subject makes it important to ask some basic questions before turning to the interview material in the book. These questions are: What exactly is a drug? How do drugs relate to medicines? How did they come onto the market, where are they now and how are they used in Sweden? What does the research on drugs look like, and how did the drug use that was criminalised become illegal? These are all questions that need to be answered to some extent in order to contextualise the interview material and position the study.

1.11 Part I

The first part of the book, after this introduction, therefore consists of a background chapter: **Drugs, Alcohol and Medicine in Sweden**. Here, I examine how drugs have become meaningful and what this has to do with class and gender. Under the heading **Drug Laws and Drug Culture**, I show how drugs first came into use in the Western world, how they spread and how different substances and preparations came to be regarded from a legal and moral perspective. Why is alcohol not obviously perceived as a drug and what role do class and gender play in the laws and moral positions related to intoxication? In the third section, **Drugs and Women**, I examine the legal market for controlled medicines and its connection to women. Why do women use more medicines but fewer illicit drugs than men? This has to do with how women's drug use has been constructed historically, and how the effects of different substances can be related to gender and class.

In 1968, the Narcotics Penalty Act came into force, and from then onwards, certain drugs became more strictly regulated. The fourth section, **Sweden's Drug Problem from the 1960s Onwards**, examines how this happened and explains how illness and social deviation have been two influential perspectives on how drug use is viewed, with roots extending far back in history. This is reflected in the remarkable gap between drug policy and drug research in Sweden since the 1980s, when repressive policies have been fiercely debated. The last section, **Qualitative Research on People Who Use Drugs**, looks into studies based on fieldwork and interviews with people who use drugs, especially women. The majority of such studies, and drug research in general, focus on socially marginalised people who use drugs. In this book, I argue that such a focus helps to shape the understanding of drugs and drug use in Sweden. When coupled only with marginalised people who use drugs, moral condemnation of drugs and drug use that builds on that research will be directed towards a specific group of people, rather than the substances and their use.

1.12   Part II

The second part of the book begins where the interviewees began their use of drugs. **The First Visits** explores how the women encountered drugs for the first time. The interviewees describe their use in spatial terms and I elaborate on the metaphor of a gateway into drugs, and the Swedish metaphor of a *knarkträsk*—a drug swamp—signifying problem-use contexts, as cultural reference points. I then look at where they went from their first encounters with drugs, and how these movements in space relate to class.

The next chapter, **Avoiding the *Knarkare***, delves into the most threatening images associated with encounters between people and drugs. The Swedish concept of a *knarkare*—a person who uses drugs— symbolises dirt and danger and is very similar to the most negative images of the working class. But the *knarkare* has its own symbols, such as the hypodermic syringe that once signified purity, the opposite of dirt. I have examined how the women relate to cultural perceptions of *knarkare* and how they move close to them or keep their distance while using drugs.

This is followed by the chapter **Obtaining Drugs**, which also deals with encounters between drugs and people, but this chapter examines how the drugs are acquired in relation to drug markets. The clash between an illegal, masculine-coded and violence-associated market and the ideal drug-induced state, which is described in terms of intimacy and community, is explored. Where does the encounter take place? On what terms? What are the roles of gender and class?

The next chapter, **Staying Appropriate**, examines how the influence of drugs is lived and embodied, and how the fusion of bodies and drugs creates proximities to and distances from other bodies and objects in time and space. How is an appropriate rhythm of restraint and release through the use of drugs kept up? How are drugs hidden or visible while they are in the body?

In many ways, children were perceived by the women as the symbolic counterpart of drugs, which then also make drug-affected bodies the symbolic counterparts of children. In **Behaving with Children,** I explore this charged relationship between women who use drugs and children, who are traditionally women's responsibility to look after. The women describe various strategies to take responsibility, for both symbolic and real-life children.

The chapter **Appropriate Drugs** deals with the interviewees' perceptions of the legitimacy of drug use. Here, the initial focus is on legally prescribed drugs. The interviewees' approach to drugs is analysed in a social context where psychiatric medication is common and often prescribed, but also involves a link to illness and control. The use of illegal drugs can then, in direct contrast to their reputation, represent health and self-control for some of the women, if they have the right resources.

This is followed by the chapter **Negotiating Addiction**, which examines the meanings of addiction from a phenomenological perspective, using Sara Ahmed's concept of lines in relation to the makings of class. How can the relationship between fear of addiction and the desire to use certain drugs but not others be understood? The women's experiences of pleasure as crucial to the development of addiction are explored, as well as the relationship between addiction and middle-class ideals of self-actualisation and development.

The chapter **Happy Using Drugs?** then addresses the charged and ethically problematic relationship between positive emotions and drug use. Such feelings are important motivations for using drugs, but are experienced and described in constant contrast to the opposite of happiness, misery. Is drug-related happiness false? How do respondents deal with their drug-induced happiness?

The chapter, **Is It Ok to Laugh?**, focuses on the drug-use-related expression of laughter. The discussion on research ethics linked to the interviewees' positive feelings evoked by drug use is deepened, with a focus on subsequent laughter and humour as aspects of drug use. The chapter explores the meaning of laughter at drug use from a gender perspective and the specificity in the pattern of the funny stories the women told. These narrations challenge the stereotype of them as mad, sad and bad in positioning them as temporarily mad, but funny and even heroic in their madness.

In the **Conclusions**, I argue that the findings of variety in how drugs are used, and the women's thought-provoking motives and considerations regarding drug use, which have been discussed throughout the book, highlight the discrepancy between drug use as a seemingly fixed and delimited problem, and the multitude of meanings and uses that it can actually have. This book calls for an intersectional revision of what drug use is, and how problems regarding drugs should be tackled, that takes social, material and cultural conditions into account. The world is not drug-free, and the changes of perspective in drug use, as well as the risks, depend upon the point in the world where that drug use takes place.

The appendix **Drugs and Medicines** is a list of the various substances and preparations used by the women participating in the study. It aims to bring these usually hidden objects into the light, thus demystifying them. This is in order to provide greater insight into what the interviewees are talking about. This chapter describes the objects' appearance, history, described effects and uses.

References

Ahmed, Sara. 2006a. *Queer Phenomenology: Orientations, Objects, Others.* Durham, NC: Duke University Press.

Ahmed, Sara. 2006b. Orientations: Toward a Queer Phenomenology. *GLQ: A Journal of Lesbian and Gay Studies* 12 (4): 543–574.

Ahmed, Sara. 2007. A Phenomenology of Whiteness. *Feminist Theory* 8 (2): 149–168.

Ahmed, Sara. 2010. *The Promise of Happiness*. Durham, NC: Duke University Press.

Antoniusson, Eva-Malin, Arne Kristiansen, Leili Laanemets, Bengt Svensson and Dolf Tops. 2005. Sprutbytesfrågan: En granskning av en forskningsgenomgång om effekter av sprutbytesprogram [The Syringe Exchange Issue: A Review of a Research Review on the Impact of Syringe Exchange Programmes]. Meddelanden från Socialhögskolan (1), Socialhögskolan, Lunds universitet.

Bancroft, Angus. 2009. *Drugs, Intoxication and Society*. Cambridge: Polity.

Berg, Daniel. 2016. *Giftets värde: Apotekarnas förståelse av opium i Sverige 1870–1925* [The Value of Poison: Pharmacists' Understanding of Opium in Sweden 1870–1925]. Göteborg and Stockholm: Makadam.

Berridge, Virginia. 2013. *Demons: Our Changing Attitudes to Alcohol, Tobacco & Drugs*. Oxford: Oxford University Press.

Bessonova, Alla, Olga Byelyayeva, Eliza Kurcevič, Maria Plotko, Fay Dennis, Kiran Pienaar, and Marsha Rosengarten. 2023. Living and Responding at the Margins: A Conversation with Narcofeminist Activists. *The Sociological Review* 71 (4): 742–759.

Björkman, Jenny. 2002. Knarkarens förvandlingar [Transformations of the *knarkare*]. *Tvärsnitt* 3: 42–51.

Bourdieu, Pierre. 2010. *Distinction: A Social Critique of the Judgement of Taste*. London: Routledge.

Boyd, Susan C. 2004. *From Witches to Crack Moms*. Durham, NC: Carolina Academic Press.

Bremer, Signe. 2011a. Med kroppen in i berättarrummet: Om närvaro och etik [Bringing the Body into the Storytelling Room: Presence and Ethics]. In *Etnografiska hållplatser: Om metodprocesser och reflexivitet*, ed. Kerstin Gunnemark. Lund: Studentlitteratur.

Bremer, Signe. 2011b. *Kroppslinjer: Kön, transsexualism och kropp i berättelser om könskorrigering* [Body Lines: Gender, Transsexualism and the Body in Narratives of Gender Reassignment]. Göteborg and Stockholm: Makadam.

BRÅ. 2018. *Narkotikaanvändning och misstankar om eget bruk bland ungdomar i Stockholm* [Drug Use and Suspected Drug Use Among Young People in Stockholm]. Stockholm: Brottsförebyggande rådet.

Buxton, Julia, Lona Lauridsen Burger, and Giavana Margo. 2020. Introduction. In *The Impact of Global Drug Policy on Women: Shifting the Needle*, ed. J. Buxton, G. Margo, and L. Burger, 1–8. Emerald Publishing: Bingley.

Campbell, Nancy D. 2000. *Using Women: Gender, Drug Policy, and Social Justice.* Milton Park: Taylor & Francis.

Campbell, Nancy D., and Elizabeth Ettorre. 2011. *Gendering Addiction: The Politics of Drug Treatment in a Neurochemical World.* New York: Palgrave Macmillan.

CAN. 2019. *Drogutvecklingen i Sverige 2019 – med fokus på narkotika* [Drug Trends in Sweden in 2019: With a Focus on Narcotics] (Rapport 180). Stockholm: Centralförbundet för alkohol- och narkotikaupplysning.

CAN. 2021. *Socioekonomiska skillnader i narkotikaanvändning bland vuxna i Sverige* [Socio-Economic Differences in Drug Use Among Adults in Sweden] (Rapport 198). Stockholm: Centralförbundet för alkohol- och narkotikaupplysning.

Chang, Judy. 2020. Women Who Use Drugs: Resistance and Rebellion. In *The Impact of Global Drug Policy on Women: Shifting the Needle*, ed. J. Buxton, G. Margo, and L. Burger, 271–286. Bingley: Emerald Publishing.

Crenshaw, Kimberle. 1989. Demarginalizing the Intersection of Race and Sex: A Black Feminist Critique of Antidiscrimination Doctrine, Feminist Theory and Antiracist Politics *University of Chicago Legal Forum* 1: 138–167 (Article 8).

Daun, Åke. 2003. *Med rörligt sökarljus: Den nya etnologins framväxt under 1960- och 1970-talen. En personlig tidsskildring* [With a Moving Searchlight: The Emergence of the New Ethnology in the 1960s and 1970s. A Personal Account of the Period]. Stockholm: Brutus Östlings Bokförlag Symposion.

de Beauvoir, Simone. 2004/1949. *Det andra könet* [The Second Sex, in original Le Deuxième Sexe]. Stockholm: Norstedts.

Dennis, Fay, Kiran Pienaar, and Marsha Rosengarten. 2023. Narcofeminism and Its Multiples: From Activism to Everyday Minoritarian Worldbuilding. *The Sociological Review* 71 (4): 723–740.

Du Rose, Natacha. 2015. *The Governance of Female Drug Users: Women's Experiences of Drug Policy.* Bristol: Policy Press.

Du Rose, Natacha. 2017. Marginalised Drug-Using Women's Pleasure and Agency. *Social History of Alcohol & Drugs: An Interdisciplinary Journal* 31 (1): 42–64.

Duff, Cameron. 2020. On the Legacy of Normalization. *Addiction* 115 (7): 1378–1381.

Edman, Johan. 2019. Drogerna: Den nya berusningspolitiken [Drugs: The New Policy on Intoxication]. One of six booklets in the collection *Det nya Sverige: Riksbankens Jubileumsfonds årsbok 2019*, ed. Jenny Björkman and Patrik Hadenius. Göteborg and Stockholm: Makadam förlag.

Edman, Johan. 2021. A Century of Dissonance and Harmony in Swedish Intoxication Policy. In *Retreat or Entrenchment? Drug Policies in the Nordic Countries at a Crossroads*, ed. Henrik Tham, 239–265. Stockholm: Stockholm University Press. https://doi.org/10.16993/bbo.j. License: CC BY 4.0.

Edman, Johan, and Börje. Olsson. 2014. The Swedish Drug Problem: Conceptual Understanding and Problem Handling, 1839–2011. *Nordic Studies on Alcohol & Drugs/Nordisk Alkohol- & Narkotikatidskrift* 31 (5/6): 503–526.

Ekendahl, Mats. 2009. The Construction of Maintenance Treatment Legitimacy: A Discourse Analysis of a Policy Shift. *Evidence & Policy* 5 (3): 247–265.

Eklund, Niklas. 2017. Naloxon nu: Civil olydnad för att rädda liv [Naloxone Now: Civil Disobedience to Save Lives]. In *Dogmer som dödar: Vägval för svensk narkotikapolitik*, ed. Niklas Eklund and Mikaela Hildebrand, 281–290. Stockholm: Verbal förlag.

EMCDDA. 2021. *Drug-Related Deaths and Mortality in Europe: Update from the EMCDDA Expert Network*. Luxemburg: Publications Office of the European Union.

Ettorre, Elizabeth. 2015. Embodied Deviance, Gender, and Epistemologies of Ignorance: Re-visioning Drugs Use in a Neurochemical, Unjust World. *Substance Use & Misuse* 50: 794–805.

Ettorre, Elizabeth. 2017. Feminist Autoethnography, Gender, and Drug Use: "Feeling About" Empathy While "Storying the I." *Contemporary Drug Problems* 44 (4): 356–374.

Fahl, Hanna. 2014. Jag sjunger om mitt liv [I Sing About My Life]. *Dagens Nyheter*, 12 oktober.

Farber, David, ed. 2022. *The War on Drugs*. New York, NY: New York University Press.

Franck, Johan, and Ingrid Nylander. 2011. *Beroendemedicin* [Addiction Medicine]. Lund: Studentlitteratur.

Friedman, Jennifer, and Marisa Alicea. 1995. Women and Heroin: The Path of Resistance and Its Consequences. *Gender & Society* 9 (4): 432–449.

Frykman, Jonas. 1977. *Horan i bondesamhället* [The Whore in Peasant Society]. Lund: Liber Läromedel.

Frykman, Jonas. 2006. Ting som redskap [Things as Tools]. *RIG: Kulturhistorisk tidskrift* 89 (2): 65–77.

Garfinkel, Harold. 1967. *Studies in Ethnomethodology*. Cambridge: Polity Press.

Göransson, Michelle. 2012. *Materialiserade sexualiteter* [Materialised Sexualities]. Göteborg and Stockholm: Makadam Förlag.

Grønnestad, Trond Erik, and Philip Lalander. 2015. The Bench: An Open Drug Scene and Its People. *Nordic Studies on Alcohol and Drugs* 32: 165–182.

Gynnå Oguz, Christina. 2017. Kriminalisering av eget bruk: framgångssaga eller dödsstöten för en human narkotikapolitik? [Criminalisation of Personal Use: Success Story or Death Knell for a Humane Drug Policy?] In *Dogmer som dödar: vägval för svensk narkotikapolitik*, ed. Niklas Eklund and Mikaela Hildebrand, 313–333. Stockholm: Verbal förlag.

Hansson, Kristofer. 2007. *I ett andetag: en kulturanalys av astma som begränsning och möjlighet* [In One Breath: A Cultural Analysis of Asthma as Constraint and Opportunity]. Stockholm: Critical Ethnography Press.

Haraway, Donna. 1988. Situated Knowledges: The Science Question in Feminism and the Privilege of Partial Perspective. *Feminist Studies* 14 (3): 575–599.

Haraway, Donna. 1991. *Simians, Cyborgs, and Women: The Reinvention of Nature*. New York: Routledge.

Heal, David J., Sharon L. Smith, Sean J. Belouin, and Jack E. Henningfield. 2023. Psychedelics: Threshold of a Therapeutic Revolution. *Neuropharmacology* 236. Unpaginated open-access document.

Heidegger, Martin. 1962/1927. *Being and Time*. Oxford: Basil Blackwell [Translation of *Sein und Zeit*].

Heilig, Markus. 2015. *Alkohol, droger och hjärnan: tro och vetande utifrån modern neurovetenskap* [Alcohol, Drugs and the Brain: Beliefs and Knowledge Based on Modern Neuroscience]. Stockholm: Natur & Kultur.

Heilig, Markus. 2017. Dogmer som dödar [Dogmas That Kill]. In *Dogmer som dödar: vägval för svensk narkotikapolitik*, ed. Niklas Eklund and Mikaela Hildebrand, 53–66. Stockholm: Verbal förlag.

Hilte, Mats. 2019. Psychoactive Drugs and the Management of Time. *Sociologisk Forskning* 56 (2): 111–124.

Irigaray, Luce. 1985. *This Sex Which Is Not One*. New York, NY: Cornell University Press.

Johannisson, Karin. 1995. *Den mörka kontinenten: Kvinnan, medicinen och fin-de-siècle* [The Dark Continent: Women, Medicine and the fin-de-siècle]. Stockholm: Norstedts.

Johannisson, Karin. 2015. *Den sårade divan: Om psykets estetik (och om Agnes von K, Sigrid H och Nelly S)* [The Wounded Diva: On the Aesthetics of the Psyche (and on Agnes von K, Sigrid H and Nelly S)]. Stockholm: Albert Bonniers förlag.

Johnson, Björn. 2005. *Metadon på liv och död: En bok om narkomanvård och narkotikapolitik i Sverige* [Methadone for Life and Death: A Book on Drug Treatment and Drug Policy in Sweden]. Lund: Studentlitteratur.

Kakko, Johan. 2011. *Heroinberoende* [Heroin Addiction]. Stockholm: Liber.

Kakko, Johan. 2017. Killing by Silence: om makt, maktens rus och maktmissbruk [Killing by Silence: On Power, the Intoxication of Power and the Abuse of Power]. In *Dogmer som dödar: vägval för svensk narkotikapolitik*, ed. Niklas Eklund and Mikaela Hildebrand, 67–80. Stockholm: Verbal förlag.

Karlsson, Niklas, Torsten Berglund, Anna Mia Ekström, Anders Hammarberg, and Tuukka Tammi. 2020. Could 30 Years of Political Controversy on Needle Exchange Programmes in Sweden Contribute to Scaling-Up Harm Reduction Services in the World? *Nordic Studies on Alcohol and Drugs* 38 (1): 66–88.

Khoury, Jamil, and Stephen Combs. 2012. *Not Quite White: Arabs, Slavs, and the Contours of Contested Whiteness*. Chicago: Silk Road Rising, https://www. youtube.com/watch?v=vHmbI2mnuwU [2023-06-20]

Kusenbach, Margarethe. 2003. Street Phenomenology: The Go-Along as Ethnographic Research Tool. *Ethnography* 4 (3): 455–485.

Laanemets, Leili. 2002. Skapande av femininitet: Om kvinnor i missbrukarbehandling [The Creation of Femininity: About Women in Substance Abuse Treatment]. Diss., Lunds universitet, Lund.

Lander, Ingrid. 2003. Den flygande maran: En studie om narkotikabrukande kvinnor i Stockholm [The Flying Mara: A Study of Eight Drug-Using Women in Stockholm]. Diss., tockholms universitet, Stockholm.

Lennartsson, Rebecka. 2019. *Mamsell Bohmans fall: Nattlöperskor i 1700-talets Stockholm* [The Fall of Mamsell Bohman: Night Walkers in 18th Century Stockholm]. Stockholm: Stockholmia förlag.

Linton, Magnus. 2015. *Knark: en svensk historia* [Knark: A Swedish Story]. Stockholm: Bokförlaget Atlas.

Lupton, Deborah. 2012. *Medicine as Culture: Illness, Disease and the Body*. London: Sage [ebook].

Löfgren, Orvar, and Billy Ehn. 2010. *Vardagslivets etnologi: reflektioner kring en kulturvetenskap* [Ethnology of Everyday Life: Reflections on a Cultural Science]. Stockholm: Natur & Kultur.

Mattsson, Tina. 2005. *I viljan att göra det normala: En kritisk studie av genusperspektivet i missbrukarvården* [In the Desire to Make Normal: A Critical Study of the Gender Perspective in Substance Abuse Treatment]. Malmö: Egalité.

McClintock, Anne. 1995. *Imperial Leather: Race, Gender and Sexuality in the Colonial Contest.* New York, NY: Routledge.

Measham, Fiona. 2002. "Doing Gender"–"Doing Drugs": Conceptualizing the Gendering of Drugs Cultures. *Contemporary Drug Problems* 29: 335–373.

Measham, Fiona. 2019. Drug Safety Testing, Disposals and Dealing in an English Field: Exploring the Operational and Behavioural Outcomes of the UK's First Onsite 'Drug Checking' Service. *International Journal of Drug Policy* 67: 102–107.

Merleau-Ponty, Maurice. 1968. *The Visible and the Invisible: Followed by Working Notes.* Evanston, IL: Northwestern University Press.

Merleau-Ponty, Maurice. 2010. *Institution and Passivity: Course Notes from the Collège de France (1954–1955).* Foreword by Claude LeFort. Evanston, IL: Northwestern University Press.

Nader, Laura. 1972. *Up the Anthropologist: Perspectives Gained from Studying Up.* Department of Anthropology, University of California. https://files.eric.ed.gov/fulltext/ED065375.pdf [2023-08-06].

Nairn, Karen, Jenny Munro, and Anne B. Smith. 2005. A Counter-Narrative of a "Failed" Interview. *Qualitative Research* 5 (2): 221–244.

Nelson, Stanley. 2021. *Crack: Cocaine, Corruption & Conspiracy* [film]. Netflix.

OECD iLibrary. 2021. *Health at a Glance 2021: OECD Indicators.* OECD Publishing. https://doi.org/10.1787/ae3016b9-en.

Olsson, Börje. 1994. *Narkotikaproblemets bakgrund: Användning av och uppfattningar om narkotika inom svensk medicin 1839–1965* [The Background of the Drug Problem: Use and Perceptions of Drugs in Swedish Medicine 1839–1965] (CAN rapportserie, 39). Stockholm: CAN.

Preciado, Paul B. 2013. *Testo Junkie: Sex, Drugs and Biopolitics in the Pharmacopornographic Era.* New York, NY: Feminist Press.

Pripp, Oscar. 2011. Reflektion och etik [Reflection and Ethics]. In *Etnologiskt fältarbete*, 2. uppl., ed. Lars Kaijser and Magnus Öhlander. Lund: Studentlitteratur.

Race, Kane. 2009. *Pleasure Consuming Medicine: The Queer Politics of Drugs.* Durham, NC: Duke University Press.

Regeringens proposition 2022/23:53. 2023. *Skärpta straff för brott i kriminella nätverk* [Tougher Penalties for Criminal Network Offences]. 2022/23:53.

Regeringens skrivelse. 2015/16:86. *En samlad strategi för alkohol-, narkotika-, dopnings- och tobakspolitiken 2016 – 2020* [A Comprehensive Strategy for Alcohol, Drugs, Doping and Tobacco Policy 2016–2020]. Skr. 2015/16:86.

Richert, Torkel. 2014. Överdoser, försörjningsstrategier och riskhantering: Livsvillkor för personer som injicerar narkotika. Diss., Malmö universitet, Malmö.

Richert, Torkel. 2017. Överdosprevention – En övergripande strategi [Overdose Prevention: A Comprehensive Approach]. In *Dogmer som dödar: vägval för svensk narkotikapolitik*, ed. Niklas Eklund and Mikaela Hildebrand, 255–280. Stockholm: Verbal förlag.

Rosenbaum, Marsha. 1997. Women, Research and Policy. In *Substance Abuse: A Comprehensive Textbook*, 3rd ed., ed. Joyce H. Lowingson, Pedro Ruiz, Robert B. Millman, and John G. Langrod. Baltimore, MD: Williams & Wilkins.

Rosengren, Annette. 2003. *Mellan ilska och hopp: Om hemlöshet, droger och kvinnor* [Between Anger and Hope: On Homelessness, Drugs and Women]. Stockholm: Carlsson bokförlag.

Rödner, Sharon, Max Hansson, and Börje Olsson. 2007. *Socialt integrerade narkotika- användare, myt eller verklighet?* [Socially Integrated Drug Users, Myth or Reality?] (SoRAD Forskningsrapport 47). Stockholm: Stockholms universitet.

Schlag, Anne Katrin. 2020. Percentages of Problem Drug Use and Their Implications for Policy Making: A Review of the Literature. *Drug Science, Policy and Law* 6. Unpaginated open-access document.

Shulgin, Alexander, and Ann Shulgin. 2019. *Pihkal: A Chemical Love Story*. Berkeley, CA: Transform Press.

Sigfridsson, Ingegerd. 2005. *Självklara drycker? Kaffe och alkohol i social samvaro* [Obvious Drinks? Coffee and Alcohol in Socialising]. Göteborg: Arkipelag.

Skeggs, Beverley. 1998. *Formations of Class & Gender*. London: Sage.

Skeggs, Beverley. 2004. *Class, Self, Culture*. London: Routledge.

Skeggs, Beverley. 2011. Imagining Personhood Differently: Person Value and Autonomist Working-Class Value Practices. *The Sociological Review* 59 (3): 496–513.

Skeggs, Beverley. 2012. Åter till frågan om respektabilitet: personvärdets moraliska ekonomi [Returning to the Issue of Respectability: The Moral Economy of Personal Value]. *Fronesis* (40–42): 64–83.

Statens Folkhälsoinstitut. 2010. *Narkotikabruket i Sverige* [Drug Use in Sweden]. Östersund: Statens Folkhälsoinstitut.

Svensson, Bengt. 1996. *Pundare, jonkare och andra: med narkotikan som följeslagare* [Pounders, Junkies and Others: With Drugs as a Companion]. Stockholm: Carlsson bokförlag.

Tham, Henrik, ed. 2021. *Retreat or Entrenchment? Drug Policies in the Nordic Countries at a Crossroads.* Stockholm: Stockholm University Press.

Travis, Trysh. 2019. Toward a Feminist History of the Drug-Using Woman: And Her Recovery. *Feminist Studies* 45 (1): 209–233.

UNODC. 2015. Status and Trend Analysis of Illicit Drug Markets. In *World Drug Report: Drug Use and Health Consequences*, 1–75. New York, NY: United Nations.

Waters, Jaime. 2015. Snowball Sampling: A Cautionary Tale Involving a Study of Older Drug Users. *International Journal of Social Research Methodology* 18 (4): 367–380.

West, Candace, and Don Zimmerman. 1987. Doing Gender. *Gender and Society* 1 (2): 125–151.

Wierup, Lasse, and Erik de la Reguera. 2010. *Kokain: drogen som fick medelklassen att börja knarka och länder att falla samman* [Cocaine: The Drug That Drove the Middle Class to Drugs and Countries to Collapse]. Stockholm: Norstedts.

Wiklund, Lisa, and Jenny Damberg. 2015. *Som hon drack: kvinnor, alkohol och frigörelse* [As She Drank: Women, Alcohol and Liberation]. Stockholm: Bokförlaget Atlas.

2

Drugs, Alcohol and Medicine in Sweden

Nicotine pouches and cigarettes, tea and wine and Absolut vodka. People crave temporary alterations of their starting point, the body's experience of the present. A quick look around reveals just how widespread such desires are. The modern world offers almost endless opportunities to alter one's state of mind.

In his book on the history of psychoactive substances in the West, *Forces of Habit* (2002), historian David T. Courtwright describes how he had a sudden realisation while in an airport:

> I found myself wondering why I was surrounded by drugs. Marlboro cartons loomed to my left, Drambuie bottles to my right, Belgian choco-lates behind me, Kenyan coffee straight ahead – everywhere I looked, I saw imported psychoactive products. How did these things get here? And why could "here" be anywhere – why did duty free shops all seem to be stocked with the same merchandise? (p. vii)

This quote highlights just how well known and widely available these products are. More than anything, however, it illustrates the everyday nature of psychoactive products—commonplace to the point of invisibility. Courtwright can write "Marlboro" instead of "cigarettes", safe in

© The Author(s) 2024
E. Eleonorasdotter, *Women's Drug Use in Everyday Life*,
https://doi.org/10.1007/978-3-031-46057-9_2

the knowledge that the reader will know what he is talking about. Duty-free shops almost exclusively sell psychoactive products, and the goods on offer are the same irrespective of where in the world the airport is located. Courtwright, a drug researcher for decades, conveys a surprising sense of not really having noticed this before. He writes that he has come to understand the trade in psychoactive drugs as one of the defining features of the modern world. Indeed, he goes so far as to call the last 500 years the psychoactive revolution (2002), and points out how people's ability to use psychoactive stimulants during this time has escalated from a single local preparation to the range available today.

It is thus within a context full of different possibilities for changing the mind that people in the twenty-first century move, which means a constant orientation either towards or away from these possibilities. Saying "no" or "yes" are, above all, everyday decisions that are part of the "obscure flows of habits and attitudes" that ethnologists Orvar Löfgren and Billy Ehn describe as characteristic of what ethnologists find when they take a closer look at people's everyday lives (2012, p. 15). However, the fact that actions are everyday does not make them less significant, quite the contrary. Such actions both create and challenge social life (ibid., p. 5). Drug use, in Courtwright's broad sense of including choco-late as well as heroin, is part of a culture of consumption that accentuates differences. Proximity to and distance from psychoactive substances are linked to the creation of identity (cf. Löfgren and Ehn 2001, pp. 64ff.). Attitudes to various psychoactive substances are thus performative acts (Butler 1990), i.e. a subjectivity that comes into being through its expression.

Alcohol consumption in Sweden is a good example of this. For most of her career, well-known etiquette expert Magdalena Ribbing advised Swedes on how to behave, in her characteristically proper way. In an interview, she looks back on her youth and describes how red wine was drunk while sitting on the floor in mahjong clothes during the 1960s (Hellqvist 2008). Criminologist and TV celebrity Leif G. W. Persson regularly speaks out about crime, but has also made a name for himself as a proponent of traditional masculinity. In his *Big Macho Book*[1] (1990),

---

[1] *Stora machoboken* (1990).

he describes joining a hunting party; one of the men treated the others to white wine and even added some to the food he was cooking. The entire party consequently assumed that the man was gay, according to Persson (pp. 202f.). Beer, brandy and slightly sweet dark-rye bread with *falukorv* sausage and butter, on the other hand, are what "real" (hetero-sexual) men consume, Persson claims, before adding racist remarks to the homophobic, cautioning against drinking rosé Champagne:

> Rosé Champagne isn't a beverage, it is a symbol for slickness. Only shady southerners drink it; upstanding northerners steer clear of it. You know what I mean. (ibid., p. 200)[2]

These examples show how alcohol (as well as the colours pink, white and red, just like food, clothes, sitting on the floor, etc.) can become tools with which to perform gender, race, age, class, sexuality and other aspects of one's identity (cf. Measham 2002; Moore and Measham 2013). Such cultural keys also affect the way in which the effect of alcohol—drunkenness—is interpreted.

Most women in the West are expected to drink alcohol nowadays. In spite of this, women are still held to different standards than men when they are intoxicated (cf. Sigfridsson 2005). The examples are many, but one serious consequence of gendered beliefs concerns sexual abuse. Numerous studies have shown that when a man has raped a woman and the case is brought to court, the verdict is often to the detriment of the woman if she happened to be drunk—but in the man's favour if he had been drinking (Nilsson and Lövkrona 2015; Wiklund and Damberg 2015, pp. 187ff.). A related problem is how women's visible intoxication is condemned. Freelance journalist Lisbeth Borger-Bendegard writes in her 1975 book *Open Letter on Women and Alcohol*[3]:

> It is considered ugly for women to drink. [...] Male alcoholics at Karolinska Hospital's group therapy often despise their female peers, even though they are being treated for the same thing. Even girls who drink

---

[2] All quotes in Swedish have been translated by me.

[3] *Öppet brev om kvinnor och sprit* (1975).

themselves find it "scarier to see a drunk girl than a drunk guy". [...] There is no equality within alcoholism. (p. 12)

Ethnologist Lisa Wiklund and journalist Jenny Damberg quote an interview with "football wife" Malin Wollin by Malou von Sivers on the latter's TV show *Efter tio*: "A mother should be there for her children, in a way. [...] There's just something so pathetic about a drunk woman!" (2015, p. 124). Analysing the cultural framework within which women drink alcohol, Wiklund and Damberg arrive at the following conclusion: "The right to make a fool of oneself when drunk is far from gender equal. A drunk woman is judged much more harshly than a drunk man" (ibid., p. 188). To which they add: "Chipping away at the taboo on women and alcohol is a way of showing that women and men do not have different roles: all human beings should be allowed to engage in every aspect of life" (ibid., p. 191).

In other words, Wiklund and Damberg suggest that it is self-evident that gender equality is best achieved through a freer approach to alcohol and women, making the right to drink a feminist issue. But the same gender balance would be achieved by increased taboos around men's drinking, which could, for example, have a dampening effect on men's violence. A report from BRÅ states that, in nine cases out of ten, men are the perpetrators of assault, threats, personal robbery and sexual offences, and that in more than half of these cases, regardless of the type of offence, they have been drunk (Olseryd 2015). However, the link between violence and alcohol or other drugs is strongest in the case of men's offences against other men. In any case, the relationship between intoxication and feminist strategies aimed at gender equality is not straightforward. On the one hand, women's freedom and self-esteem are affected by stigma and taboo; on the other hand, alcohol can be linked to health risks and violence.

This book focuses mainly on illegal drugs. But anyone who imagines that there are clear demarcations between illegal and legal drugs, or that illegal drugs have been relegated to a dark, well-defined corner on the fringes of society, may find the following text disturbing. The further the work has progressed, the more the boundaries between different drugs have appeared vague and elusive, based on cultural beliefs rather than chemical composition.

This is not just the case with drugs, however, and should perhaps not come as a surprise to a cultural researcher. Ethnologist Gabriella Nilsson has analysed popular medical texts with a focus on ideas related to healthy and unhealthy food (Nilsson 2011b). She shows how the cultural charge of food, rather than its nutritional content, is crucial to perceptions of its health aspects. Small-scale production compared to mass industrial processes and ideas linked to a safe "past" compared to a risky "present" are key concepts that sort food into good and bad based on what she believes is an underlying critique of modernity. This is a criticism that developed in line with industrialisation and tends to romanticise earlier societies, when the supply was smaller and locally produced, and portrays industrialised and urban life as threatening and hazardous to health (see also Nilsson 2011a; Johannisson 1995). In his thesis *The Threat of Pleasure: Establishing Drug Use as a Social Problem 1890–1970*[4] (1993), sociologist Sven-Åke Lindgren argues that drugs, such as pills, were constructed as a target for criticism during the period under study. He argues that drugs, with their connotations of pleasure and immoderation, manifested the artificial in contrast to the natural.

In the popular medicine texts studied by Gabriella Nilsson, modern society is presented in a way that parallels Courtwright's (2002) impressions at the airport:

> Cheap food and drink is available around the clock, wherever we are. Children can consume sweetened drinks and energy-dense food anywhere, anytime and at almost no cost. Society is deregulated and virtually invaded by opportunities for unhealthy consumption. (Nilsson 2011b, p. 208)

Whether the discussion centres on food or drugs, the modern world seems to be a place where the sheer amount of unhealthy goods is overwhelming and threateningly in one's face. Illegal drugs and the illegal drug market are part of that picture (EMCDDA 2022, p. 4). Under

---

[4] *Den hotfulla njutningen: Att etablera drogbruk som samhällsproblem 1890–1970* (1993).

the headline "This Is Where Drugs Are Sold in Town—Right in Front of Your Eyes", local Stockholm newspaper *Mitt i* interviews police officers who specialise in narcotics about the prevalence of drugs in the city (Bonnichsen 2017):

> In back alleys, in parks and in bars. Here, drugs are openly sold in the centre of town. "They're everywhere," says police officer Lennart Karlsson, who specialises in narcotics. [...] The drugs being sold and bought include everything from cannabis and prescription pills to harder drugs like heroin. Cocaine is most common out in bars. [n.p.]

According to the quotes, opportunities for unhealthy consumption, including all kinds of drugs, are "everywhere". But cultural beliefs, and thus everyday decisions, are different in different social contexts. Some people struggle with daily decisions about whether or not to use heroin and, if so, in what quantity. Others struggle with the question of whether to eat chocolate with their afternoon coffee and, if so, how big the piece should be, and still others worry about both of these issues. Anthropologist Richard Wilk writes that the moral regulation of consumption is fundamental to modern consumer cultures: "[...] if there are any universal characteristics underpinning consumer cultures it is the desire for the moral balancing of virtue and excess" (2014, p. 1).

But the fact that the everyday regulation of virtue and pleasure applies to a wide range of substances does not mean that there are no differences between chocolate and heroin. In fact, the differences between the popular confectionery ingredient and one of the world's most deadly and addictive drugs are vast. They look different, are used in different ways, can be linked to different effects and have different cultural and legal status. But so do the differences between many different illegal drugs, between different types of legal drugs and between the same drugs, i.e. the same active substances, prepared in different ways (Nutt et al. 2010; Olsson 2017, p. 28; Schivelbusch 1993). The ambiguities surrounding drugs and possible approaches to them have often been overwhelming in their scope, and I am not the first author to face this elusiveness. The philosopher, cultural theorist and novelist Sadie Plant, in the introduction to her 1999 book *Writing on Drugs*, aptly expresses how I have also felt:

> To write on drugs is to plunge into a world where nothing is as simple or as stable as it seems. Everything about it shimmers and mutates as you try to hold its gaze. Facts and figures dance around each other; lines of enquiry scatter like expensive dust. The reasons for the laws and the motives for the wars, the nature of the pleasures and the trouble drugs can cause, the tangled web of chemicals, the plants, the brain, machines: ambiguity surrounds them all. (p. 248)

Plant puts her finger on how prior knowledge, research and thinking about drugs repeatedly reach points where they seem to dissolve into too many conflicting fragments to be grasped. Where do we draw the line between frightening and non-frightening? Who determines it and why? What is sick and dangerous and what is human and healthy?

But does the accessibility of a wide range of substances automatically lead to problematic consumption? It would hardly be fair to regard the last 500 years, i.e. the period that Courtwright calls the psychoactive revolution, as a period in which health-related living conditions have deteriorated. Life expectancy has increased dramatically and there are now many more medical aids available for life crises, pain, anxiety and behavioural problems (cf. Johannisson 1990). But problems in the wake of drug use are also very present as both global and local issues.

2.1   Drug Laws and Drug Culture

What the trade in psychoactive substances looks like depends on which substance is being traded. A number of singled-out substances are subject to narcotics laws—either as controlled prescription medications or as illegal goods. Historians Brian Cowan (2005), Virginia Berridge (2013) and the abovementioned David T. Courtwright (2002) are just some of the researchers who have sought to explore why different substances and products (including opium, alcohol, coffee and tobacco) have attained such different legal and cultural statuses, and why these statuses have changed over time. To answer these questions, they highlight complex webs of international and national trade relationships, political battles, temperance movements and beliefs surrounding sickness and health, and the ways in which these factors have resulted in different regulatory systems. Berridge points out that very few substances have been subject to total prohibition: selling opiates and amphetamines, for example, is not illegal, as long as the substances are produced by registered pharmaceutical companies and prescribed by licensed healthcare providers (2013, p. 7). When I write "illegal drugs", I am thus referring to drugs that have been illegally acquired—not necessarily drugs that were also illegally produced or for which every link of the sales process was illegal.

Another example of how substances are regulated is through sales restrictions. Alcohol, which from the Middle Ages onwards has continued to be a popular substance among all social classes in Sweden, has been and still is characterised by restrictive regulations. Above all, efforts to curb its use have focused on discouraging women and workers from drinking (Jönsson and Tellström 2018, pp. 154f.; Berridge 2013). Ethnologist Håkan Jönsson and food researcher Richard Tellström describe how extensive drinking among the working class began to be regarded as a social problem in the nineteenth century. It could lead to fines or imprisonment (2018, pp. 116f.). Exactly how large the consumption was is difficult to say because the information available does not seem reasonable, which Jönsson and Tellström believe indicates that the alcoholic strength of different drinks was not the same as today. They take an example from a consumption regulation dated 1770 that specifies suitable travel costs for a traveller in a horse-drawn carriage. A journey of seven miles was considered to require two jugs of spirits per person, which is equivalent to more than five litres per traveller. "The journey could take between one and two days, depending on the nature of the road", write Jönsson and Tellström, and the researchers conclude that it was probably not 40% brandy, as such a level of consumption could have been fatal. Nevertheless, alcohol consumption seems to have been high.

In Sweden, alcohol consumption is nowadays regulated through Systembolaget—a government-owned chain of off-licences, with branches in all Swedish towns. The very first such store opened its doors in Dalarna in 1850, with the intention of curbing the alcoholism that was inflicting considerable damage on society. The mine owners united and set up a system for the sale of alcohol, perhaps more out of economic interest rather than any genuine concern for their workers' health.[5]

At the time, the temperance movement was rapidly attracting followers. These initial attempts to regulate the sale of alcohol were followed by others. The Bratt System (in which bars had to observe stringent restrictions and those who were allowed to consume alcohol were given a *motbok*—a booklet in which a stamp was added each time the owner bought anything at an off-licence) was implemented across the nation in 1919. The measure revealed that gender and class, rather than alcoholic drinks themselves, were believed to be the main driver of alcohol abuse (see Jönsson and Tellström 2018, p. 205; Edman 2019, pp. 15, 27). Women who cohabited with a man—regardless of whether they lived with their parents or husband or were live-in housemaids— were not given their own *motbok*, because they were then included in the men's household. Women living alone could get a *motbok*, but usually only a half ration. While the *motbok* system made it very difficult to obtain brandy or beer, wine—which was expensive and mainly consumed by the bourgeoisie—could be purchased in almost unlimited quantities. Jönsson and Tellström describe Bratt's view of working-class intoxication in relation to that of the bourgeoisie, as though sobriety and drunkenness had nothing to do with alcohol per se but were about certain forms of preparation in certain bodies.

> Bratt and his allies viewed bourgeois society's wine-drinking and frequent lavish business dinners in private homes and restaurants as something fundamentally different than the working class's getting drunk; as a result, it did not need to be curtailed to achieve their goal of a soberer society. (2018, p. 205)

---

[5] From the Centre for Business Industry's archive on Systembolaget. Theme: *Ursprunget* [Origins] [2023-08-02].

The Bratt system affected the amount of alcohol consumed. Jönsson and Tellström report that, in 1878, before the Bratt system was established, 6.5 litres of spirits per inhabitant were being served in company pubs in Stockholm. By 1915—when the Bratt system had been implemented in some cities—only 0.3 litres were being served, and the decline was almost as great in Gothenburg (ibid., p. 206). Systembolaget has survived until our day, with a majority of the Swedish people on its side, although it has come close to losing its popularity several times.[6]

In other words, the efforts to regulate alcohol have always ended up in its authorised sale to some pleasure-seekers, while drugs, i.e. the myriad of substances that now come under drug legislation, have travelled a different path. Drugs used for pleasure are criminalised, while controlled medicines constitute a large market. Courtwright (2002) and Schivelbusch (1993) argue that it was simply the extent of the use of tobacco, coffee and alcohol that made the sale of these drugs impossible to ban, while opium, cocaine and cannabis were only used by a small number of people, which enabled strict legislation. The word "narcotics" was first used to refer to substances such as opium that could induce anaesthesia, but as the drug conventions were expanded, it came to include psychoactive drugs "with addictive properties or euphoric effects" (SFS 1968:64, §8). However, certain preparations with such properties, such as tobacco and alcoholic beverages, have never been defined as narcotics, even though they fulfil the definitional criteria. The Swedish National Encyclopaedia puts it simply: "Traditionally, however, the addictive substances alcohol, nicotine, caffeine and organic solvents are not considered narcotics" (Nationalencyklopedin, n.d. "Narkotika").

Opium, which was the main reason for the first international control agreement, the International Opium Convention, signed on 23 January

---

[6] From Systembolaget's archives at the Centre for Business History. Theme: *Händelser* [Events] [2023-08-02].

1912 in The Hague,[7] is an example of how the meaning of a psychoactive substance can change across time. The first evidence of opium use dates back around 6,000 years, and opium played an important role in Greek, Roman and Arabic medicine (Berridge 2013, p. 9). The drug spread across Europe during the fourteenth century and, in Sweden, opium preparations such as laudanum could be bought over the counter well into the twentieth century, writes economic historian Daniel Berg (2016). Sociologist Börje Olsson writes that opium was mainly discussed in positive terms in Swedish medical journals throughout the nineteenth century (1994, pp. 50–52, 59).

According to Berridge (2013), Courtwright (2002), Shivelbusch (1993) and Berg (2016), what then unfolded and led to international agreements on increasingly powerful regulation was largely based on trade disputes between major powers (primarily Great Britain's massive and aggressive sale to China of opium grown in colonised India, but also the involvement of the USA) and the economic interests of various actors, the impact of Western temperance movements and professional battles between pharmacists and doctors. The potent opioids morphine and, later, heroin were developed in 1804 and 1899, respectively, and were widely distributed through pharmacies, before the intravenous use of morphine and heroin in particular led to a noticeable addiction problem that became too extensive to be ignored.

However, this was not the case in Sweden, where it was not until the mid-1970s that the use of heroin became a more significant problem (Olsson 2017, p. 29). For a long time, in Sweden, intravenous use of amphetamines was the most problematic drug use, which criminologists Leif Lenke and Börje Olsson argue is remarkable in an international comparison, and it is difficult to find the reason (2002). Around the 1920s, aspirin began to replace opium when the purpose of the medication was to reduce pain. Around the middle of the twentieth century

---

[7] The Convention was concluded after pressure from the USA against China and was initially aimed primarily at opium smoking by Asians, but opium use in Western countries in general was increasingly seen as a threat to workers' discipline (Berg 2016, pp. 42f.). In 1913 and 1914, the Convention was extended to include the import and export of opium, morphine and heroin and regulated domestic medical trade through prescription requirements. It also stated that any smoking of opium should be discouraged (ibid., pp. 25, 45).

and onwards, opium and alcohol appear in some respects to switch places in the social order in Sweden. Berg describes how, until then, opiate-dependent people were primarily understood as lonely and socially harmless and in need of individual care, rather than as a social problem (2016, pp. 49f.). Historian Jenny Björkman argues that, until the 1960s in Sweden, doctors and bohemians were examples of groups that were assumed to use narcotics:

> Drug users, unlike alcoholics, were assumed to come from the middle or upper class and, partly because of this, were not considered threatening or dangerous. They were not perceived as a threat to society because they were not seen as violent or untrustworthy. Quite often they were assumed to be doctors or possibly bohemians moving in the subcultures of the growing metropolises. Rather than dangerous, they were considered to be ill and, unlike alcoholics, drug addicts were consequently offered medical and hospital care. (Björkman 2002, p. 47)

In other words, people who use drugs were not stigmatised, but were seen as sickly representatives of the middle and upper classes. Meanwhile, alcoholics, according to Björkman, represented a loud, immoral and outgoing working class:

> Alcoholics were assumed to be working-class men who were usually considered dangerous both to their neighbours and to society in general. They often lacked both work and housing, exploited their surroundings and were often described as wife beaters. They thus posed a threat to a normal and socially acceptable life. Consequently, measures and treatment were aimed both at protecting society and at returning addicts to a sober life. The vagrant and anti-social alcoholics represented everything that society needed to be cleansed of, and for them compulsory care and institutionalisation were considered necessary. Through hard work and fresh air they were to be restored to sober and orderly citizens. (ibid., pp. 44–47)

According to Björkman, the alcoholics were male representatives of the working class. In Björkman's description of alcoholics, women are only mentioned as the wives who were abused by this socially dangerous group. Drugs were, she writes, "more attractive to women" than alcohol (ibid., p. 44). The article characterises societal perceptions of two almost completely different groups, but was there no overlap between them at all? Sven Åke Lindgren's thesis describes certain problematic drug use, such as morphine abuse, as more common among women than men (1993). This also applied to sleeping pills and anxiolytics, which were not classified as narcotics at the time. He writes that doctors in the 1950s were concerned about the "mass consumption" of barbiturates, a now-banned anxiolytic, and that this was described as "a new form of alcoholism" (Lindgren 1993, p. 152). While Lindgren neither considers his data from a gender perspective nor draws any conclusions from these particular findings, I would say that these examples suggest that the dividing line between society's view on alcoholism and other problematic types of drug use, as well as women's and men's use of psychoactive products at the time, was not quite as sharp as Björkman's article represents it to be.

One of the many aspects that can be confusing when discussing drugs or narcotics is that there are two main markets for them, which overlap and in which the substances that are being sold are often the same. Sweden's Penal Law on Narcotics defines narcotics as "medicines or goods that constitute a health hazard and that have addictive properties or euphoriant effects, or goods that can easily take on such properties or effects" (SFS 1968:64, §8). One of the two markets for such goods consists of the legal pharmaceutical industry, while the other is the illegal drugs market. In the former, controlled substances are sold through pharmacies to people who have been to see a doctor and given a prescription. But legally produced goods can be sold on illegally and thus cross over from one market to the other. The second market is a shadow one that mainly operates through illegal production, smuggling and dealing. One might perceive these two markets as vastly different, because they have radically different cultural meanings. But, in terms of their history, the products they sell and the pharmacological characteristics of those products, they are intricately linked with one another (see also the appendix **Drugs and Medicines**). A metric such as "drug-related deaths" (DRD), for example, which the Swedish Public Health Agency monitors and compares to similar data for other European countries compiled by the EMCDDA (European Monitoring Centre for Drugs and Drug Addiction), calls to mind illegal drugs. "Drug-related deaths" connotes unregulated products that lead to overdoses in public toilets. One of Sweden's biggest daily newspapers, *Svenska Dagbladet*, reported on drug-related deaths in Sweden under the headline "*Knark* kills record number of Swedes" (Ögren 2019). Even more clearly than the term DRD, this phrase signals that the products in question are illegal.

But Swedish DRD statistics include all lethal cases of drug toxicity, and the majority of the substances listed as having caused those deaths can have been legally produced (Swedish National Board of Health and Welfare 2016, pp. 17ff.; 2022). Victims also often legally acquired the substance they ingested, overdosing on medication they themselves had been prescribed (Swedish National Board of Health and Welfare 2016). In many cases, these overdoses are also intentional: according to the above report, suicide is the number one cause of drug-related deaths among women. "Suicide with the aid of medication" paints a completely different picture of drug-related deaths than the image conjured up by *Svenska Dagbladet*. The deceased may not have consumed excessive amounts of drugs at all during their lifetime and might have decided on a different way to end their lives if they had not had access to certain medicines.

When there is a spike in sales in the legal market, companies grow and become more successful and shareholders receive a dividend, and when psychoactive products get a foothold somewhere, this usually means they will be around for generations (Courtwright 2002, p. 98). While the illegal market is kept in check by the police, new products still manage to become popularised in this way. But, historically, illegal drugs have often made their way into society and become a set part of everyday life through pharmacies. Even the meaning of a notorious drug like heroin, which for years has been seen as unequivocally illegal and taboo, has changed over time. Just like many other drugs that are illegal today, heroin was originally developed as a medicine by a team of enthusiastic chemists, after which it found its way across the globe, prescribed and sold by doctors and pharmacies. The chemist Jie Jack Li describes how, when heroin (diacetylmorphine) was first produced in Germany, in 1897, it was regarded as a non-addictive substitute for morphine (Li

2006, pp. 162f.). It was in fact believed to be so harmless, he writes, that it was sold over the counter for the first few years, prescription-free. Ironically, aspirin—an invention of the same chemist, Felix Hoffman—was only available on prescription, as it was thought to increase the risk of heart failure. To this day, the controlled drugs that are responsible for the most deaths in Sweden, especially among women, are still largely sold at pharmacies (Swedish National Board of Health and Welfare 2016: 7; 2022). Illegally sold controlled drugs have also become more popular in Sweden; when viewed as a single group, they were the most common kind of illegal drugs in the country in 2017 (CAN 2019, p. 18).

2.2   Women and Medication

I argue that the meaning of this trend, as well as its future implications, is an understudied aspect of drug use in Sweden, and one that it is important to address, not least from a gender perspective. While more men than women use illegal drugs, women are more likely to use controlled drugs (Swedish National Institute of Public Health 2010, p. 12; Swedish National Board of Health and Welfare 2016; the Board's statistical database on medication at socialstyrelsen.se). Thus, the use of illegally or legally sold controlled medicines is a type of drug use that affects more women than men. The gender gap is so significant that there is reason to believe, based on these figures alone, that gender identity matters for how drugs are used and vice versa (cf. Measham 2002; Moore and Measham 2013, p. 16). We could interpret these statistics as suggesting, for example, that men mainly use narcotics to get high, while women use them for medical purposes. Why would men and women use the same substances for different purposes?

As described at the beginning of this chapter, intoxication among women, especially working-class women, has historically been frowned upon and stigmatised in ways that are different from attitudes to men's intoxication (Wiklund and Damberg 2015). Wiklund and Damberg quote a former bartender as saying that, up until the 1980s, women would not go out drinking unless they were accompanied by men, because "they would be told off or made to feel they had to leave"

(Wiklund and Damberg 2015, p. 26). Even in the twenty-first century, the authors say, working-class women drinking alcohol is portrayed as a real problem—in spite of low levels of problematic drinking among this section of the population and negligible instances of alcohol-related crime. Of all women, highly educated women are the ones who drink the most (ibid., pp. 74, 136f., 181). Wiklund and Damberg write that this shows that drinking alcohol is something that goes against gender norms in this particular group—but it is something these women are able to get away with due to their capital. Still, of all the women who drink, working-class women are the ones who most noticeably defy societal norms: when drinking, they go against what is expected of them, in terms of both class and gender, and risk losing their respectability (cf. Skeggs 1998). But, while women's intoxication and night life have been discouraged, medical treatments using psychoactive substances in the home and in hospitals have, conversely, been common and encouraged.

Throughout history, women's mental states have been medicalised—something to which the historian of ideas Karin Johannisson has dedicated several books.[8] In *The Wounded Diva: On the Aesthetics of the Psyche (and on Agnes von K., Sigrid H and Nelly S)*,[9] published in 2015, Johannisson takes her point of departure in the case studies of three well-known female artists to describe how female madness has been constructed throughout the ages, both to preserve repressive ideas on what constitutes "normal" femininity and by the so-called madwomen themselves. The artists Johannisson writes about are the author Agnes von Krusenstjerna (1894–1940), painter Sigrid Maria Hjertén (1885–1948) and the Nobel Prize-winning author Nelly Sachs (1891–1970). All three of these women were diagnosed with psychological ailments and treated accordingly; Sigrid Maria Hjertén died as the result of a lobotomy. Johannisson illustrates how constricting society's norms around femininity were in the nineteenth and early twentieth centuries:

---

[8] Including *The Eye of Medicine: Sickness, Medication and Society (Medicinens öga: sjukdom, medicin och samhälle)* from 1990 and *The Dark Continent: Women, Medication and Fin de Siècle (Den mörka kontinenten: kvinnan, medicinen och fin-de-siècle)* from 1995. See also Lisa Appignanesi's publication from 2009, *Mad, Bad, and Sad: A History of Women and the Mind Doctors from 1800 to the Present*.

[9] *Den sårade divan: Om psykets estetik* (och om Agnes von K, Sigrid H och Nelly S) (2015).

they made self-actualisation impossible for women and contributed to the ease with which women could be considered psychologically ill (or view themselves as such). Women diagnosed as mentally ill during the first half of the twentieth century had their human dignity violated in brutal ways: they could be locked up in mental hospitals, treated with a cocktail of alcohol, psychotherapy, ECT, lobotomy and drugs like morphine and ether. Many more women than men were lobotomised: between 1944 and 1945, for example, 58 of the 65 people who underwent a lobotomy in Sweden were women. Side effects were severe and irreversible, and the surgery often resulted in death (Johannisson 2015, pp. 139f.). Yet some patients enjoyed certain treatments, Johannisson writes:

> [The doctors'] experiments seem utterly arbitrary [...]. Patients are given large doses of sleeping aids like chloroform, chloral [hydrate], Veronal and Medinal, sedatives like bromide and the heavier opiates morphine and opium. Agnes von K loves them all. [...] Chemical experiments were part of daily life at the hospital, including extreme ones like prolonged sleep treatments. Large doses of sedatives (starting with opium or morphine) were intramuscularly injected for seven to fourteen days in a row. A patient could be kept asleep for up to 20 hours a day [...] Sometimes, Agnes von K begs to be artificially put to sleep like this. (2015, p. 133)

Agnes von Krusenstjerna's fondness for these drug treatments illustrates the shifting boundary between the medical use of controlled drugs and their use for pleasure's sake (cf. Race 2009). Johannisson writes that the entire pathology—including hysteria, a typically "female" diagnosis at the start of the twentieth century—was partially an aesthetic construct that reflected the Zeitgeist. But it did not only oppress women: some of them also used it to their advantage. Acting out one's diagnoses, Johannisson argues, can be interpreted as a "language of liberation" (Johannisson 2015, p. 16), but only under certain class-related circumstances. According to Johannisson, the symptoms of hysteria were in line with a certain aesthetic of nervosity and decadence promoted by the literature, photography, expressionist art and films of the time. Jerky movements, trembling and twisting bodies, autistic introspection and catatonic rigidity were all visual expressions of hysteria and madness (ibid., pp. 78f.). But while the misogynous pathologising was of course repressive, Johannisson points out that women's symptoms and their demands for drugs and treatment made them more difficult to deal with, not meeker.

Sociologist Beverley Skeggs shows how the pathologising of the working class has been key to the creation of the middle class (2004, pp. 4ff.), while Johannisson posits that women of all social classes have been forcibly pathologised, albeit with major differences in the ways in which this occurred and the grounds given for it. "Gender, class, convention and culture determine when a condition tips over into sickness, or when it can be tolerated as a personality trait, a quirk or a creative resource" (Johannisson 2015, p. 58).

Embracing one's diagnoses and exploiting them in creative ways, as Agnes von Krusenstjerna did, may be a privilege of certain classes only. But the intoxicating potential of drugs is accessible to anyone. How did women without any interest in or access to decadent aesthetics express their experiences of controlled drugs? Was there a similar language of liberation spoken by working-class women? One kind of medication that is often described in pejorative terms when it is used by women is sedatives in pill form. Miltown was the first benzodiazepine to be put on the market, in 1955. In the USA, it came to be associated with women, and housewives in particular—as the Rolling Stones' song "Mother's Little Helper" from 1966 exemplifies. The lyrics comment on the assumed lack of any underlying disease:

> Mother needs something today to calm her down
> And though she's not really ill, there's a little yellow pill
> She goes running for the shelter of her mother's little helper
> And it helps her on her way, gets her through her busy day

Why did women take pills like Miltown if they were not really ill? Or, if they were, what was this illness they had? Social psychology researcher Jonathan Metzl (2003) does not find it difficult to understand why women have been culturally associated with benzodiazepines: advertisements for these drugs targeted women in particular, and many more women than men were prescribed Miltown, which was said to cure frigidity, anxiety and mood swings, among other issues. But the medicine's popularity had little to do with female neurology, Metzl argues: it was based on the unreasonable ideal of the perfect housewife, which was all about men's satisfaction. Women were not just expected to perform the right kind of femininity at home; there was also significant opposition to their participation in the workforce. Metzl suggests that Miltown entailed a shift from problematic gender analyses based on psychoanalysis that did not make women more compliant in any demonstrable way, to a medicalisation that targeted a neurological function that does not differ between men and women. This, he writes, reveals that social constructs were the problem all along (2003, pp. 261f.).

The situation seems to have been somewhat different in Sweden. In her thesis *The Problem That Had No Name: Neurosis, Stress and Gender in Sweden 1950–1980*,[10] Maria Björk (2011) describes the ideal 1950s housewife as the ultimate "Woman", a natural being who represented intimacy and purity and kept the family together. But these housewives were not associated with mental illness (ibid., p. 116) because a Woman with a capital W was the antithesis of the modern world. Fulfilling their role as the anchor of the family shielded women from industrialism and the stress and hectic pace of urban life, and therefore from the main causes of psychiatric disorders. Women who not only ran a household but also had a paid position had a worse lot: Björk describes how they were trapped in an overworked Catch-22. Both jobs had to be accomplished, and both were seen as the lot of women, so women became burnt out and fell ill as a result (ibid., p. 101).

At the same time, Sven-Åke Lindgren writes (1993, p. 152), daily newspapers and trade journals fiercely debated Swedes' popping of pills, including barbiturates, sleeping aids and benzodiazepines (e.g. Miltown). Benzodiazepines were dubbed "penicillin for the soul", Lindgren writes, and sold as a cure-all for, among other ailments, insomnia, PMS, muscle cramps, headaches, behaviour problems in children and psychosis (ibid.). As for barbiturates, Lindgren states that, of those addicted to them and treated at Karolinska University Hospital's psychiatric clinic in Stockholm between 1941 and 1950, 60 were men and 120 were women.

---

[10] *Problemet utan namn? Neuroser, stress och kön i Sverige från 1950 till 1980* (2011).

Eventually, however, outrage over pill-popping was overshadowed by politicians decrying young people's use of amphetamines, which then became the most pressing issue of the day (ibid., p. 156; see also Olsson 1994, p. 179). Lindgren describes this evolution as a juxtaposition between a desire for pleasure and the fulfilment of duties, whereby chasing pleasure was seen as entailing an infinitely greater risk to society than pill-poppers' longing to soothe, sedate, anaesthetise and desensitise themselves (1993, pp. 199f.). Ever since, women have continued to consume psychoactive medicines, including controlled drugs, in larger quantities than men. In 2022, roughly 15% of women in Sweden used antidepressants, compared to 8% of men; 10% of women used sedatives and anti-anxiety medication, compared to 6% of men; and 7% of women used prescribed opioids, compared to 5% of men, according to the Swedish National Board of Health and Welfare's statistics.[11]

Both sociologist Nikolas Rose (2019, pp. 42, 45f.) and writer Lisa Appignanesi (2008, pp. 513ff.) caution against carelessly interpreting gendered differences in depression, anxiety and medication statistics without taking social conditions into account. These diagnoses are overrepresented among groups that are economically and socially vulnerable and, as Appignanesi points out, there are other factors that may underpin women's closer relationship to the healthcare sector. Seeing a doctor becomes routine for many women when they are in their teens and start using oral contraceptive pills or medication to relieve PMS; later in life, they might give birth in hospital. Medicine and public health researcher Therese Kardakis' study from 2008, "Does Gender Play a Role in the Prescription of Medication?",[12] shows that doctors are more likely to prescribe medication to women than to men with similar ailments. Kardakis argues that there is reason to believe that such discrepancies

---

[11] All of this data can be found in the Swedish National Board of Health and Welfare's publicly accessible database of medication statistics at socialstyrelsen.se. On 14 August 2023, I also downloaded information on the amounts of controlled drugs purchased from pharmacies in Sweden in 2022, aggregated by gender, via the Register Service of the Swedish National Board of Health and Welfare (which is freely accessible to the public). The data included the number of patients, pick-ups of prescriptions at pharmacies, daily doses and number of packages. A total of 649,532 men and 896,527 women purchased a controlled drug at a pharmacy in Sweden in 2022.

[12] Har genus en roll i förskrivningen av läkemedel? (2008).

stem from a stereotypical idea that women are sicklier and more sensitive to pain, while men are tougher. Sociologist Elizabeth Ettorre is critical of doctors prescribing sedatives to women. A feminist perspective, she argues, should take into account that such medication makes patients passive and dependent:

> While these drugs might help her to "stop making a fuss" [...] she is levelled out, unable to fight back and separated off from any positive form of resistance. Rather than being empowered she is "depowered". (1992, p. 70)

Ingrid Lander problematises how women's liberation is sometimes said to entail a risk that women's consumption of drugs will start to resemble men's (2003, pp. 78ff.). She argues that such a line of thought is based on a view of men as the norm (see also Measham 2002), and also cites the feminist objection that women's drug use has historically gone hand in hand with them being prescribed legal medication to help them put up with life (see also Malloch 1999, p. 353; Laanemets 2002, pp. 251ff.). This suggests that women would no longer have to use drugs if gender roles were erased—although that is based on the assumption that the motive to use them is to experience the pleasure of being numb, not pleasure as an enriching experience in a situated context. Could one kind of pleasure turn into another, and vice versa? Why, for instance, do highly educated women drink more alcohol than other women? Women's widely divergent motives for drug use appear to include both numbing and pleasure, as well as additional motives that cannot conclusively be linked to either of these—such as exploring one's self, establishing an identity or rebelling (Hilte 2019).

Criminologist Fiona Hutton (2006) and cultural studies researcher Maria Pini (2001) are two of the scholars who have shown that different drugs can play different roles in women's lives. In their ethnographic studies, they argue that the women they interviewed tended to avoid traditional spaces for alcohol consumption, because they felt that the men in these spaces acted boorishly, in line with typical gender roles. Drunkenness, the women claims, made both their own and men's behaviour more difficult to handle. Instead, the interviewees socialised in spaces where drugs like ecstasy are consumed, as this creates a different kind of environment. Still, Hutton writes, other social codes—like hugs and touching being seen as part of the experience, and the assumption that someone who is high on ecstasy will want to have sex—meant that these environments were not free from unwanted advances either (2006, pp. 44, 79ff.).

Women's Physical Morality

How does health relate to illness (an experienced lack of wellness) and disease (a diagnosed condition)? In the relationship between these two terms, illegal drug use occupies a paradoxical position. Legal use as a consequence of disease becomes illegal if a patient exceeds the prescribed consumption of their medication or offers that medication to someone else. Such illegal use can also be described as abuse and linked to sickness. When precisely illegal drug use is considered abuse varies from country to country, but in Sweden any use of non-prescribed drugs is defined as abuse, regardless of the user's intention or the amount they take (Olsson 1994). A person who follows their doctor's advice, on the other hand, taking their medication correctly and consistently, does so in order to cure illness (or at least get better). This implies that someone could just as well acquire and ingest the same product or substance illegally, with the aim of improving their health.

Many controlled substances, regardless of whether they come into someone's possession legally or illegally, are used to improve one's health and enhance one's performance (Iversen 2012; Lanni et al. 2008). Sleep, alertness, appetite, mental acuity, endurance and mood are all examples of abilities that drugs can affect in one way or another. Several substances, including amphetamines, have effects that make it easier to lose weight, for example, and achieve, as the ethnologist Fredrik Nilsson describes it, a "moral body" that, through its particular shape, embodies the bourgeois ideal of taking responsibility for one's health through exercise and diet (2011a, p. 13). Ever since the 1950s, when the first amphetamine-based diet pills came onto the market, the promise of slimness has tempted many, especially women, into the use of amphetamines (Olsson 1994,

p. 74). Rigorous body ideals have remained inescapable and have led to class-based investments in the self to increase one's value (Skeggs 2004, p. 146). In this sense, efforts to create a valuable and moral body can, paradoxically, come to encompass drug use.

In her autobiographical novel, *The Rock Blaster's Daughter Who Exploded* (2007),[13] actor, playwright and author Lo Kauppi portrays her childhood and adolescence in Stockholm and London, including her use of amphetamines. Growing up, Kauppi's life is overshadowed by her father's alcoholism. She later travels to England as a teenager, where she lives in squats and struggles with her weight, with her relationships to drugs and to other people, and to make a living. It is a fast-paced book about an existence on the margins and the struggle for personal value and meaning. Stories of theft, burglary, drug use, life-threatening physical conditions and drug smuggling are interspersed with descriptions of vulnerability, love, friendship, persistent hairdressing training and work. In this way, the novel can be said to represent a language of working-class liberation that is also expressed in images through a punk aesthetic and lifestyle, but it is an ambivalent language. She felt that amphetamines were necessary to keep her body thin enough, and lack of these drugs led to desperation, with a focus on body shape.

> When I went without amphetamines for a few days, it was like my entire body shut down. I became very bloated, tended to get cold sores, my asthma got worse and I'd be hungry all the time, except when I was binge-eating. My clothes felt all wrong. They would roll up like sausages. I wanted to slap myself and I was so incredibly tired, as though I were a hundred years old. (ibid., p. 172)

The thin body, whose ideal is based on exemplary health habits, is thus represented in Kauppi's case by someone who takes other, often dangerous, paths towards the moral body, which thus loses its connection to health. This thin body simultaneously revolts against certain societal norms and risks its life to follow others. At the same time, the above

---

[13] *Bergsprängardottern som exploderade* (2007).

quote shows how the experience of stopping drug use seems to make her sick.

Women's use of drugs has thus, to a greater extent than men's, been characterised by conflicts between adaptation and survival. Amphetamines, tranquillisers, morphine, etc., are examples of drugs that can be used strategically to comply with or break norms. The properties of drugs to make one sick or healthy, adapted or unadapted, moral or immoral—without being entirely predictable—complicate them and contribute to the difficulties of managing them, both personally and culturally. In the following section, I outline how drugs have come to be viewed since the middle of the twentieth century, and how this has changed the lives of those who use them.

2.3   Sweden's Drug Problem from the 1960s Onwards

Although opium could be used in Sweden without anyone raising an eyebrow until at least 1923 (Berg 2016), the reputation of drug use changed over the following decades. In the USA, in June 1971, Richard Nixon declared drug abuse "public enemy number one" (see, e.g., Nelson 2021), and this also marks a time of change in Sweden. Historian Johan Edman and sociologist Börje Olsson (2014) write that, since the "drug problem", i.e. problems identified as the consequences of amphetamine and morphine use in particular, was seen as an individual medical problem in Sweden until the mid-1960s, the solutions until then were based entirely on healthcare in the form of detoxification and treatment (cf. Björkman 2002). According to Edman and Olsson, however, the problem was reformulated at that time as a public and social issue, partly because amphetamines began to be used by criminals and young people (Edman and Olsson 2014, p. 509). Moral condemnation of criminals was, they argue, transferred during that movement to people who use drugs in general (ibid., p. 523).

The sociologist Dolf Tops shows how the Swedish Narcotics Care Committee of 1965–1968, whose members were primarily professionals in medical disciplines, described contemporary drug use as an epidemic, which Tops believes was a concept that had a major impact on Swedish drug policy (2001, p. 23). Psychiatrist Nils Bejerot, who inspired the police's work towards zero tolerance and control of people who use drugs (Johnson 2021; Lenke and Olsson 2002), made extensive use of epidemiological models. In his book *The drug issue and society*[14] (1969), he describes drug addiction as an infectious disease: "No debutant learns the advanced intravenous injection technique without another addict introducing him [sic] to it; it is thus a question of 'contact contagion' in a new sense" (Bejerot 1969, p. 111). Bejerot formulates a five-point action plan based on the need to eliminate drugs "as far as possible", to block the routes of transmission and to implement preventive measures "for the susceptible and at-risk but not yet infected population groups" (ibid., pp. 456–458). Those already affected were to receive treatment and "the highly infectious" were to be subjected to compulsory care and isolation (ibid.).

During this period, drug use quickly became more strictly regulated and also more highly stigmatised (Träskman 1981). In 1968, the Narcotics Penalty Act (SFS 1968:64) was adopted, which criminalised people who sold drugs rather than those using them. The maximum penalty was four years' imprisonment, but in the following year this was increased to six years and in 1970–1972 the penalty was increased further (Tham 2003). I perceive the concepts of epidemic and contagion as central both to how the criminal laws were regarded as reasonable responses to a threat to society, and to how the drug addict was symbolically stigmatised as the embodiment of this threat.

Rebecka Lennartsson describes the function of a stigma as indicating the limits of what is normal, acceptable and desirable in a society. The relationship of stigma to the law and society functions, she argues, as a way to neutralise accepted threats:

A stigma must simply have a framework of understanding based on accepted norms, truths and laws. Stigma is used to marginalize, "defuse", distinguish and often physically separate and brand individuals and

---

14 *Narkotikafrågan och samhället* (1969).

groups that are perceived as different and often threatening or dangerous. (Lennartsson 2019, pp. 35f.)

Sociologist Imogen Tyler writes that stigma is "a form of power that is written on the body" (2021, p. 9). She argues that Ervin Goffman's classic research on stigma (Goffman 1963) overlooked stigma's political role as a tool for repression (Tyler 2021, pp. 95ff.). Tyler describes stigma as a machinery that is necessary for an unjust society to be kept in place, and it fortifies social hierarchies and aids the flow of wealth upwards. Power relying on stigma is thus embedded in political economies; it distributes material resources and transforms cultural values (ibid., p. 26). Following Tyler norms, truths and laws are then not simply a cultural web that happens to produce stigma, but they have a direction, and they are a tool for statecraft intended to induce shame (see also Addison 2023).

Being subject to stigma has major consequences for the stigmatised person. Lennartsson describes "[…] reduced life chances, a judgmental attitude from society, an invalidation of experiences, opinions and competencies, and a treatment as if you were a carrier of something infectious" (2019, p. 36).

In the case of drug addicts, notions such as contagion and epidemic thus constitute both the social threat of which they themselves are victims and also what makes them threatening to society. This in turn places them in stigmatised and vulnerable social positions. Being categorised as contagious thus functions performatively, regardless of whether drug use is contagious or not. This assumed infectiousness leads to treatment as though infectiousness actually exists, reduced life chances, etc., through cultural notions as well as the institutionalised exercising of power (cf. Skeggs 2004, p. 45).

Talk of the uncontrolled spread and risk of infection signalled by the concept of an epidemic creates concern (Chitwood et al. 2009) and constitutes instructions on how people should orient themselves. If infection is spreading through society, ordinary people should keep their distance and professionals must approach those infected. Thus, there is an inherent message about the health-motivated exclusion of people who use drugs from society's everyday social life and, at the same time, the need for social intervention. The concepts of contagion and epidemic are taken from the medical field and have continued to be used for certain drug events, such as the current "opioid epidemic" in the USA (see *New York Times*[15]; Centers for Disease Control and Prevention 2022), which has led to a huge increase in overdose deaths in the 2000s. The historian of science Nancy D. Campbell (2000, p. 194) argues that women are interpreted as infectious in drug contexts to a greater extent than men, not least due to the risk of "infecting" children through reproduction (Campbell and Ettorre 2011, pp. 157ff.). Being perceived as a female drug addict is in turn a deviation that is linked to the ever-present threat of attracting the whore stigma for women, which is not based on the sex trade but on norm deviation (Ettorre 1992, p. 78; Du Rose 2015).

Thus, in the case of women, this underlying millennial stigma is combined with drug stigma, creating specific, gendered conditions for women who use drugs (Lander 2003, p. 86; Malloch 1999, p. 352; Ettorre 2007; Moore and Measham 2013). The relationship between gender and drugs is in turn further complicated by other socio-cultural structures, such as class and race (Addison 2023).[16] All four of these categories are particularly important in relation to conceptions of people who use drugs (Moore and Measham 2013; Campbell and Ettorre 2011). In this book, the focus is on the relationship between gender, class and drugs, but this does not mean that other power perspectives are irrelevant, quite the contrary. Relationships to other categorisations are crucial to what gender, class and drug use mean. That the women who are

---

[15] https://www.nytimes.com/spotlight/opioid-epidemic [2023-06-25].

[16] The concept of race is used here and throughout the thesis to denote a social construct originating from the colonial era. In Sweden, the usefulness of the word is debated because, on the one hand, race can refer to the incorrect idea that people can be divided into races based on biology. Such divisions have been rejected by biological science. It *should* therefore be an irrelevant concept. On the other hand, the understanding of the human being in the post-colonial world is based on the racist thinking that took shape during colonialism, which has given rise to continued racist violence and extreme differences between people in terms of material conditions and social rights (Gilroy 2009). In order to be able to name experiences and conditions based on racist categorisations—which form the basis for oppression as well as for privileges based on whiteness—the concepts of race and racialisation are therefore used in this book. The latter concept indicates precisely that race is not a natural characteristic but something that is constructed by being socially reproduced.

interviewed in this book are white, for example, affects how they are stig-matised and their resources to avoid stigmatisation in profound ways (cf. Addison 2023). In the same way as we can know something about class (Skeggs 2004, p. 27), knowledge about gender and race as well as drugs is produced through overlapping knowledge systems that are linked to moral systems, and that first and foremost says something about the perspective through which the knowledge is produced. In other words, in the case of people who use drugs, they came to function in the same way as whores have functioned for a long time: as representations of a lack of respectability, morality and decency (cf. ibid., p. 39). That is, the perspective is about establishing a civilised middle class, defined by its difference from the working class, as well as from drug addicts and whores, more specifically (cf. ibid., p. 118).

During the 1980s, anti-drug campaigns intensified in Sweden and criminologist Henrik Tham write that both the drug debate and official guidelines took a "hard line" (Tham 1995). This concept is also used by criminal justice researcher Per Ole Träskman: "The characteristic of Swedish drug control can be said to be that a 'hard' line has been chosen at all levels" (2003, p. 19). This hard line is thus about punishability; for example, the fact is that in Sweden it is punishable to be under the influence of drugs. Imprisonment has been included in the penalty scale since 1993 and is a prerequisite for the police to be granted extended powers to stop suspects and check their bodily fluids. This is a law that has attracted a lot of criticism (Gynnå Oguz 2017; Träskman 2003; BRÅ 2000), among other things due to the proportion of positive results in relation to the violation of integrity that a check entails. For example, only half of the young people aged 15–17 who are checked are found to be under the influence of drugs (BRÅ 2018).[17]

The social work researcher Philip Lalander also highlights the impact of the law on socially marginalised groups of people who use drugs. He believes that the fines imposed on them are counterproductive from a societal perspective, as they are often accumulated in the form of debts that will later constitute a major problem for those trying to become drug-free (2016, p. 110). The laws and their relationship to stigma

---

[17] More precisely, 57% of boys and 48% of girls showed positive test results (BRÅ 2018).

and vulnerability are a constant topic of debate and, during the time when my study was being conducted, which began in the autumn of 2015, debate articles and editorials were being published in the daily press presenting arguments for a "softer" approach, which often means taking the view that people who use drugs should receive care rather than punishment.[18] This is a debate that has recurred throughout history (see, e.g., Berridge 2013): Are drug addicts (and alcoholics) sick, or are they legitimate cases for the legal system? A follow-up question that may be worth asking is whether the perspective of drug use as a disease is an argument against the view of drug use as an epidemic and hence contagious or whether, on the contrary, it is a prerequisite. This follow-up question reveals several problematic and contradictory relationships involving both cultural and medical relationships between drug use (including narcotic drugs), disease, crime and stigma. However, it does not have any definite answers. Is it more or less stigmatising to be perceived as a sick drug user than a criminal? (cf. Ettorre 2015). Is it more dangerous, i.e. more "contagious", for the rest of society to include people who are sick or socially deviant? If the person who uses drugs is ill, when and why did they fall ill and what treatment is preferable? In Sweden, during the twenty-first century, the regulatory framework has slowly shifted towards a more and more caring and harm-reducing approach but, in practice, people who use drugs all over the world are managed through various combinations of care and punishment. It is a somewhat contradictory approach, about which Nancy D. Campbell and sociologist Elisabeth Ettorre comment:

> drug users are morally reprimanded and culturally disciplined for having a "disease of addiction" that is somehow embedded in their brains and bodies. (Campbell and Ettorre 2011, p. 14) [cf. Lalander 2016; p. 110; Edman 2019]

---

[18] De Basso et al. 2019. Decriminalize the Use of Drugs in Sweden. *Aftonbladet*, 30 January, updated 11 February [Opinion piece authored by 18 lawyers and jurists]; Svensson, Johan. 2020. It's Time to Decriminalize Drugs. ETC, 30 June [Opinion piece by Föreningen tryggare ruspolitik]; Magnusson, Lisa. 2016. Listen to the UN: Decriminalise Drug Use and Stop Moralizing. DT, August 30 [Opinion text].

Campbell and Ettorre's argument, which strongly criticises the disease perspective and the medicalisation of drug use, but at the same time presents a feminist and anti-repressive approach to people who use drugs, complicates the opposition between disease and reprehensible social deviation. Instead, they call for research—especially regarding women's drug use—that is based on feminist theory and a power-critical focus on social differences. They argue that both drug research and drug policy measures are characterised by epistemological ignorance about the needs of people who use drugs, and that drug research must develop beyond the achievements of neurochemical research, which focuses on the brain's anatomy and chemical reactions. Instead, they need to see drug use in its context in order to move forward.

> [There is a] pressing need for new knowledge about social relations in post-disciplinary societies stratified by race, class, gender, and other modes of difference, but also stratified, increasingly, by health status and categorization within multiple biomedical diagnoses and classificatory systems. (2011, p. 6)

Campbell and Ettorre's perspective is thus critical of both drug research and policy. But they also see future research as (partly) responsible for renewing and improving the conditions for people who use drugs, especially women. In Sweden, however, a large amount of research has been carried out that has not had any major political impact, which suggests that research alone cannot change the conditions for people who use drugs. Leif Lenke and Börje Olsson describe the relationship between research and politics in Sweden as hampered by an ideologically influenced political climate that has emerged in part due to the broad popular support of the temperance movements. This climate, they argue, has not allowed for the discussion of research results.

> Researchers and other drug policy experts were in many ways placed in intellectual quarantine where they remain to this day. [...] The political parties either try to avoid the topic – the left-wing parties – or take the opportunity to gain votes – the Conservatives – by sharpening their law-and-order profile. Thus, the incentives for experts to try to introduce relevant facts into the debate are rather limited. One consequence is that

public awareness slowly withers away, and anything can be presented as a fact in the debate without the risk of scrutiny. (Lenke and Olsson 2002, p. 75; see also Edman 2019, p. 38)

These researchers thus believe that drug debates in Sweden are characterised by a lack of knowledge, not only in politics but also among the public, due to an unwillingness to change views. This is a situation that has been investigated by several researchers, mainly in the fields of criminology, medicine, law, sociology and social work. This research is often highly critical of Swedish drug policy and argues for life-saving interventions and access to care (e.g. Johnson 2005; Heilig 2004, 2015, 2017; Olsson 2017; Kakko 2011, 2017) and that repressive measures have not resulted in reduced use (Tham 1995, 2003; cf. Träskman 1981, 2003). Another direction is analyses of how drug policy has been designed and is represented (e.g. Månsson 2017; Månsson and Ekendahl 2015; Edman and Olsson 2014) and the frameworks within which various social institutions operate as a result of how policy is designed (e.g. Tops 2001; Mattsson 2005; Petersson 2013; Nordgren 2017).

Researcher in social work Bengt Svensson writes in his book *Drugs Policy and Debate* (2012[19]; see also Svensson and Svensson *Drugs Policy* 2022[20]), the purpose of which is to provide a neutral account of Swedish drug policy, that most of the research conducted in Sweden is based on an anti-prohibitionist perspective, at the same time as this runs counter to Sweden's prohibitionist political stance, and that this can create problems for drug researchers' career opportunities (2012, pp. 85ff.). However, I do not perceive that the terms anti-prohibitionism and prohibitionism reflect what the two approaches stand for or the reason why they clash. Prohibitionism is about prohibition, but the question of whether drugs should be regulated by law is a different discussion from the one about how people who use drugs should be treated, whether care or other treatment should be offered and, if so, under what conditions. Instead, the point where drug research and drug policy collide seems to be about whether people can live valuable lives while using drugs, or

---

[19] *Narkotikapolitik och narkotikadebatt* (2012).
[20] *Narkotikapolitik* (2022).

whether drug use must cease in order for life to be considered valuable. This leads to questions about whether or not a person who uses drugs should be entitled to life-saving interventions, and, if so, under what conditions.

The combination of people and drugs is valued in my study in the same way as people who have not taken drugs. From an ethnological point of view, I have investigated people's everyday lives in a world where different forms of psychoactive substances are already part of everyone's bodily and psychological life and cultural lived realities (cf. Race 2009). The same substances, such as opioids, affect people in different contexts, and from my perspective, the human being themself cannot be valued differently depending on whether a substance was purchased illegally or not. I do not see how such a position could be defended.

2.4   Qualitative Research on People Who Use Drugs

Research on drug policy and its implementation and representation in Sweden serves as a starting point in this book for understanding how social institutions—such as the legal system, social authorities, healthcare and academia—relate to drugs, drug use and people who use drugs. But what do the people who use drugs themselves have to say in previous Swedish research? Swedish ethnographies on drug use are, with few exceptions, focused on problematic use. One such exception is the recent dissertation *In Her Words: Women's Accounts of Managing Drug-Related Risk, Pleasure, and Stigma in Sweden* by sociologist Oriana Quaglietta (2022), in which she seeks to counter both the marginalisation of women in drugs research and the marginalisation of pleasure and meaning in how drug use is understood and conceptualised. In order to achieve this aim, she has interviewed women who use drugs as well as dealers, with varied backgrounds and with various views on their current or previous drug use.

This focus on a deeper and more nuanced understanding of drug use, acknowledging its societal spread, is in line with my own dissertation:

"It would never have happened otherwise": On women, class and drugs[21] (Eleonorasdotter 2021), on which this book is based. But while previous researchers have mainly avoided the topic of socially integrated middle-class consumption, class and gender have been addressed by several authors. Philip Lalander's ethnographies of heroin use and street culture (2001, 2009, 2016) are one set of examples. His aim is to understand life from the point of view of marginalised people who use drugs, and hence to understand drug policy implementation, as well as the motives and effects of drug use from within. This provides a picture of how the repressive drug policies, which are disputed by researchers in the previous section, are lived as stigmatised and constrained lives.

An example of a feminist, ethnographic study is the aforementioned criminologist Ingrid Lander's thesis *The Flying* Mara[22]: *A Study of Eight Drug-Using Women in Stockholm*[23] (2003). By taking a social construc-tivist perspective, the aim is to study how the eight women relate to constructions of them as "abusing women" (ibid., pp. 4f.) and how the conditions under which they live affect them. In other words, there is a critique built into the purpose, which concerns constructions of the interviewees as less worthy. They all have experience as clients of the social services, the prison service and/or the drug addiction service. Based on Simone de Beauvoir's thesis that one is not born a woman but becomes one (de Beauvoir 1993/1949), Lander shows how these women internalise the social institutions' conceptions of them as drug-abusing women, which places the responsibility for the stigmatised social devia-tion on themselves (see, e.g., Lander 2003, p. 255; cf. Du Rose 2015). But Lander also shows how the women learn to "play their cards" (ibid., p. 267) according to the authorities' rules of the game, and in various ways to live their lives within the framework of constant control (cf. Johannisson 2015). The thesis thus provides a picture of how the exer-cise of authority towards these women is fundamentally interwoven into their lives and constitutes the prerequisite for how the construction of

---

[21] *"Det hade ju aldrig hänt annars": Om kvinnor, klass och droger* (2021).
[22] Female malevolent spirit in Nordic mythology.
[23] *Den flygande maran: En studie om åtta narkotikabrukande kvinnor i Stockholm* (2003).

social deviance takes shape, both when the women follow the guidelines and when they try to escape punishment or gain something by deviating.

Leili Laanemets' dissertation, *The Creation of Femininity: About Women in Substance Abuse Treatment*[24] (2002), is a sociological study of women in treatment, which has a descriptive and visualising purpose (ibid., p. 15). This study also approaches marginalised women for whom drug use is part of their difficult life situations. Laanemets interviews both practitioners and clients and, just as Tina Mattsson in her study *In the Desire to Make Normal: A Critical Study of the Gender Perspective in Substance Abuse Treatment*[25] (2005), takes a critical look at how the women are constructed within the care institutions and, like Lander, reflects on how these women become a specific type of woman, drug abusers, in the treatment contexts. Laanemets includes "drugs" in her study, as meaningful and complex objects that can involve both positive and negative opportunities and consequences for the women (Laanemets 2002, pp. 250ff.). This provides opportunities for effectively dissolving the category of drug-abusing women by demonstrating personal intentions and choices. She writes, for example:

> Several spoke about the fact that the reason they started using drugs was curiosity. They wanted something else and were looking for something new. (ibid., p. 191)

According to Laanemets, one interviewee, Anja, did not want to be a "perfect housewife" like her mother, but instead wanted to smoke hashish with the boys at the recreation centre.

She described her early years as one big party and, like some of the other interviewees, said that she had lived "the happy days of life" with the help of alcohol, hashish and amphetamines. The intoxication was liberating and intense (ibid.).

Curiosity and resistance to limited women's roles give "the abusing woman", to use Lander's term, a power of action that was not initially destructive, but self-affirming. However, all the interviews in the study

---

[24] *Skapande av femininitet: om kvinnor i missbrukarbehandling* (2002).

[25] *I viljan att göra det normala: En kritisk studie av genusperspektivet i missbrukarvården* (2005). The thesis is based on interviews with caregivers, not people who use drugs.

were conducted in institutions, including one compulsory care institution, where the women were housed due to their serious problems with drugs. The study thus provides a picture of the reverse potential of drugs, as limiting and harmful, as well as of the powerful control measures that can be deployed against a woman who has channelled her curiosity and desire towards violating norms in this way.

Ethnologist Anette Rosengren has studied drug-using women in relation to homelessness in her book *Between Anger and Hope: On Homelessness, Drugs and Women*[26] (2003). This is another example of ethnographic studies on women who use drugs with the purpose of analysing power. Rosengren states that she followed more than 60 women in Stockholm, mainly aged 40–60 years. Above all, the material was collected in shelters and on the streets. She writes that she wanted to seek knowledge about these women's everyday lives, beyond statistics and stereotypes, and thus contributes in a similar way to Lander and Mattsson, and to some extent Laanemets, to the fieldwork-based research that reveals the gap between research and policy. In this study, Rosengren alternates the women's statements with socially critical analyses, and drug use often appears as a reasonable action in vulnerable life contexts. For example, she writes about women's anger and resistance to social service interventions:

> The rhetoric surrounding drug use, which both the women and the staff [social services] use, includes saying that it was the craving for drugs or alcohol that took over. I myself see it as an understandable consequence of demands and violations. (2003, p. 82)

Rosengren thus complicates the relationship between vulnerability and drug use and also describes how drugs sometimes facilitate life as a homeless person. If drug use can be an "understandable consequence" of the actions of the authorities, then some of the responsibility for drug use is shifted from the person who uses drugs to the representatives of the state. If drugs can also be helpful in coping with underprivileged living conditions, they become a tool with constructive potential. Such a view differs

---

[26] *Mellan ilska och hopp: om hemlöshet, droger och kvinnor* (2003).

from, for example, Trulsson's study "*It's My Child Anyway!" A Study on Being a Drug Abuser and a Mother Separated from Her Children*[27] (1997), about women who use drugs and whose children have been taken into care by the authorities. Trulsson describes the perception that substance abuse is the reason why the women's children have been taken into care and drug use is described as "freezing" their emotional lives (ibid., p. 98). If substance abuse is the cause of the children being taken into care, even though the substance abuse is described as having been the result of social difficulties, then the state's responsibility for the resulting trauma is concealed.

Unlike Tina Mattsson, who argues that the drug abuse is relegated to the background in Trulsson's study (2005, p. 41), I see it as foregrounded. The women's reasons for resorting to drugs in their psychologically, socially and materially vulnerable situations appear to be anything but strange; rather, they are often rational survival strategies, an "understandable consequence" of the women's circumstances. Trulsson signals astonishment when she describes her realisation that abusing women also care for their children (1997, p. 1). I take this to be based on a notion of "abusing women" as fundamentally different from other women, even though Trulsson questions certain aspects of these women's deviance and finds explanations for it. I therefore interpret it as a contrarian study in relation to that of Ingrid Landers. The latter deconstructs how women are made into "abusing women", while Trulsson "makes" the abusing woman.

Both Rosengren and Trulsson highlight the deficiencies of social institutions and the needs of women from their respective perspectives, but in Rosengren's study, drug use becomes an often understandable and sometimes constructive act. In Trulsson's study, on the other hand, drug use comes into focus as a problem. In this case, the removal of the women's children appears reasonable, even though most of these already vulnerable women are described as going into crisis as a result of the loss (see, e.g., Du Rose 2015, 2017). But is it reasonable? Is there really no other

---

[27] "*Det är i alla fall mitt barn!" En studie om att vara missbrukare och mamma skild från barn* (1997).

conceivable solution than to expose mothers who use drugs to what many would consider to be the worst thing imaginable?

Research on the authorities' actions in relation to the children of women who use drugs matters in this study because one of the interviewees has lost her children, and another is worried that this will happen. The historian Nancy D. Campbell and the sociologist Elizabeth Ettorre address the emotional impact it has on women, when their children are taken into care by the authorities, or when they are at risk of this happening, and describe the contexts of mothers who use drugs as characterised by grief (e.g. 2011; see also Du Rose 2017; Boyd 2004). Ettorre uses the term abuse to describe the type of intervention that child removal constitutes (2017, p. 368). She writes herself into the research in her article "Feminist Autoethnography, Gender, and Drug Use: 'Feeling About' Empathy While 'Storying the I'" (2017), in which she draws parallels between the societal deviance of women who use drugs and her own deviance as a queer female drug researcher. In a field-journal entry after a harrowing encounter with women who had lost or were at risk of losing their children, she writes:

> I am a privileged White woman, an academic researcher. I may feel I work in a bullying, sexist, male dominated environment, but I'm deeply aware that I don't have the same hurdles that these women must overcome. It feels as if the whole patriarchal, treatment system is against them. (2017, p. 365)

The restrained rage, focusing on power structures, that characterises both Ettorre's and Campbell's work is similar to that of Rosengren and criminologist Natacha Du Rose. In Du Rose's book on women's experiences of drug policy (2015), she describes this policy as contradictory, punitive and pathologising, and as a hopeless starting point, based as it is on a view of women who use drugs as simultaneously vulnerable victims and punishable criminals (see also Boyd 1999; Anderson 2008; Chang 2020). Above all, these researchers describe living conditions and state interventions that no one, with or without amphetamines, opioids or other substances in their bodies, could be expected to accept. At the same time, there seems to be a cultural, political, ideological and social consensus that people who use drugs must be treated differently from other people (cf. Keane 2002; Fraser and Moore 2011). However, as I have shown above, this consensus runs counter to much of the research that has been carried out, even though it is often pointed out that gender perspectives are missing from drug research (e.g. Rosenbaum 1981; Ettorre 1992; Campbell 2000; Boyd 1999, 2004; Anderson 2008; Campbell and Ettorre 2011; Moore and Measham 2013). But, even where it intends to critically illuminate power differences, research on socially vulnerable people who use drugs is in line with a historical, classified direction of interest running from those who consider themselves to possess knowledge, i.e. researchers, towards those who are being studied, the "strangers" (Skeggs 2004, p. 130). This, Skeggs argues, inevitably involves moral values:

> Underlying the perspective that is taken (the interests that are held) is not just power but also morality. How people are valued (by different symbolic systems of inscription; by those who study them; by systems of exchange) is always a moral categorization, an assertion of worth, that is not just economic (e.g. good or bad; is or ought). (2004, p. 14)

Although, Skeggs writes, even if relations between researchers studying marginalised groups are problematic from a power perspective, to avoid researching such groups would mean that few people would know anything about them. Instead, she insists that the researcher must take responsibility for her position, her perspectives and the knowledge produced (ibid., pp. 130f.). In this context, I wonder what the significance is of a focus on the morally charged use of drugs when it is linked to socially vulnerable groups. That is, what knowledge is produced through this inscription?

Campbell is critical of what she calls "state ethnographies" (2000, pp. 200ff.). She argues that realistic depictions of vulnerable and stigmatised people, from the perspective of researchers and in the service of the state, run the risk of reproducing stereotypes, and thus power relations, against the will of the researcher. This is simply because some realistic depictions of drug use in socially vulnerable environments speak a highly charged symbolic language to which the academic reader cannot relate. In a similar vein, Skeggs writes that the perspectives of different actors play a fundamental role in how class is made, i.e. how class differences as such are created (2004, p. 45). "Superior" perspectives, such as those of the middle class, thus construct the working class by constructing themselves as something else (2004, p. 118). How can drug use be understood as anything other than deviant if it is exclusively studied as confined to marginalised social groups (cf. Quaglietta 2022; Taylor 1993), and alienated from the moral class? Skeggs, like Campbell, argues that linguistic signs attached to certain social groups are morally evaluative:

> Attempts by the state to deflect attention away from class inequalities, through rhetorical signs of "lone mother", "smoker", "unhealthy school", create moral divisions between worthy and unworthy recipients, the respectable and good citizen and the socially irresponsible and excluded. (ibid., p. 60)

I find that studies of "the abusing woman" run the risk of falling into the very trap of reproducing stereotypes as described by Campbell, when addiction is interwoven with descriptions of social vulnerability on all fronts. In Lander's book, for example, abuse is studied through a filter of social vulnerability and a specific approach to large quantities of drugs. A specifically Swedish conceptual ambiguity plays a role in this, as was mentioned in the introduction. The concept of drug abuse has no clear definition, but usually refers to any and all use of substances classified as drugs and not prescribed by a doctor (Olsson 1994, p. 5). In other words, drug-abuse research *could* encompass a vast amount of extremely varied drug use. Yet, for obvious reasons, sociologists usually focus on drug use as a social problem, medical researchers focus on use leading to medical problems, and so on.

But criminologist Lander and ethnologist Rosengren have also chosen to study socially vulnerable people who use drugs. These choices of perspective give their work a contradictory character: at the same time as conceptions, stereotypes and categorisations are deconstructed, people who use drugs are simultaneously constructed by the Swedish researchers discussed in this section in terms of class, even though these ethnographers have been careful to reflect human complexity. However, the problem is not, as I see it, in the individual research—how could the drug-abusing woman be deconstructed without such studies?—but arises as a result of the power imbalance of the research situation, combined with the lack of research on drug use in other social groups. By reproducing a socially anchored image of drugs as linked to certain bodies, a considerable proportion of the drug use that takes place in Sweden is thus concealed. Overall, the perspective recreates a division that is reminiscent of the Bratt system's distinction between problematic and non-problematic drunkenness, depending on class affiliation. I argue that drugs, with their links to immorality, risk, crime and disease, cannot be unproblematically linked to certain social groups in this way. In whose interests is the image that drugs are the concern of the socially vulnerable maintained? (cf. Addison 2023, p. 310).

How are drugs used when they are not part of socially vulnerable lives, and have not led to addiction? What is it that attracts people then, how do drugs change perspectives, and how are risks negotiated? What are the meanings of addiction for people who use drugs, and how is addiction avoided? Other questions that I perceive as important involve how positions and perspectives of people who use drugs, for example in terms of class, can be affected by drugs. These are questions to which I have sought answers and that I have generally found lacking in studies of women who use drugs.

The initial ideas for this thesis were inspired by the work of British criminologists Fiona Measham and Karenza Moore. They both start from an interest in how drugs are used for entertainment and depict drug use as a common phenomenon, in need of in-depth study, not least through a feminist lens (Moore and Measham 2013). What interested me was precisely these researchers' feminist and power-critical approach, which, in relation to drugs considered as everyday objects, is an unusual combination in a Swedish context. This book aims to start filling this gap.

References

Addison, Michelle. 2023. Framing Stigma as an Avoidable Social Harm That Widens Inequality. *Sociological Review* 71 (2): 296–314.

Anderson, Tammy L., ed. 2008. *Neither Villain nor Victim: Empowerment and Agency Among Women Substance Abusers*. New Brunswick, NJ: Rutgers University Press.

Appignanesi, Lisa. 2008. *Mad, Bad, and Sad: A History of Women and the Mind Doctors from 1800 to the Present.* London: Virago.

Bejerot, Nils. 1969. *Narkotikafrågan och samhället* [The Drug Issue and Society], 2nd ed. Stockholm: Aldus/Bonniers.

Berg, Daniel. 2016. *Giftets värde: Apotekarnas förståelse av opium i Sverige 1870–1925* [The Value of Poison: Pharmacists' Understanding of Opium in Sweden 1870–1925]. Göteborg and Stockholm: Makadam.

Berridge, Virginia. 2013. *Demons: Our Changing Attitudes to Alcohol, Tobacco & Drugs.* Oxford: Oxford University Press.

Björk, Maria. 2011. Problemet utan namn: Neuroser, stress och kön i Sverige från 1950 till 1980 [The Problem Without a Name: Neuroses, Stress and Gender in Sweden from 1950 to 1980]. Diss., Uppsala universitet, Uppsala.

Björkman, Jenny. 2002. Knarkarens förvandlingar [Transformations of the *knarkare*]. *Tvärsnitt* 3: 42–51.

Bonnichsen, Lisa. 2017. Här säljs knarket i stan – framför dina ögon [This Is Where Drugs Are Sold in Town—Right in Front of Your Eyes]. *Mitt i*, 25 September.

Boyd, Susan. 1999. *Mothers and Illicit Drugs: Transcending the Myths.* Toronto, ON: University of Toronto Press.

Boyd, Susan. 2004. *From Witches to Crack Moms: Women, Drug Law and Policy.* Durham, NC: Carolina Academic Press.

BRÅ. 2000. *Kriminaliseringen av narkotikabruk: en utvärdering av rättsväsendets insatser* [The Criminalisation of Drug Use: An Evaluation of the Judicial Response]. Stockholm: Brottsförebyggande rådet.

BRÅ. 2018. *Narkotikaanvändning och misstankar om eget bruk bland ungdomar I Stockholm* [Drug Use and Suspected Drug Use Among Young People in Stockholm]. Stockholm: Brottsförebyggande rådet.

Butler, Judith. 1990. *Gender Trouble: Feminism and the Subversion of Identity.* London and New York: Routledge.

Campbell, Nancy D. 2000. *Using Women: Gender, Drug Policy, and Social Justice.* Milton Park: Taylor & Francis.

Campbell, Nancy D., and Elizabeth Ettorre. 2011. *Gendering Addiction: The Politics of Drug Treatment in a Neurochemical World.* New York, NY: Palgrave Macmillan.

CAN. 2019. *Drogutvecklingen i Sverige 2019 – med fokus på narkotika* (Rapport 180) [Drug Development in Sweden 2019—With a Focus on Narcotics (Report 180).] Stockholm: Centralförbundet för alkohol- och narkotikaupplysning.

Centers for Disease Control and Prevention. 2022. Understanding the Epidemic. https://www.cdc.gov/opioids/basics/epidemic.html [2023-06-25]

Chang, J. 2020. Women Who Use Drugs: Resistance and Rebellion. In *The Impact of Global Drug Policy on Women: Shifting the Needle*, ed. J. Buxton, G. Margo, and L. Burger, 271–286. Bingley: Emerald Publishing.

Chitwood, Dale D., Sheigla Murphy, and Marsha Rosenbaum. 2009. Reflections on the Meaning of Drug Epidemics. *The Journal of Drug Issues* 39 (1): 29–39.

Courtwright, David T. 2002. *Forces of Habit: Drugs and the Making of the Modern World*. Cambridge, MA: Harvard University Press.

Cowan, Brian. 2005. *The Social Life of Coffee: The Emergence of the British Coffee House*. New Haven and London: Yale University Press.

de Beauvoir, Simone. 1993/1949. *The Second Sex*. London: Everyman's Library.

Du Rose, Natacha. 2015. *The Governance of Female Drug Users: Women's Experiences of Drug Policy*. Bristol: Policy Press.

Du Rose, Natacha. 2017. Marginalised Drug-Using Women's Pleasure and Agency. *Social History of Alcohol & Drugs: An Interdisciplinary Journal* 31 (1): 42–64.

Edman, Johan. 2019. Drogerna: Den nya berusningspolitiken [Drugs: The New Policy on Intoxication]. One of six booklets in the collection *Det nya Sverige: Riksbankens Jubileumsfonds årsbok 2019*, ed. Jenny Björkman and Patrik Hadenius. Göteborg and Stockholm: Makadam förlag.

Edman, Johan, and Börje Olsson. 2014. The Swedish Drug Problem: Conceptual Understanding and Problem Handling, 1839–2011. *Nordic Studies on Alcohol & Drugs/Nordisk Alkohol- & Narkotikatidskrift* 31 (5/6): 503–526.

Eleonorasdotter, Emma. 2021. *"Det hade ju aldrig hänt annars" Om kvinnor, klass och droger* ["It Would Never Have Happened Otherwise": On Women, Class and Drugs]. Lund: Mediatryck.

EMCDDA. 2022. *European Drug Report 2022: Trends and Developments*. Luxembourg: Publications Office of the European Union.

Ettorre, Elizabeth. 1992. *Women and Substance Use*. Basingstoke: Macmillan.

Ettorre, Elizabeth. 2007. *Revisioning Women and Drug Use: Gender, Power and the Body*. London: Palgrave Macmillan.

Ettorre, Elizabeth. 2015. Embodied Deviance, Gender, and Epistemologies of Ignorance: Re-visioning Drugs Use in a Neurochemical, Unjust World. *Substance Use & Misuse* 50: 794–805.

Ettorre, Elizabeth. 2017. Feminist Autoethnography, Gender, and Drug Use: "Feeling About" Empathy While "Storying the I." *Contemporary Drug Problems* 44 (4): 356–374.

Fraser, Suzanne, and David Moore, eds. 2011. *The Drug Effect: Health, Crime and Society.* Cambridge: Cambridge University Press.

Gilroy, Paul. 2009. *Race and the Right to be Human.* Utrecht: Universiteit Utrecht.

Goffman, Erving. 1963. *Stigma: Notes on the Management of Spoiled Identity.* New York: Simon & Schuster.

Gynnå Oguz, Christina. 2017. Kriminalisering av eget bruk: framgångssaga eller dödsstöten för en human narkotikapolitik? [Criminalisation of Personal Use: Success Story or Death Knell for a Humane Drug Policy?] In *Dogmer som dödar: vägval för svensk narkotikapolitik,* ed. Niklas Eklund and Mikaela Hildebrand, 313–333. Stockholm: Verbal förlag.

Heilig, Markus. 2004. *Beroendetillstånd* [States of Dependence]. Lund: Studentlitteratur.

Heilig, Markus. 2015. *Alkohol, droger och hjärnan: tro och vetande utifrån modern neurovetenskap* [Alcohol, Drugs and the Brain: Beliefs and Knowledge Based on Modern Neuroscience]. Stockholm: Natur & Kultur.

Heilig, Markus. 2017. Dogmer som dödar [Dogmas That Kill]. In *Dogmer som dödar: vägval för svensk narkotikapolitik,* ed. Niklas Eklund and Mikaela Hildebrand, 52–64. Stockholm: Verbal förlag.

Hellqvist, Hanna. 2008. Klart att man kan stoppa kniven i munnen [Of Course You Can Put the Knife in Your Mouth]. *Dagens Nyheter,* 20 April.

Hilte, Mats. 2019. Psychoactive Drugs and the Management of Time. *Sociologisk Forskning* 56 (2): 111–124.

Hutton, Fiona. 2006. *Risky Pleasures: Club Cultures and Feminine Identities.* Aldershot: Ashgate.

Iversen, Leslie. 2012. *Speed, Ecstasy, Ritalin: The Science of Amphetamines.* Oxford: Oxford University Press. Oxford Scholarship Online [ebook].

Johannisson, Karin. 1990. *Medicinens öga: Sjukdom, medicin och samhälle – historiska erfarenheter.* Stockholm: Norstedts.

Johannisson, Karin. 1995. *Den mörka kontinenten: Kvinnan, medicinen och finde-siècle.* Stockholm: Norstedts.

Johannisson, Karin. 2015. *Den sårade divan: Om psykets estetik (och om Agnes von K, Sigrid H och Nelly S)* [The Wounded Diva: On the Aesthetics of the Psyche (and on Agnes von K, Sigrid H and Nelly S)]. Stockholm: Albert Bonniers förlag.

Johnson, Björn. 2005. *Metadon på liv och död: En bok om narkomanvård och narkotikapolitik i Sverige* [Methadone for Life and Death: A Book on Drug Treatment and Drug Policy in Sweden]. Lund: Studentlitteratur.

Johnson, Björn. 2021. *Nils Bejerot och den svenska narkotikapolitiken* [Nils Bejerot and Swedish Drug Policy]. Lund: Arkiv förlag.

Jönsson, Håkan, and Richard Tellström. 2018. *Från krog till krog: svenskt uteätande under 700 år* [From Tavern to Tavern: Swedish Dining Out over 700 Years]. Stockholm: Natur & Kultur.

Kakko, Johan. 2011. *Heroinberoende* [Heroin Addiction]. Stockholm: Liber.

Kakko, Johan. 2017. Killing by Silence – om makt, maktens rus och maktmissbruk [Killing by Silence—About Power, the Intoxication of Power and the Abuse of Power]. In *Dogmer som dödar: vägval för svensk narkotikapolitik*, ed. Niklas Eklund and Mikaela Hildebrand, 66–78. Stockholm: Verbal förlag.

Kardakis, Therese. 2008. Har genus en roll i förskrivningen av läkemedel? En genusanalys av läkemedelsanvändningen [Does Gender Play a Role in Prescribing Medicines? A Gender Analysis of the Use of Medicines]. *Socialmedicinsk tidskrift* 85 (3): 227–233.

Kauppi, Lo. 2007. *Bergsprängardottern som exploderade* [The Rock Blaster's Daughter Who Exploded]. Stockholm: Norstedts.

Keane, Helen. 2002. *What's Wrong with Addiction?* Melbourne: Melbourne University Press.

Laanemets, Leili. 2002. Skapande av femininitet: Om kvinnor i missbrukarbehandling [The Creation of Femininity: About Women in Substance Abuse Treatment]. Diss., Lunds universitet, Lund.

Lalander, Philip. 2001. *Hela världen är din: En bok om unga heroinister* [The Whole World Is Yours: A Book About Young Heroin Users]. Lund: Studentlitteratur.

Lalander, Philip. 2009. *Respekt: Gatukultur, Ny Etnicitet och Droger* [Respect: Street Culture, New Ethnicity and Drugs]. Malmö: Liber.

Lalander, Philip. 2016. *Människor behöver människor: Att lyssna till de misstänkliggjorda* [People Need People: Listening to the One's Made Suspicious]. Stockholm: Liber.

Lander, Ingrid. 2003. Den flygande maran: En studie om narkotikabrukande kvinnor i Stockholm [The Flying Mara: A Study of Eight Drug-Using Women in Stockholm]. Diss., Stockholms universitet, Stockholm.

Lanni, Cristina, Silvia C. Lenzken, Alessia Pascale, Igor Del Vecchio, Marco Racchi, Francesca Pistoia, and Stefano Govoni. 2008. Cognition Enhancers between Treating and Doping the Mind. *Pharmacological Research* 57: 196–213.

Lenke, Leif, and Börje Olsson. 2002. Swedish Drug Policy in the Twenty-First Century: A Policy Model Going Astray. *The Annals of the American Academy of Political and Social Science* 582: 64–79.

Lennartsson, Rebecka. 2019. *Mamsell Bohmans fall: Nattlöperskor i 1700-talets Stockholm* [The Fall of Mamsell Bohman: Night Walkers in 18th Century Stockholm]. Stockholm: Stockholmia förlag.

Li, Jie Jack. 2006. *Laughing Gas, Viagra and Lipitor: The Human Stories Behind the Drugs We Use*. Oxford: Oxford University Press.

Lindgren, Sven-Åke. 1993. *Den hotfulla njutningen: att etablera drogbruk som samhällsproblem 1890–1970* [The Threat of Pleasure: Establishing Drug Use as a Social Problem 1890–1970]. Stockholm: Brutus Östlings Bokförlag Symposion.

Löfgren, Orvar, and Billy Ehn. 2001. *Kulturanalyser* [Cultural Analysis], 2nd ed. Malmö: Gleerups Utbildning AB.

Löfgren, Orvar, and Billy Ehn. 2012. *Kulturanalytiska verktyg* [Cultural Analytical Tools]. Malmö: Gleerups Utbildning AB.

Malloch, Margaret. 1999. Drug Use, Prison, and the Social Construction of Femininity. *Women's Studies International Forum* 22 (3): 349–358.

Månsson, Josefin. 2017. Cannabis Discourses in Contemporary Sweden: Continuity and Change. PhD dissertation, Department of Social Work, Stockholm University.

Månsson, Josefin, and Mats Ekendahl. 2015. Protecting Prohibition: The Role of Swedish Information Symposia in Keeping Cannabis a High-Profile Problem. *Contemporary Drug Problems* 42 (3): 209–225.

Mattsson, Tina. 2005. *I viljan att göra det normala: En kritisk studie av genusperspektivet i missbrukarvården* [In the Desire to Make Normal: A Critical Study of the Gender Perspective in Substance Abuse Treatment]. Malmö: Egalité.

Measham, Fiona. 2002. "Doing Gender"—"Doing Drugs": Conceptualizing the Gendering of Drugs Cultures. *Contemporary Drug Problems* 29 (2): 335–373.

Metzl, Jonathan. 2003. "Mother's Little Helper": The Crisis of Psychoanalysis and the Miltown Resolution. *Gender & History* 15 (2): 240–267.

Moore, Karenza, and Fiona Measham. 2013. Exploring Emerging Perspectives on Gender and Drug Use. In *Emerging Perspectives on Substance Misuse*, ed. Willm Mistral, 80–97. Hoboken, NJ: Wiley-Blackwell.

Nationalencyklopedin. n.d. Narkotika [Online resource, accessed 2023-08-02].

Nelson, Stanley. 2021. *Crack: Cocaine, Corruption & Conspiracy* [film]. Netflix.

Nilsson, Fredrik. 2011a. *I ett bolster av fett: En kulturhistoria om övervikt, manlighet och klass* [In a Bolster of Fat: A Cultural History of Obesity, Masculinity and Class]. Lund: Sekel bokförlag.

Nilsson, Gabriella. 2011b. Den fetmadrivande miljön: Kulturella föreställningar om samhället i populärmedicinska texter om övervikt och fetma [The Obesogenic Environment: Cultural Representations of Society in Popular Medical Texts on Overweight and Obesity]. *Socialmedicinsk tidskrift* 88 (3): 207–216.

Nilsson, Gabriella, and Inger Lövkrona. 2015. *Våldets kön: Kulturella föreställningar, funktioner och konsekvenser* [The Gender of Violence: Cultural Beliefs, Functions and Consequences]. Lund: Studentlitteratur.

Nordgren, Johan. 2017. Making Drugs Ethnic: Khat and Minority Drug Use in Sweden. Diss., Malmö högskola, Malmö.

Nutt, David J., Leslie A. King, and Lawrence D. Phillips. 2010. Drug Harms in the UK: A Multicriteria Decision Analysis. *Lancet* 376: 1558–1565.

Ögren, Annica. 2019. Rekordmånga svenskar dör av knark [Record Numbers of Swedes Die from Drugs]. *Svenska Dagbladet*, 18 July.

Olseryd, Johanna. 2015. *Brå: Alkohol- och drogpåverkan vid misshandel, hot, personrån och sexualbrott* [Brå: Alcohol and Drug Use in Assaults, Threats, Robberies and Sexual Offences]. Stockholm: Brottsförebyggande rådet.

Olsson, Börje. 1994. *Narkotikaproblemets bakgrund: Användning av och uppfattningar om narkotika inom svensk medicin 1839–1965* [The Background of the Drug Problem: Use and Perceptions of Drugs in Swedish Medicine 1839–1965] (CAN rapportserie, 39). Stockholm: CAN.

Olsson, Börje. 2017. Den svenska narkotikapolitiken [Swedish Drug Policy]. In *Dogmer som dödar: vägval för svensk narkotikapolitik*, ed. Niklas Eklund and Mikaela Hildebrand, 24–51. Stockholm: Verbal förlag.

Persson, Leif G.W. 1990. Om män, manlighet och manliga matvanor [About Men, Masculinity and Male Eating Habits]. In *Stora machoboken*, ed. Jan Guillou, Pär Lorentzon and Leif G.W. Persson, 199–206. Stockholm: Norstedts.

Petersson, Frida. 2013. *Kontroll av beroende: Substitutionsbehandlingens logik, praktik och semantik* [Controlling Addiction: The Logic, Practice and Semantics of Substitution Treatment]. Malmö: Egalité.

Pini, Maria. 2001. *Club Cultures and Female Subjectivity: The Move from Home to House*. London: Palgrave Macmillan.

Plant, Sadie. 1999. *Writing on Drugs*. London: Faber and Faber.

Quaglietta, Oriana. 2022. In Her Words: Women's Accounts of Managing Drug-Related Risk, Pleasure, and Stigma in Sweden. Doctoral Thesis (monograph), Department of Sociology, Lund University.

Race, Kane. 2009. *Pleasure Consuming Medicine: The Queer Politics of Drugs*. Durham, NC: Duke University Press.

Rose, Nikolas. 2019. *Our Psychiatric Future*. Cambridge: Polity Press.
Rosenbaum, Marsha. 1981. *Women on Heroin* (Crime, law, and deviance series). New Brunswick, NJ: Rutgers University Press.
Rosengren, Annette. 2003. *Mellan ilska och hopp: Om hemlöshet, droger och kvinnor* [Between Anger and Hope: On Homelessness, Drugs and Women]. Stockholm: Carlsson bokförlag.
Schivelbusch, Wolfgang. 1993. *Tastes of Paradise: A Social History of Spices, Stimulants and Intoxicants*. New York, NY: Vintage Books.
SFS. 1968:64. *Narkotikastrafflag*. Stockholm: Justitiedepartementet.
Sigfridsson, Ingegerd. 2005. *Självklara drycker? Kaffe och alkohol i social samvaro* [Obvious Drinks? Coffee and Alcohol in Socialising]. Göteborg: Arkipelag.
Skeggs, Beverley. 1998. *Formations of Class & Gender*. London: Sage.
Skeggs, Beverley. 2004. *Class, Self, Culture*. London: Routledge.
Svensson, Bengt. 2012. *Narkotikapolitik och narkotikadebatt* [Drug Policy and Debate]. Lund: Studentlitteratur.
Svensson, Bengt, and Gustav Svensson. 2022. *Narkotikapolitik* [Drug Policy]. Lund: Studentlitteratur.
Swedish National Board of Health and Welfare. 2016. *Narkotikarelaterade dödsfall: en analys av 2014 års dödsfall och utveckling av den officiella statistiken* [Drug-Related Deaths: An Analysis of 2014 Deaths and Developments in Official Statistics]. Stockholm: Socialstyrelsen.
Swedish National Board of Health and Welfare. 2022. Dödsfall till följd av läkemedels- och narkotikaförgiftningar: En statistiksammanställning [Deaths Due to Medicine and Drug Poisoning: A Statistical Summary]. www.socialstyrelsen.se.
Swedish National Institute of Public Health. 2010. *Narkotikabruket i Sverige* [Drug Use in Sweden]. Östersund: Statens Folkhälsoinstitut.
Taylor, Carl S. 1993. *Girls, Gangs, Women and Drugs*. East Lansing: Michigan State University Press.
Tham, Henrik. 1995. Drug Control as a National Project: The Case of Sweden. *Journal of Drug Issues* 25 (1): 113–128.
Tham, Henrik. 2003. Narkotikapolitiken och missbrukets utveckling [Drug Policy and the Development of Addiction]. In *Forskare om narkotikapolitiken*, ed. Henrik Tham, 5–16. Stockholm: Stockholms universitet.
Tops, Dolf. 2001. A Society With or Without Drugs? Continuity and Change in Drug Policies in Sweden and The Netherlands. Diss., Lunds universitet, Lund.
Träskman, Per Ole. 1981. Från varning till fängelse i fyratusentrehundraåttio dagar: Om kriminalisering och värdering av brott [From Warning to

Imprisonment for Four Thousand Three Hundred and Eighty Days: On Criminalisation and the Valuation of Crime]. In *Straff och rättfärdighet: Ny nordisk debatt*, ed. Sten Heckscher, Annika Snare, Hannu Takala, and Jørn Vestergaard. Stockholm: Norstedts.

Träskman, Per Ole. 2003. Narkotikapolitik och brottskontroll [Drug Policy and Crime Control]. In *Forskare om narkotikapolitiken*, ed. Henrik Tham. Stockholm: Stockholms universitet.

Trulsson, Karin. 1997. "Det är i alla fall mitt barn!" En studie om att vara missbrukare och mamma skild från barn ["It's My Child Anyway!" A Study on Being a Drug Abuser and a Mother Separated from Her Children]. Lic. thesis, Lunds universitet, Lund.

Tyler, Imogen. 2021. *Stigma: The Machinery of Inequality*. London: Zed Books.

Wiklund, Lisa, and Jenny Damberg. 2015. *Som hon drack: kvinnor, alkohol och frigörelse* [As She Drank: Women, Alcohol and Liberation]. Stockholm: Bokförlaget Atlas.

Wilk, Richard. 2014. Consumer Cultures Past, Present, and Future. In *Sustainable Consumption: Multi-disciplinary Perspectives in Honour of Professor Sir Partha Dasgupta*, ed. Alistair Ulph and Dale Southerton, 315–336. Oxford: Oxford University Press. Oxford Scholarship Online.

Part II

Ethnographies of everyday drug use

3

The First Visits

The women who feature in this book exhibit different patterns of drug use. They use different kinds of drugs, to different extents and for different purposes. But they still share certain reference points: images, experiences and concepts that are linked to drug use. They interpret their own use through the cultural meanings that drug use has acquired over time in Sweden, and through additional meanings they encountered during their travels to other countries. Based on this input, they decided at some point in their lives to acquire experiences of drug use themselves. What led them to that point, and how has using drugs changed their view of these substances over time?

3.1   A Gateway?

I meet Agnes in Dublin on a Saturday morning, the sun filtering through the large windows of the café where we are sitting. Agnes has just graduated as a psychologist and is relieved and happy that she successfully completed her studies. Now, however, she is at a crossroads, with her future path unclear. One of the decisions she will soon have to make is

© The Author(s) 2024
E. Eleonorasdotter, *Women's Drug Use in Everyday Life*,
https://doi.org/10.1007/978-3-031-46057-9_3

whether to return to Sweden or remain in Ireland. She will also have to decide whether, and if so how, to keep using drugs. Agnes tells me that she is worried about her alcohol consumption, but also critically reflects upon drug use in general.

> Sometimes I feel like quitting all of it [...] I notice how... it wasn't as clear when I was younger but now, that it's become a bit harder to express myself, you do notice that I've, like, partied a lot, and I want my mind to be clear again. Actually.[1]

In other words, Agnes does not view her drug experiences in a solely positive light. The above quote refers to her fear that drugs may have affected her intellectual acuity. Agnes gives long and self-reflexive answers to my questions and carefully considers her relationship to drugs. When we discuss the first few times she tried them, she expresses her drug use in spatial terms. It is as though drug use itself, rather than a rave scene or any other specific context for drug use, is a place to visit rather than an act of consumption (cf. Pini 2001). Speaking about a boyfriend she had back in Stockholm as a teenager, she says he was "in that world" (a social context where drugs were common), and her own use is described as something she "jumped into", almost like a pool:

> [My] friends didn't party that much, but then when I was about 14–15, I met a guy who spent a lot of time in that world. He'd lived in France before... and took all kinds of things, but yeah, mainly smoked [cannabis]. So I started smoking a lot as well then. [...] But when I moved here [to Dublin], suddenly, like, everything was around. Err, you don't make the smartest decisions when you're 20 [laughs], so I just, jumped into it, I guess.

Using the same terminology as writer Birgitta Stenberg uses in her autobiographical novel *Report*,[2] in which she refers to settings where people use drugs, primarily amphetamines, as "the other world" (2017/1969; see also Skårner 2007), Agnes describes how she was introduced to a

---

[1] All quotes in Swedish have been translated by me.
[2] *Rapport* (1969).

new "world" through a cannabis-smoking boyfriend. In the quotation, it seems that cannabis served as a so-called gateway—a term stemming from the disputed theory that using a soft drug will lead the user on to harder drugs (Kandel 1975; Lynskey and Agrawal 2018)—which revealed itself to her via a love relationship. The oft-used metaphor of a gateway is interesting because it paints a picture of a willed direction that is taken, towards a specific object within reach (Ahmed 2014, pp. 40f.). But, the metaphor suggests that object—be it tobacco, alcohol, cannabis or other "light" drugs—will forcefully direct one towards other objects that one had not intended to approach. Just as in Agnes' usage, the idea of a gateway transforms drug-taking from an activity into a place, a place that expands behind the doorway of seemingly innocuous drug use.

But Agnes does not describe her trajectory as a path upon which cannabis set her. She says that she started smoking cannabis because she herself had intentionally embarked upon a journey towards drugs:

> Back when I was pretty young, I was really, I read a lot of books and [watched] films that painted a rather uncomplicated picture of drug use. And I remember when I was younger going like "oh, I can't wait 'til I get to the age when I too can go to festivals, and…" I just felt life was so boring. Like, "why don't people get *going*?"

In other words, Agnes describes an impatient and active outreach. What she was seeking out were gateways to drug use and exciting experiences, which she hopes she will have if she approaches the "world"—a collection of things—that her boyfriend is a part of. But she also criticises her past self for having bad judgement when she finally did "jump in". The gateway (in the sense of a way into a space where drug use is happening) is embodied not by the "soft" drug cannabis that leads to "harder" drugs, but by a boyfriend. Agnes finds him in her pursuit of exciting, drug-fuelled experiences, and cannabis happens to be what he gives her access to.

Several other interviewees describe having felt a similar desire at an early age to try drugs. Madelene, who is a senior software analyst at an IT company, is one of these. She prefers opioids but, unlike Agnes, who uses drugs when she is together with friends, Madelene mainly uses them when she is alone in her flat in Gothenburg. Although she arrived at a radically different drug practice and context, however, Madelene's journey commenced in a similar fashion, with her interest being piqued at an early age.

> [...] I've always been interested in drugs in a way that others are not, I've noticed. [laughs] I was completely fascinated by the film *Trainspotting*[3]... and I and my mate, we wanted a flat like that. How many people, when you're 15, think like that? And then I decided early on that I wanted to try everything.

Alcohol and sedative medicines, taken from her aunt's bathroom cabinet, were the first drugs that Madelene tried. But she does not portray those first encounters with drugs as a determining factor for her continued use: from the start, she says, she was intent on trying "everything", and she describes longing for a physical place that would allow her to do so. Twenty years later, she uses a range of prescription opioids on a daily basis—some that have been prescribed to her, and others that she purchases illegally. She tells me that she injects heroin a couple of times a month.

Both Agnes and Madelene can be understood as regular consumers of illegal drugs according to their own statements, and it is a consumption that they have purposefully sought out since their early teens. These searches led them to an aunt's bathroom cabinet and a boyfriend active in a "drug world", and then on to other places and worlds, such as opioid intoxication in the home and MDMA and amphetamines at dance clubs and techno parties. So what happens if we understand experiences of drug use as intentional visits to imagined worlds, collective spaces consisting of fantasy, media technologies and material resources, through acts of consumption (Appadurai 1996)?

Criminologists Fiona Measham and Michael Shiner argue that, if we focus too much on agency when we study young people's drug use, we risk obscuring the important role played by structural conditions. They

---

[3] The 1996 film *Trainspotting*, based on a novel by Irvine Welsh, is about a group of people who use heroin in Edinburgh. The flat that Madelene refers to is a dilapidated and run-down place where the film's characters use heroin uninhibitedly together.

use two similar concepts, "situated choice" and "structured action", to explain that, if we want to understand adolescents' choices and actions, we need to contextualise them in relation to structural factors such as gender, race and class (2009, p. 505). These concepts are in line with Sara Ahmed's use of phenomenology, as a way to make sense of the environment and its conditions and to understand the directions of the body and consciousness in relation to them.

> Phenomenology asks us to be aware of the "what" that is around. After all, if consciousness is intentional, then we are not only directed towards objects, but those objects also take us in a certain direction. The world that is around has already taken certain shapes, as the very form of what is more and less familiar. (Ahmed 2006a, p. 545)

To begin the analysis from the body is to situate people geographically, structurally and socially; from there, orientation can take place and some objects prove to be reachable but others are not. What does this mean for Agnes' and Madelene's first experiences of drugs? The starting point for orientation is thus not only the body but also the place where the body tends to dwell. From there, the world unfolds. People intentionally orient themselves towards familiar or unfamiliar objects; the paths among these objects determine the continued directions in which bodies will move. So, the objects that are within reach lead onwards in new directions. A boyfriend who brings cannabis with him is both an intentional direction and a hopeful fantasy: what else could be within reach through a cannabis-providing boyfriend?

Passing through gateways to drug use is commonly traced back to a childhood defined by social exclusion, parents struggling with substance abuse and other kinds of trauma (e.g. Du Rose 2015; Laanemets 2002; Trulsson 1997). But neither Agnes nor Madelene described growing up in such an environment. Instead, they mentioned popular films as sources of inspiration for how they later embarked upon a path towards drugs. For these two women, their proximity to drugs was first and foremost cultural, part and parcel of popular cultural expressions. It was the films that made drugs recognisable and findable as physical objects. Both describe their class backgrounds as "upper-middle class" and their childhoods as secure, with close relationships with their relatives. The structural conditions underpinning their orientation towards drugs do not seem to be about vulnerability or social exclusion, but about cultural inspiration for how life could include drugs. So how can films like *Trainspotting*, which largely depict misery and suffering, inspire middle-class Swedish girls to use drugs? Agnes describes her orientation towards drugs as a search based on boredom, and for her as a child, drug use was situated in future, in adulthood:

> [...] I just think it's some kind of quest and that, yeah, curiosity, or as I mentioned that you go around feeling bored for a few years and hype yourself up: "soon, I'll be grown up, then I can start".

Being "grown up" seems like a practical matter for Agnes: once she is no longer held back by her legal guardians, she will be free to reach for drugs. In adulthood, she will be free to escape boredom. Despite their association with suffering, stigma and problems, the young Agnes saw drugs in a positive light, as the opposite of dullness. The structural circumstances in which Agnes and Madelene began to seek out drugs were privileged ones, from both a global and a Swedish perspective. From her secure position in an upper-middle-class family, Madelene became fascinated with the working-class misery in *Trainspotting*. She herself was not at risk of ending up on the margins of society, unless she chose to actively carve out such a position for herself.

Beverley Skeggs describes how the construction of the middle class as the moral class meant that the middle class became able to exercise moral authority, but it also made life rather boring. Anything dangerous, disruptive or sexual became the prerogative of the working class, which made it interesting and alluring to the middle class (2004, p. 22). Thus, it need not matter that drugs are associated with poverty and misery in order for them to be perceived as desirable, quite the contrary. Agnes and Madelene's class conditions did not alienate them from drugs, which instead became interesting and attractive early on. Once someone does start using drugs, however, class-related conditions for drug use generate important differences in how it takes shape when practised. Their starting points in privileged positions allowed Agnes and Madelene to approach drug use in a tentative way that did not compromise their wider directions through the middle class. As Skeggs puts it, middle-class appropriation of working-class cultural assets does not necessarily mean that what is enjoyed is the same as what is taken:

> [...] what has been extracted [from the working class] and attached to the middle-class body is [not] necessarily the same as that which was taken. It is in the relationship that the transformation occurs. (2004, p. 12)

In other words, it is in the relationship between what is taken and who takes it that the meaning of what is used arises. In spatial terms, this would mean that the entrance to drugs leads to different places depending on who walks through the gateway. Agnes and Madelene now indulge in drugs alongside their jobs as a psychologist and senior software analyst respectively. They approached and stayed around drugs without losing their class-related orientations—just as many people who use drugs with a childhood marked by social exclusion will remain in the class positions they have grown up with (Laanemets 2002, pp. 51f.; see also Olsson 1994, p. 193). Class, in other words, does not necessarily determine whether or not a person will approach drugs, but it does affect how drug-influenced directions are then mapped out. Neither do drugs' own class positions, where, for example, the heroin that Madelene uses is strongly linked to vulnerability and misery, seem to necessarily determine the ways in which lines are drawn to, between and from drugs. Instead, they appear to depend upon other factors linked to the *people* who use drugs.

Gateways to drug use exist in all segments of society; due to popular culture and a busy drugs market, they are within reach of everyone. Yet there is one factor that appears to affect a person's distance from these gateways, regardless of class-related conditions, and that is age. Drugs appear to be in cultural proximity to certain age groups, such as teenagers and young adults, but far from others, such as young children and middle-aged or older people.

Boel also describes a secure childhood and says that she had strict but loving parents. Much like Agnes, Boel mainly uses drugs at parties, but she also takes so-called microdoses when her job as a public-relations officer ("a demanding and intensive role") becomes too much to handle. But when she talks about her entry into drugs, she does not describe it as a "gateway" that she has sought in the same purposeful way as Agnes and Madelene did. Instead, she describes a more hesitant approach to the gate when it was just a step away during her younger teenage years:

> I'd say I tried drugs for the first time when I was 14, I think. [...] But I felt a bit too chicken and backed out. Then I did ecstasy at some point when I was 17 and I noticed that a lot of people started feeling bad, so I backed out again.

Right after taking her first tentative steps into a place of drug use, Boel leaves that place behind. She does so in the same way as she entered, but "backs out" instead of actually turning around. Just like Agnes, who expressly describes the use of drugs as a world she "jumps in[to]", Boel describes it in spatial terms. Her way of approaching the place where the drugs are found can also be likened to a pool. She tests the "water", like a hesitant swimmer dipping her toes in, but backs away instead of turning round and walking or jumping in. Her friends are in the same place—in youth, in drug use—and leaving the neighbourhood altogether seems like a question for the future. Her friends are in the same place—in adolescence, in proximity to drugs—and leaving this context is an issue for future Boel to consider. While Agnes describes her childhood as an impatient wait for something familiar yet unattainable, Boel portrays her teenage years as a time when drug use was waiting for her.

Notions of insidious entrances to drug use, as implied by the gateway theory, also indicate that, once in, it is difficult to get out. As Agnes depicts drug use as a body of water she happily but indiscriminately "jumps in[to]", it leads us to another common Swedish metaphor for the dangers of drugs: the image of drug use as a treacherous swamp, a *knarkträsk*.[4]

---

[4] The translation of the Swedish word *knarkträsk* is drug swamp in English, and the closest translation of *knark* is drugs. However, the word *knark* has specific connotations of problems and gravity, as it spread during the period of the 1960s to the 1980s when drugs and drug use came to be viewed as a threat to the nation, creating disruption and chaos (Linton 2015, see also the next chapter).

3.2   A Swamp?

The entrance to the drug world as longed for and sought after, or as a boundary that can be crossed and retreated from, contrasts with representations of gateways as active and insidious. In Swedish political and media contexts, gateways to the drug world are often portrayed as pitfalls or as a swamp that will suck one down in a social sense. A common metaphor for problematic drug use is *knarkträsk* (sometimes also *drogträsk* or *narkotikaträsk*), literally meaning "drug swamp". A speech made in 2018 by Stefan Löfven, Sweden's social democratic prime minister from 2014 to 2021, paints a picture of how the term is used: "Whose children suffer the greatest risk of being dragged down into a life of crime, into the *narkotikaträsk*? Those of parents already struggling the hardest in life!"[5] He shows here how the entrance to the swamp is located not only in age but also in class. The speech as a whole revolves around poverty in Sweden, historically and in the present, and the words that summarise the problems are: "Cramped living conditions. Unemployment. Crime. Poor health. Substance abuse." Taken together, these concepts provide a picture of class-related disorientation. Those who end up in the *knarkträsk* are characterised by a set of social markers that signify them as caged in by their circumstances.

The swamp metaphor indicates that drug use is not only problematic in and of itself; it is also part of an illegal and stigmatised network of relationships. The *knarkträsk* is an imagined world of everything from drugs to the sex trade, criminals and stolen goods. It has a fractured relationship with the rest of society where crime, begging, welfare benefits, healthcare and so on are meeting points. A spatial delimitation, positioning the swamp in a certain place or linking the concept to a certain body, is thus only meaningful on the basis of cultural perceptions of social conditions.

Journalist Magnus Linton has analysed Sweden's drug policy and its consequences and published his findings in his book *Knark* (2015), which also looks into the way drugs have been conceptualised—the word *knark*, which came into use during the 1960s, and derivatives of it, such

---

5 Löfven, Stefan. 2018. Stefan Löfven's speech at Järvaveckan, an Annual Political Gathering in the North-West of Stockholm. Socialdemokraterna.se, 17 June.

as *knarkare* (someone who uses drugs/*knark*). In an interview with the newspaper ETC, Linton says that the word *knark* has had a major effect on Sweden's cautionary drug policy, and combined with the word for swamp (*träsk*), it has been particularly impactful (Beeck 2015). "Phonetically, *knark* has a repellent ring to it, especially in combination with *träsk*. There's no better word than *knarkträsk* to describe some kind of abyss or collapse" (ibid., p. 17; see also Linton 2015, p. 45).

The link that Linton makes between a swamp, an abyss and collapse is rooted in the meaning of the word *träsk*, which can also refer to a quagmire: ambiguous ground that is neither stable enough to stand or build something on, nor liquid enough to swim in. It is an indeterminate in-between, which anthropologist Mary Douglas has shown signals danger (2002/1966, pp. 47ff.) and evokes a feeling of menace and unease. The idea of bathing in something that is neither solid nor liquid reinforces the link with dirt. Instead of becoming clean, someone bathing in a quagmire would become filthy and sticky. The *knarkträsk* thus acquires a temporal dimension that extends beyond having physically been in the swamp. The stickiness suggests that bodies that have visited the swamp will continue to be dirty, even after they have emerged from it. The use of the term *knarkträsk* or *knarkare* thus becomes a way of attributing blame and placing people in stigmatised and declining positions based not on drug use as such, but on drugs combined with socioeconomic status by indicating dirtiness, menace and danger.

Since the *knarkträsk* is populated by *knarkare*, entering the swamp means undergoing a metamorphosis. The person in question becomes a *knarkare*, an identity that is in turn associated with the concept of addiction, with its repetitive and chronic character. And since the entrance (or gateway) to the swamp is a downward one, exiting it means heading in an upward direction—and changing identity once again. The process of quitting drugs and becoming an ex-*knarkare* is commonly referred to as "getting clean" (see also the next chapter, **Avoiding the *Knarkare***).

But being clean is not the same as never having been addicted in the first place (Keane 2002). This complicated journey is a narrative that is not accepted by several interviewees. Worlds of drugs, such as those which Agnes describes "jumping into", do not need to be a sticky swamp—stigmatised places that do something negative to the individual—but can be perceived as places that it is possible to enter and leave without a negative change in identity. Drugs can be found in status-filled contexts, which in turn require completely different entrances than downward-angled gateways.

Pernilla, who is in her forties and works at a publishing house, is sitting on her sofa with a cup of tea in her hand. She seems to want to take the interview as an opportunity to really reflect upon her stance on drug use. She is quick-witted and has a certain theatricality about her that allows her to express things in an amusing way. We laugh a lot during the interview. She describes how surprised she was back in upper-secondary school, when she realised that drugs and drug-taking occur to a large extent in completely different contexts and bodies than the worn-down, stigmatised and dangerous ones she had been taught about as a child.

> everything I'd been told and taught [in primary school] and just how people viewed it [drug use] in general was suddenly called into question [...] to suddenly hang out with people you really like and meeting people who knew what it's like on the inside, who do drugs themselves and who are part of a context where drugs are around and stuff, and who have a completely different kind of take, like a relaxed take on it. [...] They were these expat kids who went to that school, whose parents were diplomats or worked abroad all the time [...] really had their act together and high-achieving in many ways and really, smart people, you know, that's how they came across to me. But they had a completely different approach to, to drugs.

Pernilla moved from the countryside to the city and enrolled in an upper-secondary school where a significant number of pupils came from affluent families with international ties. She describes how these pupils had "a relaxed view" of drugs, which differed significantly from the view of drugs that she had grown up with. Later on during the interview, she says "her jaw dropped" when one of her classmates talked about drugs in a very liberal way. The realisation that several of her new friends regularly used drugs was an "eye-opener". This discovery made her question everything she had been told before, even the things she had assumed were a given. Her image of drugs and intoxication thus moved from one type of body to another—from stigmatised ones to important and trustworthy ones—which resulted in a shift of meaning. Drugs made an upward class journey before her eyes, and people who use drugs took shape in unexpected ways. The countryside partying that she was accustomed to, on the other hand, free of illegal drugs but including large amounts of alcohol—suddenly seemed rather low class: "parties in the countryside, back when I was in lower secondary, were dominated by, like, loud blokes". She compares this to her friends in the city, "a quieter sort of people" who mainly smoked cannabis and whose drinking was more moderate. Looking back, she describes the drinking she witnessed while growing up in the countryside as rather destructive:

> when we were, like, 13 or 14, when everyone started… we got absolutely hammered, basically, and so of course [there were] fights, well, of course it was destructive. Because it's also a drug that really makes you act out, in a way. Alcohol causes all kinds of situations […] related to the whole puberty thing and sexuality and, you know…

From that moment onwards, illegal drugs started to play an important role in Pernilla's life. She feels that there is a discrepancy between society's view on drugs and what drugs and using drugs actually entail in practice. What she had been "told and taught" and the "take" on drugs that Pernilla describes herself as having—which were based on ideas of gateways and the *knarkträsk*—had led her to believe that everything about *knark* was dirty. But she describes how she discovered that this was not true. She looked to her friends, who were nothing like the marginalised *knarkare* in the *knarkträsk*. Nor does she mention feeling dirty herself, despite having used drugs on and off for more than 20 years.

When I head out to interview Katy, who is in her mid-forties, we meet at her office in Stockholm's Old Town. She greets me with a generous smile, one that is clearly used to welcoming visitors, and leads the way to a meeting room, closing the door on the hubbub of her workplace. The location she has chosen for our interview signals that she does not feel ashamed for her use. At the same time, however, she says that work is the setting where it is most imperative no one finds out about her drug use. Secrecy is ensured by the closed door, but also, more than anything perhaps, by Katy's social status, which makes it unlikely that anyone in the office will suspect the topic of our conversation. Katy also describes how the image of drugs and people who use drugs was repainted for her in a surprising way in her late teens, when she travelled to work as an au pair in Italy. Her previous image of cannabis was as a gateway to a life of destitution:

> because we'd all been taught how those things worked: a gateway to harder drugs and once you start, well, you'll end up on the streets. Or admitted to a psych ward.

In her new life, however, cannabis was part of different bodies than the ones she had expected:

> Over there, I suddenly got to see that "fuck, people actually do this *and* live completely normal lives!", you know. They have children and fancy jobs and earn a shitload of money and they have to be at the top of their game. And then they do this when they get home. You know. When they want to relax.

Like Pernilla, Katy also uses an expression to describe how her eyes were opened to the new insights about where drugs can be found. An order became visible that had previously been hidden by metaphors such as the gateway and the drug swamp. It is as though both women felt tricked: they had been told that drugs only existed in inaccessible, uninviting places at the very bottom of society, only to discover that drug use is common practice in an elite world they wanted to join, a world in which people have "a shitload of money" and "fancy jobs", and are seen by Pernilla as "high-achieving" and "smart".

These new insights did not challenge the image of the place of the *knarkare* at the bottom of the social order, but they discovered that drugs are not dirty in and of themselves. Rather, the people they met who used drugs were perceived as cleaner, in the sense of being better adjusted than Katy and Pernilla were themselves, who were just beginning to settle into new contexts (Douglas 2002/1966; see also the next chapter, **Avoiding the *Knarkare***). These insights became turning points for both Katy and

Pernilla, who continue to use drugs from time to time, with no plans to stop and without losing orientation within their professional jobs and careers.

3.3   Sinking into the Ground

Ahmed describes orientation in many different ways, but repeatedly compares it to feeling at home (2006b, p. 7), being at ease and thus being able to sink into the environment that surrounds us, which is in turn experienced as an extension of the body (ibid., pp. 134ff.). If the body cannot sink into the environment, and the feet cannot find any ground to sink into, this causes feelings of discomfort and a kind of nausea (ibid., pp. 138f.). Ahmed writes:

> The ground into which we sink our feet is not neutral: it gives ground to some more than others. Disorientation occurs when we fail to sink into the ground, which means that the "ground" itself is disturbed, which also disturbs what gathers "on" the ground. (2006b, p. 160)

Places are not neutral, the ground allows some feet to sink more than others, and when the feet are not allowed to sink, this means that the ground is disturbed by the feet, which in turn also disturbs those who gather there.

This way of describing experiences of disorientation stands in an interesting relation to the metaphor of the *knarkträsk*. The drug swamp implies a high possibility of sinking into the ground: this is the danger of the swamp, being engulfed by a specific, dangerous environment. As the Stefan Löfven speech I quoted earlier showed, the swamp metaphor is also used as an image of an active ground surface that pulls young people down, especially those in socially vulnerable situations. So what exactly happens to people in the *knarkträsk*; that is, in stigmatised environments linked to drugs? Ahmed's metaphor, about the possibilities of sinking into the environment as an image of orientation, seems to stand in opposition to the *knarkträsk* metaphor as a metaphor of disorientation. However, through a close examination of the marginalised and stigmatised lived reality of drug use, both metaphors can be instructive.

When I meet Hanna in a cramped office we have been able to borrow for our interview, she seems to carry her sorrow like a physical burden. Her elegant haircut and mode of dressing are testament to her interest in fashion and design, but her entire being seems cowed, beaten into submission. Hanna is in her fifties, injects heroin on a daily basis and wants to quit. Her addiction, she says, is currently dominating her life. During the interview, she speaks slowly and with hesitation; on several occasions, she mentions the loss of her children, who have been taken into care by the social services. Her current social circumstances—her financial situation (with welfare benefits and shoplifting being her main sources of income), her addiction to heroin, her housing situation (she says she is "staying at a friend's") and, not least, her grief over having lost her children—are all symbols of life in the *knarkträsk*. But the link between drugs and her current situation is not straightforward. When I ask her what she does when she is under the influence[6] of heroin, she says:

Hanna: I tend to do the things I'm most afraid of doing when I'm not on drugs. Brr! [laughs]
Emma: Such as?
Hanna: Err, it's… I guess it's, basically… basically everything I need to do.

The moments of tangible influence are when she feels most capable of action. With the help of the drug, she can orientate herself and cope with everyday tasks. In that sense, the metaphor of the *knarkträsk* as a place in which people use drugs has two sides to it. On the one hand, Hanna perceives herself to be in a stigmatised and vulnerable position, the kind of position that tends to be associated with the term *knarkträsk*. On the other, drug use temporarily leads to a swamp-free zone, where experiences of disorientation are exchanged for oriented action.

---

[6] In this context, I use "under the influence" to refer to a condition in which one's state of mind is noticeably altered as a direct consequence of using drugs, which Hanna does on a daily basis. The meaning of the phrase is difficult to pin down, however, because someone in Hanna's situation is perpetually "under the influence" of drugs, not least when they have not used any drugs for a while and are experiencing withdrawal symptoms (Heilig 2015, pp. 79ff.).

So heroin helps her feet to sink into the ground, but the same action leads to a social sinking, down into the *knarkträsk*. How did she end up here, surrounded by unfavourable living conditions? Looking back, she says, she had a completely "ordinary" childhood. Her dream was to work in fashion and design:

> I was just an ordinary, everyday girl from an ordinary, everyday home. [sounds tired, defeated] My father was a manager in the public sector and my mother is, well, working class. [...] I knew what I wanted and everything from the time I was twelve. Of course I knew. The way a teenager does. I wanted to be a fashion designer.

She situates herself as a child in class terms and describes her position as "ordinary", and from there, she points out a direction: studies, followed by a creative career. But a year into design college, something happened to that direction. She moved to a larger city and met a man whom she describes as "the wrong sort":

> *Hanna*: No [clears her throat], I met the wrong sort. Mm. Met the wrong sort, started seeing this guy who, yeah, did those things and stuff. Yeah... the wrong people. [almost inaudible]
> *Emma*: How did you support yourself back then?
> *Hanna*: At first, I, er, sold stuff and then... I started to prostitute myself. Mm...

Hanna's description of her initial drug use is not primarily about the drugs, but about the company. The man she met seems to have served as her way in, as her gateway, and the way in which she narrates her story makes it sound as though she simply found herself there one day—on the streets, with a heroin addiction. Her responses are tired and brief, and I get the impression that they have been repeated many times, to social workers, health professionals and other authorities. A normal, everyday girl moves to the big city and meets the wrong sort. It is as though she lost her way and then could not make it out of a situation that had happened to her by accident.

Why was their first encounter with drugs so different for these interviewees? For example, how did Agnes' long-awaited gateway become possible to both enter and exit, while for Hanna it led to a complete loss of orientation? How did the change take place from Hanna being "an ordinary girl" to being a heroin addict selling sex on the streets?

Looking back, Hanna describes herself as suddenly surrounded by the wrong objects: the drugs, the "wrong people" and the customers who paid for sex. The latter is a way of making a living that she talks about with a mixture of disgust and fatigue. She describes a period of disorientation, of being in the wrong space. When she recounts what happened after she started using heroin, she tells the story in a monotonous, chronological way. Life continued in the same way for about 15 years, she says, but then she became pregnant and gave birth to two children. She describes how she stayed clean for eight years after the first pregnancy by working out at the gym and spending all the rest of her time taking care of her children. Being off drugs felt like a relief, she recalls.

> I felt liberated when I was free of drugs. It was liberating to get up in the morning without needing that first fix… it was such a relief. Yeah… because this thing, it holds you prisoner.

Hanna contrasts the concept of being drug-free with being a prisoner of drug use. She now feels imprisoned again and looks back wistfully on that feeling of liberation. But she also says that after a while the children's father started abusing her.

> I was abused by my, by the father of my children. He… started to hit me. I gave birth to a daughter… my third child, and he started to hit me, and… he once abused me in front of the children, in front of all three of them. The eldest told people at day care. "Fredrik hits mummy". That's when they contacted social services.

Abuse by men is a recurring topic in studies of socially vulnerable women who use drugs. Anette Rosengren (2003) writes that most of the participants in her study of middle-aged women experiencing homelessness had been subjected to a great deal of violence—mainly perpetrated by their male partners, but also by the police, security guards and others. At the same time, she writes: "The men represent protection and love"

(Rosengren 2003, p. 207) for these (heterosexual) women. This double-edged nature of men and the emotions they provoke—protection and love on the one hand, which enables orientation, but violence and insecurity on the other, which restricts women's freedom of movement—has certain elements in common with drug use in the *knarkträsk*, not least as Hanna describes it: that which enables simultaneously locks in. The image of sinking into the swamp cannot be separated from the at-ease feeling of being securely at home, which is how Ahmed describes being oriented; but this sinking leads to a social sinking, to a place at "the bottom of society", where lack and constraint are the defining features of life. These days, Hanna no longer suffers abuse, but her children are gone and the conditions she needs to fulfil to get them back seem to be about gathering the right objects—a home and a drug-free partner, for example—and keeping others at a distance, such as heroin. Hanna repeatedly tells me that she wants to quit using heroin; when I ask her why she does not, the answer she gives me is not about security or comfort, but about time:

> *Hanna*: I take heroin because I don't have time to come off it. That's how I'd put it. Do you understand what I mean?
> *Emma*: Yes. I understand what you mean.
> *Hanna*: It's as simple as that. I never take the time for it.

So Hanna says that she keeps using heroin due to a lack of time. It sounds counterintuitive, because she has mentioned that the majority of her day is spent "chasing the cash for heroin". If the activity that takes up most of her time ceases, then the time to come off the drug should be freed up. But the way in which drug use changes perceived time is an aspect that several researchers have pointed out as under-theorised (Klingemann 2000; Klingemann and Schibli 2004; Järvinen and Ravn 2017). Sociologist Mats Hilte, who conducted a study comparing alcohol, nicotine, cannabis and heroin, argues that different drugs affect time in radically different ways (2019) and claims that these altered perceptions of time are a fundamental part of the way in which people experience intoxication. In her autobiography *How to Stop Time: Heroin from A to Z* (1999), author Ann Marlowe specifically discusses the relationship between heroin use and time. She describes heroin as providing a sense of living in an eternal present, while the past and the future cease to exist. Throughout her book, Marlowe, who used heroin for years, keeps returning to the drug's ability to change time and make it stand still. During the come-down, there is no other way to resist the passage of time than to take another dose of heroin.

Hanna's life is characterised by grief due to the ever-present awareness of the loss of her children, who were taken into care and placed with a foster family. In her situation, it is not at all surprising that she would be drawn to something that has the capacity to stop time. When she says that she does not have the time to come off it, she is referring to the time when she is not on heroin; that is: when she is not in the state that she says she needs to be in to get anything done. In a way, taking time to venture into the *knarkträsk* that surrounds the protective bubble offered by heroin means enduring time itself—not just by detoxing (and thus enduring a period of agony), but also by allowing one's experience of time to change, allowing it to pass without the ability to act. But Hanna is in a place she does not want to be, and that is where she remains trapped when she suspends time by taking heroin. From an outsider's point of view, it looks as though she is stuck in the *knarkträsk*. Hanna herself, however, views the drug as the one thing that allows her to do "basically everything" that needs to be done. Spatially and temporally, heroin appears to be both a solution and a dead-end.

The interviewees thus describe drug use and time under the influence in terms of places or worlds, which can also be understood as places where time works differently (Hilte 2019). As I have shown, the interviewees are strongly influenced by the socioeconomic structures that surround these places and the various objects found there. This relates to radically different directions, ways of understanding and relating to their own drug use. I have looked at the metaphors of the *gateway* and the *knarkträsk* as common Swedish portrayals of the idea that drug use will, over time, result in a downwards slide. My research, however, shows that the interviewees perceived themselves as having entered a variety of places, internal as well as the social worlds of drugs. Pernilla and Katy journeyed upwards from the entrance, into high-status circles. For Hanna, the entrance led to a place of disorientation and violence. Agnes and Madelene yearned for it and actively sought it out. During Boel's teenage years, it was something that was ever-present and possible to repeatedly enter and exit.

Different social settings provided these women with different class-related opportunities to visit exciting yet sometimes dangerous worlds, where it is not only drugs that are close by but also collections of objects. These worlds take on different shapes as extensions of the body. Some interviewees temporarily dwell in them in the physical sense, while others have become stuck there, as though the drugs world and the body have become tangled up in each other and can no longer be separated (cf. Skeggs 2004, p. 177). I have analysed the metaphor of the *knarkträsk* as a term for class-related disorientation, and this metaphor does not apply to the majority of drug practices of the women who took part in my study. But even when I considered the swamp metaphor as a way of referring to a stigmatised and marginalised life, closer inspection showed the link to drugs to be more complex. Using drugs creates a protective bubble inside the unpleasantness of life in the drug swamp, which is characterised by harsh class conditions, a bubble from which the route out is tortuous and it is difficult to extricate oneself.

References

Ahmed, Sara. 2006a. Orientations: Toward a Queer Phenomenology. *GLQ: A Journal of Lesbian and Gay Studies* 12 (4): 543–574.
Ahmed, Sara. 2006b. *Queer Phenomenology: Orientations, Objects, Others.* Durham, NC: Duke University Press.
Ahmed, Sara. 2014. *Willful Subjects.* Durham, NC: Duke University Press.
Appadurai, Arjun. 1996. *Modernity at Large: Cultural Dimensions of Globalization.* Minneapolis: University of Minnesota Press.
Beeck, Malin. 2015. Räkna med normkrasch [Expect a Collapse of Standards]. *ETC*, 11 October: 16–18.
Douglas, Mary. 2002/1966. *Purity and Danger: An Analysis of Concepts of Pollution and Taboo.* London and New York: Routledge.
Du Rose, Natacha. 2015. *The Governance of Female Drug Users: Women's Experiences of Drug Policy.* Bristol: Policy Press.

Heilig, Markus. 2015. *Alkohol, droger och hjärnan: tro och vetande utifrån modern neurovetenskap* [Alcohol, Drugs and the Brain: Beliefs and Knowledge Based on Modern Neuroscience]. Stockholm: Natur & Kultur.

Hilte, Mats. 2019. Psychoactive Drugs and the Management of Time. *Sociologisk Forskning* 56 (2): 111–124.

Järvinen, Margaretha, and Signe Ravn. 2017. Out of Sync: Time Management in the Lives of Young Drug Users. *Time & Society* 26 (2): 244–264.

Kandel, Denise. 1975. Stages in Adolescent Involvement in Drug Use. *Science* 190: 912–914.

Keane, Helen. 2002. *What's Wrong with Addiction?* Melbourne: Melbourne University Press.

Klingemann, Harald. 2000. "To Every Thing There Is a Season": Social Time and Clock Time in Addiction Treatment. *Social Science & Medicine* 51 (8): 1231–1240.

Klingemann, Harald, and Daniela Schibli. 2004. Times for Healing: Towards a Typology of Time-Frames in Swiss Alcohol and Drug Clinics. *Addiction* 99 (11): 1418–1429.

Laanemets, Leili. 2002. Skapande av femininitet: Om kvinnor i missbrukarbehandling [The Creation of Femininity: About Women in Substance Abuse Treatment]. Diss., Lunds universitet, Lund.

Linton, Magnus. 2015. *Knark: en svensk historia* [Knark: A Swedish Story]. Stockholm: Bokförlaget Atlas.

Lynskey, Michael T., and Arpana Agrawal. 2018. Denise Kandel's Classic Work on the Gateway Sequence of Drug Acquisition. *Addiction* 113 (10): 1927–1932.

Marlowe, Ann. 1999. *How to Stop Time: Heroin from A to Z*. New York, NY: Anchor.

Measham, Fiona, and Michael Shiner. 2009. The Legacy of "Normalisation": The Role of Classical and Contemporary Criminological Theory in Understanding Young People's Drug Use. *The International Journal on Drug Policy* 20 (6): 502–508.

Olsson, Börje. 1994. *Narkotikaproblemets bakgrund: Användning av och uppfattningar om narkotika inom svensk medicin 1839–1965* [The Background of the Drug Problem: Use and Perceptions of Drugs in Swedish Medicine 1839–1965] (CAN rapportserie, 39). Stockholm: CAN.

Pini, Maria. 2001. *Club Cultures and Female Subjectivity: The Move from Home to House*. London: Palgrave Macmillan.

Rosengren, Annette. 2003. *Mellan ilska och hopp: Om hemlöshet, droger och kvinnor* [Between Anger and Hope: On Homelessness, Drugs and Women]. Stockholm: Carlsson bokförlag.

Skårner, Anette. 2007. *Skilda världar? En studie av narkotikamissbrukares sociala relationer och sociala nätverk* [Worlds Apart? A Study of Drug Users' Social Relationships and Social Networks]. Skriftserien 2001:5. Göteborgs Universitet.

Skeggs, Beverley. 2004. *Class, Self, Culture*. London: Routledge.

Stenberg, Birgitta. 2017/1969. *Rapport* [Report]. Stockholm: Norstedts.

Trulsson, Karin. 1997. *"Det är i alla fall mitt barn!" En studie om att vara missbrukare och mamma skild från barn* ["It's My Child Anyway!" A Study on Being a Drug Abuser and a Mother Separated from Her Children]. Lic. Thesis, Lunds universitet, Lund.

4

Avoiding the *Knarkare*

People wash the world. Sweeping, sanitising and making it clinically clean. People like you and me have no place in squares, parks or other public spaces. People like you and me my friend, people like you and me litter. (Adolfsson 2004, p. 39[1])[2]

As I have argued, *knark* (drugs) can refer to any drug, but the *knarkare* (a person who uses drugs) and the *knarkträsk* (drug swamp) always refer to marginalised social contexts, rather than to anyone or any network of people who use drugs. Still, *knarkare* seemingly refers to anyone who has ever used a drug, and any person who uses drugs could potentially risk being identified as a *knarkare*. So what does it mean to be identified as

---

[1] In her autobiography *Kårnulf Was Here: A Homeland Portrayal in Four Parts and Two Conversations* (2004), Josefine Adolfsson describes her childhood and upbringing in Lund, during which she and her closest friends consumed large quantities of tranquilisers, in particular. The book is a depiction of how class-related vulnerability, in this case the vulnerability of girls, cannot be handled by adult society and leads to marginalisation. At the same time, it becomes clear how irresistible anti-anxiety tablets can be when anxiety and worry are ubiquitous problems that shape everyday life.

[2] All quotes in Swedish have been translated by me.

© The Author(s) 2024
E. Eleonorasdotter, *Women's Drug Use in Everyday Life*,
https://doi.org/10.1007/978-3-031-46057-9_4

such? How do the women negotiate the symbolically charged figure of the abuser and the *knarkare* in relation to their own drug use?

The Swedish Tenants' Association's[3] magazine, *Hem och Hyra*, twice asked its members "What kind of neighbour bothers you the most?" The first time 49% and the second time 33% answered "*knarkare*", which thus came first in both surveys, ahead of categories such as "criminals", "noisy young people" and "motorcycle gangs" (Lundmark 2008; Ljungqvist 2017). Julius von Wright, editor-in-chief of the magazine *Alkohol och Narkotika*,[4] criticises the ways in which stereotypes are uncritically reproduced in these articles and questions the purpose of measuring prejudice (von Wright 2017). However, precisely because the surveys do so, they provide information on the cultural meaning of the concept of the *knarkare*, and how notions of the *knarkare* influence how spaces are organised. The *knarkare* is kept at a distance, and it is assumed to make people uncomfortable to be close to them. Self-defined former users of drugs are asked in the articles to comment on how unpleasant they have been as neighbours, alongside quotes from people who have been tormented by neighbouring persons who use drugs. The articles give the impression that the *knarkare* is a fixed, well-defined character, and that thefts, needles in the sandbox and faeces on the basement floor characterise the kind of environment they create around them—a kind of *knarkare*, in other words, who is easy to spot because of the damage they cause to their surroundings.

In her article "The Shifting Shapes of The *Knarkare*",[5] historian of ideas Jenny Björkman describes how the "traditional" Swedish image of the *knarkare* is a "homeless, prostituted, injecting drug user" (2002, p. 43), just like the portraits in Stefan Jarl's documentary trilogy about

---

[3] The Tenants' Association, which was founded in 1923, protects the rights of tenants and has more than 500,000 members.

[4] *Alkohol och Narkotika* is published by the Swedish Council for Information on Alcohol and Other Drugs (CAN), a hybrid organisation that combines grassroots movements with cooperation with the authorities. CAN was founded in 1901 and was inspired by the UK's Band of Hope movement.

[5] Knarkarens förvandlingar (2002).

socially marginalised people who use drugs.[6] In this description, homelessness becomes an indication of a further spatial demarcation between the *knarkare* and others, and based on *Hem och Hyra's* articles, it seems anything but strange that the *knarkare* would lose their home. In Björkman's definition, however, the *knarkare* is characterised by their vulnerability and the damage they inflict upon themselves. What both definitions have in common is dirtiness: in the sense of both a lack of hygiene and social taboos which, according to Mary Douglas' theory of purity and danger, need to be kept at arm's length (2002/1966). In short, the *knarkare* poses a threat and is a danger that must be kept at a distance from other people (cf. Ettorre 2015, p. 801). How is this work done by people who use drugs themselves, and their surroundings?

Historian Johan Edman and sociologist Börje Olsson write that drug problems began to be formulated without reference to specific substances after World War II, in Sweden. Drug use then became a coherent problem, and people who use drugs began to be discussed in medical journals as a defined group (Edman and Olsson 2014, p. 508). Author Birgitta Stenberg has claimed that it was she and poet Paul Andersson who came up with the word *knarkare* in the 1950s, albeit as a definition of people who use amphetamine, just like they themselves did. The reason was that they thought that they made a crunching noise— "knrk knrk"—when they chewed (Lindstrand 2001, p. 49). The word *knark* was later expanded to include all sorts of drugs, which made it a useful descriptor for the entire group that Edman and Olsson write about. I perceive the contemporary meaning of the word *knark* as generally synonymous with the terms drugs and narcotics, which primarily refer to illegally purchased substances.[7]

---

[6] Jarl's first film, *Dom kallar oss mods* ("They Call Us Misfits", 1968), was followed by *Ett anständigt liv* ("A Respectable Life", 1979) and *Det sociala arvet* ("Misfits to Yuppies", 1993). These documentaries, distributed by Folkets Bio, depict the lives of marginalised adolescents in Stockholm, focusing mainly on Kenta Gustavsson and Stoffe Nilsson, a pair of friends. Nilsson overdoses on heroin and passes away while the second documentary is being filmed.

[7] As I mentioned in the introduction, controlled medicines can become illegal if they are sold on or given to someone other than the person for whom they were prescribed. They can also be used for a different purpose than that for which they were prescribed—which is technically legal, but places their use in the grey area between legitimate and illegitimate use. Even when used as prescribed, however, controlled medicines can be regarded as *knark*/drugs by those who use them, or others. The relationship between the concepts of *knark*/drugs and controlled

4.1   Invisible Dirt

Although representations of the *knarkare* paint a picture of a coherent character that is noticeable and visible, my empirical material shows that the line between *knarkare* and non-*knarkare* is unclear. Angela says:

> if you say…"I've taken speed [amphetamine] today," people think "Ah! She's one of those *knarkare*.[8] Taking speed all the time." […] everyone's kind of afraid to be seen as a drug abuser or something, so it becomes this confidential thing.

In this quote, the person Angela calls a *knarkare* does not come into being through visible harm to herself or those around her, but through speech. According to Angela, talking about a single occasion of use can be perceived as an implicit message about a long-term relationship with drugs. Angela's intention, to talk about something temporary, takes on a different meaning for the intended listener, who hears a story about permanence and identity. This shift in meaning can be traced in part to a temporal ambiguity in the word "use". The person who uses is in a close relationship that could mean they may potentially use again. Use can thus be understood as constant if it is presented as potential (Ahmed 2019, p. 29). In the case of illicit drugs, repeated use is associated with dependency, i.e. compulsive use, and the concept of addiction, which literally expresses the use as improper. A pronounced proximity to drugs can therefore create a shift in meaning to include developed notions of compulsiveness and problems; that is, the person who use drugs becomes an addict/a *knarkare*. This means that Angela only talks about her use in confidence. The level of trust in a relationship can thus determine whether or not language will turn someone into a *knarkare*. But what happens, then, in situations in which someone needs to mention that

---

medicines is thus unclear and context-dependent, which is something I explore in greater depth in the chapter **Appropriate Drugs**.

[8] Angela uses the term *tjackpundare* here, which has its own history stemming from a term for a specific, manic condition that can result from high amphetamine intake (see Rylander 1969; Iversen 2012, chapter 2). However, in the context of this interview, the term is synonymous with the meaning of *knarkare*.

they have used drugs, without having been able to first establish a bond of trust?

Pernilla describes an occasion when she became more affected by cannabis than she had anticipated, at a friend's house just before she had planned to go home. She describes how it was an unpleasant experience involving feelings of anxiety and dizziness, and when she imagined how she would be treated by those around her if she went out on public transport, she judged that it simply would not work.

> [H]ow the hell am I even going to get home on the tube and bus? [...] Oh God, that's not possible. And then I'm not going to go "yeah, I'm wasted and stoned out of my mind [high on cannabis]." How do you ask for help when you're under the influence of drugs? Yes, because things are different then. You've got to consider other risk parameters because you know that you're under the influence of something that's not entirely socially accepted in all contexts. So, if things go wrong, I think people might be more likely to ignore you.

If "things go wrong", that is: if Pernilla had started to feel worse in public space, she would have needed to ask for help and approach another person. However, being a lonely woman in the city, feeling bad, under the influence of drugs, is a provocation, challenging norms and conventions of how femininity should be done (Lupton 1999, p. 165). Pernilla feared that it would not be a good idea to announce that she was on drugs when she was already not feeling well, and decided that she should avoid a situation where she might have to. The question: "How do you ask for help when you're under the influence of drugs?" encapsulates the way in which different approaches to drug use structure the urban environment and create a gap between the few who use drugs and the majority who do not. Should these drugs make her feel bad, Pernilla expects that people will ignore her. They might view both her and the state that she is in as a threat; if they approached her, they would risk also becoming dirty themselves (Ahmed 2014, p. 87).

Instead, Pernilla decided to sleep on her acquaintance's sofa. There is relief in her voice when she tells me that, fortunately, he was someone with a lot of experience of drugs himself:

[T]hat person's really, he's done all kinds of different drugs and stuff in his life. So he just went "oh, no problem". You know? "Have a seat. Would you like some water?"

The difference between the expected rejection in public space and the helpful treatment from another person who uses drugs shows how the dirty *knarkare* comes into being when drugs are revealed to be present in certain social spaces, but not others. As Pernilla had the opportunity to choose which space to be in, she was able to avoid becoming dirty.

Mary Douglas describes how notions of purity and danger are tools of cultural orientation (2002/1966). She uses these terms to highlight that which our society finds acceptable or unacceptable, respectively, and argues that the latter is more about an aversion rooted in fear of the incomprehensible, the disorderly, of things that are in an unexpected place, than the actual characteristics of the condemned substance itself. In the chapter "Secular Defilement" (2002/1966, pp. 36ff.), Douglas describes shoes on the dining table or dishes in the bedroom as examples of misplaced objects that, in their expected places, do not evoke the same feelings of discomfort. The point is that dirt is not intrinsically dirt in and of itself, but it is the beliefs attached to it that make it dirty when in the wrong place (ibid., pp. 44f.).

If this reasoning is transferred to a drug context, an epidural anaesthetic during childbirth or a glass of champagne at a birthday party can be examples of when substances such as opiates and alcohol are considered pure—i.e. culturally accepted—substances, integrated into everyday life. But these same substances become dirty and dangerous in other places, such as a syringe in a public toilet or an alcoholic drink in a plastic cup next to a beggar (cf. Moore and Measham 2013, p. 87). The transformation into dirt occurs irrespective of factors such as the amount of matter or its bacterial count.

Douglas also illustrates that ideas about dirt and impurity forge rules for gendered bodies: women and men are not allowed to freely touch each other, for example. The rules are different in different places, but they exist everywhere, both in legal texts and as social contracts, in the Western world as well as in the "primitive" societies that Douglas studied. These rules serve to maintain order—an order that establishes and preserves power structures by keeping the sexes apart and distinguishing between them, and that legitimises its necessity with the feeling that it is preventing everything from dissolving into chaos.

4.2   Keeping the Abuser on the Margins

Douglas' view of order is thus constructed in terms of ideas about dirt and purity: the dirtier something is, the lower it ranks in the hierarchy of power. *Knarkare* are an example of an impure group, the kind of group that Jonas Frykman and Orvar Löfgren describe as individuals who have been and continue to be marginalised by society: "Ideas of dirt are ever present in our thoughts about people who, for varying reasons, we view as foreign or odd" (Frykman and Löfgren 2019, p. 157). The concept of marginalisation illustrates that ideas about dirt are linked to spatiality. That which is on the margins, on the periphery, is not at the centre, where the starting point is. The person who imagines dirt and the margins is thus looking from the perspective of the centre. If they have used drugs, however, and happen to mention that they did, others might view them as being on the margins.

Katy tells me that she has no problem with these premises. She reflects upon transparency and the laws governing drugs, describing them as things that are not primarily for her and her friends, but are needed for the sake of other people who use drugs. She says:

I don't feel the need to be some front-line activist [...] I don't need them [drugs] that much that I [...] demand the freedom to be more open about it, and talk about it. I don't. [...] I mean, of course using [drugs] is a violation of the law. But we've never had to deal with, you know, ending up in a situation in which we, well, end up in court, or, you know, we've never, we've never had to pay any fines. Because we try to handle it so discreetly that it doesn't... so that I feel that within the framework I can be quite open. So I'm probably not going to fight for a more liberal drug policy, but I understand the issue. Then again, maybe not everyone is like us...

I interpret Katy as understanding Sweden's drug laws to be designed for other kinds of people who use drugs, not for her social circle. Nor does she have any issue with the fact that her actions are technically a crime, because she does not expect to have to face any practical penalty. This, according to her, is because she is discreet. Discretion stands in contrast to the non-discreet, the deviant—in this case represented by the *knarkare*—and requires both material resources and an embodied ability to pass. Ettorre writes:

> Regardless of how deviant behavior is defined, it always manifests itself in the substance/materiality of the "deviant's" body. Simply, individuals who deviate from the ideal, from "consensualized" norms, are seen as being socially and morally inferior and their social and moral trouble making is embodied. (2015, p. 795)

A marked body cannot (any longer) be discreet, and then, the practical application of the law may become necessary, according to Katy. In her view, laws serve to protect society from troublemakers, rather than from drug use. Perhaps she also means that laws are needed to dredge people who have "succumbed" back up from the *knarkträsk* through legal means, for their own sake. But the moral as well as the legal blame in such reasoning is placed unilaterally on the person who uses drugs who gets into trouble with those drugs, the person who can no longer be discreet and who is therefore considered to need the framework of harsh, criminal measures that is the practice.

Katy's approach demonstrates how stigma around people who use drugs can be constructed independently of how drugs themselves are viewed. Instead, questions about drugs become questions about people. This shift sometimes becomes a subject for debate, as with the slogan "*Knark är bajs*" (literally "Drugs Are Faeces", 2003–2007) of the national campaign Mobilisation Against Narcotics, which urged adolescents to give drugs a pass. In an interview in *Vice* magazine (Hagman Rogowski 2017), Björn Fries, who served as the government's Anti-Narcotics coordinator from 2002 to 2007 and was part of the team behind the campaign, says that he feels some people misunderstood it:

I know many thought the campaign didn't quite strike the right tone – "surely *knarkare* aren't faeces?" And no, of course they aren't. But that's not what the slogan said. It wasn't about people who face social exclusion, substance abuse, poverty, perhaps mental health issues. We didn't view drug users as faeces – but people interpreted it that way.

But can the term *knark* (drugs) really be separated from "social exclusion, substance abuse, poverty [and] mental health issues", or is *bajs* (faeces) an apt synonym for dirt as a way of referring to the interplay of the above factors? The *knarkare* is not just anyone who uses drugs: they are a dirty representative of the combination drug + human—and a slogan like "Drugs Are Faeces" brings to mind precisely this dirty character.

If the *knarkare*'s defining characteristic is their dirtiness, then people who use drugs can be expected to engage in negotiations about what is dirty and clean for them; that is, what is order and what is chaos? But how does symbolic dirt work? Can drugs dirt be scrubbed off?

4.3 Dirt and Freedom

When I ask Carolina what it was like to be a woman in the problem-use context she used to inhabit when she used amphetamines, she chooses the word "dirty" to describe the unpleasantness and panic she felt at the time:

> well obviously I *am* a woman, so I never got to experience it from any other perspective, but it's… this… intense shame, being incredibly dirty, sort of, and that I felt extremely… whorish.

Using drugs made Carolina feel as though she became a dirty person. But instead of a *knarkare*, she became a whore—yet another symbol of contagiousness. This is no coincidence; rather, it is in line with the commonly held assumption that women who use drugs also always sell sex (Du Rose 2015; Ettore 1992, p. 78). Carolina stresses that she never did sell sex in the sense of offering sexual services for a certain amount of money. On the contrary: the feeling that this was expected of her was frustrating, because she would rather have been a dealer:

> it was really hard for me to, you know, … to do business [deal drugs]; for example, I often wanted to sell things on and stuff, but people never trusted me with that. Because, because I was a girl. Even though I insisted on it. Instead, I was forced to earn my cash elsewhere.

This division of roles in drug-using contexts has been described in detail elsewhere, for example by Lisa Maher in *Sexed Work*, her 1997 study of drug-dealing on the streets of Brooklyn, NYC. Maher shows how race, class and gender all structure the market and how women, especially racialised women without a safety net, are either excluded from the market or given jobs that pay very little or put them in danger. A large proportion of women therefore sell sexual services to support themselves. Sociologist Torkel Richert (2009), however, who studied the Swedish women frequenting a needle-exchange centre, paints a somewhat different picture. His research shows that the largest proportion of these women's income derived from legal sources, such as welfare benefits, and that a lower number than predicted sold sex (2009, p. 374). Richert also found that it was more common for women to deal drugs than had previously been assumed, which he believes might mean that male dominance is being eroded in the drug market (ibid.; see also Rosengren 2003, p. 66; cf. Fleetwood et al. 2020).

Carolina describes her feeling of whorishness as stemming from a way of acting that could be described as a strategic performance of femininity (cf. Skeggs 2004, p. 16). Instead of being demanding when negotiating access to drugs, she took on the submissive role that she felt was expected of her as a woman, even though a variety of jobs already provided her with the money she needed. She describes feeling like "a bootlicker" around a dealer who had abused her friend, for example, and that she was often nice to people she despised. She wanted to be angry and hostile towards this abusive dealer, but acted in a friendly way instead because she "was afraid that […] the source [slang for dealer] would be turned off". It is with anger, sadness and lingering self-loathing that Carolina discusses the dirty feeling of what she calls whoring.

I felt like a terrible person, being like this, very nice [...] to sort of go
on anyway and socialise and be nice because you, because I wanted....
something.

Her story shows that the feeling of whorishness stuck with her as a
woman. This reflects both Björkman's criteria for what constitutes a
knarkare and the cultural assumption that women who use drugs are
automatically sexually available (Du Rose 2015). Derogatory Swedish
words like *knarkarhora* ("*knark* whore") and *sprutluder* ("needle hooker")
show that *knarkare* is not a gender-equal category, but divided into a
moral hierarchy, in which women who both use drugs and sell sex are
at the bottom. Regardless of whether Carolina had sold sex or not,
whoredom seems to have been impossible to escape, given that she
wanted to continue using drugs and therefore maintain good relations
with the dealers, who according to her interview responses were all men.
The sleazy feeling was a gendered consequence of drug use. The feeling of
whoredom in her case is related to her demonstrated niceness and stands
in direct opposition to Ahmed's concept of the killjoy (2010, pp. 50ff.).
Carolina did not kill joy, not other people's, and not her own drug-
related joy. But she wanted to do so and writhed under the feeling of
whoredom that was the alternative.

Ahmed writes that joy and not causing trouble can be ways of avoiding
that which we are unable to bear (ibid., p. 64). For years, Carolina felt
that being nice was just such an avoidance of something that she did not
think she could cope with, to fall out with the "source" and see it "turned
off". But she also felt that she could not cope with allowing the situation
to continue. In the interviews, she returns to saying that she wants to be
able to approve of what she does, which she is able to do now that she has
repositioned herself far away from the sources. But she cannot take back
the niceness that has already taken place, and it still feels like a dirtiness
she cannot wash away.

Carolina also talks about the hygienic connotations of feeling dirty.
During our first interview, she describes a situation a few months after
she had tried amphetamines for the first time:

> So it was like I suddenly woke up again, sort of, and found myself in this
> fucking disgusting flat, which I'd been using every day for several months
> then, and I was absolutely riddled with anxiety and worry and anxiety
> and heartburn and things, and the place smelt like piss and... well, you
> can imagine. And I just went, like, "urgh, how the hell did this happen?"

The overwhelming anxiety she describes feeling in that moment makes
me unsure whether the smell of urine was a one-off occurrence that she
happened to notice, or part of her everyday life at the time. If she was
living an everyday life that was dirty, in the sense of smelly, it made me
wonder how that worked with her jobs, in terms of employability. I asked
her about this during a go-along interview:

> She stops and says after a short pause that it was probably more of a
> feeling, when it came to herself. The smell of pee in a drug den, visits to
> places full of "food, piss, blood" happened more often at the beginning,
> she says.
>   "Filthy on the inside and on the outside, it just became too much. It
> was about the dirt on the inside. The drugs and the fact that I couldn't
> look at myself in the mirror. That I lied, was filled with lies."
>   She repeatedly says emphatically that she had so much she wanted
> to do and that she was always thinking about leaving the drug life. She
> "didn't want to do it" and panicked about realising year after year that
> she was still there. (Field Diary)

So there was a dirty aspect to the drug life that involved smells and
"food, piss [and] blood" in the wrong places. But, above all, Carolina
emphasises what she calls "the dirt on the inside", which consisted of
amphetamines and the fact that she did not want to do what she was
doing and lied about it. It is therefore partly about matter in the wrong
place: amphetamines in her body, where they were not supposed to be,
which led to (and continues to lead to) an unpleasant feeling of dirtiness.
When she talks about dirt during our interviews, it is a multifaceted dirt.
Her use of amphetamines, her bootlicking and her lies are all perceived
as having taken place in her body, as dirt.

I see what she describes as feelings of anxiety and panic about both
wearing the dirt and the time aspect, that she remained in the dirty

contexts for so long, as co-constructors of the dirt. Her whole body was matter in the wrong place, moving in the wrong directions. In a way that is well known and widely debated in addiction research, her intention was simultaneously to move away from the amphetamines and to get more (see, e.g., Heilig 2015, pp. 34ff.).

While Carolina was in her long period of daily use, she felt that she was dirty, i.e. labelled as condemned. Now, without illegal drugs in her body, she is clean, but still suffers from having been dirty for so long. She seems to carry her former dirt like a weight, a physical burden that continues to affect her. The cleanliness is upheld through the Twelve-Step Programme, one day at a time. In the present, she is "clean", but she describes her addiction as a chronic disease that must be constantly monitored and combated in order to be contained (cf. Keane 2002, p. 163). This means that she puts a lot of effort into staying clean, from both drugs and lies. She gives a detailed account of her past mistakes, does not drink alcohol and says that she does not want to use medication, even though an ADHD assessment she is undergoing may lead to controlled medication being suggested. Overall, she gives the impression of being guided by high-held purity ideals (cf. ibid., p. 163). Yet dirt threatens around every street corner. A beer would count as a relapse, into the dirt. Being identified as clean in Douglas' sense no longer seems to be an option; rather, Carolina views herself as chronically marked by dirt.

Her fragile cleanliness is linked to a specific kind of freedom: being "drug-free", a state of consciously staying away from drugs in a physical sense. Carolina often uses this term, talking about how she was drug-free before she started using amphetamines, about a former boyfriend who was a "drug-free abuser", how she later became drug-free, how she stayed (was) drug-free during the treatment period and how she is now still drug-free. The term denotes a strategic approach to drugs, rather than freedom from them.

My interpretation of this is that the "free" in drug-free (similar to the clean in "getting clean") implies other conditions than those Carolina has to deal with. For her, using drugs is not just about using substances that are nearby, but has taken the form of embodied shame (Campbell and Ettorre 2011, pp. 182, 200). Dirt manifests, not by orienting herself towards drugs—drugs are the starting point to which she actively and continuously needs to relate, while performing cleanliness. If the lines of addiction form circles or loops that keep bringing one back to drugs (see the chapter **Negotiating Addiction**), then a "clean" line is about continually leaving drugs behind, without losing contact with the starting point. Freedom and cleanliness become conditional ideals, situated beyond the line that is anchored in the *knarkare*. Carolina's situation can be compared to having a chronic disease, such as diabetes. As with the diabetes patients in a study by Gabriella Nilsson and Kristofer Hansson (2016, p. 264), who are offered freedom *with*, but not from, the disease, conditional upon good behaviour and careful medication, freedom from the dirt/*knarkare* is not an option. The *knarkare* is the starting point, and a former *knarkare* can free themselves from drugs but not from dirt.

Madelene describes how her rejection of alcohol is interpreted as such "freedom", which is based on addiction:

> People have a hard time accepting that some people don't drink, [...] they always automatically assume you have an alcohol problem. But... that bothers me. Because I really don't. [pauses] I've never had any problems with alcohol. I just choose not to drink because it's, it doesn't taste that great, and it doesn't make me feel good.

In Madelene's situation—as a person who uses a large number of anti-anxiety drugs and heroin—the surrounding world's interpretation, as she perceives it, of her dislike of alcohol leads to frustration. She describes her use of medication and drugs as self-imposed directions, which she occasionally refrains from taking. She therefore feels in control, but repeatedly mentions occasions when such control has been difficult to maintain and is sometimes lost. In other words, she is fighting against the experience of addiction, but she proudly emphasises that she has won the battle and decides for herself about her intake of drugs and medicines.

However, these struggles are hidden from the environment, and instead, her rejection of alcohol in social situations is interpreted as though it was a compulsory direction. She feels misunderstood as unfree.

4.4   Disgusting Syringes

If particular ways of talking about drugs in certain circles immediately conjure up the spectre of dirty drug use, then syringes are the ultimate material symbol of the *knarkare* (Lalander 2016, p. 92). Needles in a children's sandbox connote a violent clash between innocence and danger. The women I interviewed had clear opinions on syringes: those who did not inject drugs immediately shook their heads when I asked whether they ever had. Using syringes was a line they would not cross. The two interviewees who did inject, on the other hand, Hanna and Madelene, painted a complex picture of syringes' connotations of dirt and purity.

Madelene, who injects heroin from time to time and sometimes dissolved tranquillisers, describes her attitude as a negotiation around methods of introduction, with each alternative having different advantages and disadvantages:

Emma: What are the negative aspects of heroin?
Madelene: [considers] Mm, well, it's the needles, isn't it? They're just so disgusting.
Emma: I see... But you wouldn't consider administering it in any other way?
Madelene: Well, I've tried [sounds dismissive] smoking it, but that doesn't do anything for me... I guess that's the problem. [...] I think you fall in love with the feeling that comes after [injecting]. Like, you know it's coming then. When you smoke, it's different. It's like, instead of this [demonstrates how the high hits her], you've got to deal with foil and get all dirty and... it feels less discreet as well, in a way.

For Madelene, the different methods are evaluated from the perspectives of discretion and effect. Although she finds the injections disgusting, the rapid and strong effect means that she prefers injections to smoking from sooty aluminium foil sheets, a practice that she describes as less discreet. In the quote, it is smoking that Madelene refers to as dirty. At the same time, the syringes are repulsive to her and she only uses them reluctantly.

The disgust that she describes may seem obvious in relation to the syringe as a symbol of the dirty *knarkare*, but the meaning of the syringe has changed, in terms of clean and dirty, in relation to time and place. When the hypodermic needle was invented in the 1850s, it was marketed as a sophisticated, clean and safe way to inject medicines (Plant 1999, p. 6; Berg 2016, p. 66). It became popular to inject morphine, which had been extracted from opium in 1804 but had previously been taken orally. In New York, according to a 1908 magazine article, ornate gold syringes presented in cases were available as morphine kits from the best jewellers (Palmer and Horowitz 2000, p. 72). The swift highs that these new hypodermic needles could bring, coupled with chemical break-throughs at the time, led to enthusiasm about the potential of injection. Syringes became a symbol of a medical expertise that replaced more non-specific medicines, like opium (Berridge 2013, p. 113). Drug addiction was one of the problems that the injection of other drugs seemed to cure. In turn, doctors tried to cure opium addiction with morphine injections and then tried to cure morphine addiction with cocaine and heroin. It turned out not to work. One example of optimistic belief in drug injections as a cure for addiction was Sigmund Freud's morphine-addicted friend Ernst von Fleischl-Marxow, who began to inject cocaine, upon the former's advice, only to become more ill and ultimately die (Freud and Byck 1974, pp. xvii, 117, 155–158; Plant 1999, p. 72). When syringes eventually came to be associated with addiction and degeneracy, they fell off their pedestal. Sven-Åke Lindgren describes syringes' status in the 1950s:

> In terms of iconography, it is the syringe that comes to symbolise drug abuse. Syringes jabbed into tied-off arms, women giving themselves injections into their thighs, loaded syringes, syringes and needles and substances in glass ampoules, jars and pipes… These kinds of illustrations and hand-drawn vignettes are by far the most prevalent. What we have here is a tool that has fallen into the wrong hands: an initially benevolent invention that went astray and became an instrument in the service of the forces of evil. (1993, p. 166)

Lindgren's analysis focuses on the way in which syringes veered "off line" (cf. Ahmed 2006, pp. 65ff.). The syringe was meant to serve society, but in the wrong hands it was led astray. Lindgren calls the directions that the syringe was meant to take "benevolent", but the images he studied depict it as being in "the service of the forces of evil". Between the lines of the above paragraph, there is a sense of regret over the syringe's unworthy fate. This change must be analysed from a class perspective. It was when the working class started using injectable drugs, in the 1960s, that syringes fell from grace. This led to symbolic, downwards class journeys for syringes as well as for drugs and people who use them (Lindgren 1993, pp. 165ff.).

The experience of manifesting a socially vulnerable injecting drug user in the present day is illustrated by Hanna, when asked about where she uses drugs:

Emma: Where do you prefer to take heroin?
Hanna: Well, as far away from people as possible.
Emma: Alone?
Hanna: Oh yes. [pauses]
Emma: Why?
Hanna: Because, because… you can't use a syringe among people, every-
one… everyone knows that. [Inaudible]

You cannot be seen holding a syringe, Hanna says, because "everyone knows" it is not possible. The knowledge that the syringe is a dirty, stray object—something that a person is not to be seen with—makes heroin injections a solitary practice. They have to be performed in private, as far away from other people as possible. At the same time, they give off no odours and can be more discreet—less dirty—than smoking, for those who have a door to close. Madelene can close her apartment door, but for someone in Hanna's situation, having a home is less of a given. The only closable doors in the public domain are toilets, which have everything you need: the ability to close the door and be alone, unseen, but also without the possibility of getting help if something goes wrong.

4.5   Conclusion

As I have shown, Mary Douglas' theory of how cultural notions of dirty and clean create order can make visible how *knarkare* and the *knark*-whore are created and kept at a distance from the rest of society. Class-related conditions and power structures interact intersectionally and create degrees of dirtiness. Various kinds of symbolic, drug-related dirt structure people who use drugs hierarchically. Through utterances, acts and objects, someone who uses drugs can fall, or avoid falling, into the category of the abuser, the *knarkare* and/or the whore. But dirt is simply matter out of place, and in the right place, something that would be dirty elsewhere can become uncharged, like Pernilla's cannabis-related sickness or a syringe in a hospital.

On the whole, women who use drugs, and the emotions they express, are on the margins of several of the hierarchical systems that define dirt (Campbell and Ettorre 2011). Without taking class into account, however, these systems make no sense. *Knarkaren* and the whore can come to define a person, as it did for Carolina, but with the right resources this can be avoided through discretion. Even though the terms "abuser", *knarkare* and *knarkarhora* ("*knark* whore") can serve as slurs, they do not refer to just any deviant, drug-using woman, but specifically to people who embody social exclusion, as Björkman (2002) and *Hem och Hyra's* articles illustrate (Lundmark 2008; Ljungqvist 2017). Dirt and cleanliness can be located in different places and manifested in different situations, but they take on a spatial character when they become linked to a classed context, what I called the drug swamp in the previous chapter, a place that most of the interviewees sought to avoid.

References

Adolfsson, Josefine. 2004. *Kårnulf Was Here: En hembygdsskildring i fyra delar och tva° samtal* [Kårnulf Was Here: A Homeland Portrayal in Four Parts and Two Conversations]. Stockholm: Bokförlaget Atlas.

Ahmed, Sara. 2006. *Queer Phenomenology: Orientations, Objects, Others.* Durham, NC: Duke University Press.

Ahmed, Sara. 2010. *The Promise of Happiness.* Durham, NC: Duke University Press.

Ahmed, Sara. 2014. *The Cultural Politics of Emotion*, 2nd ed. Edinburgh: Edinburgh University Press.

Ahmed, Sara. 2019. *What's the Use? On the Uses of Use.* Durham, NC: Duke University Press.

Berg, Daniel. 2016. *Giftets värde: Apotekarnas förståelse av opium i Sverige 1870–1925* [The Value of Poison: Pharmacists' Understanding of Opium in Sweden 1870–1925]. Göteborg and Stockholm: Makadam.

Berridge, Virginia. 2013. *Demons: Our Changing Attitudes to Alcohol, Tobacco & Drugs.* Oxford: Oxford University Press.

Björkman, Jenny. 2002. Knarkarens förvandlingar [Transformations of the *knarkare*]. *Tvärsnitt* 3: 42–51.

Campbell, Nancy D., and Elizabeth Ettorre. 2011. *Gendering Addiction: The Politics of Drug Treatment in a Neurochemical World.* New York, NY: Palgrave Macmillan.

Douglas, Mary. 2002/1966. *Purity and Danger: An Analysis of Concepts of Pollution and Taboo.* London and New York: Routledge.

Du Rose, Natacha. 2015. *The Governance of Female Drug Users: Women's Experiences of Drug Policy.* Bristol: Policy Press.

Edman, Johan, and Börje Olsson. 2014. The Swedish Drug Problem: Conceptual Understanding and Problem Handling, 1839–2011. *Nordic Studies on Alcohol & Drugs/Nordisk Alkohol- & Narkotikatidskrift* 31 (5/6): 503–526.

Ettorre, Elizabeth. 1992. *Women and Substance Use.* Basingstoke: Macmillan.

Ettorre, Elizabeth. 2015. Embodied Deviance, Gender, and Epistemologies of Ignorance: Re-visioning Drugs Use in a Neurochemical, Unjust World. *Substance Use & Misuse* 50: 794–805.

Fleetwood, Jennifer, Judith Aldridge, and Caroline Chatwin. 2020. Gendering Research on Online Illegal Drug Markets. *Addiction Research & Theory* 28 (6): 457–466.

Freud, Sigmund, and Robert Byck, eds. 1974. *Cocaine Papers by Sigmund Freud.* New York, NY: Stonehill.

Frykman, Jonas, and Orvar Löfgren. 2019. *Den kultiverade människan* [The Cultivated Human Being]. Malmö: Gleerups.

Hagman Rogowski, Theo. 2017. Berättelsen om "Knark är bajs" [The Story About "Drugs ar faeces"]. *Vice*, 27 December.

Heilig, Markus. 2015. *Alkohol, droger och hjärnan: tro och vetande utifrån modern neurovetenskap* [Alcohol, Drugs and the Brain: Beliefs and Knowledge Based on Modern Neuroscience]. Stockholm: Natur & Kultur.

Iversen, Leslie. 2012. *Speed, Ecstasy, Ritalin: The Science of Amphetamines.* Oxford: Oxford University Press. Oxford Scholarship Online [ebook].

Keane, Helen. 2002. *What's Wrong with Addiction?* Melbourne: Melbourne University Press.

Lalander, Philip. 2016. *Människor behöver människor: Att lyssna till de misstänkliggjorda* [People Need People: Listening to the One's Made Suspicious]. Stockholm: Liber.

Lindgren, Sven-Åke. 1993. *Den hotfulla njutningen: att etablera drogbruk som samhällsproblem 1890–1970* [The Threat of Pleasure: Establishing Drug Use as a Social Problem 1890–1970]. Stockholm: Brutus Östlings Bokförlag Symposion.

Lindstrand, Örn. 2001. Birgitta Stenberg: "Knark fick jag gratis" [Birgitta Stenberg: "I Got *knark* for Free"]. *Socialpolitik* (2): 48–50.

Ljungqvist, Rikard. 2017. Grannarnas skräck: En narkoman [The Neighbours' Fear: A Drug User]. *Hem och Hyra,* 5 December.

Lundmark, Anneli. 2008. Knarkare värsta grannen [*Knarkare* the Worst Neighbours]. *Hem och Hyra,* 27 August.

Lupton, Deborah. 1999. *Risk.* London: Routledge [ebook].

Maher, Lisa. 1997. *Sexed Work: Gender, Race and Resistance in a Brooklyn Drug Market.* Oxford: Oxford University Press.

Moore, Karenza, and Fiona Measham. 2013. Exploring Emerging Perspectives on Gender and Drug Use. In *Emerging Perspectives on Substance Misuse,* ed. Willm Mistral. Hoboken NJ: Wiley-Blackwell.

Nilsson, Gabriella, and Kristofer Hansson. 2016. Berättade fantasier om förr, nu och framtiden i vården av barn med diabetes [Told Fantasies About the Past, Present and Future of Caring for Children with Diabetes]. *Socialmedicinsk tidskrift* 99 (3): 261–270.

Palmer, Cynthia, and Michael Horowitz. 2000. *Sisters of the Extreme: Women Writing on the Drug Experience.* Rochester: Park Street Press.

Plant, Sadie. 1999. *Writing on Drugs.* London: Faber and Faber.

Richert, Torkel. 2009. Injektionsmissbrukande kvinnors inkomstkällor och anskaffning av droger [Injecting, Drug-Abusing Women's Sources of Income and Acquisition of Drugs]. *Nordisk Alkohol- & Narkotikatidskrift* 26 (5): 365–394.

Rosengren, Annette. 2003. *Mellan ilska och hopp: Om hemlöshet, droger och kvinnor* [Between Anger and Hope: On Homelessness, Drugs and Women]. Stockholm: Carlsson bokförlag.

Rylander, Gösta. 1969. Centralstimulerande medel ur historisk, klinisk och medicinsk-kriminologisk synpunkt [Central Stimulants from a Historical, Clinical and Medical-Criminological Point of View]. *Svensk Juristtidning*: 302–315.

Skeggs, Beverley. 2004. *Class, Self, Culture*. London: Routledge.

von Wright, Julius. 2017. Svårt bli av med (begreppet) "knarkare" [Hard to Get Rid of the (Concept of) "*knarkare*"]. *Alkohol & Narkotika*, 7 December.

5

Obtaining Drugs

Proximity to drugs is necessary if they are to be used, but illegal drugs are not necessarily available in the contexts where interviewees want to be. Proximity to drugs can also be a sensitive issue, as the previous chapter showed. So how do women acquire drugs? In this chapter, I take a closer look at the different ways in which the women orientate themselves so that the drugs are close enough to be introduced into their bodies.

5.1 Out on the Town

When Nanne recalls smoking marijuana as a hippie in the city of Malmö during the 1970s, she gives a picture of how the street drug market has changed.

> *Nanne*: There used to be dealers on Gustav Adolf Square, right in the middle of Gustav Adolf Square. That was before they moved to the car park next to the police station. [laughs]
> *Emma*: What did the police do then?
> *Nanne*: Nothing. [pauses]
> *Emma*: When was this?

Nanne: The seventies. Then they decamped to Kungsparken. Swedes hardly knew what cannabis *was* in the sixties. It was legal.[1] And the sheer number of 'em on Gustav Adolf Square!
Emma: Yeah?
Nanne: Ooh yes! Chock-a-block. And then the police station's car park.[2]

Nanne chuckles when she recalls how dealers used to shift their wares in the car park next to the police station on Davidshall Square, in the centre of Malmö, during the seventies. She finds it remarkable that they used to do business in places that today constitute the teeming heart of Malmö's shopping district. We are curled up on the sofa in Nanne's terraced house in the sleepy, seaside district of Limhamn in Malmö, sipping coffee and nibbling on biscuits. Remembering back, she startles from time to time, laughing in wonder as she searches her memory and recalls the past. Gustav Adolf Square, Nanne says, and later the police car park were places where people used to hang out and she enthusiastically describes the various qualities of hash on offer:

you'd buy these small slabs. There'd be Moroccan [hash] and Afghan, and there'd be… all these different kinds. You knew what country it was from. […] Lebanese, that was… top-class stuff. [laughs] That one was black.

While her tone is casual, there is an undercurrent of pensiveness and defiance in her voice. Nanne, a 65-year-old white woman, views her memories of the seventies through the lens of how it is now, imagining what it would be like if drugs were still being dealt in those squares in a similarly bohemian way today, and concluding that it would be absurd. When the media reported on the cannabis trade in Malmö during the time when I was conducting the interviews, the focus was usually on the trade's link to gangs, crime and bloody acts of violence.[3] International studies of street trade in the 2000s paint a

---

[1] Nanne's claim that cannabis used to be legal in the 1960s is incorrect; Sweden's Penal Law on Narcotics was adopted in 1968 (SFS Swedish Code of Statutes 1968:64).

[2] All quotes in Swedish have been translated by me.

[3] See, e.g., Erberth, Moreno and Rasmusen. 2018. Knarkande överklassen som betalar Malmös gängkrig ["Drug-Using Upper-Class Financing Malmö's Gang War]. *Expressen*, 7 August; Gustaf

picture of drug markets that bear little resemblance to Nanne's laid-back hippie experiences. Campbell and Ettorre write that "what was once a largely innocuous, consensual, consumer market has been transformed into what is routinely described in policy terms as a war zone" (2011, p. 22). Criminologist Letizia Paoli (2002) and sociologist Sandra Bucerius (2007) report that the illegal drug market in modern-day Europe is highly racialised, gendered and riddled with violence (see also Nafstad 2011). Norwegian sociologist Sveinung Sandberg also stresses the racialised structure of the drug market:

> The lowest and most dangerous positions are increasingly taken over by foreigners, both those who immigrated recently and second and third generation migrants. (2008, p. 609)

Nanne posits that "cannabis isn't a drug", which is her way of saying that she is not of the opinion that using cannabis should be illegal. But her quote at the start of this chapter shows that the drug trade has changed—and with it the cultural meaning of being in the vicinity of the cannabis market. Or, as Ahmed writes:

> What is at stake [...] is not only the relation between the body and "what" is near, but also the relation between the things that are near. [...] Orientations are binding as they bind things together. What puts objects near depends on histories, on how things arrive, and on how they gather in their very availability as things to do things with. (2006a, p. 558)

Orienting oneself towards a drug means orienting towards a cluster of objects: the drugs themselves and the objects, including people, that surround them, which have all, in different ways, arrived at the same place. What was within Nanne's reach when she was a hippie is now foreign and distant, because the objects that surround the drugs sold on the streets these days are no longer the same.

These days, cannabis that is meant to be smoked does not cross Nanne's path, despite her liberal attitude to the drug. Instead, she buys

---

Tronarp. 2019. Teorin: Tonåringar skjuts – i kampen om knarkhandeln [Teenagers Being Shot—In Battle Over Drug Trade]. *Aftonbladet*, 17 November.

CBD oil online and has a prescription for opiate painkillers to relieve the ache in her hips. The post office and the pharmacy thus constitute the meeting points towards which Nanne orients herself.

In parallel to the pharmacy trade, the illegal street market for drugs has prospered and becomes more ruthless with each subsequent attempt to shut it down (Tham 2003; Farber 2021). It is a particular scene in which one can expect a certain set of objects, all aligned with each other, and approaching these objects is risky. Pharmacies' commercialised retail environment, with its colourful packaging and smiling personnel in white coats, means that Sweden's two main drug markets are worlds apart. Comparing them, it is easy to lose sight of the actual substances' effects and chemical make-up.

A Gendered, Classed and Racialised Street Market

The drug market does not only have a racialised structure but also a classed and gendered one (Buxton et al. 2020; Maher 1997; Grundetjern and Sandberg 2012). In his analysis of 20 men who sold drugs on the streets of Oslo, Sveinung Sandberg (2008) uses Bourdieu's concept of habitus to explain how the social space of the drug market is created by men who, through early bodily experiences of violence and exclusion—such as war, being refugees, being subjected to racism and/or experiences of living on the streets—have gained a symbolic capital that can be transformed into money and status in the context of Norwegian drug sales. Sandberg argues that the young men who sought out the open drug trade scene found both commercial and socially viable ways to manage their "street capital", in contrast to the marginalised position of being racialised, poor and lacking viable cultural capital in white societies (Sandberg 2008; Sandberg and Pedersen 2011). Sandberg cites their readiness to use violence and their American hip-hop artist-inspired performative masculinity (2008, p. 612) as examples of their gendered capital, which they acquired by living through violence and marginalisation. When these men draw on this habitus to increase their capital, however, it simultaneously entrenches their position at the bottom of both the drug-trade hierarchy and a racialised society.

While (impoverished, racialised) men have become the face of the drug trade in the West, however, the cultural perception of women in the Scandinavian drug market centres around a completely different activity: obtaining drugs. Feminised terms for a person who uses drugs—such as *tjackhora* ("speed whore"), *knarkarluder* ("junkie hooker") or *sprutluder* ("needle hooker")—link drug use to another activity, selling sex and the stigmatised identity of a whore. Certain drugs in particular, such as heroin, are widely associated with the sex trade, as Elizabeth Ettorre writes:

> Whether or not a woman heroin addict has ever exchanged her body for drugs or money for her habit, she is characterized as an impure woman, an evil slut or a loose female. (1992, p. 78)

Ettorre suggests that, since women's bodies have always been judged on the basis of ideals shaped by historical, scientific, medical and capitalist ideas, women who use drugs are not only forced to try and live up to these ideals, but also to do so from a marked position (or a position in which they risk becoming marked). She emphasises that a marked body that deviates from the norm is regarded as socially and morally inferior, and concludes that any feminist analysis of women's drug use must pay attention to embodiment (2015, p. 795).

Ettorre's focus on embodiment aligns with the phenomenological perspective, which begins with the body moving through a certain space—a place with a past and a present, which affect how the body is interpreted. Ahmed describes how spaces that have historically been spaces of whiteness—such as the academic world—have been shaped into whiteness. When such spaces are visited by a racialised body, others already in the space take note, which can make the non-white visitor feel uncomfortable or conspicuous (2007, p. 157). In a male-dominated drugs world, women stand out, and their feelings of discomfort help to preserve the shape of these spaces. Writing about women's dual deviance, Ettorre concludes that "'normal' embodiment is foreclosed to women drug users" (2015, p. 794). I interpret Ettorre's term "women drug users" as referring to the class-related position of the abuser and the *knarkare*, someone who cannot be discreet.

Obtaining drugs, in other words, is a challenging act, not least for women. So how do women navigate between the different worlds they encounter when obtaining drugs, such as the drug market and the contexts where they use drugs?

5.2   In One's Own Social Circle

Most of the women I talked to said that they avoided the open drug market, but neither did anyone say they engaged in online purchasing, which has been described as a potentially attractive market for women buyers, due to the relative anonymity and possible avoidance of face-to-face meetings (Fleetwood et al. 2020). Instead, the women referred to the street market when they discussed the option of obtaining drugs from strangers. Madelene, for example, reluctantly imagines what it would be like to foray into the open, illegal drug market to purchase heroin:

> I think I'd be pretty terrified if I were forced to head to Brunnsparken – something I would never do. But I'd be just as afraid of the police as I would be of the dealers.

Purchasing drugs in public would remind her that her actions are illegal and a punishable offence. She has no desire to put herself in such a situation. Instead, she gets her drugs from a man she knows and who therefore is not perceived as a threat. Without that familiarity, she says, she would never buy illegal drugs. When I ask her whether she thinks she will ever stop using heroin, she responds:

> if I reached a point in life where I wouldn't be able to. Like when I worked abroad for extended periods of time. It's not like I went looking for a new dealer in Milan just because I happened to be there for a year. Then I just don't bother. Or when I'm working in the US, it's not like [laughs at the mere thought] I'd ever dare do anything like that.

So Madelene orients herself away from the open drug market. For an encounter to take place, drugs have to be available via something or someone with whom she is familiar.

Thea describes her drug purchases in a similar way, without specifying which drugs she is talking about (not heroin, however, since she does not use heroin):

> *Thea*: I'm not that fond of the whole drugs-buying thing, really, I actually find it quite stressful… Doing deals is awful, really. [laughs]
> *Emma*: How do you buy drugs then?
> *Thea*: No, I get them through… people I know. Because I've been around for a while, I've got […] I have friends who… I know who's got stuff.

Thea describes "doing deals"—negotiating and conducting illegal transactions with strangers—as "awful". During another interview, she tells me that she is uncomfortable in heteronormative settings in general, being a queer woman and a political and progressive artist (cf. Brennan 2020). She insists on spending her time exclusively in environments in which she feels safe.

> I already only engage with a… limited circle of people. [tentative laugh] A circle that I've cultivated myself [takes a breath], both on purpose and… not on purpose. So life will be tolerable. I avoid heterosexual settings. I do everything I can to avoid them. Have done so for many years, really. Or, a long time. A very, very long time. Because I need to.

Perhaps part of the reason why she finds "doing deals" so awful is because it requires her to step outside of the familiar, queer settings where she tells me she needs to be for life to be tolerable. The queer interviewees in criminologist Fiona Hutton's (2006) study also describe uneasiness in nightlife settings that strongly emphasise heterosexuality as the norm. Hutton quotes the women she talked to as saying they prefer not to buy drugs from male dealers:

> Investigation around the source of the drugs taken by female clubbers showed that it was mainly from friends or "friends of friends" that ecstasy

was obtained, not from the stereotypical, dangerous, unscrupulous male dealer. (Hutton 2006, p. 79)

Despite the different ways in which they use drugs, both Madelene and Thea mainly purchase them from acquaintances—a pattern that reflects Hutton's study. By doing so, my interviewees ensure that the objects around drugs constitute a familiar collection towards which they orient themselves.

But how did the drugs arrive there (Ahmed 2006b, p. 37)? When cocaine comes up in our conversation, Thea reflects upon that very issue:

It's all unethical, of course, but cocaine is incredibly unethical. Chemicals can be created in a lab. Best-case scenario, MDMA even comes from a legal lab. But most of it comes from… Cocaine is transported in people's, you know, rectums.

Between the lines, Thea is saying she *hopes* the MDMA (and other chemically produced drugs) that she uses will have been produced and transported in ethically justifiable ways, but that she does not believe this is often the case. The issues for which cocaine is notorious—drug cartels resorting to violence, trafficking the drug via impoverished bodies—pose an ethical dilemma for her. Ahmed writes that queer phenomenology not only needs to take into account a body's orientation towards certain objects, but also these objects' backgrounds: how they arrived where they are, encountering that body. From the perspective of the body, a person's orientation towards a certain kind of drug encounter will determine what that person's drug use will look like. For Thea, the drugs path to the places where she encounters them is in the background. She can only picture fragments of their journey, like legal laboratories or drug mules smuggling cocaine in their rectums. But even if she had wanted to, it would have been difficult, perhaps impossible, for her to discover how a drug had actually made its way into her hands. When she orients herself towards drugs by turning to acquaintances in her social circle, however, she can avoid both the discomfort of "doing deals" and being reminded of drugs' potentially unethical journeys. Thus, both Thea and Madelene consciously turn their backs on the drug market that Campbell and

Ettorre (2011) describe as "a war zone", and the kinds of places where Sandberg's racialised interviewees face violence and exclusion. They travel familiar paths. Instead of meeting different worlds, they meet familiar faces along the way: people who serve as a link between the drug market and buyers who prefer to remain in their own social circle. It is a drug world embedded within the world they themselves inhabit.

The end buyer and end consumer can be one and the same person, but this does not necessarily need to be the case. Drugs can also transition from being a commodity in a market to being part of a gift economy.

5.3   Drugs as Gifts

For a person to be able to use something, that thing needs to be within their reach: the body needs to be in the vicinity of the thing it wants to use. But for a person to be able to use a drug in their vicinity, additional proximity is required: the drug needs to be actively inserted into the body. Ettorre criticises drug researchers for parroting the idea that "true substance abusers" are men who decisively take action, while women merely play passive supporting roles (1992, p. 17). This creates a simplified picture of women as passive and motionless. Yet the interviewees talk about intentions and how those intentions incited movement: burning desire, strategies to get their hands on drugs, travel, nightlife and parties. The women I talked to turn towards certain drugs and away from others, avoiding them or consuming them and allowing themselves to be influenced. These encounters occur because drugs move towards them, but also because they themselves simultaneously move towards drugs. Several of the women reported that the majority of the drugs they use are given to them, which adds an additional layer of complexity to these encounters. How can we interpret this receiving of drugs in the context of gender? How do drug gift economies work?

Agnes does not seem concerned when she tells me how she obtains the drugs she uses:

Agnes: I've got almost everything for free… all the time.
Emma: Who gives you drugs then?

> *Agnes*: [reflects] I can barely remember how I… whether they were bought, to be honest. Most of the time it was with friends, through friends… but if we bought anything… I never did. I'd give my friend money, and then she would just go off, like. I never bought any myself or had any at home or anything.

Based on this quote, it may seem that Agnes is relatively inexperienced with drugs. She says that she does not really know how the drugs get to her and, on the occasions when she has paid for them, the transactions have been through intermediaries. But Agnes has been using drugs for ten years, to such an extent that she herself, her family and her friends have all been concerned about her health. How does this add up? Agnes says the acquisition happens in the background, and it is so non-central that she does not even remember how it happens. Even when friends buy drugs on her behalf, they take the money and walk away. To her mind, the drugs seem to present themselves as expected objects within a narrow field of vision, and she has not noticed how they got there. In this way, Agnes' drug use resembles the philosopher Edmund Husserl's phenomenological practice at his desk, as theorised by Sara Ahmed. Ahmed describes how, when Husserl discusses objects, he exemplifies with writing paper and other writing equipment. The examples are no coincidence, according to Ahmed, because Husserl is a philosopher who writes on paper.

> what we can see in the first place depends on which way we are facing. What gets our attention depends too on which direction we are facing. (2006b, p. 29)

Husserl thus focuses on his own work when he keeps his face turned towards the writing paper. Without looking, he also describes himself as knowing what is in the parts of the room he cannot see, behind him and outside the room. In contrast, Ahmed writes, Husserl does not pay attention to the labour behind his ability to write—the labour of making the table, cleaning it and taking care of his children, whom he can hear through the wall, for example (ibid., pp. 30–31). Writing is the focus and the desk is obviously in front of him, as he is a philosopher. I will return to the way in which Agnes simply assumes that people will give her drugs and to her comment about never having had any drugs in her own home, but first I would like to explore the relationship between gift economies, gender and class in greater depth.

When it comes to gifts, there is extensive ethnological and anthropological research theorising the social and cultural systems of which giving and receiving are part. Perhaps the most influential gift theorist, anthropologist Marcel Mauss, examines different gift systems in his book *The Gift*, first published in 1925 (2002[4]). Understanding these as relationships of which the objects commonly perceived as "gifts" are only part, he concludes that, unlike goods in a market, gifts are never free. They come with obligatory demands for reciprocation, which he interprets as related to their spirituality in a so-called total system. By this, he means that the gift relationship is part of a system that includes everything from religion and myth to legal, economic and social structures. The gift reflects something of the donor who, in a spiritual sense, becomes part of what is given, and this spiritual part wants to return to its origin, that is, the original donor (ibid. 2002, pp. 13–16). The relationship involves three basic requirements: to give, to receive and to reciprocate. The latter obligation ties individuals, families and groups together, forging relationships and solidarity.

When it comes to women in drug-related contexts, there are strong beliefs about the sexual availability of drug-using women (e.g. Du Rose 2015, pp. 26ff.). It is therefore easy to imagine that gift economies in drug contexts are gendered and sexualised in such a way that men provide drugs and women reciprocate with sex. This is in line with Mauss' view of heterosexual relationships—namely, as a relationship which has always meant that men continuously reciprocate women's provision of sex through gifts (2002, p. 93). In the drug context, such an exchange would take on a morally charged character through the ways in which drug-using women are conceptualised. In Swedish, these are manifested, for example, in concepts that denote drug-using women, such as *knarkarhora* ("*knark* whore") and *sprutluder* ("needle hooker"). The term "whore" is traditionally used, as shown by Frykman (1977)

---

[4] First published in 1925 as *Essai sur le don*.

and Lennartsson (2019), to denote an unclean and therefore threatening female position, rather than to describe a woman's exchange of sex for money. And the terms that denote drug-using women appear to do just that, giving them far-reaching meanings of dirt, menace and sex trafficking. Conceptions of drug-using women as sexually available also exist within some drug-using contexts, as Carolina points out. She says that the men who provided amphetamines expected her to be "nice", and also describes how this type of socialising could turn into both unwelcome sexual advances and reluctant sexual acts.

> just obvious things that I experienced, like… sexual situations that didn't feel quite right and… and stuff and it just seemed almost like a given in that… world, sort of. Like, maybe, you know, being with someone who… gave you drugs…

Sociologist Torkel Richert (2009) writes about women who inject regularly, and that women more often than men state that part of their drug consumption consists of gifts. More than half of the 188 women Richert interviewed had been offered drugs in the past two weeks, and of these, 95% had received drugs from at least one man, while 40% had received drugs from at least one woman (ibid., p. 377). He suggests that these gifts may relate to some extent to the expectation of receiving sexual favours, but also points out that more men than women use drugs and that there seems to be a more general "culture of treating one another" (ibid., p. 376) in the drug contexts he has studied.

Unlike Agnes, Madelene and Thea, but much like the women in Richert's study, Carolina was part of a socially marginalised context, where drugs are sought in the vicinity of violence and crime. The "world" that Carolina mentions in the above quotation is a world with a class-determined relationship structure that includes both orienting intoxication experiences and disorientation in relation to the rest of society, and a criminal, violent market trade. Agnes, Madelene and Thea, on the other hand, describe their drug use as places defined by highs that are removed from that world, albeit still with a charged connection to it. Both Agnes and Carolina mainly use amphetamines. But the ways in which they obtain them—the points where they meet drugs—are strikingly different. Carolina had arranged her life in a manner that ensured she would always be able to pay for the drugs she took. She tells me that she made sure to make ends meet, despite her drugs habit negatively affecting her ability to work, by switching jobs before her drug use could be revealed:

> I [worked] in restaurants. In the kitchen mostly, as a cook and pantry cook. Kitchen assistant… You just go from job to job and keep going that way. That's what allows you to keep finding work, switching all the time.

The aim behind Carolina's strategy of always having a steady job as a source of income was to make herself as immune as possible to sexual pressure and expectations. She recounts, for example, how some men who sold drugs tried to convince her to give heroin a try, thinking it would make her give up her restaurant jobs and instead "take a job" with them as someone who, as she describes it, would act as a kind of sexually available maid in exchange for drugs.

> there were people who tried to persuade me to do it [use heroin] because it's good to have a girl who hangs around the flat and gets hooked [addicted to the drug], and then they can be there and do the dishes and clean and all that sort of thing… and then it's not … like, prostitution, selling sex or something like that. But it's still a borderland, you know. [A man] wanted to convince me to … [use heroin] "come on, that's what you need. I can see it in you. Just a little bit. Come on", and so on.

In other words, Carolina was forced to pay attention to her surroundings and could not focus on drugs and drug experiences undisturbed. She also had to turn to a string of jobs and purchases and had to take a stand on various offers in order to obtain drugs.

Agnes' situation is completely different. She does not seem to worry at all, either about finances or acquisition. She describes how she orientates herself towards contexts where the drugs come to her under pleasant circumstances—parties, festivals and clubs—while Carolina reluctantly puts on a smile for "the source", spending time in "disgusting flats". It is easy to analyse the entire difference as related to the concept of addiction: a person who is dependent on another's help may be willing to associate with the person who can help (Lebra 1975, p. 557). Carolina also uses the word addiction to define her use. In the chapter **Negotiating Addiction**, I discuss this concept in more detail, as a definition of a compulsive approach which means that drugs continue to be used "despite negative consequences" (Heilig 2015, p. 35). But Carolina does not mention any radical changes in her social circle once she started using amphetamines. And Agnes' concern about her use is precisely about negative consequences linked to overdoses, health and relationships, etc. The concept of addiction thus has some connection to their use in both cases. However, the encounters they describe between drugs and bodies seem to take place in two different worlds. These worlds are built on relationship structures within classed contexts, which results in different perspectives on what is valuable and how exchanges can take place (Skeggs 2004, pp. 10ff.), where drugs are in the vicinity of different collections of objects. Skeggs writes that:

> valuing always works in the interests of those who can name it as such. Their perspective on what counts as legitimate puts valuation into effect. In this evaluation process a distinction can be drawn between use-value and exchange value. Making legitimate (making things valid) places the thing (be it person or object) that is being valued in the realm of dominant categorizations. As it is inscribed with value it becomes part of the symbolic economy. The moral evaluation of cultural characteristics is central to the workings and transmission of power. (Skeggs 2004, p. 14)

In line with Skeggs' argument, the availability of amphetamines to the interviewees is related to Agnes and Carolina being ascribed different value in two different class contexts. Agnes, like Husserl, is valued by herself and those around her from a perspective that expects others to provide certain services in exchange for her presence as symbolic capital.

In Carolina's social circle, on the other hand, giving away drugs is done with the expectation that sex or other services will be offered in return. Are drugs a gift then, or is it trade? If men around her expect

Carolina to perform the "*knark* whore" when she uses drugs, perhaps what she is being given is not a spiritual part of a soul, but rather a carefully calculated amount of drugs of a certain value, as payment for her labour. Carolina knows the dealers, who make a living from their business, and knows what amphetamines cost. But that knowledge and the social capital that her drug use entails have no value other than its use value, a non-accumulative capital. Agnes, on the other hand, takes drugs both for pleasure and as part of her identity as a valuable woman who does not shy away from risks and likes to party (Skeggs 2004, p. 23), which makes drug use an accumulative capital for her. Ironically, no payment is needed at Agnes' parties, while Carolina's efforts to preserve her integrity in the social circles she frequents do cost.

It appears that Mauss' description of trade as fundamentally voluntary and gift economies as coercive is thus refuted. But Mauss does not argue that these two systems are separate. Gifts, as parts of a total system, intertwine what is bought and sold with what is given and received in rituals that are valid in specific contexts.

Mary Douglas summarises this relationship in her foreword to *The Gift*: "gift complements market in so far as it operates where the latter is absent" (Douglas 2002, p. xviii). In Carolina's case, drugs are first and foremost commodities within a market, while Agnes views them as gifts, removed from any market.

What then is the nature of the symbolic reciprocity that Agnes provides, and can it be compared to Husserl's? In the case of women, gift theories are confusing. Mauss describes gifting as a way to gain and maintain respect, but especially between men. In his studies, women are sometimes seen as commodities to be exchanged, sometimes as economic partners. Skeggs writes that the whole idea of being an owning individual emerged from a privileged perspective, specifically that of men with access to circles of distribution of symbolic values and with an interest in distancing themselves from the "masses" (2004, p. 7). Economic transactions in the form of exchanges of objects, including other people such as women and slaves, she writes, consolidated the differences between men who own themselves and can own objects, and those who cannot, thus laying the foundations for a class society. This is also known to be a heteronormative society, where much energy is spent on explaining and maintaining differences between men and women. Starting from a critique of Freud's analysis of women as castrated, deficient men, feminist theorist Luce Irigaray writes:

> In our social order, women are "products" used and exchanged by men. Their status is that of merchandise, "commodities." How can such objects of use and transaction claim the right to speak and to participate in exchange in general? (1985, p. 84)

Feminist demands for equality have partially levelled the playing field since Irigaray's text was written in 1984, and I understand that most women in the twenty-first century in Sweden do not accept the idea of living on men's terms, but see themselves as subjects who act and negotiate. But the heteronormative order is still based on femininity and masculinity as subordination and superiority, passivity and activity, with femininity thereby becoming a state of deficiency. Can femininity be anything else? (Dahl 2017).

I perceive women's positions as fluid in relation to the market, between objectification and trading partners, as the example of Carolina shows. As discussed in the chapter "Avoiding the *knarkare*", she was not allowed to participate in the sale of drugs. It was instead to sell drugs herself that she worked regularly in order to pay for herself, which thus meant that she was encouraged to accept gifts, with the subsequent expectations of sexual and domestic availability. This could be described as pressure to move from being an active trader/exchanger to rendering herself passive within a gendered exchange system, where addiction was used as a repressive strategy. In other words, excessively coercive expectations of controllability meant that Carolina could not allow a gift/sex trade system to operate, but working in a restaurant and paying for herself also meant proximity to a drug market in which she could not participate on equal terms.

For Agnes, however, the drug market as a gendered place is not present; she remains at a distance (see also Hutton 2006, pp. 49ff. for a description of the significance of gender in relation to drug markets at dance clubs). Agnes instead gets her drugs through a gift system that she enjoys and takes for granted. From Carolina's point of view, as the world unfolds for her, drugs are bought and "donated" within the same marginalised drug world. From there, she sees no alternatives to an acquisition that involves sexism. Agnes, on the other hand, allows herself to be offered drugs under other conditions, and then, the drugs are as taken for granted as the desk in front of Husserl. She is a woman who is invited to partake when she goes out, but not a woman who owns drugs and takes them home.

Although the givenness of having drugs in front of you without thinking about how they got there can be likened to sitting at your desk and practising philosophy, activities made possible by social conditions, there are nevertheless differences between Agnes and Husserl. Agnes does not own the drugs as Husserl owns his paper and pen, because ownership would imply a different, gendered, market relation. Instead of being a woman who is mainly invited, she would become a woman who owns drugs and can distribute them herself. Agnes emphasises that she is not such a woman. If, on the one hand, femininity provides access to drugs, it also becomes a prerequisite for femininity not to own, but to be invited.

Women's Reciprocity

But are offerings only about gender? Not all drug gifts are given by men to women. The general "culture of treating one another" that Richert (2009) mentions is uneven, both in his statistics and in my material, which indicates that sharing between friends or the concept of a culture of treating does not provide the whole picture. Men offer more, and women are more often invited. It is also difficult to invite without owning, which Agnes says she refrains from doing. I therefore wish to examine both the relationship between drugs, femininity and passivity/activity, and bidding culture as a context in relation to gender and class. However, I can only start from the interview responses in the material, which provide a picture of how the women describe their experiences of the gift economy to a researcher. These have been more about the fact that the drugs are donated than how this happens. Angela says:

> I don't really buy amphetamines, people always treat me to them when there's a party or... An occasion or things...

And Pernilla told me how she obtains drugs:

> As for amphetamines and cocaine, people usually treat me. Mm, I mean, yeah, I would say so, or like, we'll decide that we'll get our fix together and then, like, all of us get the fix, but it'll be someone else who actually does the deal, although I do buy cannabis myself.

So Pernilla seems to have a different approach to different illegal substances. Amphetamines and cocaine either cross her path as gifts in certain settings, or someone else will purchase them. Cannabis, on the other hand, is something she also purchases herself. Meanwhile, Dora has yet another relationship to cannabis:

> I don't tend to buy it myself, no. I mainly get it from others, like friends, you know?

So the women I talked to (actively) seek out settings in which drugs are available. In some of these settings, drugs come to them without any financial strings attached. This could be interpreted as meaning that the women orient themselves based on a certain feminine vulnerability (Dahl 2017), bypassing the risky drug market. But does accepting gifts automatically mean they turn themselves into passive objects? When the women I quoted above talked to me about being given drugs, they did not sound concerned; much like Agnes, it seemed as though they considered it a given that they would receive such gifts, or at least it did not seem to be an issue to them. Here is an excerpt from Tone Schunnesson's hit autobiography from 2016, *Tripprapporter*:

> Don't buy drugs. Just get them. Learn that you can get anything for free. You never owe anyone anything. Just get and get and get until you can hardly take any more. (p. 152)

Schunnesson's impatient demands partly resemble Agnes' attitude and contain no trace of either vulnerability or passivity. In some relationships, drugs are expected as gifts, a circumstance that Schunnesson takes to extremes. Why does she feel entitled to these gifts?

In their study of women flight attendants' work, sociologists Melissa Tyler and Steve Taylor use Mauss' concept of an "exchange of aesthetics" to highlight a central and under-theorised aspect of women's work (1998, see also Petersson McIntyre 2016). They posit that both customers' and employers' expectations of women's bodies to look and behave in a certain way (always being willing to serve, for example, which Tyler and Taylor call "compulsory altruism") are actually obligatory gifts on the part of women (ibid., p. 169). Aesthetics and altruism, they claim, are made part and parcel of the flight as a commodity, which is why the women's gifts are regarded as having been paid for, not as something that needs to be repaid. At first sight, Schunnesson's demands look like a demand for gifts with a refusal to reciprocate. But her attitude could also be interpreted as the other side of the coin of an exchange of aesthetics, a bodily performance of femininity in "the night-time economy", which requires labour (see, e.g., Nicholls 2019). In that sense, her demand for drugs could be read as a feminist demand to be repaid for the aesthetic gifts she is obligated to give. In the feminist classic *Femininity* (1984), writer and journalist Susan Brownmiller describes femininity as just that: a gift.

> Femininity pleases men because it makes them appear more masculine by contrast; and in truth, conferring an extra portion of unearned gender distinction on men, an unchallenged space in which to breathe freely and feel stronger, wiser, more competent is femininity's special gift. One could say that masculinity is often an effort to please women, but masculinity pleases by displays of mastery and competence while femininity pleases by suggesting that these concerns, except in small matters are beyond its intent. (p. 4)

What Brownmiller describes as the gift of femininity, making men feel stronger, wiser and more competent by affirming them as such—together with Tyler and Taylor's description of aesthetics as women's obligatory gifts—paints a picture of a patriarchal fantasy (Dahl 2017, p. 43), in this case a patriarchal dream relationship. A possible gift economy would be that drugs (or other gifts) are given in the hope of such a relation-ship. Irigaray writes that attempts to perform femininity expose it (and masculinity) as a masquerade that serves to entrench male systems of representation. The problem, she says, is that when it comes to markets, especially markets for sexual transactions, women's only choices are either to play on their femininity and thereby lose themselves, or to be left out, without access to the market (1985, p. 84). While there does not appear to be a way for women to allow their femininity to exist in the market, Irigaray does propose a disruptive queer strategy. Instead of asking what women really "are", and whether she is an object or a subject, Irigaray advocates disruptive exaggerations of femininity:

> repeating/interpreting the way in which, within discourse, the feminine finds itself defined as lack, deficiency, or as imitation and negative image of the subject, they should signify that with respect to this logic a disruptive excess is possible on the feminine side. (ibid., p. 78)

A disruptive excess of the feminine is thus a way of stirring up a dichotomous division of gendered meanings. In the quotation from Schunnesson, above, the reception itself can be interpreted as exagger-ated femininity. She accepts and does not stop accepting, but demands more without indicating any (further) reciprocation. The power over the evaluative perspective thus becomes a struggle for the primacy of values, where Schunnesson claims an almost unlimited value that questions the legitimacy of any other judgements. Irigaray's interpretation opens up the possibility that gift economies, even if they take place within heteronor-mative contexts, precisely in line with women as recipients and men as active givers, include room for resistance.

But is excess the only way to queer femininity? Is there really no way for a woman to accept a drug gift from a man without either playing on femininity or being marginalised?

Most interviewees describe certain drug-use occasions as intimate, shared contexts, where the focus is on a common experience. Can a phenomenological perspective, based on the situated body with its possi-bilities for extension, reveal a different, potentially queering, community through drug use? Angela describes a party where the participants produce an intimate, shared spatiality based on shared drug use (cf. Pini 2001, p. 103):

first, the party gets going. People chat, there are all these sensory impressions [...] Mm. And then the crowd thins out, some people disappear, and then you go deeper, by being awake, I mean... For a really long time, that is: by not going to bed but taking speed instead... And then, all of a sudden, you've got the time to paddle out onto the lake. [Has shown me pictures of people paddling canoes.] And, there's this intimacy as well. You get a... what's it called? Like, this island that's suspended in time. Because everyone has disappeared into the kingdom of sleep by, by then, but you're left on this island of wakefulness. And... everyone on that island is grateful because we have [carefully articulates] each other and "we chose to be here", you're part of a community and you, there's this kind of shared affection, like "here we are, on this deserted island. Together." And it gets really... Also because it's a crime, it becomes this shared secret as well.

The island metaphor takes on a literal meaning here. The island is a physical, and at the same time a perceived, place for intimate community. Those who belong to this group, whose togetherness Angela describes in terms of intimacy, affection and community, linked to the illegality of amphetamines, are separated by wakefulness. The other partygoers are asleep. She describes gratitude "[for having] each other", and for how those who are close have chosen to be together. The gift system, in terms of intimacy, seems to be manifested through a reciprocation in terms of togetherness. Those who are close in intoxication have given their presence to a mutually intimate situation.

Phenomenologist Merleau-Ponty theorises the body as simultaneously both active and passive, subject and object. The body is sentient while becoming known and he describes this as the body's dual belongingness to the world (1968, pp. 137f.). In this way, the body is vulnerable and impressionable at the same time as it affects and is affected. He further writes that, although people store previous experiences and therefore to some extent do what they usually do, by living/dwelling together, the instituted is simultaneously receptive of elements and significances and may diverge from the past as it initiates the present. There is thus an unpredictable innovativeness in togetherness. Thus, could there be a subtle, or even subversive, possibility of a queering dissolution of social orders in the endeavour to experience temporary intense togetherness through drug use?

Homeliness

In her book *Club Cultures and Female Subjectivity*, with the instructive subtitle *The Move from Home to House* (2001), Maria Pini foregrounds a similar description of intimacy and community to the one Angela gives, regarding women's raving (see also Kavanaugh and Anderson 2008, on solidarity in the rave scene). Several of Pini's interviewees describe raving, most commonly including the use of amphetamines and ecstasy, as making them feel at home. "Amy" says: "When I discovered rave, I just finally found a place that felt like home – like being in the bosom of my family" (Pini 2001, p. 15).

Pini's analysis is directed specifically towards the rave scene, and while most interviewees use drugs, some have stopped, or sometimes go to raves without using any, and she theorises this "other world" as being the dancing community, rather than the drug use. In my material, descriptions of feelings of homeliness were common in all kinds of settings and seemed to be related to experiences of altered consciousness together with others, which shaped an intimate space.

Sociologist Deborah Lupton writes that taking risks for pleasure, for example through extreme sports, certain crimes or drug use, can spiritually bind people together.

> The pleasures of risk-taking also inhere in the ways in which risk-takers may find a communal spirit with other like-minded souls. To engage in risky activities may bind people together closely in this common pursuit, particularly if they identify each other as being members of the elite group of skilled, tough-minded individuals who can cope successfully with edgework. (1999, p. 157)

Risk-taking, she believes, can forge a team spirit and even, at least for a brief while, dissolve the self:

participants may lose a sense of their autonomous selves, becoming, at least for a brief time, part of a mass of bodies/selves with a common, shared purpose. (Ibid.)

We could view Lupton's "mass of selves" as a temporary dwelling that simultaneously institutes and is instituted, and which therefore offers queer opportunities to dissolve one's body into a single shared body, which is also described in spatial terms by Angela, as an "island of wakefulness". From there, the world unfolds towards common purposes, such as canoeing. But does this (only) have to do with risk-taking? The ravers in Pini's study do not describe their dancing as primarily a risk-taking activity, but still they foreground intense experiences of becoming part of a mass. "Amy" describes how she can "merge into somewhere strange with people I don't really know and get so close and be so calm and comfortable within a crowd which is all losing it together". "Catherine" narrates how she feels "belonging and love" on the dance floor, and that it is important "having the crowd do it together and go mental". "Jane" describes raving in terms of "doing something more personal with hundreds of other people and getting really close to those hundreds of other people" (2001, pp. 109f.).

Pernilla tells me about a more serene kind of drug use: smoking cannabis with her friends. Like Angela, she uses spatial expressions in combination with intimacy:

personally, I find cannabis, hmm… sweet, precisely because it's… relaxing and helps me unwind, but also because of the fact that you can just sit and, like, listen to music and chat about stuff and, you know… you have a lot of fun precisely because you're part of, like, the same kind of bubbles, sort of, which feels really special and intimate.

The people who use drugs together are described by both Angela and Pernilla as sharing an experience of intimacy that is translated into spatiality through an experience of closeness to each other during the intoxication, which is expressed as islands by Angela and bubbles by Pernilla. The drug intoxication and relationship-building make the islands and bubbles into extensions of the body (Ahmed 2006b, p. 58), which experiences a range of positive emotions that together provide connotations of homeliness (ibid., p. 7).

Pernilla uses words like "relaxing", "unwinding", "fun", "special" and "intimate". Angela says that she and the others who are on amphetamines are "grateful that they have each other"; she too uses the word "intimate", as well as the phrases "shared secret" and "affection". This potentially queer, homely state of sharing a body/spatiality seems to be connected to altered states of consciousness, which are connected to drug use. However, these experiences only occur after the drugs have already been obtained. So drugs first have to be brought into these spaces, by people who frequent the drug market or have established some other link to it. And the drug market, where violence, vulnerability and all kinds of risks abound, does not appear homely. Someone in the group must be the person who maintains these links. Sociologist Kristian Mjåland, in his study of prisoners' "culture of sharing" drugs, explains their willingness to smuggle drugs into the prison and give them away partly by the respect it can earn: "Prisoners accrue respect by importing drugs because it symbolizes 'nerve', resistance to the system, ambition and connections to organized drug networks outside prison" (2014, p. 338).

This quote suggests that one could gain respect among those who use drugs by taking the risk of serving as the link between the contrasting drug market and the bubbles and islands where the people who use the drugs feel at home. Intimacy also stands in contrast to gift-giving situations that are neither intimate nor confidential, like the ones Carolina and Schunnesson so vividly depict. Drawing on the concepts of intimacy and politeness, anthropologist Takie Sugiyama Lebra (1975) discusses gift economies in a way that highlights the contradictions between different gift-exchange situations. She criticises the work of anthropologist and gift theorist Marshall Sahlins (2004/1965), rejecting the claim that reciprocity would be based on static relationship structures: instead, she argues, gift economies are ever changing and dynamic. We can achieve intimacy by getting to know someone over a prolonged period of time, or by sharing certain experiences (Lebra 1975, p. 552). But the state of intimacy is never guaranteed.

I interpret the intimacy that the above women are describing as a community in which one's own body can be temporarily dissolved (at least partially), which means that intimacy can be a queer condition. But, while intimacy may be an ideal drug-induced state, with the spirituality of drug gifts dissolving in the group's spiritual togetherness, the women I talked to also mentioned a whole host of problems that can make gifts precarious and/or take on unexpected forms. Most of them stressed the importance of being in the right company when taking drugs—a warning that could often be traced back to the shifting nature of gift economies.

Gifts Causing Trouble

If the intimate context is one of reciprocity, there is also a vulnerability in the maintenance of these structures. When Pernilla discusses her approach to the uncontrolled content of drugs, she describes a readiness to accept whatever she is given:

> *Emma*: Do you think about it? Purity and...
> *Pernilla*: Yes. In theory. In practice, when someone goes "d'you want some?", not so much. [laughs] Unfortunately. I wish I could... No, I'm not that picky when someone's offering.

The recipient of a gift is not expected to demand quality. But, regardless of what is being offered, the recipient enters into a relationship which in turn can be perceived as an agreement. As Lebra reminds us:

> a gift or favor is not only a token of affection or esteem held by the donor for the receiver but is convertible into one of these and other social values to be conveyed in the reverse direction. (1975, p. 555)

A further quote from Tone Schunnesson shows how the legitimacy of perspectives within a gift economy can shift. She repeats the advice to never buy one's own drugs, but this time continues by describing how the way the environment responds to this requirement can change. She writes:

never buy your own drugs. You can get anything you want for free. Which works for a few years until everyone gets tired, everyone got tired of me. Snapped at me in a taxi: "Why can't you chip in for once." (2016, p. 162).

Sahlins defines negative reciprocity as "the attempt to get something for nothing" (1972, p. 195). In the above quote, Schunnesson herself seems to view her demand as a kind of negative reciprocity, because she says drugs should be given to her "for free". Feminine aesthetics and a willingness to serve are rarely considered gifts, as Tyler and Taylor write; instead, they are a capacity that is expected of women (1998, p. 165), which means they are not acknowledged as accumulative capital. For Mauss, the aesthetic aspects of gifts are important and "extremely numerous" (2002, p. 49), but also inextricably linked to legal, economic and religious exchanges within a total system—an interlinkage that could be analysed through Bourdieu's concept of symbolic capital (1986).

But Mauss also highlights something else that indicates a certain forging of community. He argues that there is a common interest in aesthetics that extends beyond morality and self-interest:

everything, food, objects, and services, even "respect", as the Tlingit say, is a cause of aesthetic emotion, and not only of emotions of a moral order or relating to self-interest. (2002, p. 101)

The intertwining of the ways in which aesthetically pleasing contexts are desired and designed together with the specific conditions of women's expected endeavours provides a breeding ground for frustration and perceived impoliteness. What can be considered as donated, what should be reciprocated, and how?

Whatever abilities and qualities a person may display in a drug-use context, these need to be recognised by the other participants as reciprocal so that payment or referral to the drug market is not required. Consequently, there is a pride in not having to buy drugs, as shown, for example, by Agnes when she says that she never buys drugs or "has [them] at home". She can trust that the drugs will come to her when she gets to the right context. But there are also limitations to being invited. Such a position creates distance to the drug market but at the same time limits movement in line with women's desires (cf. Polanyi 2001/1944). As long as there is moderation and satisfaction with what is offered, practised and experienced, reciprocity follows a pattern that strengthens the community. However, if a desire for more drugs or a desire for a specific drug is involved, the women must move closer to a person with the resources to satisfy that need, either in the form of a gift or in exchange for money.

Boel describes an unpleasant experience from her teenage years, involving a guy in her circle of friends who was giving her drugs instead of selling them to her:

> *Boel*: I never had to buy anything. I got it, I got it. And it wasn't as if I asked for it either, I got it.
> *Emma*: But then, he thought that you...
> *Boel*: Mm. That I owed him things. I just said no, no, then you can... then I can manage. Then it's good, like, and he was just like "but please, you can keep that" and I was like, "Ok. But. Then I'll go now. I'll go now. And you stay here." But he, he was a pretty skinny guy and I'd trained in martial arts so maybe he gave in for that reason.

In this quote, Boel shows how the gift implied certain unspoken expectations of reciprocity, which she was not prepared to fulfil. This created a situation that involved the risk of violence, as she suggests by mentioning her physical strength and comparing it to that of the drug dealer. But at the beginning of the quotation, she also suggests a certain pride in being a recipient of gifts, someone who does not have to ask for drugs, which is complemented by her pride in firmly refusing when the donor's expectations turn into demands.

The interviewees who want to be able to choose the drugs, time and place independently of others, and those who feel they need the drugs regularly, also buy them for themselves. This implies a proximity to the drug market, which is characterised by risk but also by opportunities to show "nerve".

Boel, who usually buys her drugs herself, has no problem owning drugs, quite the contrary. But this does not make the acquisition unproblematic. She describes her purchases as risky projects and that she uses men to gain an advantage in buying situations. Her tone is convincing when she says:

[If] I bring a big, muscular friend along and introduce him as my brother, I know I'll get the good stuff, from the top, the top shelf, like. It's not even hard.

Performative masculinity is described as a commercial advantage here, one that may be used strategically. Boel describes this strategy as an easy part of the drug trade. All she needs to do is make sure she is around the right kind of bodies: strong and/or masculine ones.

As Pernilla shows, however, different kinds of behaviour work in different contexts. She buys cannabis herself and stores it at home, smoking it in specific situations: at home, in the company of close friends. Amphetamines and cocaine, on the other hand, she is usually treated to, at parties or when out clubbing with friends.

Overall, the interview material illustrates that positions and places are fluid, that shared spaces can become inhospitable, gifts can turn into advance payments, intimacy can turn into periphery, and politeness can turn into unwanted sexual advances. Whether women approach the drug market or allow themselves to be treated, obtaining drugs is a gendered, racialised and classed activity, but with potential ability, in a best-case scenario, to lead to a certain world characterised by intimate homeliness.

References

Ahmed, Sara. 2006a. Orientations: Toward a Queer Phenomenology. *GLQ: A Journal of Lesbian and Gay Studies* 12 (4): 543–574.
Ahmed, Sara. 2006b. *Queer Phenomenology: Orientations, Objects, Others.* Durham, NC: Duke University Press.
Ahmed, Sara. 2007. A Phenomenology of Whiteness. *Feminist Theory* 8 (2): 149–168.
Bourdieu, Pierre. 1986. The Forms of Capital. In *Handbook of Theory and Research for the Sociology of Education,* ed. John G. Richardson, 241–258. Westport, CT: Greenwood Press.

Brennan, A. 2020. Queer Feminine Identities and the War on Drugs. In *The Impact of Global Drug Policy on Women: Shifting the Needle*, ed. Julia Buxton, Giavana Margo, and Lona Burger, 213–216. Emerald Publishing: Bingley.

Brownmiller, Susan. 1984. *Femininity*. New York, NY: Linden Press/Simon & Schuster.

Bucerius, Sandra. 2007. "What Else Should I Do?": Cultural Influences on the Drug Trade of Migrants in Germany. *Journal of Drug Issues* 37: 673–697.

Buxton, Julia, Lona Lauridsen Burger, and Giavana Margo. 2020. Introduction. In *The Impact of Global Drug Policy on Women: Shifting the Needle*, ed. Julia Buxton, Giavana Margo, and Lona Burger, 1–8. Bingley: Emerald Publishing.

Campbell, Nancy D., and Elizabeth Ettorre. 2011. *Gendering Addiction: The Politics of Drug Treatment in a Neurochemical World*. New York, NY: Palgrave Macmillan.

Dahl, Ulrika. 2017. Femmebodiment: Notes on Queer Feminine Shapes of Vulnerability. *Feminist Theory* 18 (1): 35–53.

Douglas, Mary. 2002. Foreword. In *The Gift: The Form and Reason for Exchange in Archaic Societies*, Marcel Mauss. London: Routledge.

Du Rose, Natacha. 2015. *The Governance of Female Drug Users: Women's Experiences of Drug Policy*. Bristol: Policy Press.

Ettorre, Elizabeth. 1992. *Women and Substance Use*. Basingstoke: Macmillan.

Ettorre, Elizabeth. 2015. Embodied Deviance, Gender, and Epistemologies of Ignorance: Re-visioning Drugs Use in a Neurochemical, Unjust World. *Substance Use & Misuse* 50: 794–805.

Farber, David, ed. 2021. *The War on Drugs*. New York, NY: New York University Press.

Fleetwood, Jennifer, Judith Aldridge, and Caroline Chatwin. 2020. Gendering Research on Online Illegal Drug Markets. *Addiction Research & Theory* 28 (6): 457–466.

Frykman, Jonas. 1977. *Horan i bondesamhället* [The Whore in Peasant Society]. Lund: Liber Läromedel.

Grundetjern, Heidi, and Sveinung Sandberg. 2012. Dealing with a Gendered Economy: Female Drug Dealers and Street Capital. *European Journal of Criminology* 9 (6): 621–635.

Heilig, Markus. 2015. *Alkohol, droger och hjärnan: tro och vetande utifrån modern neurovetenskap* [Alcohol, Drugs and the Brain: Beliefs and Knowledge Based on Modern Neuroscience]. Stockholm: Natur & Kultur.

Hutton, Fiona. 2006. *Risky Pleasures: Club Cultures and Feminine Identities*. Aldershot: Ashgate.

Irigaray, Luce. 1985. *This Sex Which Is Not One.* New York, NY: Cornell University Press.

Kavanaugh, Philip R., and Tammy L. Anderson. 2008. Solidarity and Drug Use in the Electronic Dance Music Scene. *Sociological Quarterly* 49: 181–208.

Lebra, Takie Sugiyama. 1975. An Alternative Approach to Reciprocity. *American Anthropologist*, New Series 77(3): 550–565.

Lennartsson, Rebecka. 2019. *Mamsell Bohmans fall: Nattlöperskor i 1700-talets Stockholm* [The Fall of Mamsell Bohman: Night Walkers in 18th Century Stockholm]. Stockholm: Stockholmia förlag.

Lupton, Deborah. 1999. *Risk.* London: Routledge [ebook].

Maher, Lisa. 1997. *Sexed Work: Gender, Race and Resistance in a Brooklyn Drug Market.* Oxford: Oxford University Press.

Mauss, Marcel. 2002. *The Gift: The Form and Reason for Exchange in Archaic Societies.* London: Routledge.

Merleau-Ponty, Maurice. 1968. *The Visible and the Invisible: Followed by Working Notes.* Evanston, IL: Northwestern University Press.

Merleau-Ponty, Maurice. 2010. *Institution and Passivity: Course Notes from the Collège de France (1954–1955).* Foreword by Claude LeFort. Evanston, IL: Northwestern University Press.

Mjåland, Kristian. 2014. "A Culture of Sharing": Drug Exchange in a Norwegian Prison. *Punishment & Society* 16 (3): 336–352.

Nafstad, Ida. 2011. Changing Control of the Open Drug Scenes in Oslo: Crime, Welfare, Immigration Control, or a Combination? *Journal of Scandinavian Studies in Criminology & Crime Prevention* 12 (2): 128–152.

Nicholls, Emily. 2019. *Negotiating Femininities in the Neoliberal Night-Time Economy: Too Much of a Girl?* Cham: Springer Nature.

Paoli, Letizia. 2002. Flexible Hierarchies and Dynamic Disorder: The Drug Distribution System in Frankfurt and Milan. *Drugs: Education, Prevention and Policy* 9: 143–151.

Petersson McIntyre, Magdalena. 2016. *Att älska sitt jobb: Passion, entusiasm och nyliberal subjektivitet* [Loving Your Job: Passion, Enthusiasm and Neoliberal Subjectivity]. Lund: Nordic Academic Press.

Pini, Maria. 2001. *Club Cultures and Female Subjectivity: The Move from Home to House.* London: Palgrave Macmillan.

Polanyi, Karl. 2001/1944. *The Great Transformation: The Political and Economic Origins of Our Time,* 2nd ed. Boston, MA: Beacon Press.

Richert, Torkel. 2009. Injektionsmissbrukande kvinnors inkomstkällor och anskaffning av droger [Injecting, Drug-Abusing Women's Sources of Income and Acquisition of Drugs]. *Nordisk Alkohol- & Narkotikatidskrift* 26 (5): 365–394.

Sahlins, Marshall (1972). *Stone Age Economics*. Chicago: Aldine Atherton.

Sahlins, Marshall. 2004/1965. On the Sociology of Primitive Exchange. In *The Relevance of Models for Social Anthropology*, ed. Michael Banton, 139–236. London: Routledge.

Sandberg, Sveinung. 2008. Black Drug Dealers in a White Welfare State: Cannabis Dealing and Street Capital in Norway. *British Journal of Criminology* 48: 604–619.

Sandberg, Sveinung, and Willy Pedersen. 2011. *Street Capital: Black Cannabis Dealers in a White Welfare State*. Bristol: Bristol University Press.

Schunnesson, Tone. 2016. *Tripprapporter* [Trip Reports]. Stockholm: Norstedts.

Skeggs, Beverley. 2004. *Class, Self, Culture*. London: Routledge.

Tham, Henrik. 2003. Narkotikapolitiken och missbrukets utveckling [Drug Policy and the Development of Addiction]. In *Forskare om narkotikapolitiken*, ed. Henrik Tham. Stockholm: Stockholms universitet.

Tyler, Melissa, and Steve Taylor. 1998. The Exchange of Aesthetics: Women's Work and 'The Gift.' *Gender, Work & Organization* 5 (3): 165–171.

6

Staying Appropriate

Beverley Skeggs (2012) describes the concept of respectability as closely linked to norms of propriety. By respectability, Skeggs means a practice that is usually gendered, and that involves emotionally charged work of judgement about where the boundaries of propriety lie and about staying within them (2012, pp. 64f.). This work aims to establish value by being/ becoming a proper person. She describes the requirements for propriety as historically inherited norms linked not only to gender but also to class, which impose an affective responsibility on certain people; that is, respectability is perceived as a mandatory norm, and loss of respectability means a loss of personal value.

How is propriety maintained during drug use? In this chapter, I explore how time and place are negotiated in relation to proper and improper drug use. I then examine the spatial relationship in the women's lives between children and drugs, both highly charged symbols linked to norms of propriety.

© The Author(s) 2024
E. Eleonorasdotter, *Women's Drug Use in Everyday Life*,
https://doi.org/10.1007/978-3-031-46057-9_6

6.1   Keeping the Rhythm

I conduct my first interview with Dora in her kitchen in Gothenburg. Dora comes across as a cautious, conscientious person, and tells me that she is interested in drugs but simultaneously afraid of them.

Cannabis is the only drug she has tried so far, despite having been offered other drugs on several occasions. She says she turned down amphetamines, for example, because she worried they would make her schizophrenic and because she does not trust chemically produced drugs.

> *Dora*: I just feel like all this white powder… could be anything, really, or, you know…
> *Emma*: So white powder –
> *Dora*: – equals bad. [laughs][1]

Several studies have suggested a potential link between schizophrenia and the smoking of cannabis (cf. Allebeck 2007; Manrique-Garcia et al. 2012; Månsson 2017), and these have been repeatedly publicised in the media. But cannabis does not "equal bad" for Dora because most of her friends—students mainly, from different fields of study and with busy social lives—use cannabis. This makes it an everyday, unremarkable part of life for Dora. However, she also calls smoking cannabis a stigmatised pursuit. I wonder how it is that something can be both stigmatised and everyday, and she describes how the time of day is crucial for controlled, non-stigmatised use:

> *Dora*: many of my friends are very high achievers, and I think they think a little bit that… if you start smoking in the middle of the day and… it might happen once in a while, but if you were also seen, by someone else, that they would think "oh, she's really lost it". […] "she's really not taking responsibility for her…", whatever commitments you have.

Dora does not want to seem like a person who does not take responsibility for her commitments, which is why she does not smoke cannabis during the day, a time associated with work or studies. The friends who sometimes smoke with her at night are the same people she is afraid

---

[1] All quotes in Swedish have been translated by me.

might consider her as having "lost it" if they were to catch her smoking during the day. I interpret the expression "losing it" as closely related to Ahmed's use of the term "out of line", which describes both the drawing of a non-normative line that can be perceived as strange (queer), and an experience of disorientation (2006, pp. 66f.). But times of abstinence are followed by times when she can allow herself to use cannabis.

Richard Wilk describes this rhythm as one of the cornerstones of modern-day consumer societies:

> The rhythm of restraint and release marks time in the lives of consumers; every day is divided into periods of work and breaks to consume coffee, lunch, snacks, and tobacco. Work is followed by leisure, during the day and in the week in the form of the weekend break. [...] This cycle connects our [...] consumption to work in a direct way, and is based on a moral scheme in which the pleasures of consumption are earned through the pain and the sacrifice of unrewarding, disciplined labour. (Wilk 2014, p. 14; see also Nichter and Nichter 1991)

This rhythm, Wilk posits, preserves a moral balance between pleasure and sacrifice. That balance differs between contexts: different substances may be consumed, for example, in different amounts. Dora's suggestion that it is the time of day when one uses cannabis that determines whether or not such use is appropriate is in line with Wilk's rhythm theory, in which daytime equates to work while evenings and weekends are moments that may be relaxing and pleasurable.

Sociologist Mats Hilte, however, paints a different picture. In his analysis of how the use of cannabis, heroin, tobacco and alcohol affects the user's perception of time in relation to the environment, Hilte divides time into social time, which means shared time that corresponds to schedules and calendars, etc. (2019, p. 115), and subjective time, which is about the experience of time. In the case of both cannabis and heroin, people who use these drugs are reported to experience time as slower during intoxication. Hilte further argues that legal substances can be synchronised with shared social time in a different way than illegal substances can, because the latter are not accepted by the majority society.

Coffee and cigarettes are legal substances and therefore part of socially sanctioned rituals and practices for taking time out and suspending the passage of normative time. This is not the case with illegal substances such as heroin or cannabis. The use of heroin and other narcotic drugs is generally considered a deviant act in the West, argues Hilte, and there are therefore no socially accepted practice or rituals for using these drugs to manipulate the subjective experience of time (2019, p. 114).

However, Dora's perception of what is appropriate indicates that cannabis can form part of socially sanctioned recreational rituals within a context that is hardly socially marginalised, but one that she describes as "high achieving" and which appears to be morally oriented. It, therefore, appears that the illegal drug cannabis can be included in social time in such a way that subjective perceptions of time under the influence, if it occurs within the socially accepted time window, can form part of a social, shared time that is synchronised with subjective time (cf. Hilte 2019, pp. 115ff.). The time shared with other people who use cannabis under the influence then comes to occupy an intermediate position. The subjective, displaced perception of time is shared with others in a limited social context during a certain period of time, a "bubble" or an "island", in Pernilla's and Angela's words, which is adapted to the fixed points and commitments of general social time.

The rhythm of enjoyment and sacrifice is thus maintained in different ways by different people, nor does it have a precise temporal structure. Its boundaries are unclear, making it difficult to form judgements about the appropriateness of using or abstaining. Below, Dora describes an evening that demonstrates these unclear boundaries.

For our go-along interview, I had asked Dora to take me to a place that was important to her drug use. On the way there, she recounts an occasion when she met some friends in a large park on a bright summer evening for a picnic. We visit the park and in my field diary I describe my impressions:

She tells me she likes this place, because she associates it with summer, BBQing and having a good time. […] We walk over to where she and her friends laid out their blankets. As she talks, she recreates the scene by pointing and showing which direction they faced. They arrived around four or five in the afternoon, she says; at the time, several families with young children were seated on the grass nearby. One of her friends had baked a carrot cake with marijuana in it; several of them had a slice. Later, several other people she didn't really know joined in as well; some of them decided not to have any cake. There is unease in her voice as the describes their decision.

I interpret her unease as stemming from the reality that the shared spatiality and experience during drug use (which I described as "intimacy" in the previous chapter) cannot materialise in the same way when some of those who are present do not join in. If drug use is the prerequisite for such a space, then those who are not part of the space risk disturbing its homeliness (cf. Ahmed 2010b, pp. 56, 58). Dora can get high if others are high as well. Around people who are not high, however, she risks becoming improper. Dora herself ate half a slice and initially experienced some positive intoxication effects, but then took another bite and gradually experienced increasingly unpleasant feelings and visions, and finally suffered several hours of vomiting. She herself links her emotional states to the influence of the drug, but mainly to the social situation, the behaviour of some of the people who had not eaten the cake, and the importance of time and place.

Everything began with a game of croquet. Another excerpt from my notebook reads:

> Her arms felt weird and she felt as though she had lost some control. But she still wanted to "act normal"; she mentions the facts that it was light out and that there were still families around as reasons why she felt being high would not be appropriate. So she continued to play, but started laughing and throwing her ball around. Her behaviour drew people's attention; eventually, her friends suggested she go and sit down on the blankets.

The nearby families and the late-afternoon sunlight created a milieu in which being high was inappropriate. At the same time, however, the whole picnic and get-together with close friends had been planned as an occasion during which being high would be appropriate. Summer evenings symbolise a time when release is permitted. But as the sun was still up, it signalled that it was still day. The time and the objects around her resulted in an ambivalent environment, in which Dora tells me she felt insecure and conspicuous.

The situation she describes exists in the space between night and day, the familiar and unfamiliar, joy and fear. The effects of the drug sound distressing enough in and of themselves. But, as Dora tells her story, she focuses on how uncomfortable she found it to be around sober people and have them witness her being high, because this meant they might find her improper.

She repeatedly tells me how some of those who were present and who had not eaten any cake found her behaviour funny.

> She tells me she dislikes it when people see her at times like that, that she wants to seem proper and gives a lot of thought to that.

As mentioned above, Dora tends to avoid getting high during the day. She does not want to be considered improper or seen as someone who is "losing it". Yet, on that particular evening, she threw her croquet ball around, laughed and called attention to herself. In a way, being "out of line" (in the sense of not being in sync with others) also means that one is "out of time" (Ahmed 2014, p. 50). Ahmed describes how, when one fails to keep a steady pace, one becomes more visible; and this conspicuousness can in turn be interpreted as clumsiness:

> When we are out of time, we notice the other's timing and pace; in noticing the other, the other might appear as awkward and clumsy, as not willing to be helpful [...] Indeed, the feeling of clumsiness can be catchy: once you feel clumsy, you can feel even clumsier; you can even lack the coordination to coordinate yourself with yourself, let alone yourself with others. (2014, p. 50—note that Ahmed is not referring to the experience of being intoxicated/high)

When Dora's intoxication occurs in front of sober people and families with children, she feels what can be described as being "out of line" as well as "out of time". Her body and movements under the influence of cannabis are not intoxicated in a positive sense, but strange and clumsy. I interpret her laughter and the way in which she throws her croquet ball around as a sign that she feels uncoordinated, both with herself and with the environment, and in the midst of her intoxication she can find no way to regain control.

Ambivalence about time, whether or not intoxication is appropriate, is thus influenced by families with children as symbols of daytime and responsibility. In addition, her own company includes non-intoxicated people who disrupt the intimate spatiality. She therefore also feels "out of place" (cf. Ahmed 2006, p. 135; 2010b, p. 60). Perhaps the group could have created a spatial intimacy that Dora would have experienced as sufficiently suitable for intoxication, despite the families with children, if the sober people had not disrupted that intimacy, i.e. the creation of place? In any case, when neither intimacy/spatiality nor time is assured as appropriate, this leads to discomfort for Dora, who feels inappropriate and indecent.

She describes it as a relief when the families with children finally went home and it started to get dark. The time for intoxication moved more and more towards legitimacy. Despite this, the intoxication became more and more unpleasant. She says that she cried and threw up, that it was horrible and that she thought it would never end. I perceive her choice of location for the go-along interview as related to the fact that the experience made a strong impression that she is still trying to process. It was a particular event that frightened her, but it has not led her to give up cannabis. The highs that she describes during our interviews seem generally unpleasant, with associated feelings of anxiety and fear. This makes me wonder whether the rituals surrounding the intake of cannabis need to be analysed, at least in part, separately from the effects. My field notes for this part contain my questions and Dora's answers:

You describe smoking pot [marijuana] as a social thing, but you describe the effect as becoming introverted and withdrawn. How does that work?

She answers that it is the sharing of the joint that is social. She repeats that it is. And that she wants to have friends around her with whom she feels comfortable.

I say jokingly: So you're introverted together? A bit like yoga? She laughs and answers in the affirmative. "A bit like that."

A division emerges between talking about smoking a joint, saying yes and taking the joint, as social and everyday, "no big deal", something that most people are considered to do. On the other hand, the highs she experiences evoke both pleasant and unpleasant feelings, including the risk of stigma, acting strangely, paranoid experiences, etc. I perceive that Dora's attraction to cannabis use is largely about participating in a social community, an intimate context that follows a rhythm in which cannabis use is defined as the opposite of sacrifice and discipline, in Wilk's words. But, in the cannabis rush, she is worried about not having followed the rhythm in a proper way. Rather than a desire for the high as such, she orients herself rhythmically, enjoys allowing herself to indulge and then makes an effort to get through the high properly. The rhythm thus becomes uneven, and the intoxication itself does not represent "release", but rather a type of "restraint".

The joint or carrot cake containing marijuana can also be interpreted as "happy objects" in Ahmed's sense (2010a, pp. 21ff.). She writes that happiness is attributed to certain objects, which are understood as good objects. We collect such objects around us and thus create a "horizon of likes" (ibid., p. 24). People who like the same things also gather nearby; Ahmed takes fan clubs and hobby groups as an example, and says that we often like people who like the same things as us. We thus align ourselves with others by investing in the same objects as causes of happiness, thus forming affective communities (ibid., p. 38). But being in a community that is centred on a particular object does not always mean that feelings of happiness arise. The opposite, negative feelings in relation to the object, can then mean experiences of alienation and being "out of line". Ahmed writes:

> So when happy objects are passed around, it is not necessarily the feeling that passes. To share such objects (or have a share in such objects) would simply mean you would *share an orientation towards those objects as being good.* (2010a, p. 44, italics in original)

When the joint or carrot cake is passed around, Dora wants to share the happiness by orientating herself towards these objects as being good, but then she does not always feel that being under the influence of cannabis is much fun. The goodness of the object does not match the impression it makes. Experiencing the wrong emotions associated with the joint/carrot cake is, therefore, not just about loss of control in front of the sober. The investment in the object as a cause of happiness is shattered, and Dora becomes "out of line" with the other people who used cannabis.

Another aspect of Dora's uncomfortable experience is how it is gendered. Sara Ahmed reminds us that rooms have a history and a present, and writes that rooms become extensions of the bodies that visit them. They have been shaped by the bodies that have already passed through them (Ahmed 2010b, pp. 56ff), and this affects how they receive new people. They may appear open and permissive, but expectations of what the bodies in the rooms should look like create places where some bodies become part of the room. Bodies that deviate appear alien and visible, and alienation becomes an uncomfortable feeling for those who do not fit in (Ahmed 2006, p. 133). Public space was long considered to be reserved for men, "public woman" in the late nineteenth century literally meant prostitute (Svanström 2000). Drugs and intoxicants also have a history of being men's business in the public sphere (Berridge 2013). When I ask Dora whether there are differences between men's and women's use of cannabis in her social circle, she again refers to time, but also to publicity:

> *Dora*: Mm… maybe that men do it more often… during the day, and more around people and so on, that they don't spend as much time thinking about how it makes them look, perhaps?
> *Emma*: Why do you think that is?
> *Dora*: Well, maybe it's about propriety, the fact that you should, or that you don't want to be seen as improper and irresponsible. And like, not having your shit together, kind of. That you're, losing… That's how the environment might see you.

The spatiality of a shared intoxication, what I have called intimacy, thus constructs a context-dependent social time that is also subjective. I would, therefore, argue that the boundaries of social time and subjective time in relation to drug use are more fluid and situated than Mats Hilte (2019) assumes in his study. The "environment" that Dora refers to is important for her as a way of judging whether the intoxication is appropriate, but as I understand it, this judgement can also stem from people who share an intoxication that is positioned in the right time and place. Dora does not take the joint/carrot cake in order to deviate, but rather to align herself with the rhythm between sacrifice and duty based on her situated starting point, i.e. she takes the joint precisely in order to relate to social time. However, this behaviour is affected by gendered uncertainties about the appropriate time and place, along with the effects of cannabis, which in her story about the park became unmanageable. Uncomfortable feelings lead to alienation, both from the non-cannabis affected and from the other intoxicated people, and Dora felt misplaced, i.e. non-aligned, which she formulates as impropriety. In other words, propriety, i.e. respectability and value, is contrasted with an inappropriate rhythm, but it seems difficult to assess in advance what constitutes such a suitable rhythm, which can offer sustained decency.

When does an "evening", when cannabis use is a proper activity, start? How can one keep intimacy intact, i.e. how can one avoid sober participants? And how close can a person under the influence of drugs get to a family with children without losing their propriety?

6.2   Hiding

For a person under the influence of drugs, public space during the day, where the influence is illegal and stigmatised, can become a space where much is about hiding. The psychoactive substances can affect the expression of the body in different ways, creating "embodied deviance" that is visible from the outside (Campbell and Ettorre 2011). Such a body is marked by stigmatising beliefs, and the interviewees describe different strategies to counteract the drugs' effects that they know can become visible to others when someone is under the influence of the drug they have taken. Carolina's use of amphetamines, for example, made her hyperalert, and by extension the use of the drug produces a typical, nervous body language which she describes as a source of shame in the public domain. She contrasts this with the sense of freedom she experiences in other timed spaces where she can be left alone, and in yet other spaces where drug use is about social interaction.

I used to climb scaffolding a lot and go up to the roof. And sit or lie
there. For example. And then... so in these morning hours... between
three and five, because then it's so quiet, calm. It was like a parenthesis...
I mean, nobody else, there weren't many others awake, just me and the
birds and the city, and then you can walk around and move freely and
nobody's watching and so on, but as soon as the day starts to dawn again,
around six o'clock or so, and the morning traffic and morning people and
so on, then I become aware of reality and aware of the day, what I have
to do during the day, maybe have to get more so that I can go to work
or whatever. Or aware of... that people can see me. And see that I'm
under the influence and then I have to cover up and hide myself and
feel ashamed. But that particular time between three and five somewhere
there was always... a little, quiet freedom like that.

In my conversations with Carolina, she often returns to explaining that
she did not want to use amphetamines, but still did so almost daily for
eight years. This use became a solution to the anxiety problem that she
still lives with, now without using illegal drugs, but it was a solution that
she was ashamed of and did not want to continue. In other words, for
her, visible drug use was not only about the law and the stigmatising
view of others, but also about self-loathing related to her inability to
stop using the drug. Concealment, therefore, became an advanced and
demanding practice:

I didn't want anyone to see that I was under the influence. So I had a
few different tricks. Fake glasses, for example. That's good because then
you can't see the eyes so well. Er, cap. Cap and hat. But sunglasses are the
world's fucking dodgiest thing, it's ok if it's sunny, but then as soon as
you come in or the sun goes behind clouds, it's the world's dodgiest thing
to walk around with sunglasses. It looks so dodgy. Hehe. [laughs and
dramatises with her body] But such things. Maybe I could wear make-up
sometimes. Tanning in a solarium so you look a bit fresh.

The masking that Carolina describes was not about hiding the problematic behaviours associated with drugs, such as personality changes,
antisocial behaviour, violence or acute medical conditions. It was about
hiding enlarged pupils and the worn appearance caused by inadequate

nutrition and lack of sleep. Carolina perceives these as signs, in the environments where she wants to hide her use, of a person who uses drugs and is associated with problems, whether or not any problems have occurred. A body that shows such signs is not welcome in the workplace or in public spaces, but with a mask she can pass as a person who is allowed to be in these places. But it is not only the appearance of the body that must be hidden. The amphetamine's energising effect made it necessary for Carolina to act in reverse, to act tired among other tired people:

> Or also try to behave like the others, so you were like there, in the morning traffic and going somewhere, and everyone is sitting there and is so tired in the morning. Then I also tried to look so tired in the morning and yawned a bit, like [yawns]. Although I had been awake for a... day and wasn't tired at all, you still [yawn] try to blend in. Look at how others behave, because it was embarrassing if someone suspected something or said something.

Carolina's behaviour in the morning traffic shows that her concealment is based on a strong need to be an invisible and expected part of the rooms she is inhabiting. When she says that it would be "embarrassing" if someone suspected something, I interpret this not as being about the risk of being reported, but about the risk of being seen as a person whose alertness and lack of sleepiness could be due to drug use. This would signal an alienation and an intrusion by someone who deals with criminal and stigmatised people and products, but still insists on riding the bus to work with the morning-tired. Dora's statement that being under the influence of drugs during the daytime could be interpreted as not fulfilling one's duties and commitments has a reverse meaning for Carolina, who resorts to "tricks" to avoid being revealed as someone trying to fulfil duties and commitments under the influence. I ask if what she says means that she felt pressure to be perceived as not being under the influence of drugs even by complete strangers:

> Yes [...] Absolutely. And among people I knew, it was definitely like that, where you really had to lay it on and try to pretend like hell in the workplace when you arrived in the morning: "Uhh [yawns loudly] I'm so

fucking tired", and so on. Even though you absolutely weren't, or hadn't slept or something like that: "oh I've slept so well". So, all the time that lie and… the image that would… or if I went together with another knarkare who was like this, obviously a drug user. "Damn, how embarrassing [whispers], damn, how embarrassing, he's walking around here flapping and oh, I'm dying, how embarrassing".

In this quote, Carolina expresses the fear of being seen as someone who uses amphetamines, which for her means being someone who has failed to stop using amphetamines. This is true in public spaces among strangers, but also among people she knows who are not part of the contexts in which amphetamine use is accepted and creates cohesion. On the one hand, she follows a normative line that, in her stories, primarily takes her to and from various jobs and through them. The spaces crossed are public spaces and the restaurants in which she works, where the risk of expressing something that will reveal her is always imminent. At the same time, she reluctantly draws a line that deviates, moving through friends' and acquaintances' flats, parties and onto rooftops. There, the rules of the game are different and expressions of amphetamine influence are expected, or do not matter. It is as though she is pushed away from normative lines, and onto deviant lines, by feelings of impropriety. At times and in places where amphetamine use is not allowed, the price of accidental disclosure is high. Carolina felt ashamed, she was risking her job, her relationships and "getting caught" by the police. In short, her whole life situation was constantly at stake.

In other words, the rhythm of restraint and release in consumer societies may well include drugs. Marginalisation is not primarily about the drug's relationship to the law but about social context, time and place, and the fact that drug use can only be expected at certain times and in certain places. But women's drug use seems to be in constant danger of slipping beyond the narrow and elusive windows of the right time and place where use is permitted, and ending up off line, which means experiences of impropriety. The body in such improper places must be carefully monitored to avoid or limit harm, and drug use as a release can become a situation of intoxicated, strict restraint where what is at stake is human value.

References

Ahmed, Sara. 2006. *Queer Phenomenology: Orientations, Objects, Others.* Durham, NC: Duke University Press.

Ahmed, Sara. 2010a. *The Promise of Happiness.* Durham, NC: Duke University Press.

Ahmed, Sara. 2010b. Vithetens fenomenologi. *Tidskrift för genusvetenskap* (1–2): 49–69.

Ahmed, Sara. 2014. *Willful Subjects.* Durham, NC: Duke University Press.

Allebeck, Peter. 2007. Cannabis och schizofreni: Finns ett orsakssamband? [Cannabis and Schizophrenia: Is There a Causal Link?] *Socialmedicinsk tidskrift* 84 (1): 27–31.

Berridge, Virginia. 2013. *Demons: Our Changing Attitudes to Alcohol, Tobacco & Drugs.* Oxford: Oxford University Press.

Campbell, Nancy D., and Elizabeth Ettorre. 2011. *Gendering Addiction: The Politics of Drug Treatment in a Neurochemical World.* New York, NY: Palgrave Macmillan.

Hilte, Mats. 2019. Psychoactive Drugs and the Management of Time. *Sociologisk Forskning* 56 (2): 111–124.

Manrique-Garcia, Edison, Stanley Zammit, Christina Dalman, Tomas Hemmingsson, Sven Andreasson, and Peter Allebeck. 2012. Cannabis, Schizophrenia and Other Non-affective Psychoses: 35 Years of Follow-Up of a Population-Based Cohort. *Psychological Medicine* 42 (6): 1321–1328.

Månsson, Josefin. 2017. Cannabis Discourses in Contemporary Sweden: Continuity and Change. Diss., Stockholm University.

Nichter, Mimi, and Mark Nichter. 1991. Hype and Weight. *Medical Anthropology* 13: 249–284.

Skeggs, Beverley. 2012. Åter till frågan om respektabilitet: personvärdets moraliska ekonomi [Returning to the Issue of Respectability: The Moral Economy of Personal Value]. *Fronesis* (40–42): 64–83.

Svanström, Yvonne. 2000. *Policing Public Women: The Regulation of Prostitution in Stockholm 1812–1880.* Stockholm: Atlas.

Wilk, Richard. 2014. Consumer Cultures Past, Present, and Future. In *Sustainable Consumption: Multi-disciplinary Perspectives in Honour of Professor Sir Partha Dasgupta*, ed. Alistair Ulph and Dale Southerton. Oxford: Oxford University Press. Oxford Scholarship Online.

7

Behaving with Children

In the previous chapter, Dora described the presence of parents and children in the park as a disruptive factor, one that resulted in unease. Such a charged relationship between drugs and children is a recurring pattern in the interviews—most of the women describe children as the symbolic opposite of drugs. This is in line with Nancy Campbell's analysis of how drug use by women has come to be seen as something that is destructive of women's maternal instinct and as posing a threat to children (2000; cf. Du Rose 2015). How do the participants navigate children and drugs? This chapter analyses the strategies the women use to combine drug use with being women, who are traditionally positioned as responsible for children.

Boel illustrates the clash between children and drugs during a go-along interview that retraces the steps she took while using LSD one summer night. As we make our way through Malmö towards the modernistic Västra Hamnen neighbourhood by the sea, Boel eagerly recounts how she felt that night and reflects upon the way in which the hallucinogenic high affected her perception of both the city and her own body. Here is an excerpt from my field diary:

© The Author(s) 2024
E. Eleonorasdotter, *Women's Drug Use in Everyday Life*,
https://doi.org/10.1007/978-3-031-46057-9_7

She says that she wants to bombard herself with impressions when she uses drugs, and that this particular place was perfect: the views it offered "turned it into Disneyland". She bends down towards a manhole and takes a deep breath of the sulphurous air wafting from it. [...] She relives the emotions she felt that evening and straightens back up, spreading her arms and speaking with enthusiasm. "I wanted to feel my body! Hear myself breathe. Really feel that I'm a living organism."[1]

We pause on a street corner overlooking the ocean, just as she did that night, when she first received a text message and then a phone call from a friend who was awake, breastfeeding her child. She describes herself as "shocked" and what happened as a "full-on clash", reenacting the events by raising her eyebrows and staring at an imaginary telephone. The reasons they each had for being awake at the crack of dawn—one because of LSD, the other due to a newborn baby—led to their two different worlds intersecting. The child and the drug use met each other unexpectedly (although at a safe physical distance), yet still to shocking effect.

Angela's long and rambling account of a trip to Colombia in her youth is another example of someone unexpectedly encountering a child while they are under the influence of drugs. She tells me that she travelled to Colombia to study, but ended up bingeing on the endless cheap drugs the country had to offer. After a while, she realised that she could make a living selling marijuana to other students and tourists, so she put her studies on hold. The story becomes more fragmented as she describes how she began to use crack and moved in with someone with a shared interest in drugs. All of a sudden, however, she found herself staring at a child who stood out clearly against a blurred background:

Angela: And then I discovered, this was maybe a month into things, we were sitting in a circle... and watching boxing on the telly, and all the people around me were these fucking mafia blokes. [...] And the reason I discovered it was because there was this young boy serving us... And I reacted to the fact that he was a child. Who was there, serving these men, and I thought: whose child is this? Are there *children* living here? And then I realised it was their little, you know, sex slave. And I snapped

---

[1] All quotes in Swedish have been translated by me.

out of it then, like, shiiit – how did this happen?! [...] It wasn't about trying to, you know, save him, it was just about trying to get out of there myself.

Emma: You realised you wanted to get out of there?

Angela: I realised something had changed in my environment. Something had gotten really [bad], so slowly, that I hadn't even reflected on it. You know, crack cocaine, it makes you stop caring, stop reflecting on things, I think.

In Angela's story, too, the child is a symbol of a different world. His proximity affects her, more strongly than the crack cocaine itself does. In the above quote, she describes how she reacted when she first saw the child. Her reaction, she says, made her "snap out of" things, as though she was seeing her environment for the first time. The fact that there was a child in the middle of a drugs environment at first surprised her, then horrified her when she realised the child in question was also being sexually abused. This discovery in turn led to certain thoughts and reflections, and her own hurried departure. The problem that Angela outlines here is not so much about drugs' proximity to the child, but rather about the abuse the child is suffering in a context where she only then starts to feel like an outsider. In this way, the child represents a different world, a different collection of objects than the one she had slowly become accustomed to. She describes drugs as having enabled her to feel at home and let her feet sink into an environment to which she is a stranger once she wakes up and opens her eyes. In a sense, the crack in her body served as a material prerequisite to turn the space she was in into an extension of her body.

Jonas Frykman, drawing upon Mary Douglas' theory of dirt and purity (2002/1966), writes that taboos relating to the demarcation between one's own body and what is not the body are the strongest (Frykman and Löfgren 2019, p. 161). Viewing a space—an intimate space in which people use drugs—as an extension of the body can help us to understand why Angela's experience made her leave instead of trying to save the boy. To this day, more than 20 years later, there is anger and indignation in her voice when she remembers the event. She seems sickened by the fact that she herself was part of this space, which suddenly felt foreign to her. Her encounter with the child became an alarm bell that remains burnt into her memory, its ring warning her that she had to leave.

In certain situations, Angela and Boel are described as orientating themselves so that the worlds of drugs and children, or environments in Angela's words, are kept separate. When juxtaposed, these worlds can appear crystal clear, there can be a "total clash", as Boel puts it, which demands distance.

The above is a clash between symbols, which differs from situations in which relationships with children (in the sense of young human beings) are the focus. I asked the interviewees how they would reason about drug use in relation to their own or related children, even if no children were planned. I posed this question to gauge whether my interviewees' moral take on drug use would change if a (hypothetical) child were in the picture. On several occasions, the interviews took interesting and thoughtful turns at this point. I interpret this to mean that the moral weight of the issue requires more and/or different perspectives to be taken into account than those that were considered relevant in the case of the interviewees own drug use.

Katy has a stepchild who is in their teens, which means they might soon come across drugs in their social circle. She says that she feels it is up to her as the child's stepmother and someone who uses drugs herself to inform the child in a way that prepares them for such an event. Previously, Katy has described her knowledge of drugs and the knowledgeable company she keeps as being the factors that make her own drug use safe:

> *Katy*: [Me and] my friends, we know what we're doing, they're psychologists and doctors and they do their jobs, you know. [...]
> *Emma*: Do you think you'll stop using drugs at some point? If so, when?
> *Katy*: No. I don't think so. I've, we've talked about it in our social circle, because we're all in our forties now. Many of us have children, who're getting older... But I guess we've also talked about how damn nice it is. When we *do* do it. It's just too nice to quit.

However, when I ask her what advice she plans on giving her stepchild, she responds, to my surprise, by quoting her own parents:

I'll probably say what my own parents once said to me: "No one will force you to take anything; if you do [use drugs], you have to take responsibility for it." And "if a drug makes you feel bad, come home. No matter what you've taken. Because we're here for you."

How can it be that Katy, who has emphasised her experiential knowledge as a safeguard, says that she wants to follow the same lines in her own child-rearing as her parents, two people with no experience of drug use? Katy does not offer her experienced company when it comes to testing drugs. This means that, if the child chooses to use drugs, they will have to repeat the uncontrolled (disorientated) period that Katy herself went through before gaining her current knowledge.

We used to be like "God, we should be careful now" and… and now it's more like, you know, we know how we… we know how much to take, we know what it does to us, we know what the worst-case scenario is, things like that…

There is a discrepancy between the emphasis on safe drug use as a matter of knowledge: "[Me and] my friends, we know what we're doing", and concerns about what could happen, that is brought up once more in the case of children. There again, the one-way entrance to the *knarkträsk* threatens. Katy does not want to be responsible for leading a child to that entrance; she plans on telling her stepchild that it is all up to them. In the case of the child, it does not seem important whether the drugs are purchased and taken under the controlled conditions that Katy advocates for herself. It is not possible to know what drugs "does" to this particular child, and therefore, we do not know what "worst case scenario" could arise; in other words, what kind of entrance the child may become familiar with. On the other hand, Katy wants to make it possible for the child to come back home if things go badly, before they suffer an irreversible fall (down into the *knarkträsk*).

It would not be compatible with the appropriate behaviour of gender, age or social status for Katy to take an overly liberal approach to drugs in relation to children. She states that she has no plans to go into descriptions of the various drugs and their effects together with the child. This could have provided prior knowledge of the risks, but it might also have created curiosity. Instead, if the child decides to try drugs, they need to have these experiences on their own.

When I ask Thea the same question, she carefully considers how she would navigate the issue if she had a child. She starts by saying that she would never use drugs around her hypothetical child, referring to the hard time some of her friends had because their parents used drugs in problematic ways. She does not consider herself traumatised by her father's cannabis smoking, however, and guesses that she would probably "smoke weed" (cannabis) even if she had a child. Next, she reflects upon the consequences of not referring to real-life experiences when discussing the issue:

> I would still want to discuss it with the child, though. Precisely because I don't think it's helpful when it becomes this ghost, the way it is in Sweden today. It doesn't do anyone any good when there's no discussion, no rational discussion. Usually, it's all just "No! Danger. Danger. Danger." You know, "once you start, you're hooked, you'll end up on the streets." But then when they grow older, when they have to make certain decisions, when someone sooner or later offers them drugs... [...] If it's this massive taboo, the way people deal with the issue in this country, it can become a scary thing. But anything frightening and forbidden is always alluring... [pauses]

Thea's argument centres on how Sweden's abolitionist approach has turned drugs into something frightening, into a "ghost", that might make people feel inclined to try drugs, drawn to their fear. But the ghost metaphor simultaneously implies that we are talking about a figment of the imagination: something that might frighten us but will never pose any real danger. Thea puts her finger on a tricky question that I was forced to grapple with myself during my study: Does talking about them make drugs more or less appealing?

The minute we start discussing drugs, we draw them closer and raise awareness of their possible risks and benefits, but also to the fact that drug use is an option: the line between clean and dirty becomes blurred. Choosing to only discuss their drawbacks, as the Swedish authorities (and authorities elsewhere in the world) have historically done, is an attempt to ensure that illegal drugs remain distant and dirty (and illegal). But the abundance of films, books and songs that also portray the positive effects of drugs is a constant threat to their categorisation as dirt. Regardless of the strategy a parent adopts to guide their child through this land-scape, there *will* thus be risks, whether born of their familiarity or lack of familiarity with drugs.

Angela's tone is serious when she says that she tends to tell her children that "drugs are a struggle"—something she really wants the children to understand. By saying this, she is making it clear that drugs are not just about getting high and having pleasurable emotions: using them can also lead to discomfort and problems. She does not want her children to be fooled into thinking they can consume drugs without being prepared for what doing so might entail. As a mother who uses drugs, this is her way of taking responsibility. Her approach is based on an assumed prox-imity between children and drugs, rather than an attempt to keep the two apart. While Dora considered herself "out of place" when she was under the influence of drugs around young families, Angela gives us a drug-influenced insider perspective on young families, from her point of view as a mother. For her, drugs are not necessarily the polar opposite of work and obligations. On the contrary: to her, certain drugs and types of drug use (but not others) are prerequisites for being able to accomplish what she needs to in life.

When her children were very young, she says, there was a time when she was not doing well. This was followed by a period during which she used amphetamines and alcohol as "normalisers"—a word she uses to indicate that she felt better when she was under their influence and was able to function (cf. Sandell 2016) with their aid. She structured her use of these substances around the times when she had to drop off/ pick up her children from day care and take care of them herself. Drugs were thus a constant part of the rhythm between pleasure and sacrifice, between partying and obligation. She would spend the weekends that her children were not with her partying (and consuming large amounts of amphetamines and alcohol). Sleeping pills marked her transition to the following week. On weekdays, she would continue to use amphetamines, but in lower doses—"to be able to be a good mother". This rhythm of consumption was thus not about using or abstaining (cf. Wilk 2014), but about switching between different types of use. To Angela, these years were a good time in her life, a period that worked well—the only drawback being that her substance use was visible to others.

> You know, the kids saw that mummy was starting to feel happy again. Mummy had a life. Mummy was [facing the world?], it wasn't just all harsh reality, like. So, for me, it was perfect. [...] But then people told me you can't go out into the streets, it shows. [...] So that summer, I was forced to stay inside with the kids. Mio had just learnt to crawl [...] while I looked like a complete *pundare*.[2] So I had to stay at home, which wasn't great, but...

Here, the perception that "it shows" is reinforced because Angela's young children are with her, which makes the situation even less acceptable. When I meet her, Angela seems to have openly embraced what I would call a punk lifestyle, one that disregards propriety. There is a cigarette perpetually glued between her lips, she laughs unabashedly and is dressed in the typical black garb of a punk, her clothing frayed and carefully assembled. I interpret her words in the above quote as meaning that she would not have minded looking "like a complete *pundare*" at that time in her life, even during the day. But because the children were with her, she took her friends' advice to heart. She guessed that other people in her surroundings would be outraged if they saw her out and about with her children while she was on drugs. Her solution was to stay inside.

I interpret Angela's approach as based on her experience that drug use can be both pleasurable and problematic. It seems to me that she neither wants to withhold from her children the aspects of drug use she enjoys herself, nor keep her own use a secret from them. But that does not mean that she never worries about their relationship to drugs. She tells me that she has seen many others who used a lot of drugs struggle for long periods of time. This is why she warns her children not to heedlessly become involved in something they might end up struggling with. She also worries about how the authorities would react if they found out that

---

[2] A Swedish slang term for addicted person who uses amphetamine.

she—a mother—uses drugs. On one occasion, I ask her as diplomatically as I can whether she ever worries that she will lose custody of her children. She stiffens and does not immediately reply. Then, in a strained voice, she eventually responds in the affirmative, without elaborating. It is clear that this is not the first time she has considered the issue and that it is something she is concerned about.

Katy has a completely different attitude to children's place in relation to her own drug use. She makes it very clear to me that she never uses drugs around children, and illustrates how the conversation tends to go when she and her friends discuss whether or not to use drugs: "Are there any children around? No? All right. Who's buying?" In other words, there should never be any children in spaces in which drugs will be used. One reason why it can be inappropriate to have children around while under the influence of drugs is that being high can make it difficult (even impossible) to take care of others. Women in particular are not simply expected to steer clear of children while using drugs; they are expected to remain fully sober, so they can take care of the children (Wiklund and Damberg 2015). In general, women are expected to abstain from psychoactive substances that have visible effects; however, this does not apply to the kinds of substances they are prescribed just to get through the day (Dollar and Hendrix 2018; see also Ettorre 1992). Angela, for example, does not only buy amphetamines illegally but has prescriptions to use amphetamine-based medicines, as well as other controlled medications. Criminologist Natasha Du Rose describes the difference between these two types of drug use as a matter of lacking versus regaining morals:

> Legal drugs are prescribed to women by "experts" with medical authority to serve a normalising function as "coping mechanisms", but are constructed as deviant and immoral when self-administered. Women who use illegal drugs are considered irresponsible, irrational and selfish. However, once they comply with their drug use being administered through the medical profession within the treatment or criminal justice systems, regardless of the relative addictiveness or harmfulness of the drugs prescribed, their normality, rationality and responsibility is considered to be restorable. (2015, p. 62)

In terms of intoxication that is intended to relieve feelings of responsibility and duty, Measham describes the concept of "controlled loss of control" (2002, p. 359) as a planned loss of control within a certain framework. Time, place, drug, dosage, company and other conditions can be planned as a context in which a certain loss of control is permitted to occur. Taking responsibility for children, in such cases as Katy describes, is about planning a break from responsibility. In such situations, it would be irresponsible to be near any children, because their planned-for lack of responsibility presupposes freedom from the responsibility for children that women are expected to take when they are around. However, the loss of control could also mean that actions and experiences may be frightening or even dangerous for the child. Thus, not being close to children during drug intoxication may be related to caring for the child, while, conversely, using drugs in a way that is perceived to enhance motherhood may also be related to caring for the child.

If bodies are shaped by the objects around them (Ahmed 2007, p. 152), then Angela's children will be shaped by drugs. They might not necessarily actively focus on drugs, but they are expected to notice and be familiar with them. Drugs are part of the children's point of departure, their home, from which their lives unfold. Drugs thus become familiar objects, reference points for onwards orientation. Katy expects the children in her life to come across drugs, just as they will come across many other objects, but hopes that her stepchild will simply pass them by, ignoring them rather than approaching them the way she did. Either way, the child will never encounter both drugs and Katy at the same time, she says. As a result, drugs come to represent the foreign, the unfamiliar.

As I have shown, the interview material reveals that the women's sense of responsibility is at the centre of the charged relationship between drugs and children. Throughout, the women's different answers concern different ways of paying attention to and taking responsibility for children. Responsibility can be taken through a willingness to talk about drugs, like Thea, who thinks that children need to be able to take a stand, and by encouraging personal responsibility, as Katy does. In some situations, taking responsibility is expressed as a charged spatial issue, which may involve distancing one's own drug-affected body from children, as in the example of Katy. But responsibility can also be expressed as making sure that one is under the influence of appropriate drugs, as in the example of Angela. Due to the widely varying nature of drug use, and the motives for it—for example, for pleasure, social reasons or pain relief (Hilte 2019, p. 112), to feel like "a living organism" (Boel) or to "be a good mother" (Angela)—drug use can be either rejected or valued, but always in dialogue with strong notions of dirt and purity; that is, orders that have consequences for the shaping of constellations of children, women and drugs.

References

Ahmed, Sara. 2007. A Phenomenology of Whiteness. *Feminist Theory* 8 (2): 149–168.

Campbell, Nancy D. 2000. *Using Women: Gender, Drug Policy, and Social Justice*. Milton Park: Taylor & Francis.

Dollar, Cindy Brooks, and Joshua A. Hendrix. 2018. "I'm Not a Traditional Woman": Tranquilizer Misuse as Self-Medication Among Adult Women. *American Behavioral Scientist* 62 (11): 1562–1585.

Douglas, Mary. 2002/1966. *Purity and Danger: An Analysis of Concepts of Pollution and Taboo*. London and New York: Routledge.

Du Rose, Natacha. 2015. *The Governance of Female Drug Users: Women's Experiences of Drug Policy*. Bristol: Policy Press.

Ettorre, Elizabeth. 1992. *Women and Substance Use*. Basingstoke: Macmillan.

Frykman, Jonas, and Orvar Löfgren. 2019. *Den kultiverade människan* [The Cultivated Human Being]. Malmö: Gleerups.

Hilte, Mats. 2019. Psychoactive Drugs and the Management of Time. *Sociologisk Forskning* 56 (2): 111–124.

Measham, Fiona. 2002. "Doing Gender"—"Doing Drugs": Conceptualizing the Gendering of Drugs Cultures. *Contemporary Drug Problems* 29: 335–373.

Sandell, Kerstin. 2016. Living the Neurochemical Self? Experiences After the Success of the SSRIs. *Distinktion: Journal of Social Theory* 17 (2): 130–148.

Wiklund, Lisa, and Jenny Damberg. 2015. *Som hon drack: kvinnor, alkohol och frigörelse* [As She Drank: Women, Alcohol and Liberation]. Stockholm: Bokförlaget Atlas.

Wilk, Richard. 2014. Consumer Cultures Past, Present, and Future. In *Sustainable Consumption: Multi-disciplinary Perspectives in Honour of Professor Sir Partha Dasgupta*, ed. Alistair Ulph and Dale Southerton. Oxford: Oxford University Press. Oxford Scholarship Online.

8

Appropriate Drugs

"WE CAN'T STAND IT!" we say.
"I can give you diazepam," They say.
"HELP US," we say.
They are being ruthless and that outrages us.
(Johanna Gustavsson "We Are This Place or This Condition"[1] 2017,
p. 34)[2]

Orders of dirt and cleanliness based on time, place, context, class and gender are, as I have shown, fundamental elements of the women's drug use practices. But what role do the drugs themselves play in attitudes towards drug use? How are the boundaries drawn and what constitutes a legitimate drug use practice for the women? In this chapter, I examine

---

[1] *Vi är den här platsen eller tillståndet* (2017) is a book by artist Johanna Gustavsson which has also been performed as a "headphone show". It is based on one or two women who are alternately referred to as "I" and "we", and depicts a vulnerable, aggressive and violent form of drug use that simultaneously involves strong intimacy and solidarity. The book is a class-critical narrative focusing on the body and emotions from the perspective of drug use and marginalised living conditions.

[2] All quotes in Swedish have been translated by me.

© The Author(s) 2024
E. Eleonorasdotter, *Women's Drug Use in Everyday Life*,
https://doi.org/10.1007/978-3-031-46057-9_8

how the interviewees' various arguments can be understood in relation to the concepts of illness, health and personal responsibility, and to a society increasingly influenced by the possibility of altering states of mind with the help of psychoactive drugs.

8.1   Medicines

Most Swedes will be prescribed medication by a doctor countless times in their lives and will pick it up at a pharmacy: it is an entirely legal, everyday process. As I mentioned before, more women than men in Sweden use controlled psychiatric drugs, while the opposite is true for illegal drugs (CAN 2019; Swedish National Institute of Public Health 2010). In 2022, antidepressants alone were used by approximately 15 per cent of women in Sweden (Swedish National Board of Health and Welfares statistical database at socialstyrelsen.se). This might lead to the assumption that the interviewees would view the consumption of psychoactive prescription medication as a legitimate and appropriate practice, and that illegal drugs with the worst kind of reputation, like heroin and crack (cf. Petersson 2013, pp. 412f.), would occupy the other end of the scale. But the issue is more complex than that. Whether or not the women see drugs as legitimate depends on factors extending beyond legislation and medical science, their views can only be understood from a broader perspective. This section and the next discuss the interviewees' stances on medicines in relation to the concepts of sickness, health and personal responsibility, but also in relation to compliance and potential resistance.

I am sitting in a cafe with Angela on a sunny day, at a table overlooking Björns trädgård Park in Stockholm, discussing her relationship with the medication she takes. In a frustrated voice, she says:

> You can go along with it and feel like, because help is available, you're obligated to regulate yourself. They talk about it like there are solutions. Like you've been offered solutions and then it's up to you whether you... [inaudible].

Angela describes expectations that she will "regulate [her]self" with the help of medication and her own experience of feeling obligated to do so (cf. Boyd 2004; Du Rose 2015), mainly with reference to anti-anxiety sedatives and amphetamine-based products to relieve the symptoms of ADHD. When Angela claims that people expect her to regulate herself, I understand her as meaning a combination of a perceived sense of general expectations plus actual insistence by the healthcare professionals who treat her and the social workers she is in contact with because her children have disabilities.

The historian Nancy D. Campbell believes that women's use of different substances is met with the same expectations of adaptation that they are expected to display in other areas of life—that is: the expectation that they will use certain products to help them fulfil their duties, while simultaneously making sure their drug use never prevents them from carrying out those duties. Campbell writes that the extent to which women adapt themselves determines the rights they are granted:

> Women's rights depend on the degree to which women fulfill their responsibilities as contingent workers, consumers, and caretakers. Women purchase their autonomy at the price of good behavior and social conformity. (2000, p. 4)

Angela does not want to conform, as evidenced by both her distinctive style and her statements, but neither does she want to lose custody of her children. Her frustration with her medication is not rooted in any aversion to mood-altering substances and their effects as such; all her life, she has experimented with and used both prescription and illegal drugs. Nor does the way in which she views herself clash with the diagnoses she has been given—of ADHD, anxiety and depression. When I interview her, Angela often refers to these diagnoses, as explanations for why she has acted, acts and thinks in certain ways. Every once in a while during our conversations, she will mention her neural health, basing her analyses of herself on it and saying, for example: "yeah, so my brain, because I've got these autistic tendencies and stuff, that's why [...]". So Angela largely views herself as a neurobiological subject, yet feels reluctant to regulate herself with medication. Where does this resistance come from?

Sociologist Nikolas Rose (2003) argues that medicines such as those Angela describes being offered as a solution are psychiatric healthcare strategies that have become routine ways of rewiring humans' subjective capacities since the mid-twentieth century (cf. Campbell and Ettorre 2011). Rose portrays psychiatric, commercial medication as an integral part of a changed world, in which humans have come to understand themselves in new ways. He believes that a new ontology has emerged, based on the view that the brain is the centre of the self. He links this ontology to what he calls well-developed, liberal and democratic societies, which he says have turned into psychopharmacological societies. People in these societies (of which Sweden is one) now view themselves as neurochemical selves inhabiting a neurochemical world (Rose 2003, p. 46). Rose is critical of this increasing use of psychiatric medication, calling it an adaptation to the neoliberal and capitalist norms, values and assessments that he argues are embedded in these medicines (ibid., p. 59). Seeking the cause of mental health problems in individual brains makes people responsible for their own well-being, responsible for "regulating themselves" in Angela's words. This takes the focus away from circumstances such as class-related conditions and workplace stress. The fact that the cause of depression, for example, can be rooted in economic conditions, unreasonable working conditions or social conditions, he argues, is overlooked when the focus is on the treatment of brain chemistry (Rose 2003, 2019). Consequently, the cures offered are about balancing neurotransmitters or numbing emotional sensations through the intake of prescription drugs, while grief, stress and anxiety may be explained by the material and social situation. I will return to this criticism at the end of the chapter.

Another approach is presented by Skeggs, who uses the concept of "the optimizing interested self" (2004, p. 63) to demonstrate a valuable model of the self in a capitalist economy, which functions as a neoliberal subject. "The optimizing interested self" is a split self, which is both morally responsible for taking care of itself, and a rational model that understands its value on the market. The combination of an optimising interested self and a self that understands itself as a neurochemical subject provides a picture of what the expectations that Angela feels may look like. The self-regulation that she feels is expected of her is a requirement for achieving such a valuable self, which is internalised through expectations of taking responsibility. But this responsibility, Skeggs writes, cannot be taken by everyone.

> Self-regulation then is a matter of establishing a moral code under which the self can be assessed as being or becoming responsible. Forms of ethical conduct are a form of labour and governance imposed upon the self by the self. The self becomes obliged to "become" in a particular way: But all ways are not open to all, and some positions are already classified as in need of help, of being irresponsible, of having deficit culture, or of being pathological. (2004, p. 73)

So I take it that Angela understands herself, at least in part, as precisely a neurochemical subject within a discourse that locates the causes of thoughts, feelings, emotions and behaviours in the brain. Consequently, this means that she directs her efforts towards the brain, using psychoactive substances of various kinds when she wants to change her behaviour. But this does not mean that she unquestioningly accepts the medication prescribed for her. She does not aspire to the ideal of "the optimizing interested self". She proudly talks about her disability allowance and about risky and experimental adventures, relationships and parties. At the same time, she wants to be a good mum and feel good. Throughout the course of this study, Angela tells me about her anxiety, about going off her medication and then taking it again, reducing and increasing her dosage. Sometimes, she uses illegal drugs, and she drinks quite a lot of alcohol. I understand that, for her, the use of psychoactive substances is a legitimate practice insofar as its regulation is in line with her changing intentions, regardless of whether she has been prescribed the substances or not.

One interpretation of Angela's way of handling her substance use would be that these objects start to mean something to her when they appear along the lines she is following. Depending upon how they are encountered, and how they are experienced after she has ingested them, they mean different things. An encounter can give her the feeling that she is on the right path or a sense of disorientation. Ahmed writes:

> How does [...] "matter" matter? It is crucial that "matter" does not become an object that we presume is absent or present: what matters is shaped by the directions taken that allow things to appear in a certain way. (2006, p. 165)

Matter, according to Ahmed, becomes significant not by being, or not being, this or that object, but by the directions taken that allow things to appear in specific ways. For Angela, the meaning of the drugs and medicines is shaped by the directions, towards and through the drugs, that she sets out on her way forward. From that path, the drugs and medicines appear to be useful in different ways at different times. The perceived obligation to regulate oneself is contrasted, for example, with the possibilities of creating forbidden, intimate drug-use spaces with friends, as described in previous chapters. A person who has regulated themselves according to external instructions may not want to go to an all-night party, for example. Following a line through the medication prescribed by a doctor does not necessarily mean that she will get where she wants to go, where she feels orientated.

Angela has some trust in the health professionals who prescribe medicines and encourage her to use them. For example, she says:

> then they convince me that I [emphasises the remaining words] have to understand that not taking my medication hurts me more... than taking medication. That it wears me out to be, to feel bad.

However, the underlying theme of this quote is that Angela's ambivalence towards the drugs is also because she sees them as harmful, even though the healthcare staff say that it is even more harmful not to take them. Reluctance and ambivalence lead her to constantly make new decisions about whether or not to take the medicines she is prescribed, negotiations that are also ongoing during the interview period. This difficulty in deciding whether the drugs are good or bad for her health is an ambivalence she shares with many patient groups. Ethnologist Åsa Alftberg's study of older people's attitudes to medicines reveals similar anxieties, noting: "A medicine cannot be said to be *either* curative *or* harmful, it is *both* at the same time" (2015, p. 6, italics in original; cf. Derrida 1993).

This makes medicines a constant source of concern. Questions about the potential dangers and benefits of medicines, combined with increasing expectations that patients will take an active role in their own treatment, make for a challenging situation (Hansson 2007). Patients must weigh potential benefits against potential harms and hope that the decisions they make will lead to an improvement. In Angela's case, sometimes she sees illegal drugs as potentially better, at other times she takes greater or lesser quantities of her medicines than have been prescribed.

So how, then, can we tell what constitutes a medicine and what constitutes a drug? Where does one end and the other begin? While visiting the Sorgenfri medical centre in Malmö, I came across an information sheet that provides a picture of the healthcare sector's attempts to define (il)legitimacy (Berman et al. 2005). Patients are asked to fill in a run-of-the-mill form ahead of a blood test to check for vitamin deficiencies. The form includes the question: "Do you use any drugs?" and suggests that patients refer to the back of the page to determine which box they should check (yes or no). Under the title, "List of Drugs", the first half of the back of the page, cites a number of illegal drugs; the rest of the page lists a number of controlled drugs. "NOTE: NOT ALCOHOL!" is written in bold, capital letters immediately below the title. The lower half of the page provides an indication of how dividing controlled drugs into legitimate versus illegitimate substances requires the user to assess themselves by questioning their intention. According to the text, prescribed medicines become drugs if the patient takes them with the intention to "have fun, feel good, get 'high' or find out how [they] will be affected". But the text emphasises that pills do not count as drugs "if they were prescribed by a doctor and if the right dose is taken". A medicine could thus make a patient "feel good" without being considered a drug, but would turn into a drug if it was the patient's *intention* to "feel good".

Historian Virginia Berridge describes how such distinctions between intentions, linked to drug use, were already being made in the nineteenth century. The use of opiate-based drugs for the purpose of intoxication was then called "luxury use" (2013, p. 15). The concept of luxury use indicates that such use was perceived as non-essential, but as something that some people could indulge in. A psychoactive substance could thus be used to a greater extent than a medical condition requires, and thus have a different use. The medical centre's form, on the other hand, indicates that the substance *itself* changes when the intention is to experience effects beyond those intended. It becomes a drug, when it was previously a medicine.

Sara Ahmed uses the concept of "forness" to illustrate how an object can be defined by its use. She gives the example of birds laying eggs in a postbox, and how the laying of eggs turns what used to be a postbox into a nest.

> Something is what it provides or enables, which is how what something "is" can fluctuate without changing anything at the level of physical form. [...] To refer to something as a postbox is to refer to a use of a thing or even a use not a thing. (2019, p. 35)

Thus, to refer to something as a postbox is to refer to its use, which maintains the notion of the postbox in that it is used as a postbox. This, she says, can lead to confusion if that same postbox is used for something else that the shape allows it to be, such as a nest.

> Describing what something is for is a partial account of what it can be. *Forness helps reveal the partiality of an existence.* (2019, p. 35, italics in original)

In the case of medicines, the definition by use is as clear as a postbox. Medicines are for healing, while drugs are for drugging oneself. Thus, when the patient's intention was to be drugged, what were previously medicines become drugs, through the way in which they are used. But the medicine's function—its ability to cure, for example by helping someone who suffers from anxiety to feel better—and using that same medicine in an inappropriate way to "feel better", that is: drugging oneself, is not quite as different as a postbox and a nest. Whether a product is used to heal or to drug oneself, the outcome is confusingly similar, and this shifts the focus onto the person using it. A postbox is used by humans, while a nest in a former postbox is used by birds small enough to slip through the slot at the front. A *what* change can thus be a *who* change (ibid., p. 34). The person using the drugs must judge their character by employing the same judgement that determines what the intention of the drug or drug use was. Was it a medical patient or a drug user who used it?

I interpret the health centre's differentiation between terms as a way of absolving medicating patients of the stigma that drug use would entail. But this differentiation also shows that patients are forced to make a difficult choice, drawing sharp lines where the reality is blurred and fluid. Several of the controlled drugs that are listed, for example, are used precisely for anxiety, that is: to feel good. Patients like Angela need to ask themselves what their intentions are. It becomes a question of knowing who they themselves are in relation to feeling better, if they are to be able to determine whether or not the medicine was a drug according to the information sheet. Angela and several other interviewees are constantly navigating through these identity-creating fields of different behaviours and intentions that construct medicines and illegal drugs from the same materials.

There is also a large and growing interest in the alternative use of currently illegal medication, and investigations are being conducted into whether what are now considered drugs could have a different "forness" than drugging. In Sweden, and around the world, research on psychedelic drugs is ongoing. For example, the hallucinogenic club drug Ketamine is attracting interest due to its potential usefulness as a cure for depression (Tiger et al. 2020; Kvam et al. 2021). At the same time, MDMA, LSD, and psilocybin mushrooms are being researched as potential cures or aids in diagnoses of such conditions as post-traumatic stress disorder, depression, anxiety and addiction (Brown 2023; Liechti 2017; Lundgren 2023). Altogether, such uses construct a thicket of non-intoxication-motivated uses of drugs, which are usually sold illegally, and narcotic and prescription medicines, where their "forness" runs counter to use as temporary opportunities for release and (potentially controlled) loss of control. Instead, their use is aimed at functioning in society (cf. Sandell 2016). How, then, does the orientation between and through these substances take place?

Alftberg discusses the concept of "poor adherence" (also called "poor compliance"), a term used by the healthcare sector. She problematises it as a "normative term that highlights the relationship between the ideal and practise, that is: the relationship between the doctor's prescription and how the drugs are handled by the individual who uses them" (2015, p. 4). The concept thus focuses on the direction indicated by the doctor and the patient's propensity to follow it.

From the healthcare sector's point of view, as well as that of the law, Angela's consumption could be described as "poor adherence". The lines she follows are based on directions that are progressively pointed out, sometimes in line with healthcare instructions, and sometimes not. But while her adherence may be poor, it is not non-existent.

A Troublesome Brain

From time to time, Angela takes the doctor's recommendations to heart. She sometimes tells me when we meet that she is drinking alcohol in moderation, taking her medication and staying away from drugs. However, she often describes having anxiety. In those moments, she views her body as "troublesome", to use Signe Bremer's words (2011, pp. 43ff.). Bremer uses the term "troublesome body" in her study of transgender individuals, in the sense of bodies that do not fit into the expected templates of the healthcare system. She uses it to illustrate how, for example, masculine-coded body lines on a person who perceives herself as a woman can be difficult to recode. The body can be perceived as refusing to allow itself to be recoded by means of clothing, for example. In such cases, Bremer explains that it can lead to the healthcare investigators who make decisions about gender reassignment not perceiving the person who wants such reassignment as credible (ibid., p. 103).

The concept of "troublesome bodies" highlights body parts that the patient wishes would follow prescribed lines, but do not. The body thus goes against both the patient's wishes and the healthcare system's expectations of how it should be expressed. "By defying normalisation and at times refusing to do what we want, [the body] makes trouble" (ibid., p. 45). In my own research, I have discerned a neurological troublesomeness in people whose treatment plans failed to regulate their brains. Angela has a brain that does not react to medication in the way it should:

it "defies normalisation". Sometimes, medicines do not make her feel better. I interpret her words, quoted near the beginning of this chapter, as expressing a sense of guilt for failing to adjust her dosage until everything is all right: "you've been offered solutions and then it's up to you". Often, it is Angela's very attempts to fix the shortcomings of her medical treatment that lead her down crooked paths. Her goal is always the same: to feel good, in different ways. Yet she also wants to quit her medication. When it does not work, she walks away from it; when it does, she finds herself facing a paradox. I ask her about her recurring decisions to quit her medication, to which she replies: "When I stop taking my medication, I often do so because I… maybe… yes, because I… you know, I feel good".

From a bodily point of view, it does not make sense for her to take medication that might harm her when she is feeling good. In the same vein, Alftberg describes how the potential dangers inherent in medication versus its ability to heal creates tension for its users, who begin to notice the way their body reacts to it:

> One therefore constantly monitors one's body, and symptoms and sensations outside of the ordinary cause one to focus on the medication and its impact on the body. The body and the prescription are thus sometimes pitted against each other, with the individual forced to decide which he or she should heed and act on: the experiences of one's own body or the medical prescription. (2015, p. 4)

Alftberg reveals that approximately half of all patients who are long-term medication users do not use their medication in the way that was recommended. This means that "poor adherence" is a common problem. In Alftberg's quote, as well as in Angela's statements, a line that runs through the body is visible, a line that is able to eclipse the doctors' guidelines, and then she can think about using the medicines again. Her reluctance to take medication, therefore, also seems to be related to the link between these medicines and deficiency states. Introducing medicines into the body to remedy a deficiency becomes an option when she has previously given up those medicines and feels bad, but their use clashes with experiences of feeling good and being healthy and thus complete. Karin

Johannisson writes: "To be ill is to allow feelings of weakness and inadequacy. It is to establish a language between the body, the self and society" (1995, p. 8). As in Alftberg's study, the language established between body and self focuses on risk and health, but in Angela's case, I interpret the focus as being on how communication with the third party, society, is experienced. The medication becomes a way for society to tell Angela what she needs, and she resists this. At times, she tries the prescribed line, and at other times she stakes out her own. Angela questions the ability of medication to bring about and maintain sanity when the drugs are in her body, both when she is well and when she is not. Her attempts to take control of her own well-being with medicines in varying doses and with illegal drugs take on an experimental character, resisting compliance.

Madelene also finds herself in a similar situation of disbelief, hope and alternating adherence and non-adherence to prescribed drug treatments. When she lists the drugs she has been prescribed to alleviate depression and reduce anxiety, the list is long. They include various SSRIs[3] for depression, but also several drugs, opiate-based and variants of benzodiazepines, to reduce anxiety. These are classified as highly addictive and can also cause fatal overdoses. When I ask her how it is possible that she could have received these drugs, which should only be prescribed with "caution" (see fass.se[4]), she replies:

How did I get it? It's so easy. I get exactly what I want. [...] or I didn't ask for it. It was suggested after a burnout. Which I had.

When I question the high dosages she is on, she says:

But he always adds "SIC" to my prescription, you know, you know, that you can exceed.

---

[3] Selective serotonin reuptake inhibitors, see **Appendix**.

[4] The Swedish site fass.se contains prescribing and patient information for licensed medicines and is comparable to medicines.org.uk (UK) and www.usp.org (USA). Information about how opioids and benzodiazepines should only be prescribed with caution is presented right next to the name of the drug, when searching, for example, on Xanor (Xanax in the USA), one of the medications Madelene uses [2023-08-08].

By "SIC", Madelene is referring to her doctor adding a specific abbreviation to her prescription to allow for large withdrawals that exceed the recommendations for controlled drugs. When I express surprise at the number of drugs prescribed to her—she says there were 27 at one point—she replies:

> Yes. I don't know if they used me as some kind of guinea pig or something but, they didn't work. I tapered them off [incrementally decreased her dosage to zero] myself all the time, so that, it was just, madness.

Madelene's case puts the term "poor adherence" in a different light. In Angela's case, the prescribing of drugs appears to be part of treatment plans (even when they do not work), based on caring purposes, but Madelene specifies so many drugs that the prescribing doctor's prescriptions do not appear to be guidelines. Instead, the doctor's adherence comes to the fore when she says: "I get exactly what I want". If her statement is true, the doctor's legitimacy can be questioned. Madelene describes the way in which she tapers off her medication of her own volition as a responsible way of navigating an uncontrolled number of prescribed medicines, but also of navigating towards illegal drugs, like the heroin she uses.

Thus, Angela and Madelene do not take responsibility for their drug use by following the doctor's instructions to the letter, but by using their own bodies as their point of departure to experience and judge their use. However, feeling good does not mean that their use stops; instead, their use may have other intentions than addressing deficiencies, as medicines and drugs also have the potential to elevate states of mind in various ways. Conversely, illicit drugs may consist of the same active substances as medicines, and thus be used for curative or "regulatory" purposes. This also applies to some substances that are never, or very rarely, prescribed as medicines in Sweden, such as LSD and cannabis. So what is the role of such illegal use in the women's lives, and how does it relate to other kinds of drug use?

8.2   Drugs as Medication

That people are, in Angela's words, "obliged" to take personal responsibility for their lives and health is a neoliberal ideological paradigm (Gilbert 2008; Campbell and Ettorre 2011; Du Rose 2015). One aspect of this paradigm is using medicines as prescribed, another is not using illegal drugs. Someone who does not conform to this paradigm can be viewed as belonging to a group that puts its health at risk. In a report on socioeconomic differences in drug use, the Swedish Public Health Agency links this group to disease and death:

> Drug use increases the risk of harm from both a medical and a social perspective. Both morbidity and mortality rates are much higher among drug users compared to the general population. (Public Health Agency 2021, p. 11)

In other words, using illegal drugs is presented as an act that is diametrically opposed to taking responsibility for one's own health. Some people who use drugs contest this juxtaposition, claiming that it is precisely because they take responsibility for their own health that they have approached illegal drugs. The global battles over whether cannabis should be legal or not often involve such arguments. For example, Nanne says: "from the time I started smoking pot [cannabis] when I was 18 until I got pregnant, I was almost never sick". On another occasion, she triumphantly announces over the phone that her doctor said it should be illegal *not* to recommend CBD oil for pain management. In these statements, she takes a stand in favour of the medical use of cannabis preparations, with her doctor vouching for the oil. She contrasts this with the side effects she experiences from prescription opioids and other painkillers. She describes some of the drugs she has tried as having unpleasant effects: "Uneasiness, fatigue, stomach ache, cramps and just no! It just feels wrong in the whole body". When Nanne talks about cannabis and the prescribed medicines, she emphasises the terms "chemical" and "natural" as distinguishing markers for artificial preparations and plant extracts or plant-based preparations, such as marijuana and CBD oil. It is clear that "natural" for her has positive connotations (cf.

Lindgren 1993). Looking at it that way, the combination of human plus psychoactive substance can be interpreted as human plus nature, while introducing artificial products into the human body is a clearer embodiment of human + technology: a half-dead, half-alive technobody, a cyborg with monstrous features (Preciado 2013, pp. 44f.).

The latter stands in contrast to a natural, namely herbal, aid that helps the body to function. Nanne is open about her use of CBD oil to relieve pain—something that is not, in fact, illegal in Sweden. Legislatively, CBD oil is a grey area, as Sweden's Medical Products Agency has ruled that it is usually a medicine rather than a foodstuff, but medicines may only be sold if their efficacy has been proven by peer-reviewed studies.[5] When I ask if there is anyone she would not want to tell about her use, she laughs cockily and says: "No, I write [about it] on Facebook directly". As mentioned earlier, she also argues in favour of using THC-containing cannabis, even though she no longer uses it herself. I read a pride in her alliance with the natural world.

Even though there has not been quite as vocal a pro-cannabis movement in Sweden as, for example, in the USA, where many states have legalised medical marijuana, Nanne is not alone in believing cannabis to be therapeutic. In one notorious case from 2014 to 2015, Swedish tattooist and young father Jens Waldmann was charged with and found guilty of growing and using marijuana to treat his chronic depression. He was given a conditional sentence with community service, but has since continued to advocate for cannabis use, considering a career as a "cannabis influencer" (Höglund 2021). Like Nanne, Waldmann contests the belief that a healthy lifestyle as a member of a well-functioning society would not be compatible with the particular kind of drug use he would like to engage in. Waldmann compares himself without cannabis—someone who is depressed and cannot function, who only wants to sleep and is unable to work, regardless of whether he takes the benzodiazepine sedatives his doctor has prescribed him—to a well-functioning marijuana smoker who has no problem working and sleeping. Waldmann's final words in a pre-trial interview with *Jnytt*, the

---

[5] See "Cannabidiol – CBD" (only in Swedish) on the Medical Products Agency's homepage, lakemedelsverket.se, for up-to-date information [2021-02-25].

online version of local newspaper *Jönköping Nu*, were: "I just wonder what society would gain from me going to prison…" (Johansson 2014; see also Foltmar Elfton 2014).

Neither Nanne nor Waldmann questions the paradigm of taking responsibility for one's own health: what they want is to create new distinctions within that paradigm. They compare responsible personal drug use to other types of use. In the *Jnytt* article, Waldmann calls himself "a normal, functioning human being and parent" who is afraid of "being written off as a junkie" and "lumped together with addicts" when he goes public with his use. His goal, in other words, is not to question the stigma attached to "junkies", but rather to redraw the boundaries of the concept itself. He argues from a socioeconomic perspective, focusing on health and the image of a well-functioning human being who happens to also use cannabis—the opposite of the junkie. Waldmann says that he is ill but that cannabis makes him better, not that it turns him into a junkie. In other words, both Nanne and Waldmann prefer cannabis to the medication offered by doctors, for the sake of their own health and thus also for the good of society.

But while cannabis is hotly debated in the media, other debates are drawing different lines between medicines and harmful drugs.

Illegal Chemicals

The discourse on cannabis as a natural rather than a chemical medicine is just one of many blurred lines when it comes to the healing properties of illegal drugs. Boel, who, like Angela and Madelene, uses drugs both to function and to lose control, distrusts the SSRIs she has been prescribed for depression. She says:

> I once got a prescription for Zoloft [a common SSRI] about twelve years ago. Felt like crap and quit three days later. "What is this shit?" They went: "Yeah, but here are five other meds to counter the side effects." I don't have to deal with that when I buy MDMA.

She not only questions her medication's ability to help her, but also raises its side effects as a negative factor. Medicines are thus portrayed as both bad and harmful, and their side effects, in turn, serve as starting points for increased medication needs. But Boel's arguments are not about chemistry. She sees MDMA, which, like SSRIs, is produced in a lab, as more effective than SSRIs and free from side effects. I ask her what her take is on consuming chemical products.

> it depends on the way you look at it, whether you view the chemical as something that contaminates your body. Then it's an attitude. Then it ruins the effect of the chemical. The way I see this chemical is just that it stimulates other chemicals in my body, makes them react in a certain way.

So Boel sees MDMA as a chemical product that stimulates substances that are inherent to her body, which is different from how she views SSRIs. What she calls "an attitude" could also be described as her bodily starting point, from which she then embarks upon a journey in a certain direction. Her use of SSRIs is part of a system, in which she needs to submit to being labelled ill and being prescribed whichever medicines her doctor selects for her. MDMA, on the other hand, is something that she—who is capable of committing a crime and getting in touch with the drug market—buys herself. The line she draws is based on the attitude that she does not need anyone else, and differs from another line she finds less appealing: allowing herself to be labelled and medicated.

Submission to control and responsibility for self-monitoring, Skeggs argues, is fundamental to how class has been constructed historically and how class positions continue to be defined (2004, p. 178). The ideal "optimizing interested self" is expected to be in control of itself and has to manage its resources in a way that strengthens its individuality. So Boel defines her class by making her own assessment as a healthy and rational person, and thereby avoids the control to which she would have been subjected as part of a pathological group (Skeggs 2004, pp. 10, 20, 73ff.).

MDMA can also be intoxicating, producing hallucinations and feelings of euphoria (Iversen 2012). This could be another reason why Boel feels MDMA serves her better than SSRIs, which do not have any intoxicating effect. However, even if illegally acquired products did not get her high, Boel would still rather use them to be able to cope with work when she feels bad. She tells me about the way she handled a difficult period by taking micro-doses of ecstasy.

> *Boel*: I've micro-dosed both ecstasy and acid [LSD]. I micro-dosed ecstasy last winter, when I was completely swamped at work. And I was forced to keep my shit together even though everything was falling apart. [...] One of my colleagues was fired, my boss had a breakdown, and I had to take on both of their jobs. And become, like, my own colleagues' boss. And, I went home and cried. [Sad voice, thinking back] And then I realised like, okay, how am I going to do this? [Happy, hopeful voice] I'll micro-dose.
>
> *Emma*: Okay. Did it work?
>
> *Boel*: Yes! It went really well.
>
> *Emma*: Which worked better?
>
> *Boel*: E [ecstasy]. Definitively. For sure. Acid makes you a bit more withdrawn. [...]
>
> *Emma*: How much is a micro-dose then, give or take?
>
> *Boel*: Hard to say with E. [...] I crushed it, into extremely small pieces. Tiny, tiny, tiny, just such small bits it was like... dust.
>
> *Emma*: But it still had an effect on you?
>
> *Boel*: Mm. Absolutely. It stops you from... from being so easily thrown off. I became a little more stable.
>
> *Emma*: All day long?
>
> *Boel*: All day long.

Boel thus describes how micro-doses of ecstasy, in portions so small that she describes them as grains of dust, helped her during working days when she was under great pressure. The route she chooses, which becomes an embodied experience, from the acquisition to the end of the working day, is different than if she had chosen to go to a doctor for help with stress management. The who-question is thus linked to the what-question, even though the "forness" of the substances, to address depression, may be the same. The deviant line does include breaking the law, but she is never identified as sick and copes with her workload as a "stable" and capable self. The chaotic working conditions, under the influence of an illegal grain of dust, cannot disturb her. In other words, illegal drugs become preferable according to the neoliberal paradigm of taking responsibility for one's own health.

Performance Enhancers

Healing or drugging (in the sense of wanting to become intoxicated in a way that does not increase one's self-control) are thus not the only two possible "fornesses" of medicines and drugs. The "forness" that Boel calls micro-dosing refers to the way in which certain psychoactive substances can be used as cognitive performance enhancers, also called nootropics. This is a "forness" that has an unclear boundary with medicines. Is it a deficiency that is being corrected, or something that enhances a completely healthy person's ability? What do illness and health mean? A fourth "forness" in turn complicates the boundaries between intoxication and performance enhancement. Pernilla describes the effect of amphetamines and cocaine when she is out dancing: "you become awake in a different way, it's more like a heightened reality in some ways". When the intention of drug use is to sharpen the senses in a pleasurable, intoxicating experience, the difference between what could have been helpful for pilots flying long distances, for example (Iversen 2012), and what is taken for pleasure, is the difference between a performance-enhancer and a drug. Again, the change in *what* also becomes a change in *who*. Is it a worker or a party-goer who is using the substance?

According to some researchers, drugs that can increase concentration, boost self-esteem, reduce fatigue and/or create other changes are becoming increasingly popular as cognitive performance enhancers (Schifano et al. 2022; Lanni et al. 2008).

As problems are increasingly treated with psychopharmaceuticals—in Sweden, prescriptions for antidepressants increased by 32% between 2010 and 2022 (Swedish National Board of Health and Welfare's statistical database at socialstyrelsen.se)—even people without any documented psychological issues have become interested in enhancing their brain functioning. Products used to improve performance include prescription-free herbal remedies sold at health stores, medicines prescribed to patients with established concentration difficulties (including amphetamine-based or amphetamine-like products like Ritalin, Concerta, Medikinet and Elvanse, among others), illegal drugs such as micro-dosed LSD or ecstasy, and amphetamines, either illegally produced or prescribed by a doctor but then sold on to others seeking to stay awake for many hours, for example (Lanni et al. 2008; Ragan et al. 2013). Antidepressant medication too, like SSRIs, can be seen as performance-enhancing, because it can improve well-being and boost performance, for example by improving concentration and regulating sleep, even if that person is not suffering from depression (Lanni et al. 2008).

Lanni and her co-authors conclude their review of different studies on the (often dubious and/or unresearched) cognitive effects on healthy people of both legal and illegal substances with a rather agitated appeal. They suggest that researchers embrace the possibilities of pharmaceuticals to modify people's mental capacities and conduct more research in the area.

> Perhaps it is time to face with an open mind the fact that our mental abilities are at least in part based on biochemical reactions amenable to pharmacological modulation. If we are willing to benefit of this possibility without harm, serious researches and study programs under the Control of national research agencies have to be implemented in this field. (pp. 209–210)

These researchers argue that, because the use of performance-enhancing drugs is already so popular—despite the uncertainties of a poorly controlled legal market and an even less controlled illegal market, and despite the fact that the little research that has been done has often shown questionable results—research institutions need to take responsibility and pave the way for a regulated market.

Ragan et al., who conducted a review of studies examining the prevalence and efficacy of various substances used for performance enhancement, disagree with Lanni et al.'s argument. They argue that neither the extent of people's use nor the effects of performance enhancers have been sufficiently investigated to conclude that their use is widespread and increasing. In addition, they argue that the risks associated with cognitive enhancement drugs make it unlikely that research institutions would invest in the ethically controversial development of drugs that do not serve a medical purpose (Ragan et al. 2013, p. 592).

The claim that even people without a diagnosis might be very interested in cognitive modification is in line with Rose's theory that humans view themselves as neurochemical beings who have adapted themselves to a neoliberal world order (2003). Lanni et al. appear to want to present this new subjectivity as a reasonable starting point for the scientific community's future research. But the very fact that people's mental capacities can be chemically altered leads to existential questions about human beings' relationship with their bodies. To what extent can psychoactive substances be added to the body without "taking over"?

In her cyborg manifesto, Donna Haraway posits the post-humanistic idea that technology does not have to be scary and coercive: it could instead be a prerequisite for subversive opposition to the neoliberal order (1991, pp. 149ff.). She writes that we do not need to either dominate or deify technology because it is already part of our bodies, part of what it means to be human.

A cyborg body is not innocent [...] Intense pleasure in skill, machine skill, ceases to be a sin, but an aspect of embodiment. The machine is not an it to be animated, worshipped, and dominated. The machine is us, our processes, an aspect of our embodiment. (ibid., p. 180)

If the drug-using body is interpreted as a cyborg—part human, part technology—among other cyborgs who do not know what it means to be human in any other way than in symbiosis with technological solutions, then the use of psychoactive drugs does emerge as a possible adaptive tool in line with a neoliberal world order. Amphetamines as a tool to stay awake and make it easier to endure monotonous tasks can, for example, facilitate night work and long working days (Iversen 2012), or make it easier to clean the house (Campbell 2000). At the same time, using medical technology could be an act of resistance: a way of trying to stretch the cyborg's limits and expand its capacities, rather than submissively adapting to life in a neoliberal world. Haraway compares the cyborg's technological features to potent growths on injured bodies:

For salamanders, regeneration after injury, such as the loss of a limb, involves regrowth of structure and restoration of function with the

constant possibility of twinning or other odd topographical produc-
tions at the site of former injury. The regrown limb can be monstrous,
duplicated, potent. We have all been injured, profoundly. We require
regeneration, not rebirth. (1991, p. 181)

Haraway calls the desire for rebirth a hopeless and sentimental longing to
return to a state that never existed. The subversive power is instead found
in regeneration, in rebuilding the body from its broken condition. This
is an optimistic perspective on neurochemical creatures' potential in a
neurochemical world: while Rose's Foucauldian analysis paints a picture
of patients in the hands of the psychiatric care apparatus, Haraway gives
the guilty, monstrous cyborg, the medicating patient–subject, a power of
action based precisely on its fusion with technology.

Rose sees the neurochemical world as a framework that determines
the conditions under which subjects can understand themselves. Still,
he argues that a freer psychiatric healthcare apparatus, in which patients
have a greater say and care is largely provided within patient groups,
would reduce demand for medication (2019, p. 186). But I perceive
his description of people as neurochemical subjects as contradicting his
claim that—as long as conditions, that is: the world, remained unal-
tered—patients would not want as many psychoactive substances if they
were able to decide for themselves. Boel's narrative, as well as those
of Angela, Madelene and Nanne, instead depicts a cyborg-like way of
managing feelings and moods through drugs and medicines. Life sometimes brings these women anxiety and pain, but they also derive pleasure
from their ongoing experimentation with different doses and products.

Researchers who advocate acceptance of humankind's opportunities to
enhance its cognitive functioning through psychoactive products because
they believe there will always be a craving for these products reflect
Haraway's cyborg theory. But, while the benefits referred to in the article
by Lanni et al., such as improved concentration and increased alertness,
are predictable and in line with a neoliberal paradigm, there is an unpre-
dictability in the potential of the monstrous cyborg. The "forness" of
products can be multifaceted.

8.3   Legitimate Hedonism

Some interviewees refrain from using anything that could have any kind of curative and/or performance-enhancing effect. When I ask Pernilla whether she will be using performance enhancers in her new job, she answers with a slightly indignant laugh: "Fuck that [laughs], I'm not going to drug myself for work. I only do that for pleasure". By saying this, she signals that she is healthy and does not need anything to "fix" her. She considers drugs a supplement that do not prevent her from living her life, as long she only consumes them on carefully selected occasions. She does not perceive the drugs she takes (mainly marijuana, amphetamines and cocaine) as health-promoting but as something that should only be used by a person who is healthy to begin with. This is also why she does not intend to "drug [herself] for work". I interpret her statement as a political critique of a society in which people put their health on the line for the sake of their careers by striving to attain the ideal of "the optimizing interested self" (Skeggs 2004, p. 63).

For Pernilla, drug use becomes legitimate not because it functions as medicine; rather, she justifies it by asserting a healthy but risk-taking position. She links drug use with risks of physical and psychological harm, as well as relationship issues and dependency. Agnes, who enjoys amphetamines, also gives examples of how she adopts a conscious, risky position when she uses drugs: "your heart can stop beating and, the risk of schizophrenia is really high with amphetamines. [...] your coronary artery can be torn, off [...]". For these women, taking drugs means subjecting themselves to something that could make them ill and therefore requires a healthy and responsible user.

Boel takes an approach that occupies a mobile position between those of Nanne, Pernilla and Agnes. For Boel, the drugs she uses (mainly MDMA and LSD) are both harmful and curative. She says that the daily micro-doses of MDMA have gotten her through difficult periods at work due to their medicinal properties, but that drugs also serve as an aid to "let go of control" and take a break from high-performance work. Thus, depending on the situation, she, like Angela, uses them both in order to be a more effective part of society and to revolt against it. She emphasises even more clearly than Pernilla that she sees herself as a strong person who can cope with drug use, and finds several ways to develop what it means to be a person who is neither a junkie nor in medical need of a curative substance, but rather a person who is capable of using a drug even though it might be dangerous. In the following excerpt, she describes both the kind of people who are suitable and the kind who are unsuitable to do drugs with, explaining that this suitability depends on whether someone takes drugs to fix a problem or to complement who they already are.

> The right company is people who are not afraid of themselves. [...] If they have a lot of issues and can't even handle a beer, there's no point in sitting there when they start taking other things. If they have a hard time at work, they have a hard time at home, so you know they're not going to be comfortable. They're going to be really annoying. [Thinks] Those people can often lose their footing a little in this nice feeling.... Or they discover the difference between their reality and this [drug buzz], and then they lose it. I... prefer to... be around people who just think everything about them is enhanced. "I become more of me and my surroundings become more of what they are."

Thus, for Boel, it is about being healthy enough to handle drugs. If neurochemical subjects are required to manage their feelings with the help of psychoactive drugs, then the drug-using company that Boel avoids is described as having added something inappropriate when drugs are taken with a "forness", i.e. evokes a sense of "feeling good", when life without the drug is difficult. According to Boel, the cyborg should not replace something that is missing, but only desire more of what already exists. For her, "having a hard time" is a bad reason to get high. Yet, having a hard time might actually be a powerful incentive for a person to want to change the way they feel; some might even see it as an obligation to, as Angela puts it, "regulate oneself". This results in a catch-22: those with the strongest desire to alter their state of mind are seen as unfit to use certain drugs.

Ahmed writes about the word "use": how objects can be considered useful, such as doors and chairs, but in fact address a limited group, namely the people who have a suitable form and functionality to use those objects (2019, pp. 57ff.). Those who are unable to use the chairs and doors become "misfits", they do not fit into the environment. In Boel's description, the usability of drugs is limited to those who are mentally fit to use them, which seems difficult for potential users to determine since those who have a great need to alter their minds must refrain. Once a drug has been used, the person who used it reveals themselves to be "comfortable" or a "misfit" within the group. Thea's analysis is similar to Boel's; in a discussion about the hallucinogenic LSD, she says that she too feels it is inappropriate for someone to use drugs when they feel bad. But her story is based on her own experiences of discomfort and the way in which she herself takes responsibility.

> you reinforce things in yourself, that's what I mean, that's why I'm precise and careful and cautious when I take something. Because, it can reinforce something bad. If you're not stable and you feel bad, then it becomes difficult. The last thing you should do is take LSD or something, then you get one of those, monsters. Like your brain is on fire.

To prevent LSD from conjuring up monsters and setting the brain alight, the starting point must be stable when taking it. For Thea, such a starting point is about temporary states of mind when she perceives intake as appropriate, and the ability to use drugs in a rewarding way is about being able to judge when such occasions occur. Instead, Boel describes how she gets through unpleasant experiences by embracing them, and the ability to handle drugs is described as a permanent feature:

> I never lose it in the sense that, like, I become one of those people who just want to flee [...] On the contrary, I want to stay even more and really get into things. When I'm in it, I really want to know, feel that, I want to soak up all the beauty right where I am, sort of. And I want to see things just as they are, even the ugly, the awful – fuck, if it's awful I want to face that it's awful.

Boel describes herself as someone who is unswayed by the shifts in the high of the drug from beauty to ugliness, reality to euphoria. In such representations, a weak person who feels worse by using drugs is contrasted with an image of a strong and capable drug-using person. To be fit to use drugs, someone who uses them needs to be in such good health that they can handle something that could harm others. They exist at the far end of a scale that ranges from the vulnerability of a junkie to something that, in Boel's description, resembles invincibility. Thea, on the other hand, suggests that the ability to avoid vulnerability is more about being able to determine whether one is sufficiently invincible from the start to be fit for drug use.

8.4   Responsibility for Oneself

But are they really talking about invincibility? Because I interpret their quotes as an aspect of their significantly more apparent and oft-referred to fear of "getting hooked", "losing it", and being out of control. Their words can be interpreted as an expression of hope that the strategies they employ—scheduling when they use drugs, choosing the right drugs, their attitude to drug use, etc., in other words: taking responsibility for their own lives—will suffice to make everything go well, and an expression of gratitude when, looking back, things did indeed go well. Even Boel and Katy, the two interviewees most intent on constructing images of themselves as strong women, describe unpleasant situations in which drugs made them feel bad. They give detailed accounts of how, on these occasions, they took responsibility for the situations. Katy explains that she can hear the voice of a psychologist friend in her mind, reassuring her when she reacts with fear during a cannabis rush. She lets her friend guide her, while also telling herself more brusquely to snap out of it:

> And then it's like I hear her, inside of me, "let's take a deep breath now", and then I identify: "what is it I'm feeling?" Where I think it's coming from. Why it's affecting me right now. I guess I always have a pretty open inner dialogue […] it's probably a combination of my need for control, that I have to go "okay, now you've got to calm down." Kinda. "You're gonna take this one step at a time, and then…" It can happen sometimes, because everything's different, some [drugs] are stronger than others, that you smoke something and you're like "oh Christ, what was this?" You know. But… then I can also just [tell myself] "this will soon be [over], just wait an hour and it'll disappear". So… I've got my strategies.

Katy describes a strategy that is a combination of an understanding attitude towards herself and strict self-control that does not allow any frightening feelings to take over. Boel too describes a mixture of understanding and control when it comes to dealing with the days after she has taken MDMA. Once again, she emphasises the importance of being a person who is capable of taking MDMA; her words are a lecture on how to understand and handle the comedown:

> It's also important, I think, to inform your, the people you're closest with of how you're doing during those days. So you get the support you need. That's really important, I think. And that you don't get anxious, you know I think that when drugs are associated with anxiety or childhood taboos, then you should really stay away from them because then you'll just feel bad during those, days. But if you don't have that then it's... You're... a little, sensitive, you're a little exposed. You're kind of like you don't have any skin, like all your nerves are on the outside, sort of. And of course you might, start crying and you might feel bad and you might get angry but that's just when you don't, play along. You've got to understand that, the days after you do drugs, the drugs are playing you. And you've got to keep up.

These quotes from Katy and Boel reveal that it is not just the (mental) health of the person who uses drugs that matters: they also see friends who are therapists, friends who are understanding, a good childhood and the means to hide out from the world as prerequisites for being able to weather the unexpected effects or aftereffects of drugs in a good way. Not having any skin, as Boel puts it, paints a picture of an extremely vulnerable state that requires a special setting. This highlights once again how class matters for their ability to handle drug use. Social and material vulnerability and a starting point as a member of a pathologised social group, as Skeggs describes the conditions of the working class, is a radically different points of departure for a skinless person who feels exposed than if that same person had been in a strong position and able to designate a space to sit out their temporary vulnerability. But, instead, the women seem to interpret the life circumstances of people who use drugs as personal mental abilities. Without professional advisers, temporal and spatial locations that can make it easier to cope with feeling skinless, and the freedom to wait for unpleasant states to pass, the person who uses drugs seems to run the risk of being judged as mentally unfit to use them.

Tales of personal strength and of coping with the effects of drugs are told in a way that depicts the interviewee as taking responsibility. Thus, the interviewees express acceptance of the paradigm of individual responsibility for one's health, presenting it as an argument for their right to use drugs (cf. Rödner et al. 2007, p. 52). Someone who fails to take responsibility should not be using drugs, they claim. Responsibility entails knowing the effect that these substances will have and how one's body and mind will react to ingesting them. However, this is often not possible, for several reasons. One is that illegal substances tend to be unregulated, which means they may contain unwanted ingredients and it can be difficult to get the dosage right. This is different from alcohol and regulated medication. Another reason is that the effects of psychoactive substances can differ depending on the consumer's state. In addition, a reasonably pure version of any particular drug must be tried before the person who uses it can know anything at all about how they react to that drug. Responsibility must, therefore, be temporarily released and replaced by the hope that things will go well, if drug consumption is to take place at all. This hope relates partly to the quality of the drugs, but, as Katy explained, varying quality can be an acknowledged factor— "sometimes you smoke something and you're like 'oh Christ, what was this?'"—that people who use drugs need to be able to handle when things do not go as planned. Responsibility, therefore, ultimately appears to be about possessing personal qualities that become an expression of a self with the capacity for self-monitoring (Skeggs 2004). But it is also about access to tools and conditions. The person who uses drugs must not only have the knowledge needed to choose the right drugs at the right time and limit their intake, but also have the right background, as Boel described it: "if drugs are associated with anxiety or taboos from childhood then you really shouldn't use them". Being able to handle the drug in a good way, such as managing a period of not having skin, is thus a matter of having access to a web of resources.

For these women, the legitimacy of drug use and pharmaceutical use is about the directions they have taken and how the preparations take shape from there. But these directions are often ambivalent; the drugs' "partiality" (Ahmed 2019, p. 35), i.e. their multiple meanings and uses, mixes up intentions and transforms the women's starting points into questions about who they are. Blurred boundaries between drug users, patients, professionals and pleasure-seekers make the judgements about what, when and how to use important positions that construct the self. Both from a healthy and a sick position, "the optimizing interested self" can be something to strive for or to oppose. The women are navigating through a psychopharmacological society (Rose 2003) with a sense of responsibility—a responsibility that is about assessing, in advance, the ability of one's brain and of products to align themselves with one's chosen directions.

References

Ahmed, Sara. 2006. *Queer Phenomenology: Orientations, Objects, Others.* Durham, NC: Duke University Press.

Ahmed, Sara. 2019. *What's the Use? On the Uses of Use.* Durham, NC: Duke University Press.

Alftberg, Åsa. 2015. *Mellan vanor och faror: Ett kulturanalytiskt perspektiv på äldre människors bruk av läkemedel* [Between Habits and Hazards: A Cultural Analysis Perspective on the Use of Medicines by Older People]. Working Papers in Medical Humanities, 1, Lund University Libraries, Lund.

Berman, Anne H., Hans Bergman, Tom Palmstierna, and Frans Schlyter. 2005. *Drug Use Disorders Identification Test (DUDIT).* Karolinska Institutet. Center for Psychiatric Research.

Berridge, Virginia. 2013. *Demons: Our Changing Attitudes to Alcohol, Tobacco & Drugs.* Oxford: Oxford University Press.

Boyd, Susan. 2004. *From Witches to Crack Moms: Women, Drug Law and Policy.* Durham, NC: Carolina Academic Press.

Bremer, Signe. 2011. *Kroppslinjer: Kön, transsexualism och kropp i berättelser om köns- korrigering.* [Body Lines: Gender, Transsexualism and the Body in Narratives of Gender Reassignment]. Göteborg and Stockholm: Makadam.

Brown, Katie. 2023. Legalizing MDMA for PTSD Treatment: Phase 3 Clinical Trial Results. *Psychiatrist.com,* 23 May.

Campbell, Nancy D. 2000. *Using Women: Gender, Drug Policy, and Social Justice*. Milton Park: Taylor & Francis.

Campbell, Nancy D., and Elizabeth Ettorre. 2011. *Gendering Addiction: The Politics of Drug Treatment in a Neurochemical World*. New York, NY: Palgrave Macmillan.

CAN. 2019. *Drogutvecklingen i Sverige 2019 – med fokus på narkotika* [Drogutvecklingen i Sverige 2019 – med fokus på narkotika] (Rapport 180). Stockholm: Centralförbundet för alkohol- och narkotikaupplysning.

Derrida, J. 1993. The Rhetoric of Drugs: An Interview. *Differences: A Journal of Feminist Cultural Studies* 5 (1): 2–25.

Du Rose, Natacha. 2015. *The Governance of Female Drug Users: Women's Experiences of Drug Policy*. Bristol: Policy Press.

Foltmar Elfton, Rasmus. 2014. The Dad Trying to Legalise Medical Weed in Sweden. *Vice.com* [2023-06-13].

Gilbert, Jeremy. 2008. *Anticapitalism and Culture*. Oxford: Berg.

Gustavsson, Johanna. 2017. *Vi är den här platsen eller tillståndet* [We Are This Place or This Condition]. Göteborg: Self-Published.

Hansson, Kristofer. 2007. *I ett andetag: en kulturanalys av astma som begränsning och möjlighet* [In One Breath: A Cultural Analysis of Asthma as Constraint and Opportunity]. Stockholm: Critical Ethnography Press.

Haraway, Donna. 1991. *Simians, Cyborgs, and Women: The Reinvention of Nature*. New York, NY: Routledge.

Höglund, Gunnar. 2021. Tatueraren Jens tog timeout efter domen – nu vill han bli cannabisinfluencer: "Fruktansvärt trött på de stela reglerna" [Tattoo Artist Jens Took Time Out After the Verdict—Now He Wants to Become a Cannabis Influencer: 'Terribly Tired of the Rigid Rules']. *Jönköpingsposten*, 17 April.

Iversen, Leslie. 2012. *Speed, Ecstasy, Ritalin: The Science of Amphetamines*. Oxford: Oxford University Press. Oxford Scholarship Online [ebook].

Johannisson, Karin. 1995. *Den mörka kontinenten: Kvinnan, medicinen och fin-de-siècle* [The Dark Continent: Women, Medicine and the fin-de-siècle]. Stockholm: Norstedts.

Johansson, Lasse. 2014. Jens Grew His Own Medical Marijuana. *Jnytt*, 6 August.

Kvam, Tor-Morten, Lowan H. Stewart, Andreas Wahl Blomkvist, and Ole A. Andreassen. 2021. Ketamine for Depression—Evidence and Proposals for Practice. *Tidsskrift for Den norske legeforening*, 25 October.

Lanni, Cristina, Silvia C. Lenzken, Alessia Pascale, Igor Del Vecchio, Marco Racchi, Francesca Pistoia, and Stefano Govoni. 2008. Cognition Enhancers

Between Treating and Doping the Mind. *Pharmacological Research* 57: 196–213.

Liechti, Matthias E. 2017. Modern Clinical Research on LSD. *Neuropsychopharmacology* 42 (11): 2114–2127.

Lindgren, Sven-Åke. 1993. *Den hotfulla njutningen: att etablera drogbruk som samhällsproblem 1890–1970* [The Threat of Pleasure: Establishing Drug Use as a Social Problem 1890–1970]. Stockholm: Brutus Östlings Bokförlag Symposion.

Lundgren, Johan. 2023. PSIPET—The Effect of Psilocybin on MDD Symptom Severity and Synaptic Density. Department of Clinical Neuroscience, Karolinska Institutet. https://ki.se/en/cns/psipet-the-effect-of-psilocybin-on-mdd-symptom-severity-and-synaptic-density [2023-08-10].

Petersson, Frida. 2013. *Kontroll av beroende: Substitutionsbehandlingens logik, praktik och semantik* [Controlling Addiction: The Logic, Practice and Semantics of Substitution Treatment]. Malmö: Egalité.

Preciado, Paul B. 2013. *Testo Junkie: Sex, Drugs and Biopolitics in the Pharmacopornographic Era.* New York, NY: Feminist Press.

Public Health Agency. 2021. Narkotikaanvändningen och dess negativa konsekvenser i Sverige [Drug Use and Its Negative Consequences in Sweden]. www.folkhalsomyndigheten.se/publicerat-material/ [2023-06-13].

Ragan, Ian C., Imre Bard, and Ilina Singh. 2013. What Should We Do About Student Use of Cognitive Enhancers? An Analysis of Current Evidence. *Neuropharmacology* 64: 588–595.

Rose, Nikolas. 2003. Neurochemical Selves. *Society* 41 (1): 46–59.

Rose, Nikolas. 2019. *Our Psychiatric Future.* Cambridge: Polity Press.

Rödner, Sharon, Max Hansson, and Börje Olsson. 2007. *Socialt integrerade narkotika- användare, myt eller verklighet?* [Socially Integrated Drug Users, Myth or reality?] (SoRAD Forskningsrapport 47). Stockholm: Stockholms universitet.

Sandell, Kerstin. 2016. Living the Neurochemical Self? Experiences After the Success of the SSRIs. *Distinktion: Journal of Social Theory* 17 (2): 130–148.

Schifano, Fabrizio, Valeria Catalani, Safia Sharif, Flavia Napoletano, John Martin Corkery, Davide Arillotta, Suzanne Fergus, Alessandro Vento, and Amira Guirguis. 2022. Benefits and Harms of 'Smart Drugs' (Nootropics) in Healthy Individuals. *Drugs* 82: 633–647.

Skeggs, Beverley. 2004. *Class, Self, Culture.* London: Routledge.

Swedish National Institute of Public Health. 2010. *Narkotikabruket i Sverige* [Drug Use in Sweden]. Östersund: Statens Folkhälsoinstitut.

Tiger, Mikael, Emma R. Veldman, Carl-Johan Ekman, Christer Halldin, Per Svenningsson, and Johan Lundberg. 2020. A Randomized Placebo-Controlled PET Study of Ketamine's Effect on Serotonin 1B Receptor Binding in Patients with SSRI-Resistant Depression. *Translational Psychi.atry* 10: article 159. Unpaginated open-access document

9

Negotiating Addiction

As the previous chapter showed, both compulsive and recreational drug use can be linked to different ways of doing class, with different outcomes. The key concepts for successful middle-class behaviour are control, time management and resources. If any of these are missing, drug use leads to unsuccessful middle-class enactments, or else the use was never intended to generate such capital. In this chapter, I examine addiction as an enactment of drug use in the light of Beverley Skeggs' class theory.

Skeggs writes that research lacks the tools to theorise subjectivities other than those conceived as worthy middle-class subjectivities, which are based on certain epistemological assumptions about what people strive for.

> Theories of the good and proper self (the governmental normative subject, be it a reflexive, enterprising, individualising, rational, prosthetic, or possessive self) or even the self produced in conditions not of its own making, such as Bourdieu's habitus, all rely on ideas about self-interest, investment and/or "playing the game". (2011, p. 496)

© The Author(s) 2024
E. Eleonorasdotter, *Women's Drug Use in Everyday Life*,
https://doi.org/10.1007/978-3-031-46057-9_9

She argues that lack of interest in self-optimisation or "playing the game" is unexplored working-class positions. Instead, such lack of interest is woven into (middle-class) descriptions of the working class as worthless (2011, pp. 503ff.). The working class, Skeggs argues, also does not have the resources to develop a self that can be described as valuable through capitalist metaphors, such as investment, inheritance, profit and loss. From such a perspective, the working class appears paralysed and dependent (2004, p. 187). Skeggs does not explicitly refer to dependence on drugs per se when she describes the middle class's construction of the working class as dependent. But, as I will show, class is inextricably linked with issues such as drug dependence, addiction and substance use disorders. This, in fact, is an issue that could perhaps shed light on the reasons why those in lower socioeconomic and educational positions use drugs more frequently and in larger quantities (CAN 2021[1]). Namely: How can a person in a neoliberal world, whose drug use has become problematic, quit using drugs if they lack the resources and/or the desire to become a "governmental normative subject", interested in optimising and investing in their self?

When drugs are used in line with the performance of an optimising middle-class self, they sometimes function as more or less temporary prostheses, something that is needed to "play the game". Such a need for drugs in order to maintain or increase personal value (in Ahmed's words: to align oneself, and remain in line, with normative ideals, 2006, p. 66) contrasts with addiction, that is: the need for the drug itself and the drug's intoxication, despite the fact that its use does not optimise the user, causing them trouble instead.

Addiction is defined by addiction researcher Markus Heilig as "continued use despite negative consequences" (2015, p. 35). These negative consequences may include loss of one's home, work and relationships, which thus indicates a downward class journey over time, regardless of the point from which the addict started. In other words, the optimising middle-class self and the dependent self seem to move in diametrically opposite directions in class society.

---

[1] CAN's study lumps together highly addictive and less addictive drugs into a single category; it would have been interesting to gather more details about how these different types of drugs affect different social groups.

But while some addictions can indeed lead to the kinds of losses listed by Heilig (Laanemets 2002; Lewis 2017), the consequences of addiction are not set in stone. Becoming addicted to drugs does not automatically mean that one will lose one's home, for example. Which negative consequences an addicted person will experience depends upon the assets and resources they have at their disposal.

If addiction is about "continued use despite negative consequences", then it is a concept of time. Addiction does not refer to a single instance of drug use that has led to negative consequences, but rather to a prolonged process that also extends forward from the present, through the word "continued". Thus, an ongoing addiction has already occurred, but it is still present and will continue. An addicted person is thus crossed by a line that runs both backwards and forwards in time. Nevertheless, several interviewees define addiction as a point that one passes, something that risks occurring as a result of a single act. This point then takes the form of an accumulated line (cf. Ahmed 2006, pp. 178f.) that arises and extends backwards as well as forwards, but might not have arisen if that particular point had not been passed. What does addiction mean when viewed from different distances to such points, and what does class have to do with that meaning? How is a line of addiction that unfolds forwards as well as backwards experienced? And how can non-dependent, dependent and inactive dependencies be understood?

This chapter examines different interviewees' perceived proximity to addiction and the directions that are pointed out from there, from different ways of staying at a distance to being inside addiction. The lines drawn are discussed in relation to will, class and direction.

9.1   The Will to Perform Class

Pernilla reflects upon the question of whether there are any drugs she cannot imagine using, and the answer indicates that it is the risk of addiction, and its connection to certain drugs, that is decisive for her drug use practices.

There are many different drugs. I'd say I'm pretty... selective. Take crack, for example. It's the most disgusting thing I've seen, just how incredibly quickly it induces addiction. The way it utterly and completely changes who you are, as a person.[2]

During trips to the USA when she was younger, Pernilla met people who had started using crack. She was horrified at how quickly they became addicted and how the drug changed their personalities. Pernilla expresses addiction—a timeline through the body—as a matter of spatiality: a state of proximity to a certain object (crack) that induces addiction. The Swedish term for addictive, *beroendeframkallande*, literally means "addiction-inducing". It suggests that addiction lies dormant in the body, and that it is the characteristics of an object that can awaken the addiction. This, Pernilla says, is why she avoids crack.

It is not just any kind of addiction that Pernilla fears crack would induce. By nature, humans depend on the supply of a range of substances—oxygen, water, certain nutrients—to stay alive; for many people, everyday medicines too are life-sustaining. A crack addiction, on the other hand, can alter, or even shorten, one's life. The addiction that Pernilla is wary of is thus one that could result in more changes than simply becoming addicted. It is an addiction that has to be initiated to be able to commence, and Pernilla believes that ingesting crack could lead to negative changes in her life. This is why she feels the need to avoid crack—as opposed to the drugs she likes to use, such as cocaine and amphetamines.

How should we interpret this line that Pernilla has drawn, expressed in terms of avoiding crack? Below, I examine two different addiction research perspectives that theorise addiction as will from a psychosocial perspective, and as defective will from a neurological perspective. To understand why my interviewees sometimes reject and sometimes approach drugs, I discuss both perspectives in relation to phenomenology and Ahmed's concept of lines (2006).

---

[2] All quotes in Swedish have been translated by me.

Drug researcher Ted Goldberg's psychosocial perspective on addiction, which he defines as "problematic use",[3] focuses on will:

> In the psychosocial school of thought, recreational consumption and problematic consumption are two essentially different things. When consumption is problematic (rather than recreational), all fundamental areas of life – one's living conditions, physical health, mental health, social relationships, financial situation, self-image, etc – deteriorate. Most citizens do not want that to happen; they want to create a good life for themselves and their loved ones. (2012, p. 60)

Goldberg thus makes a sharp distinction between recreational consumption that can be part of "a good life" (cf. "the optimising self", Skeggs 2004, pp. 62ff.) and consumption that negatively affects all important areas of life. He suggests that some people *want* to engage in problematic consumption, while others do not, and that the two forms of use are therefore essentially different. According to him, a person who uses drugs in a problematic way and the person who uses drugs recreationally are headed in different directions, but does this mean that the "essence" of use, which I interpret as the drive to use, is definitely divided and separate? Would it be enough for Pernilla to be sure that she wants a good life, in order to then be able to test crack unproblematically? Or is a desire to consume certain drugs problematic by definition? In other words, does the "nature" of the drugs, i.e. their properties, have anything to do with it? Pernilla mentions another drug she does not want to try, namely heroin.

---

[3] Goldberg defines "problematic consumption" as follows: "A *problematic consumer* is a person who prioritises a psychoactive substance (regardless of which one it is) so highly it becomes [...] a *central activity*. They allow the drug to dominate their everyday life. In comparison, problematic consumers award a low priority to aspects of life most people would give precedence, such as one's family, relationships, work, financial situation and health" (2012, p. 58, italics in original). I would say that Goldberg's concept is synonymous with the way in which addiction tends to be described by, for example, Heilig (2015, p. 35). But drug consumption can also be problematic on an individual occasion or without an addiction in terms of a perceived, urgent need having arisen, which could have made the definition broader. However, according to the definition above, Goldberg is referring precisely to compulsive and repeated problematic consumption, although his focus is on the will to consume, rather than a will that is compromised, as I discuss in this chapter.

Heroin. I would probably not… dare, precisely because they say that once someone's had a taste of that high, they immediately want to go there again. I think I have a lot of respect for addiction, for addictive stuff.

Pernilla is thus afraid that, if she were to try heroin, she would acquire a new will that she did not have before—a development she expresses in both spatial and temporal terms. She fears that experiencing the high of heroin would make her want to "go there again". Between the lines, she suggests that she is afraid this new will would be more powerful than her other wills, and thus lead to addiction. Wanting to "go there again" also illustrates how the line of addiction is not a straight one: it is a loop, one that keeps returning to the same point, over and over again. The loops of addiction lead one away from optimisation, in the sense of personal development and success. Instead, they spiral towards the next hit of drugs.

What is addictive according to Pernilla is thus not the objects or addictive substances themselves, heroin and crack, but the experiences of intoxication located in time and space. Experiencing the world through crack or heroin are experiences that she fears could lead to new desires and directions, towards certain places where the body would spend time instead of being in others. Sara Ahmed writes:

> "orientations" depend on taking points of view as given. The gift of this point is concealed in the moment of being received as given. Such a point accumulates a line that both divides things and creates spaces that we imagine that we can be "in". (2006, p. 14)

From one perspective, the world seems to develop in a particular way that offers certain possibilities, but from another the world looks different and other things seem attainable. The space that is available seems obvious from the point from which it is viewed, and orientation takes place from there. If Pernilla resists heroin and crack, life does not unfold from such intoxications, and she can stay in line with her current perspectives.

If orientation from a certain point takes place in relation to what appears to be possible and attainable from there, the areas of life that

Goldberg judges to be the most important, "living conditions, physical health, mental health, social relations, finances, self-image, etc." (2012, p. 60), also end up in a dependent position in relation to the addicted person's other life conditions. What can be maintained, and how this is done while the addict devotes a lot of time to his or her addiction, becomes a question of capital in Bourdieu's sense, or resources in Skegg's sense, which in addition to capital also includes cultural resources that have no accumulative value (Skeggs 2004, p. 17). Regardless of drug dependency, the conditions concealed behind the abovementioned areas of life relate to people's different living conditions, which means that notions of "a good life" do not look the same for everyone. For example, poverty, poor health and problematic social relationships are a radically different starting point for addiction-related "negative consequences" than extensive financial assets, good health and a strong social network.

Many famous personalities throughout history have lived their lives as both successful and addicted. The poet and critic Samuel Taylor Coleridge (see e.g. Plant 1999), the novelist Thomas de Quincey (2003/1822), poet and writer Charles Baudelaire (see Plant 1999), songwriter and singer Billie Holliday (see Palmer and Horowitz 2000), singer and actress Judy Garland (see e.g. Iversen 2012, chapter 5), rock musician and actor Elvis Presley (ibid.) and rock artists Courtney Love (Carr 2017) and Lady Gaga (ARTPOP by GAGA 2013) are a selection of famous people who have had the opportunity to engage in both optimisation and addiction, either simultaneously or alternately (cf. Berridge 2013, pp. 160ff.). In several cases, their addictions have involved serious consequences, including death. But during their active and successful lives, addiction was part and parcel of their activities. It could be argued that, for them, the desire for a good life has meant both professional accomplishments *and* problematic drug use. Rather than being oriented in different class directions by definition, the loops of dependence are stuck in class-related lines based on conditions, capital and claims for optimisation.

I will come back to the role of (free) will and addiction's relationship to certain drugs and class, but first I would like to examine addiction from another point of view—as exemplified by Carolina, who does not refer to addiction as an act of will.

Carolina describes her addiction as clashing with her will, which is to "do things in life", rather than starting from it. As previously mentioned, she used amphetamines as a daily practice for eight years, has undergone twelve-step treatment and has since been involved in Narcotics Anonymous (NA). In other words, she has extensive experience both of being addicted and of talking about it in specific contexts where addiction is understood within an institutionalised conceptual apparatus. She tells me how her addiction manifested itself once it had arisen, after she had tried drugs for the first time.

> [T]hen I just, kept using. And, like, went to school on Monday, lied – and I'm the kind of person who never lies. Lied to my teacher: "I think I was drugged this weekend, I should go home", and then I just immediately headed home to him [her boyfriend], looked for his stash and used again. It was like it came automatically, so it just, kept going. This was, like, a week before I graduated from upper-secondary.

This quote illustrates how her use became "automatic"; what started as a conscious choice "just, kept going". The way Carolina puts it, it sounds as though someone else was in the driving seat. Carolina, who hates to lie, lies and skips school so she can use more amphetamines. She describes the events as though she suddenly found herself at a point from which the looping line of addiction immediately unfolded and actions that she would usually find unthinkable suddenly appeared reasonable.

While Goldberg argues that problematic use is based on volitional actions, neuroscientist and physician Markus Heilig describes addiction as a state in which the will is suspended:

> The most striking thing about people who seek out treatment for problems with alcohol or drugs is [...] how their motivational engine somehow seems to have broken down. [...] I have never yet met a patient who valued getting drunk more than having a job or a home. Yet countless patients can easily and repeatedly risk these things for a chance to drink or take drugs. [...] This inability to direct behaviour towards desired goals is at the heart of compulsive substance use. (2015, p. 34)

Heilig describes the brain as broken and the addict's actions as compulsive, painting a picture of a state beyond their control. But he retains a loophole for himself by writing "countless patients" instead of "the patients", which allows for exceptions. Some patients do not risk their homes for their addictions, partly because some homes are simply not at risk of being lost, but may some addicts not allow their homes to be risked either? His interpretation of the term thus involves some uncertainty about what it might mean: that the ability to direct behaviour towards desired goals may not be completely eliminated? In any case, this quote from Heilig emphasises an image of the addict as a compulsive consumer, a person who has fallen out of the rhythm between pleasure and duty (Wilk 2014), where duty represents the motivational machinery. The addict may become unable to steer their behaviour in the desired direction in the long term—doing/not doing what is required to keep their job and home, for example—which highlights its difference from the short-term nature of pleasure. The rhythm thus involves not only an alternation between sacrifice and relaxation, but also between the present and the future (ibid., pp. 9f.), long and short lines that must coincide in a way that prioritises the long lines in order for the rhythm to work.

From the points that are passed while following short lines, such as recreational drug use, it must be possible to imagine how these lines can be drawn to points along the long line, and the lines must coincide well enough for life to proceed towards long-term, normative goals. However, Carolina does not express her use as either playful or wilful. In relation to Heilig's motivational machinery metaphor, the "automaticity" that she describes manifests as an error rather than a will, a compulsive movement that leads her astray.

In other words, the self must follow lines towards normative goals, otherwise addiction/problematic use has occurred, according to both Heilig and Goldberg. But the two different ways of describing addiction and problematic consumption—from a neurological and psychosocial perspective—collide in terms of will. Simply put, the clash can be described as a question: Does the person who is addicted or uses drugs problematically want to use, or is the will/motivation machinery broken? (The latter seems to be in line with Pernilla's and Carolina's images, as well as experiences of addiction.) How can this question be analysed from a cultural analysis perspective?

The queer theorist Eve Kosofsky Sedgwick (1993) writes about the relationship between the will and the concept of "addiction". Sedgwick argues that, since the medicalisation of so-called dependency states through the term "addiction" has come to cover everything from the use of drugs and tobacco to food and exercise, it has proved impossible to identify what it actually means (ibid., pp. 131f.). It can be about the intake of a foreign substance, but also about the body's own substances; about uncontrolled activities but also about extremely controlled activities characterised by willpower. She believes that the discourse is based on an imagined dichotomy between absolute free will and compulsiveness, which are actually inherent in each other.

Sedgwick argues that hope for the addict is constructed as the existence of the free will to stop using, which is threateningly overshadowed by the fact that the person has previously been forced by the addiction (which is chronic and has not ceased) and has acted compulsively. At the same time, there is comfort in the fact that unwanted behaviour was precisely compulsive, not free will, but this is overshadowed by the fact that at any given moment—if free will exists—the person could have chosen differently (ibid., pp. 134f.).

Instead of "addiction", Sedgwick advocates the concept of "habit", although she believes that this concept is difficult to use:

> It is extraordinarily difficult to imagine an analytically usable language of habit, in a conceptual landscape so rubbled and defeatured by the twin hurricanes named Just Do It and Just Say No. (ibid., p. 140)

I also see that an everyday word like habit risks belittling people's struggles to extricate themselves from painful states of addiction. But Sedgwick wants to use the word as a complex expression that names the movement by linking "habitus", "habit" and also "habitation":

> [A] version of repeated action that moves, not toward metaphysical absolutes but toward interrelations of the action – and the self acting – with

the bodily habitus, the appareling habit, the sheltering habitation, every-thing that marks the traces of that habit on a world that the metaphysical absolutes would have left a vacuum. (ibid., p. 138)

For Sedgwick, the term "habit" thus implies a movement, not towards a particular drug but towards the behaviour itself, and in this interpre-tation it includes the habitus of the body as well as expression and a sheltered place to be. Moreover, Sedgwick indicates that the habit leaves various traces that absolute compulsion or free will cannot comprehend. This can be compared with Ahmed's description of directions that shape the body if they are repeated and that depend not only on how we direct ourselves but also on how we are directed by what we see in that direction (2006, p. 15f.). That is, what is expected of us, how we are addressed and treated, for example, and what is then made possible. I interpret Sedgwick as saying that habit (cf. habitus and performativity) takes a different approach to the subject's context (thoughts, relation-ships, material assets and so on) than addiction, which also includes a relationship to time. Short and long lines coincide in these habits, our repeated, everyday events. From the position of the body, habits provide a number of fixed vantage points from which the future can be imag-ined and lines drawn. "Free will" thus becomes linked to what can be imagined from the vantage points of habit.

If we go back to Pernilla's reasoning about the concern that using heroin could lead to wanting to "go there again", the question of *when* the will changes is also important. Is it in connection with the choice of drug, or when the drug has already been taken? When does the moti-vational machinery break down, or when does problematic use become desirable? Goldberg argues strongly that problematic use can be linked to stigmatisation and historical vulnerability among people who use drugs in a problematic way (2000). However, the example of Pernilla's avoidance of heroin and crack demonstrates a concern with the char-acteristics of the drugs, which she describes as "addictive stuff", that extends beyond such an explanatory model. Her understanding of addic-tion, as someone who has never experienced it, is not unequivocally in line with Heilig's concept of "broken motivational machinery", but involves the imagined ability of drugs to change the will so that the body takes new directions.

So what are these places and perspectives that Pernilla does not want to make her own? The people she mentioned who used crack were part of a structural context of which she does not want to be part. She says, among other things:

> I've seen too much of the social structures around it [crack]. People stealing from their own mothers and then selling their loot for another hit of a shitty drug made of residual products.

Crack is thus not attractive to Pernilla as a perspective-creating object because, from her outsider perspective, it is part of a social context that she perceives in negative terms. Crack is described as a "shitty drug" and its very materiality—extracted from "residual products"—as inferior to other drugs made from previously unused raw materials. Recycling, in this context of cocaine-containing residues, thus lacks the charge of reuse and environmental sustainability and contributes to Pernilla's disdain for crack as rubbish. It fuels her outrage over the drug's effects, the way that it makes people rob their own mothers so they can indulge in the rush of crack once more. The scenario is a clear picture of the non-respectability and moral inferiority associated with the intake of a certain substance. For Pernilla, allowing such a drug into her body thus entails the risk of taking the step from defining the morally inferior to constituting it. When Pernilla makes these arguments about drugs she does not want to try, I ask her why cocaine and amphetamines feel okay.

> *Pernilla*: Well, there I think it's a matter of me having been in so many contexts in which people use them. Before even trying them, I already knew people weren't addicted. If I'd spent time in social circles in which every other person used heroin from time to time, maybe I would have seen it [heroin] differently too. There's something about that drug that makes you go "well, it *would* be exciting to give it a try", but then I also think [...] well, you know, the risks. [...] It feels too hard, too dirty, in a way to become... I mean, dirty in the sense that it's like "poof"...
> *Emma*: So the fact that you've seen these social structures and...

Pernilla: Yes, it's partly that and then also how it seems to affect your behaviour when you use [it]… or something. I guess I like being *present*…

I interpret the hard and dirty aspects that Pernilla does not want to deal with as a description of the environments she associates with these drugs, which are usually portrayed as marginalised, violent and dirty. That drug use can look like this is also something she says she has witnessed herself in the case of crack, manifesting as dysfunctional relationship structures linked to a desperate need for the drug in combination with a lack of money. In addition, she describes the effects of the drugs as rendering a person no longer able to be "present", an expression to which she returns in various parts of the interview. I interpret "being present" as synonymous with being in tune with one's environment and in line with the directions staked out before use. The fear of no longer being in tune is thus not about falling out of tune as an experience of disorientation, which can be caused, for example, by unpleasant or strong drug effects and which she talks about in other terms (e.g. as being "cuckoo"), but about new experiences of orientation and new directions from there. She does not want to move away from the long lines; rather, she wants to be present and aligned.

So, for Pernilla, the desire to have a good life and the drive to optimise herself and be in line means that she does not use certain drugs because she associates them with addiction, rather than with recreational use. The will to experience a good life is about a will that leads her to refrain from using these drugs, and this line is drawn even before use is even considered. A line towards crack and further into addiction is thus defined at the same time as it is regarded as a point, in the form of an object to be avoided. Some drugs are expected to produce such strong effects that Pernilla is doubtful whether they can be used without changing a person's long-term perspective. These objects are described as points on already defined problematic lines, and she contrasts them with her own use of amphetamines and cocaine, which she has not only used herself but has also seen others use without any problems. But, while both of these drugs are common recreational drugs, they are also known as problematic, addictive substances (Iversen 2012; Wierup and

De la Reguera 2010). In other words, there is an inherent uncertainty about how the world will develop from a certain point, whether addiction will occur and hence turn the point into a line in the form of a loop. Birgitta Stenberg's addiction, for example, which lasted for several years, was to amphetamines. In the documentary *All the Wild Ones*[4] (Belfrage and Gustavsson 2012), Stenberg describes one of her first amphetamine rushes:

> It was so magnificently beautiful. I said to Palle: is it like this? This is how it is, he said. Exactly like this.

Later, she adds:

> You have to remember that these things that look so dirty when it comes to narcotics – dirty quarters, dirty needles and… – you wouldn't voluntarily put up with that if there hadn't been an infinite answer in, in narcotics.

Stenberg unabashedly links her wild life to drug use and shows in the quote how the world can look from a drug-using versus a non-drug-using perspective. That which looks dirty and filthy from one angle can be magnificently beautiful from the other. Pernilla's fear of addiction could be interpreted using Stenberg's terminology. If something magnificently beautiful were to unfold after taking crack or heroin, she also knows how dirty and filthy it would look from the outside. The longing for the temporarily magnificent is, therefore, held back by an aversion to the dirty, an aversion that keeps her anchored within the perspective of the long lines. These perspectives are shaped by norms about what constitutes a good life. But, since the contexts in which Pernilla uses amphetamines are not dirty and return to or never leave the long lines, the grandiose can be enjoyed without the risk of dirtiness. But the question is: If enjoyment and the desire to go there again are crucial for whether or not addiction occurs, how grand can it be allowed to be without a drug being perceived as difficult to resist? That is, for the will

---

[4] *Alla vilda* (2012).

to be replaced by a new will, or, according to Heilig, for the motivational machinery to break down.

Some of my interviewees recounted their experiences of pleasure in precisely those terms: as experiences of risk.

9.2   Does Pleasure Equate to Addiction?

Thea is one of those who believe that their own use of certain drugs involves risks of addiction. She believes that the opioid-based drugs for back pain, which she is sometimes prescribed and sometimes buys illegally, pose such a risk. She also tells me how friends who started taking the opioid heroin changed, and even died from their use, which deters her from trying the drug herself. She describes herself as "interested in drugs", and has tried many different ones, both legal and illegal, since her youth. She says:

> I can also, well, quite honestly, sometimes I take it on an empty stomach. Then I get a little more high, and that's nice. [...] so there is a risk that I could become dependent on it.

Taking opioid-based drugs on an empty stomach, instead of after a meal, enhances the experience of the effect. Thea says she gets "a little more high", and that it feels good. I understand her concerns about addiction being linked to the longing for niceness, to experience effects beyond the pain relief. This is a desire that was problematised in the previous chapter in relation to an information sheet from a health centre, where the *intention* of the intake is described as decisive for whether a drug-classified medicine is a drug or not. Thea feels that the desire to get a little higher, or the fact that she takes painkillers in such a way that she not only numbs the pain but also gets high, could indicate that she is aiming for an illegitimate pleasure, and it is this that she feels could lead to potential addiction.

However, the drugs are causing her body to become constipated, which in itself is associated with pain, health risks and anxiety. Thea's intestinal system has been damaged as a result of various surgeries, leading to several intestinal disorders. As a result, she lives with periodic back pain and periodic constipation due to painkillers, but the latter periods are not so long or frequent that she worries about the risk of addiction. She has approached addiction in such a way that she has been able to recognise it as a risk due to experiences of pleasure. The risk is kept at a distance by practical circumstances; the painful constipation caused by opiates negates the point of using them to treat back pain, and therefore, she has not had to make decisions about consumption based solely on a risk assessment from an addiction perspective. But she says that she does do so in relation to other drugs, again with a focus on pleasure, for example in connection with her first use of MDMA. This comes to mind in a context where she discusses fears. One fear that she perceives as common among other people is that addiction will occur on the first use of a drug. She says:

> [P]eople have a lot of fears and stuff about, addiction or, the whole addiction thing.... Without knowing that it's not as simple as trying something and becoming hooked. That's not even the case with heroin. I felt that way maybe, the first time I took MDMA, when I was 19. [...] then I just had this thought: "ok, this was... I've never felt this good in my entire life. There's a potential danger in this." [laughter].

Thea describes how she linked positive feelings during this occasion of drug use to danger. The danger was that she felt better than she ever had before. In other words, what she describes is an experience of optimisation. Even while in the intoxicated state, she realised that she would either have to accept returning to a less optimal state, or try to maintain the MDMA influence over time. I perceive the attraction of the latter option as the "danger" in this argument, because repeated use is associated with addiction. For Thea, addiction as a danger thus took the form of an experience of feeling extraordinarily good together with the drug, a fusion that she nevertheless perceived as impossible to maintain without sacrificing other things that she would eventually be deprived of. What was so extraordinarily good about Thea in that moment was due to the drug and, if she wanted to remain in the experience, she would become dependent on the drug being provided. She, therefore, had to make a decision to feel worse again shortly afterwards to avoid becoming even worse in the long run. If the person who uses drugs, in Pernilla's words, "wants to go there again" too often, this optimisation transforms into its opposite. There is, therefore, an inherent loss in such an intoxication, which must be accepted in order to avoid addiction.

MDMA does not appear to have high addiction potential (Iversen 2012, chapter 8, pp. 16ff.), which Thea also mentions in another context. It is a drug that loses its effect after only a few doses, but I perceive what Thea describes as a danger of addiction, the unparalleled positive state, to be a fundamental idea within how the concept of addiction is conceptualised. The formula for addiction then becomes: the drug involves surprisingly strong experiences of pleasure. The relationship with the drug is crucial for a person to continue feeling so good. The person who used drugs "wants to go there again", the drug use is repeated and the one who uses drugs becomes an addict.

In other words, according to this formula, the addict is a pleasure seeker. Markus Heilig writes about the search for the cause of addiction and dismisses such a formula:

[A]re drugs' effects all that matter? Hardly. Most people appreciate that social inhibitions ease after a couple of drinks at a cocktail party. Most people who try cocaine experience euphoria. And yet, for most people who try these drugs, substance use will not become a problem. (2015, p. 29)

Thus, according to Heilig, enjoyment in itself does not explain why some people who use drugs continue to use despite negative consequences. Instead, Heilig argues that only some individuals develop dependence, and that this takes time. One important factor is "drug craving", which he defines as "a strong and overwhelming desire for the drug even after prolonged abstinence", which constitutes "the driving force behind continued substance use despite negative consequences" (2015, p. 35). Thus, as I interpret Heilig, the danger that Thea identifies when she tries MDMA for the first time consists of an admittedly hard-to-believe pleasurable experience, but which in most people does not lead to compulsive use as long as drug cravings do not develop. When this has happened—and research cannot determine in advance whom it may affect, but according to Heilig it requires repeated use—the addiction is a fact. Thea's interpretation of the pleasure as dangerous argues against such repeated use. The danger consists of an imagined future scenario that involves repeated use, which Thea describes herself as having already rejected as a viable way to go while she was in the intoxication situation. Instead, she orientates herself away from the danger. Enjoyment seems to have acted as a warning bell, rather than as a direction towards uncontrolled repeated use.

Heilig also mentions another symptom, "drug-seeking behaviour", meaning the physical movement towards the drug which in addiction becomes a repetitive movement. He states that his research has shown how this can be linked to stress and "negative thoughts" (2015, pp. 84ff.). Both the concepts of drug craving and drug-seeking behaviour describe how bodies and objects approach each other, on the body's initiative. They give a picture of a craving behaviour enacted towards drugs, and an active seeking behaviour, respectively. Odd behaviours that some bodies, oddly enough, engage in. But the negative thoughts that can be linked to such drug-seeking behaviour indicate that there is something significant in these objects, which is the reason for the search.

Can craving be described as a desire to escape negative thoughts? Heilig also argues against such an interpretation of addiction. He writes, for example, that people who become addicted but stop using drugs (including alcohol) have elevated anxiety levels during withdrawal, but thereafter do not report greater anxiety than the normal population (ibid., pp. 92ff.). Nevertheless, they are at risk of experiencing cravings and relapsing into addiction. But he also writes that the lasting changes in the brain to which compulsive use is believed to lead involve a bodily balancing act, where the brain reacts antagonistically to prolonged euphoric experiences. He compares this to the brain's reaction to a hangover, but describes the addicted brain's reaction as stronger and more prolonged. Addiction, he says, means that people permanently react more strongly to stress than they did before, which often leads to relapse. This reasoning leads back to the negative thoughts, but also out of the brain, to stressors in life.

Thus, regardless of how and whether the brain changes, the prognosis is better for an addict who is free of stress, and the reason for the onset of addiction is linked to the effects of drugs on stress and negative thoughts. Thus, Heilig argues that patients' experiences of euphoria are not in themselves a warning sign; instead, the experiences of drug cravings and drug-seeking behaviour are signs that the addiction has already been established, which usually requires high and prolonged consumption. I interpret him as saying that a feeling, drug craving, drug-seeking behaviour and the body's movements towards drugs, together define what addiction "is". But how can repeated consumption in a given moment be distinguished from addiction? From a neurological perspective, the transition from use to addiction is shrouded in mystery. From Thea's perspective, the euphoria is noticed immediately after the first intake, but it functions more as a warning bell not to use again (soon) than as a gateway. This contrasts with Carolina who, after her first intake, felt that use had already become automatic.

Thea distinguishes between the lines by arguing that there was an important aspect in the contrast between euphoria and her well-being in the potential danger she experienced during her first MDMA intoxication. For example, she says that, then, at the age of 19, she had "never felt this good in my entire life", which in the context of how she describes her well-being as a young person implies a longed-for experience of feeling better. For example, a major problem factor was that she had not started her trans process and felt bad, uncomfortable in her body.

Her 19-year-old self wants to feel good, but perceives such a state as necessarily linked to long-term changes, such as the gender reassignment she later undergoes. From the body's point of view, a prolonged MDMA high looks unsustainable. In contrast, she perceives opioids as more risky from an addiction perspective. Freedom from pain is a state that is experienced positively, and she can also get "high". I perceive her as though, from within the intoxication as well as afterwards, she makes judgements about danger, where the positive effects of the intoxication on her mood signal the risk of addiction. In both cases, practicalities limit her use—Thea and the drugs are separated.

The purpose that Katy describes for her cocaine use is a desire to stay awake for longer. She says that she loses interest in social situations when she gets tired in the evenings, and therefore uses cocaine primarily to feel alert. She says that she does this only rarely and in small doses. According to her, the purpose of her drug use is, therefore, something as mundane as feeling awake. Nevertheless, she also recognises a danger in the euphoric aspects of drug use. When she talks about the time she tried crack without knowing what it was, she says:

> It was… it was amazing. Really. You got, like, super alert, it's short, intense periods. But … it was probably, unfortunately, the best thing I've ever tried. I think.

The reason why she regrets that crack was the best thing she ever tried is because she never wants to try it again. Even though it was the best drug she had used, she describes the occasion with irritation in her voice. She emphasises that she would never have tried it if she had understood that it was crack and not "regular" cocaine. It happened with a boyfriend who smoked his cocaine in foil, which she describes as "a bit dodgy". She also first calls what he was using cocaine, but then specifies that it was crack. She describes their approach to the drug as different:

> I'm not an addiction kind of person […] Which might also be why I do it. Because I know I'm in control of it. And as soon as I notice that I, as I did with crack, that I notice that "oh God, wow, *this*", then it's like "uh oh, alarm bells". And then I won't take that one again.

In this way, Katy also approaches something that she perceives as the risk of addiction, and comes close enough to metaphorically hear warning bells ring. A question here is whether the warning bells came from the drug experience itself, or whether they were rather related to what she already knew about crack, which is burdened with a bad reputation as a highly addictive drug for the racialised poor, especially in the USA (Nelson 2021; Wierup and De la Reguera 2010, pp. 241ff.; Campbell 2000; Maher 1997). Above all, she expresses embarrassment at having crossed a line that she did not intend to cross because she did not realise that the cocaine was crack. In a spatial sense, it was the crack that crossed her border under a false name. Katy put some kind of pipe to her lips and drew crack smoke into her body.

I interpret the degree of intimacy with drugs as an aspect of use that extends beyond risk assessments of health impact and also pleasure. The intimacy of bringing the drugs into contact with the body, together with the various risks (legal, health, social) and the intense pleasure sought, could be the basis for strong experiences of integrity violation and disgust in a situation like the one Katy describes, when an unwanted drug turns out to have taken the place of the desired one (cf. Lupton 1999, pp. 131f.). When, on top of that, the unwanted drug also carries connotations of class stigma and puts one at risk of a life-altering addiction, the experience might even feel like an assault by the "lower" drug world that Katy never wanted to have anything to do with (cf. Ahmed 2014, p. 86).

The astonishing class journey between bodies that Katy saw the drugs make when she started travelling around the world as a teenager, from vulnerable and excluded to respected and desirable bodies, does not apply to all drugs, but adheres perhaps especially to cocaine. When Katy strongly distances herself from crack but continues to use cocaine, she inscribes herself in a classed discourse that distinguishes between the two drugs of the same origin and those who use them. Magnus Linton describes cocaine as a drug with positive connotations, associated with mental acuity and successful people. It is "the drug for those who don't like junkies" (2010, p. 20, see also p. 29). Crack, on the other hand, despite its origins in and similarity to cocaine (see chapter on "Drugs and Medicines"), is strongly linked to the very definition of the junkie: loss of control, prostitution and poverty (Maher 1997). The shorter and even more intense high associated with crack is perceived by Katy as dangerous because it was the "best she had ever had", but the radically different class connections may also have played a role. Katy wants cocaine in her body, but not crack, and the intensely pleasurable experience does not mitigate the discomfort, rather the opposite.

I interpret the interviewees' fear of feeling *too* good as an indication that these experiences involve more than just euphoria. Katy did not want to use crack again, and Thea felt that the use of MDMA was risky and assessed that any future use must be under careful self-monitoring.

The euphoria involved orientation away from repeated use and therefore did not lead to addiction. Instead, potential new experiences of orientation and new wills seem to constitute the risk of pleasure, which would consequently affect the body's movement patterns, what Markus Heilig calls drug-seeking behaviour. If such new desires and perspectives completely took over, people would not seek help for drug addiction. Instead, the new wills and perspectives often seem to clash with other wills and with the expectations and demands of their surrounding environment. Addiction appears to be a paradoxical experience of the world unfolding in different directions, with certain lines that enable orientation, sometimes in the form of loops, coming to the fore for different people. In Carolina's description of such an experience, its use became automatic and required eight years of struggle to find her way back to other lines. Pernilla is heedful of certain drugs she views as addictive, while Thea and Katy have caught glimpses of addiction in moments of overwhelming pleasure. In all of these stories, addiction seems to lie beyond a sharply drawn line: it has either already occurred or remains at a distance. Did my interviewees experience any other close encounters with addiction?

9.3   In and Out of Addiction

Eve Kosofsky Sedgwick defines the cultural significance of the transition from drug use as an activity to addiction as follows:

> In the taxonomic re-framing of a drug-user as an addict, what changes are the most basic terms about her. From a situation of homeostatic stability and control, she is propelled into a narrative of inexorable decline and fatality, from which she cannot dis-implicate herself except by leaping into that other, even more pathos-ridden narrative called "kicking the habit". (1993, p. 131)

Thus, according to Sedgwick, addiction denotes not just a condition but a narrative of "inexorable decline and fatality". Her description is a comment on texts found, for example, in treatments based on twelve-step programmes. A message formulated in different ways in the Narcotics Anonymous literature is: "We are people in the grip of a continuing and progressive illness whose ends are always the same: jails, institutions, and death" (1986, p. 1). "An addict" is thus characterised not only by their actions but also by an already imagined, deviant life trajectory. The addict is expected to move through time according to a preconceived downward chronological progression that terminates when the person either dies or stops using. But Sedgwick also writes that "kicking the habit", that is, quitting drugs, or "getting clean", has its own dramatic narrative. In short, in such a reading, the concept of addiction constructs subjects in life-changing ways.

Angela, however, rejects the idea of addiction as a compulsive state. She describes how she has been both close to and inside what is called addiction, but says she has realised that *identification* as an addict is required for the addiction to be reified. She thus opposes the "re-framing" that Sedgwick describes. She says:

> I mean, I've read articles saying that this addiction people talk about... That love helps cure addiction and that people who were given morphine ahead of surgery don't go through the same withdrawal at all as someone who sees themselves as an addict. And it's the same for me, I haven't, like... Or, that is, I've always understood that you... need to change things up [mumbles] I think people might be looking for an identity, like "now I'm part of this group, now I'm adopting this style, now I'm getting an... addiction. Then we [become], now I become an addict."

Angela believes that, if love can ward off addiction and withdrawal looks different depending on the context in which drugs were consumed, this indicates that it is not the drugs themselves that are key when it comes to addictions. The argument that one has to "change things up" is a reference to how she quits using a certain drug when she starts to feel a need for that drug in particular. Switching from one drug to another entails a change of perspective, a refusal to identify with a certain drug-related way in which the world can unfold.

While Agnes too tells me of her proximity to addiction, she herself has not taken responsibility for these changes of perspective. Instead of backing out, she has remained where she was and acted on her longing for drugs and her drug cravings. But when she has turned to drug-seeking behaviour, her friends and other circumstances have stopped her, which she considers lucky.

> *Emma*: You mentioned before that amphetamines are very addictive. Have you experienced that yourself?
>
> *Agnes*: Mm. Absolutely. I think it's enough to take them a few weekends in a row, and you can end up in trouble. Yes, it's very easy to romanticise it. And you don't realise that yourself, but you don't see it as something dangerous any more. That it goes from having tried it and just "oh my God, what have I done?" to, it's something normal. […]
>
> *Emma*: But have you ever had a hard time not taking it?
>
> *Agnes*: Well, I've been really lucky with a lot of these things because I think that, if I'd had the opportunity… I *think* things could have gone pretty badly. […] But now I always, like, when I wanted to go out again the day after or do something, there's always been someone who's told me to stop, so yes, I've been lucky. But I think it's incredibly hard to put a stop to things yourself.

On the one hand, Agnes describes drug-seeking as a wilful action from a perspective where drug use and the return to drug use seem normal. During the interview, on the other hand, this behaviour, which sometimes appears normal, is described as dangerous and the fact that factors in her environment stopped her as luck. Addiction, therefore, appears to Agnes as an imminent risk; she orients herself in loops, but thanks to an obstructive environment, other lines enter her field of vision and the loops are straightened out.

It is at this abstract point where use occurs or ceases, between lines and loops, to use the terms of this chapter, that Sedgwick argues substances and behaviours become "addictive" or not, according to the medicalising discourse of which she is critical. She calls the point "The ability to […] *choose (freely) health*" (1993, p. 132, italics in original). Such a notion of free will, she argues, conceals social conditions behind a moralising imperative. Angela's drug changes and Agnes' obstructive environment show that loops and lines can coexist, and that the options of death or "kicking the habit" are not the only ones possible. For both Agnes and Angela, loops and lines seem to alternately appear as the perspectives from which the world unfolds. For Angela, it is a strategy of forming winding lines that diverge towards other targets when the loops become visible. For Agnes, it is about being in the right context. Are these contexts really about luck, or has she targeted them, in a similar way to Pernilla, with the intention of escaping addiction and keeping the lines in sight?

9.4   The Will to Quit Using Drugs

At *Brukarföreningen*, the *Users association*'s syringe exchange at Globen in Stockholm, there was a note on the noticeboard with the text: "Don't look back cuz you're not going that way!", with a sun on it (Observation 22 November 2017). This is an orientation instruction. I interpret it as containing both a request not to look back upon undesirable events that may provoke unpleasant feelings and obscure the view away from the drugs, and simultaneously a request not to move in a loop, via drugs.

As an instruction, it is negative, focusing on the direction to be avoided. When I ask Hanna, who says that she wants to and will stop using drugs, what she will do instead, she firmly answers that she wants her children back. Since she lacks a home of her own and also seems to want to stop prostitution and shoplifting, I ask where they will live and how she will support them. I want to hear how she envisages other lines than loops, but I receive only delayed and evasive answers. Among other things, she says:

> Um… [pause] You know… usually you don't have options when it comes to work, you don't have much choice in life. You don't have that. You have to… take what you… can get in life. Isn't that so?

The lack of choice in life that Hanna imagines means that the pursuit of self-developing optimisation does not seem relevant in her thoughts about the future, her life beyond heroin. The metaphor of long lines loses its relevance. She imagines herself not going anywhere but holding onto her children and taking what she can get.

Drug addiction appears to be a familiar room in which Hanna finds herself, but she wants to leave that room and close the door behind her. Then she will get "clean" but at the same time she will find herself in unfamiliar territory where she cannot orientate herself. The instruction not to look back can therefore also be interpreted as an invitation to force oneself to orientate away from the familiar, regardless of what happens. Ahmed describes a person's orientation in a dark unfamiliar room as groping for recognisable objects (2006, p. 7). A wall, for example, which sooner or later leads to a door. For Hanna, it is precisely the familiar objects that risk leading her back to the door she came out of. I perceive that Hanna's perspective during the interview, from the starting point in her body, is firmly focused on her children. Before she can reach them, however, she has to make it past heroin—the very thing that enables her to get anything done at all (see the chapter **The First Visits**). She is thus trapped in a looping Catch-22. Without heroin in her body, she cannot reach for them, so she turns towards heroin. When she turns around again, under the influence, her children are pulled away by society.

Carolina, who has not used drugs for eight years, describes new ways of orientating herself, away from the loops. Her story reads like a tale of exceptional determination. She portrays her experience of coming off drugs as a long and persistent struggle to gain access to treatment. In the end, what she describes as "eleven months of active attempts" (involving both her father and another relative) led to a place at a rehabilitation centre. A twelve-step programme was what would help her, she believed:

> we really insisted on twelve-step treatment. My dad too managed to get sober thanks to the twelve-step programme. So, like, we had *proof* that this was something that worked.

The name of the twelve-step programme itself indicates a spatial movement in a certain direction, through twelve numbered steps. Carolina's struggle was thus about getting help to orientate herself, to move physically and mentally, in line with a specific programme. She found the toughness of the twelve-step programme helpful and has continued to follow it through the twelve-step-based organisation Narcotics Anonymous (NA).

But does the twelve-step programme mean moving in completely new directions? NA's texts show that it is not that simple. The organisation brings together people who, in a group, but one at a time, talk about the worries that plague them after they stop using. Some participants have not used drugs for decades. Others may have decided to stop just a few hours earlier. What is required to participate is "a desire to stop using drugs" (NA 1986, p. 1). The people who gather are directed to the space where the drug use would have been, which is not a void but a mental place of memories, feelings and problems, and, with their involvement in NA, also a physical place for a community of people who formerly used drugs (Heilig 2015, pp. 266f.). Can NA be understood partly as a gathering place for mourning what is lost when drugs are no longer used? The people who gather are committed to the cessation of an activity, sometimes for the rest of their lives. This involves a new activity that is intended to facilitate a shift away from drugs, and towards other desired goals, but requires movement along a line that, like addiction, continually folds back into a place where drug use is central. In this way, a drug-using perspective is retained to some extent.

I ask Carolina what happens when one has reached the final step.

> No but, you know, you do all of the steps, and then… you can go through them again, and again, and now I have "sponsees". I have a sponsor who supports me, and I've started sponsoring a few girls myself. So then I go through the steps with them and learn even more myself and start seeing additional things I have to work on.

She describes the movement as loops: the twelve steps recommence from step one, and other people are led through the same steps. Through these loops, Carolina says she is alerted to new aspects of herself and her life that she has to work on. Under the headline "Recovery and Relapse", NA formulates this looping movement as follows:

> Complete and continuous abstinence, however, in close association and identification with others in NA groups, is […] the best ground for growth. […] We may tire mentally in repeating our new ideas and tire physically in our new activities, yet we know that if we fail to repeat them we will surely take up our old practices. (1986, p. 4)

This orientation through the repetition of new ideas and activities seems to offer a necessary substitute for movement back towards actual drug use, which would otherwise be too tempting. The loops resemble a bodily habitus, a movement that the twelve-step programme understands as permanent. The choice available to people who used to use drugs is whether to allow the loops to include physical drugs or just talk about drugs.

If drug intoxication is an alteration of the starting point from which one's world unfolds, the twelve steps are returning points, or points of connection to those previous points, but where the focus is on developing the self. By exploring what life was like when they used drugs and making plans for the future, with drug use as their point of departure, the person who formerly used drugs approaches the same points they passed before, but sees them in a different light. In the NA text *Another Look,* the organisation writes "In recovery, through the help of a Higher Power and the steps of NA, anything is possible" (1992, p. 2). The vantage point from which one looks in this case is based on the experience of drug use and the repetition of the steps, from which all possibilities are described as attainable.

Helen Keane criticises such a revision of the starting point as an illusion of freedom of choice, while being an essentially predetermined self-realisation project according to specific templates. She writes:

> The healthy and productive life of recovery is a particular mode of existence that comes about not from natural processes of healing or growth, but from a concerted and multifaceted project of self-production. (2002, p. 158)

Keane argues that, according to the twelve-step programmes, the recovering addict is different from both addicts and non-addicts, because the recovering addict has embarked upon a journey that leads to a particular spiritual awakening and a free and harmonious interior. But freedom, on the other hand, is based on a profound inwardness within a regulative discourse of freedom (see also Rose 2019) that requires the recovering person to engage in rigorous self-monitoring and a series of daily practices, such as honesty, sobriety, self-examination and regular meetings.

What is possible is limited to normative endeavours to transform the inner self (Keane 2002, p. 172) and free it from delusion. According to the twelve-step programmes, the alternative to addiction thus appears to be an optimisation strategy, a focused interest in self-development, in a lifelong relationship with the loops of addiction.

Beverley Skeggs, as described earlier, locates a central aspect of class difference in the self. She discusses how the ownership of the self and the ability and authority to police it is a fundamental middle-class privilege that is constantly made through self-representation, which can be contrasted with how the working class is considered to be in need of policing, and how personal experiences and narratives are interpreted as expressions of a generalisable "otherness" (2004, p. 37). In such an analysis, spending time and effort on formulating a complex interior becomes a making of class distinctions, "interiority as a form of superiority" (Skeggs 2011, p. 497). Such a self-reflexive and performative way of constructing oneself as valuable is institutionalised as a starting point for how a good citizen should be—Skeggs describes this as "compulsory individuality" (2004, p. 57)—while the creation of the working class is seen as a form of surveillance. It is, and always has been, about constituting a deficient counterpart, a backdrop of meaninglessness against which valuable middle-class selves can be measured (2004, p. 118). However, Skeggs argues that there are other ways of establishing and perceiving value, which—as I mentioned earlier—can include, for example, care and love, non-market values that are invisible to a middle-class gaze when they are not accompanied by capital.

For those who do not find resources for self-realisation in their situation, such as Hanna, it becomes difficult to formulate alternatives to the loops. If a person does not think of themselves as a progressive self-actualisation project, how can subjectivity be understood at all in a capitalist class society? The purposeful loops of dependency look threateningly clear compared to a desire to just be with one's children.

References

Ahmed, Sara. 2006. *Queer Phenomenology: Orientations, Objects, Others.* Durham, NC: Duke University Press.

Ahmed, Sara. 2014. *The Cultural Politics of Emotion,* 2nd ed. Edinburgh: Edinburgh University Press.

ARTPOP by GAGA. 2013. Lady Gaga—Interview on Z100 Radio (11/11/2013) [Part 2]. In *Elvis Duran and the Morning Show.* https://www.youtube.com/watch?v=FP_9eXhcF4g&t=70s [2023-08-10].

Belfrage, Lisa, and Marianne Gustavsson. 2012. *Alla vilda* [film]. Stockholm: TriArtFilm.

Berridge, Virginia. 2013. *Demons: Our Changing Attitudes to Alcohol, Tobacco & Drugs.* Oxford: Oxford University Press.

Campbell, Nancy D. 2000. *Using Women: Gender, Drug Policy, and Social Justice.* Milton Park: Taylor & Francis.

CAN. 2021. *Socioekonomiska skillnader i narkotikaanvändning bland vuxna i Sverige.* (Rapport 198). Stockholm: Centralförbundet för alkohol- och narkotikaupplysning.

Carr, Alan. 2017. Courtney Love Talks about Her Battle with Drugs. In *Alan Carr: Chatty Man.* https://www.youtube.com/watch?v=z9kO183ZD9w [2023-08-10].

de Quincey, Thomas. 2003/1822. *Confessions of an English Opium Eater.* London: Penguin Classics.

Goldberg, Ted. 2000. *Narkotikan avmystifierad: Ett psykosocialt perspektiv.* Solna: Academic.

Goldberg, Ted. 2012. Vad händer om vi legaliserar narkotika? *Socialvetenskaplig tidskrift* 19 (1): 56–64.

Heilig, Markus. 2015. *Alkohol, droger och hjärnan: tro och vetande utifrån modern neurovetenskap.* Stockholm: Natur & Kultur.

Iversen, Leslie. 2012. *Speed, Ecstasy, Ritalin: The Science of Amphetamines.* Oxford: Oxford University Press. Oxford Scholarship Online [ebook].

Keane, Helen. 2002. *What's Wrong with Addiction?* Melbourne: Melbourne University Press.

Laanemets, Leili. 2002. Skapande av femininitet: Om kvinnor i missbrukarbehandling. Diss., Lunds universitet, Lund.

Lewis, Marc. 2017. *The Biology of Desire: Why Addiction Is Not a Disease.* London: Scribe.

Linton, Magnus. 2010. *Cocaina: en bok om dem som gör det.* Stockholm: Bokförlaget Atlas.

Lupton, Deborah. 1999. *Risk.* London: Routledge [ebook].

Maher, Lisa. 1997. *Sexed Work: Gender, Race and Resistance in a Brooklyn Drug Market.* Oxford: Oxford University Press.

NA. 1986. *NA White Booklet.* Narcotics Anonymous World Services.

NA. 1992. *Another Look.* Narcotics Anonymous World Services.

Nelson, Stanley. 2021. *Crack: Cocaine, Corruption & Conspiracy* [film]. Netflix.

Palmer, Cynthia, and Michael Horowitz. 2000. *Sisters of the Extreme: Women Writing on the Drug Experience.* Rochester, VT: Park Street Press.

Plant, Sadie. 1999. *Writing on Drugs.* London: Faber and Faber.

Rose, Nikolas. 2019. *Our Psychiatric Future.* Cambridge: Polity Press.

Sedgwick, Eve Kosofsky. 1993. *Tendencies.* Durham, NC: Duke University Press.

Skeggs, Beverley. 2004. *Class, Self, Culture.* London: Routledge.

Skeggs, Beverley. 2011. Imagining Personhood Differently: Person Value and Autonomist Working-Class Value Practices. *The Sociological Review* 59 (3): 496–513.

Wierup, Lasse, and Erik de la Reguera. 2010. *Kokain: drogen som fick medelklassen att börja knarka och länder att falla samman* [Cocaine: The Drug That Drove the Middle Class to Drugs and Countries to Collapse]. Stockholm: Norstedts.

Wilk, Richard. 2014. Consumer Cultures Past, Present, and Future. In *Sustainable Consumption: Multi-disciplinary Perspectives in Honour of Professor Sir Partha Dasgupta*, ed. Alistair Ulph and Dale Southerton. Oxford: Oxford University Press. Oxford Scholarship Online.

10

Happy Using Drugs?

Agnes and I talk about the positive effects that drugs can have. She describes what it is like to use amphetamines:

> And then, it's this hit of pure happiness, yeah. Extreme energy, for a pretty long time. But the best effect is probably that it makes you feel so natural and confident. I would say. Music can sound a lot better too, I feel.[1]

That drug use can lead to experiences of happiness and other positive feelings may not surprise anyone. It is, after all, an implicit purpose of drug use in general. But when these feelings of happiness are put into words, something happens. The feelings described contrast with stories about drugs as dangerous and destructive, their inherent unhappiness.

Most of the research that has been conducted on drug use has focused on unhappiness rather than happiness. Drug-use-related unhappiness is also a well-established cultural image, including the assumption that any happiness one might experience when using drugs is temporary and

---

[1] All quotes in Swedish have been translated by me.

© The Author(s) 2024
E. Eleonorasdotter, *Women's Drug Use in Everyday Life*,
https://doi.org/10.1007/978-3-031-46057-9_10

false. Ulf Ellervik—chemist and author of popular science books such as *Evil Chemistry* (2011) and *Pleasure* (2013)[2]—describes in a lecture how amphetamine use "tricks us into thinking we are happy" (My notes, 18 January 2017) by mirroring dopamine, which he identifies as "the molecule of pleasure", one that rewards us when we engage in survival behaviours, such as eating or having sex. According to Ellervik, getting high on amphetamines is a kind of (self-)deception, because it rewards us for unnecessary behaviours in the same way as for necessary ones. The reasoning then includes the feelings to which these behaviours give rise: they are genuine when linked to evolutionarily necessary practices, and false when they are not. From such a perspective, biological responses are aligned with normative conceptions of how happiness is achieved. Ahmed calls such beliefs promises of happiness (2010, pp. 27ff.). Approaching the right objects and keeping one's distance from others implies an underlying promise that the path leads to happiness. Approaching unhappy objects thus equates to turning towards unhappiness. This is an image of the perceived relationship between happiness/unhappiness and objects which, in the case of drugs, is widespread in society. Multiple Swedish municipalities provide similar information about drugs on their websites, cautioning against their use. The municipality of Grums, for example, writes: "Abuse becomes a shortcut to false happiness, a happiness that does not stem from having done something good".[3] In these texts, too, a false emotional experience is linked to bad actions, namely drug use, which is contrasted with good actions and genuine happiness.

In this chapter, I examine how the women in the study relate to drug-induced happiness and theorise how this form of happiness can be understood in comparison with normative understandings of what happiness is and the relationship between happiness and unhappiness.

There are risks in doing so. Sara Ahmed writes that happiness and unhappiness are perceived to be contagious and, in the same way as someone may keep their distance from a person who is unhappy to

---

[2] *Ond kemi* (2011) and *Njutning* (2013) in the original.

[3] https://www.grums.se/stodomsorg/stodforbarnochunga/ungochintemarbra/riskbrukochmiss bruk.5531.html [2023-08-12, Swedish only].

avoid becoming infected, they may seek to get close to a person who is perceived to be happy, with the hope of experiencing happiness themselves (Ahmed 2010, pp. 39, 97).

Linking drug use to unhappiness or happiness is, therefore, not just a neutral statement of fact, but a figure of speech that can influence people's directions. If drug-use-related happiness is perceived as being just like any other form of happiness, there is a risk that people will move closer to both drugs and the people who use them. This in turn increases the risk of exposure to the negative effects associated with drugs.

10.1 Distance and Closeness

The women describe difficulties in communicating drug-related happiness in different ways. When Katy says emphatically that "it's not something you talk about, and it's not something I talk about, either, anywhere", this secrecy stands in stark contrast to her descriptions of wonderful and easy-going parties where she uses cocaine with friends. Her silence is partly out of consideration for others who might be unhappy to hear about drug-related happiness. Katy's parents, for example, would feel sad rather than pleased if they learned about her drug happiness, she says. Parents would generally read unhappiness into drug use for the interviewees. Agnes tells me about her mother's reaction when she discovered that her teenage daughter smoked cannabis:

> my mum walked in on us when we'd been smoking in my room and made it sound like we'd been… doing heroin. "How will you be able to afford cannabis? Next thing you know, you'll start prostituting yourselves!"

Agnes' mother interprets cannabis smoking through a fearful understanding of all drugs as being associated with addiction and sex trafficking. This seems exaggerated and clueless to Agnes, who believes that her mother lacks knowledge about drugs and has a black-and-white view. I understand her to mean that the colour black represents drugs and unhappiness, while white is drug-free and happy. Agnes calls for a more nuanced approach.

Katy does mention that it sometimes happens that drug effects are commented upon, outside the circle that uses them together. In the right company, she can imagine saying that she had "a little help along the way". According to this expression, the drug is described as facilitating movement along a certain path, an intended path that has led her to the happy mood that is the reason she wants to put her use into words.

But does the person who says they had a little help along the way feel that they got ahead? Those who are told seem to have reason to wonder how the person who used drugs got where they are. This reflects a spatial distance that can be perceived as existing between people who use drugs and people who do not.

In this way, distance turns out to be a key concept in how drug-related emotional experiences affect relationships with others. Two people can be in the same room but, according to the women, the drug use of one or both of them can create strong feelings of distance or, conversely, intimacy. Agnes describes feelings of distance in relation to people who do not use drugs as linked to identity, an identity that therefore also includes drugs:

> Drugs are one thing, they're substances, but there are also the experiences, they're connected, but I think the identity is perhaps also connected to the substances with all that they entail, the experiences that come with them. [...] it's very difficult for someone who has taken a lot of drugs to connect with people who haven't.

In this quote, Agnes discusses how the combination of human and psychoactive substance is perceived by the person who uses drugs herself, as a unit that together experiences things that would not have been possible without drugs. Preciado describes techno-bodies, i.e. associations between bodies and pharmacological and technological objects, as monstrous (in a hopeful, Harawayian sense), irreversible implosions of modern dichotomies between, for example, nature and culture (2013, pp. 44f.).

Such a body, in Agnes' narrative, becomes an experience, from a first-person perspective, of having become permanently different through previous fusions. Agnes understands the monstrous nature of this fusion between the body and dead matter, not as a negatively characterised identity, but as a starting point for enriching experiences. The drugs have thus given rise to meaningful views from other vantage points, aligned with certain other people's (techno-bodies') feelings for/through similar objects (Ahmed 2010, p. 38). These are thus experiences and feelings that cannot be shared with people who have never used them. Not being able to "connect" becomes a marker of distance. Agnes again:

> So I would never have been able to meet someone or get close to someone I wasn't able to talk to about these things. It would never have worked. Like, er, at all. So I would never be able to get close to anyone at my current job, for example.

The sensation of distance from people without drug experience is contrasted with how Agnes describes closeness to others while intoxicated. One example is a love story:

> When I took MDMA for the first time in Berlin, it was with this guy I was dating a bit, who was an addict. I was 20 or 21, I think … and it was, well, it was such a rush that came in two or three seconds. And we'd just met and were quite in love, so it was very intense. It was an extreme relaxation, for several hours. We'd just met and yet we took a bath together and talked about our innermost secrets and there was an extreme naturalness in our being, all the time, which is… well, now I realised why it's fun to take it. It's that people become so natural, it's not a facade any more. I don't care so much about people's status, what they've done in life, I think all people are quite interesting, but it's hard to bring that out. And drugs make that quite easy. You can take anybody and give them a drug and then this extremely sincere person comes out and it's really interesting.

This scenario is straight out of a film: two young lovers in a bathtub telling each other their innermost secrets. What stands out (but does not make it any less cinematic) is that the lovers are high on MDMA, the man is said to be abusing heroin, and the woman, a psychologist, describes it as the height of authenticity.

In this quote, Agnes attributes the synthetic drug MDMA with the ability to bring out what she describes as the "natural" in people. This is further described as a sincerity, free from the facades that obscure what is natural and interesting in people. She thus conveys an image of drug use that stands in sharp contrast to the image of drug-related happiness as false. Instead, she perceives the positive feelings experienced during drug intoxication as linked to the ability of drugs to induce a naturalness that would otherwise not have been there, or would not have been able to emerge. According to Agnes, these are also conditions that later, when the intoxication has subsided, create a distance from others who have never experienced that influence.

Drug intoxication, as well as experiences of such intoxication, need to be shared so that the naturalness, sincerity and so on can be experienced as creating closeness. Those who are not intoxicated themselves may instead experience feelings of distance from an affected person, as the example of Katy shows.

Concepts such as facades, authenticity, naturalness and help along the way all point to experiences of how an inner life, especially an emotional life, is imagined or perceived to be affected by drugs. Drug-related happiness becomes a state that is experienced from a different body than the one that a person had before the drugs were used. The perspective changes, orientation takes place in different ways and person who uses drugs will perhaps always carry memories and possibilities of orientation that had not been there before.

Drugs can thus generate a particular point of view, from which drug-related feelings of happiness are within reach. But drug-related happiness is a happiness that also has a distinctive relationship with its opposite. It can make others unhappy, be interpreted as unhappiness, or be interrupted by experiences of unhappiness when the high wears off. How does the meaning of happiness connect to unhappiness for the interviewees, and how does it affect their images of drug use?

10.2 Unhappiness

Ahmed writes that the original meaning of "happiness" was "lucky", giving the word connotations of temporary and random events, rather than diligent endeavour. However, in a more recent context, feelings and descriptions of happiness have increasingly come to be associated with morally recognised paths to happiness according to normative ideals (2010, pp. 22f.; cf. pp. 88ff.). A bad person can be lucky, but it is more difficult to think of them as happy.

Unhappiness, Ahmed argues, is an understudied area in philosophy, but she examines the genealogy of the word. She claims that it can teach us something about the history of happiness, but I also see that the meanings of the word unhappiness paint a familiar picture of the *knarkare* or *knarkarhora*, who are exemplary illustrations of the word. Ahmed writes:

> In its earliest uses, unhappy meant "causing misfortune and trouble". Only later, did it come to mean "miserable in lot or circumstances" or "wretched in mind". The word wretched also has a suggestive genealogy, coming from wretch, referring to a stranger, exile, or banished person. The wretch is not only the one driven out of his or her native country but is also defined as one who is "sunk in deep distress, sorrow, misfortune or poverty", "a miserable, unhappy or unfortunate person", "a poor or hapless being", and even "a vile, sorry or despicable person". (ibid., p. 17)

The "wretch" has much in common with the *knarkare*: the sad, poor and marginalised character I imagined at the beginning of my thesis project as one of the iconic visible drug users, with the other being the rich and famous user. Ahmed's etymological study also encapsulates the active role of the wretch or *knarkare* and the madness that the *knarkare* on the street represents.

Wretchedness is not (only) about being "miserable" and "sunk in deep distress", but also about causing "misfortune and trouble" and being "wretched in mind", which together could constitute what might be described as a "despicable person", or a person who for obvious reasons is not happy but unhappy. A person who falls into such a category is often invisible. An unpleasant category is unpleasant to think about, and the very act of categorisation makes the preconception of unhappiness seem given, tiresome and inevitable.

However, Ahmed also writes that "the familiarity of a scene of suffering should not stop us from describing the suffering of a scene" (2010, pp. 98f.). She thus calls for descriptions of the inherent suffering within familiar scenes, ones that have been described so many times that we know what they look like, without ever having understood what they *feel* like. Such a scene is embodied by the unhappy *knarkare*, whose wretched life and death are scripted as inevitable consequences of their actions. The term "wretched", by both representing and causing suffering, places blame on the person identified as such, making it difficult, or even impossible, to mourn them.

If drugs can only contribute to false or monstrous forms of undeserved happiness, then drug-related happiness also becomes an expression of wretchedness. The unhappy *knarkare* and the happy one are both representations of the not-entirely human figures that I have previously shown are kept at a distance in society. This in turn creates an ambivalent relationship between the interviewees and drugs as happy or unhappy objects (Ahmed 2010, pp. 21ff.). Ahmed examines how the relationship between happiness/unhappiness and objects can be theorised, and quotes Spinoza, among others:

> We call a thing good which contributes to the preservation of our being, and we call a thing evil if it is an obstacle to the preservation of our being: that is to say, a thing is called by us good or evil as it increases or diminishes, helps or restrains, our power of action. (ibid., p. 23)

This quote states that the effect of objects is what determines whether they are judged to be good or bad, but Ahmed points out that such a judgement is based on evaluation and how the evaluations in turn affect which objects we approach: "To be affected by something is to evaluate that thing. Evaluations are expressed in how bodies turn towards things" (ibid., p. 23). As a result, she adds, happiness can play a significant role in shaping our immediate environment:

> Objects that give us pleasure take up residence within our bodily horizon. We come to have our likes, which might even establish *what we are like*. The bodily horizon could be redescribed as a horizon of likes. (ibid., p. 24)

She thus argues that liking creates our bodily horizons and becomes part of who we are. Such a way of theorising drugs is complicated by the rhythm between pleasure and restraint, as described by Richard Wilk (2014). The liked objects can become disliked if they become too numerous and/or are too often present. In other words, drugs as happy objects can abruptly fall out of favour with the one who uses them and slip into a socially defined category of unhappy objects, just when/if they come to define the bodily horizon. This change shows that the path to happiness is not only related to approaching the right objects, but also to enjoying them in moderation and experiencing moderate amounts of happiness in their vicinity (Ahmed 2010, pp. 36f). In other words, a happy life involves the regulation of desires, which distinguishes morally good people from bad ones. The difference can be linked to will and self-regulation (i.e., middle-class ideals, cf. Skeggs 2004, p. 73) versus bodily desires at the "behest" of objects (Ahmed 2010, p. 36; 2014, p. 80), in this case when someone cannot resist drugs.

In spite of the fact that every single woman I talked to described experiencing feelings of happiness as a result of their closeness to drugs, I still got the sense that they viewed drugs as unhappy objects when they had come to define someone's bodily horizons.

Therefore, despite the fact that all the interviewees described happy feelings as linked to proximity to drugs, a perception of drugs as unhappy objects was evident in situations where they have come to define a person's bodily horizon. One question from the interview guide was "Are you a typical XXX user? What is a typical XXX user like?" where the XXX was replaced by the name of the interviewees favourite drug or drugs. In response to the first question, only Hanna indicated in a sad tone that she herself was probably a typical heroin user. This coincides with the fact that she was also the only person who stated that she was currently abusing drugs. The word "typical" can be interpreted in different ways. For example, a person who emphasises MDMA as a drug with many benefits and positive effects could be assumed to think that typical users were lively and social people. But the question was not necessarily interpreted that way.[4] Instead, Agnes, for example, interprets "typical" as meaning that the person uses the drug (amphetamines) to a very great extent and manifests a negative image of use:

> I've got this friend [who] uses a lot. It's really hard to have a conversation with him. He's just, at it all the time. And... yes, cognitive impairments, [laughs] I would say. Restless...

Boel has a different image of the typical user, in her case of MDMA, whom she refers to in a slightly patronising tone. She says that she does not think that she herself is a typical MDMA user and continues:

> A typical MDMA person, I think, is mainly, for all kinds of reasons, someone who's trying to escape the norm. Who perhaps has problems with the norm and thus rebels against it by using.

Boel compares this kind of person to people who enjoy themselves when using MDMA and who feel that "everything about them is enhanced"—which is how, on an earlier occasion, she described herself and the people she prefers to socialise with while using drugs. Despite their own use of drugs and the fact that both Boel and Agnes emphasise use as an important part of their lives, albeit in different ways—Boel describes use as something she could very well do without, while Agnes thoughtfully concludes that she actually sees drug use as part of her identity—both individuals associate "typical use" with a person who uses the drug in a way that causes harm, or as a way of escaping problems. From their perspectives, the typical drug user thus does not appear to be a happy person. For drugs to be used in ways they consider advantageous, the use has to be atypical.

---

[4] I think that a similar question about, for example, typical drinkers, athletes, politicians or musicians would also have generated responses that focused on the respondent's ideas about a small and hardly representative group of practitioners who spend a lot of time engaging in their activity of choice. The point here, however, is the negative way in which my interviewees viewed typical drug users and their relationship to unhappiness/happiness.

So using drugs is about navigating happiness and unhappiness, which are four different feelings: drug-related happiness, drug-related unhappiness (which cannot be mourned) and then other kinds of happiness and unhappiness. None of the four can be fully separated from the others. Happiness and unhappiness can serve as each other's antithesis, but can also overlap and run into each other, as Thea explains:

> *Thea*: what drugs can be [about] for me, is that I've lost so much of myself because of… physical things that have happened to me, and how… burnt out I am, mentally. So I want to get back, myself. Yes, get my joy back, it's like a reminder…
>
> *Emma*: Can you tell me about a time like that?
>
> *Thea*: […] I took some MDMA, by myself. Then I took a little more, when I felt it started having an effect. Yes. I spent some time with myself. In bed, under the blankets. [laughs] And, kind of worked on getting in touch with myself.
>
> *Emma*: Was it a positive experience?
>
> *Thea*: It was. Ideally, you want to have someone who, someone else who makes you feel safe. You know, it works better then… But yes, I would say that, it was a positive experience, although it was also… it was also mixed with a kind of sadness, a… relaxed sadness, there was simultaneously this kind of sorrow, a… relaxed sorrow.

Thea's starting point for drug use with the aim of regaining or being reminded of joy is the painful physical and mental conditions caused by the series of failed gender-affirmation surgeries that she has undergone. The quote above mentions an occasion that was experienced both positively—Thea desired the proximity to MDMA, even though she would have liked to be accompanied by a safe person—and as grief. This grief involved, among other things, terrifying and painful hospital stays and the physical challenges and problems caused by the surgery. In the story, she performs another repeated, familiar scene of unhappiness, namely her transitioning process. Thea can mourn this process by using MDMA, which not only puts her in touch with her sorrow but also brings up positive feelings. Navigating happiness and unhappiness thus does not necessarily draw a line between dichotomous experiences; in Thea's case, it takes on the shape of a strategic path, via drug-related happiness, that allows her to approach or return to experiences of non-drug-related unhappiness. Thea felt that she needed to mourn them in order to be able to regain her joy, and used MDMA to enable that process.

In her piece *The Alphabet of Feeling Bad* (Cvetkovich and Michalski 2012), the artist and researcher Ann Cvetkovich writes: "It's important to question what counts as Happiness, and to make room for feelings of Unhappiness that express the desire for a different kind of world". For Thea, drugs served as a way to find the courage to approach unhappiness, and thus as a point from which the world unfolds in a way that allows change.

The above quote is inspired by Sara Ahmed's notable discussion of unhappiness and feminist "killjoys", who can be, for example, people who do not laugh at something they do not perceive as funny (2010, p. 65). Such behaviour can ruin the mood of a room, and people who do not laugh, or perhaps question the joke, thus kill joy and become killjoys. Ahmed shows how happiness and joy are given conventions that can put pressure on people who are oppressed by what is presented as funny, and that laughter can be a practice that maintains power.

However, the feminist aspect of a critical stance towards joy is not just about laughter, but is also relevant to normative life events that are expected to bring happiness, such as marriage, making one's husband happy, organising one's home and family in particular ways and so on. If, in Thea's case, there was a strategic idea of connecting to herself and experiencing grief during intoxication—a getting-in-touch that led to a change in her bodily point of departure and, by extension, of the way in which the world unfolds—women's use of drugs, as discussed before (Ettorre 1992; Malloch 1999, p. 353), has often been about numbing oneself in order to be able to put up with the world as it is. Different drugs have different effects, which allows for vastly different and even conflicting opportunities to experience feelings. The interviewees' ways of navigating between and through happiness and unhappiness are thus connected to different ambitions to maintain or deviate from normative lines.

10.3 Drugs as Happiness

The charged status of drugs as unhappy objects makes their use a thoughtful practice for interviewees, which is defended in various ways. Ahmed writes: "you can be affectively alien because you are affected in the wrong way by the right things" (2010, p. 67). When it comes to drug-related happiness, I interpret my interviewees as experiencing the opposite. They are emotionally alienated by being affected in the right way, but by the wrong things, but allied with others who approach drugs in the same way.

In the following, I describe three different patterns of navigating alongside drugs in the interview material, in relation to normative lines and through and between different forms of happiness and unhappiness. These are about: being made happy by the drugs as though it were the right thing; refusing to accept unhappiness induced by normative demands to approach the right things and instead using the drugs as happy objects; and the inability to access the right thing, which induces unhappy feelings. In the latter case, drugs become ambiguous, simultaneously happy and unhappy objects.

An Almost Normative Happiness

If normative lines are accepted as the right path to the goal of being happy, where, for example, striving and status-filled work are important promises of happiness, then drug use becomes a question of how it can be incorporated into such established notions of what the path to happiness should look like.

Madelene, who has been injecting heroin to varying degrees for years, tells me she now uses the drug a few times a month. "I don't *like* taking it […] in a group. I take it by myself and watch a film or something. That's how I use it. I use heroin the way others have a glass of wine on a Saturday", she says, but adds: "And that isn't accepted".

Katy also makes comparisons with wine. She says that she does not see any reason to stop using drugs, which in her case means mainly cocaine and cannabis: "I don't really see why I would do that. It's like I would stop drinking, a glass of wine". She describes a typical evening when she smokes cannabis:

> it might be if I've had a really stressful day, and I've got a shitload of things to think about and, I can't sleep and my head's spinning.... and for me, like, my well-being is all about getting sleep. So that... then I can have my own little moment, when I light some candles and watch a [TV] series and smoke a little and just be myself.

The fact that it is the two hard-working single women who draw pictures of themselves as though they were relaxing after work with a glass of wine while using drugs is not a coincidence. Wine in Sweden has a history of being a more expensive alcoholic beverage reserved for the wealthy, beginning in 1702 when the Wine Merchant's Society formed a guild (Jönsson and Tellström 2018, p. 94) to the Bratt system's distinction between the unproblematic wine drinking of the bourgeoisie and the booze drinking of the working class (ibid., pp. 204f.) and on to the present day. The more widespread wine appreciation of the twenty-first century includes descriptions of grapes and wines that employ words like "refined" and "complex" (Nehls 2009, p. 130).

In other words, wine can signal good taste and respectability. Madelene's and Katy's modes of enjoyment thus follow normative lines, along which they place contested objects and argue for their appropriateness. Katy argues that cannabis has helped her to handle her demanding job. The drug then takes on the role of a market assistant in the literal sense, an object that not only guides one along happy lines shaped by a neoliberal labour market but also actively prevents unhappiness and the inability to work. She says:

> my work is incredibly intense, all project-based, I never have any time off, I can finish a project on Friday and then start the next one on Monday. And I'm supposed to fire on all cylinders, it's always like this when I start a new project, just one month and you're expected to deliver, so I think I haven't hit the wall *because* I smoke. Because then, just, then I disconnect everything.

For Katy, it is thus all about following the line that is expected of her, a professional line clearly born of a liberal market economy that requires flexibility and results. Pleasure in the shape of cannabis use manifests itself as a quiet time for herself, with the aim of getting her ready for work again.

Forbidden Happiness

While Boel uses drugs to help meet her job's expectations of efficiency, she also uses them at parties, as an expression of a rebelliousness for which she says there is no place in everyday life. Her identification as non-normative comes up from time to time during our conversations, and Boel makes links to her sexuality. When asked if she feels that it matters that she is a woman in relation to drug use, she answers that it does, and she says that the rules regarding women's morality are stronger, but then adds that these do not fully apply to her because she is a lesbian:

> *Boel*: I think my orientation matters, absolutely, absolutely, absolutely, absolutely, absolutely. I don't have to relate to a boyfriend's view of my lifestyle. And my parents, of course, it's not like I tell them that I, but … when it turns out that I have other, when I make other choices in life …. they don't react as strongly… as they might have done if I were straight.
> *Emma*: Why not then?
> *Boel*: Well, they don't because they assume it's part of my orientation. "I don't know what it is but it's probably your thing", I don't know. "That's what you people do. You go to clubs, you do different things, you poke each other." You know. I don't know, *I don't have to deal with any of those expectations.*

Her parents know that Boel is a lesbian, but not that she uses drugs. But their knowing about and accepting her lesbianism makes Boel believe that her parents would also accept her drug use as part of her deviant life choice. Ahmed describes people's different choices of happy objects as rooted in what she calls the idiosyncratic nature of these choices. People choose different things for the same purpose: to be happy (2010, p. 119). But not all choices are comparable entities that can be substituted for each other. Opting out of heterosexuality moves the person beyond the normative proximity that can unite people's choices into a single form. Boel feels that lesbianism has given her space beyond the normative demands that would have been placed on her if she had been straight, but at the same time she has been moved to a space where her parents do not expect to understand her choices. In other words, the promises of happiness familiar to the parents do not apply to the daughter, who goes her own way, and the parents accept this.

Boel seems sure of her direction, but during the interviews, doubts also emerge as to whether her free, non-normative space is really worth its price in terms of distance from the normative. For example, during a go-along interview, she describes a night out that ended with a skinny dip in the sea in the morning. From the field diary: "She says that in the middle of the dip in the sea she thinks of her mother, and that she had an existential crisis: 'What would my mother say? She's so proud of me, and I do drugs and bathe naked'". The distance to her parent suddenly becomes painful. I interpret her as wishing at that moment that she had instead acted in a way that her mother could recognise as a path to happiness. When she suddenly sees herself through her mother's eyes, the feeling of pleasure in swimming naked in the sea, while high on drugs, becomes a feeling of being off line, around the wrong objects, which then leads to a feeling of shame.

Instead of the Right Kind of Happiness

Carolina's first encounter with amphetamines was an experience of calm. She describes getting it from her boyfriend and his friends and then walking away:

> *Carolina*: I… woke up, sort of. At a neighbour of theirs, and was so very calm and comfortable in my body. And I sat and looked through a record box that he had, with lots of different records, and I had often been, like, prevented from doing things fully, before. And very much so that you can't think a thought to the end and can't read, that I have to jump back in the text, that kind of thing…
> *Emma*: That you were impatient?

> *Carolina*: Yes, or what should I say that I kind of … but, when I sat there and browsed, I could really … it was calm. It was quiet around me and I could look through all the records. I was somehow calm and very focused, and thought it was very quiet, all around. In my head, it was. It wasn't quiet, it was at an after party. But silence in the sense that I could sit and do what I was doing. It was really nice.

The amphetamines made Carolina feel at peace, she felt that she could focus and the world around her seemed to quiet down. This was "nice", she says, so she started using amphetamines more often. Soon, she did not want to be without them. At the same time, however, she says that she had a nagging feeling of aversion towards the pleasure, a longing for something different. When I ask her why she never injected the drug (she ate the powder wrapped in cigarette paper, or mixed it in drinks), she responds by saying:

> Because I really didn't want it to be the best thing in life. There were people around me who went, like: "come on, it's the best, it's pleasure like you've never experienced it". And I just went "but I don't want that pleasure! I don't want it to be the best thing in life." You know?

For Carolina, the pleasure itself becomes a terrifying thought. Like Thea's and Katy's experiences of drug-related pleasure as warning signs of addiction, Carolina does not want to try anything that would make amphetamine use even more pleasurable. The increasingly hated amphetamines risk taking on the role of the nicest thing of all, as a reminder that she cannot access the ways she wants to be happy. She describes the frustration of not getting onto the courses she applied for and barely making ends meet in terms of housing and finances. So she orientated herself towards the promise of happiness, a normative line, but was not given a place there.

She often lost her jobs and had failed to get into university. As she describes how the amphetamine rushes affected her—calm, quiet and beautiful—they appear to be preconditions for orientation. But the stories of how she constantly puts herself out into an otherwise messy world are characterised by struggle and loss. In this situation, she felt that too much drug-related pleasure could become a definitive direction, "the best thing in life", pointing away from what she wanted to do. Instead, she kept her consumption within a framework that simultaneously kept it limited, but also limited her, because she did not feel that she could live without it. Despite not injecting, she suffered the effects of heavy and repeated consumption. She describes how she became paranoid and depressed and that it changed her way of moving her body. Setting boundaries against injecting seems to have protected her from the pleasure she did not want to experience, but not from the painful consequences of drug use.

For Hanna, who describes no boundaries against pleasure, the daily heroin injections formed a similar pattern. She only hints with unfinished sentences that heroin use can be pleasurable. When asked if there are any positive aspects of heroin, the answer is that it serves as pain relief, which relates to her missing her children. She says: "It *can* do, it can…. It numbs the pain, it numbs the pain. Quite simply. The physical and psychological". But then she says that she has no physical pain. She states in a matter-of-fact voice: "Mental pain occurred with the children". This refers to the social services taking them into care. The kind of cushioning through heroin that Hanna describes, of pain caused by trauma and abuse, is defined by Natacha Du Rose as "a pursuit of pleasure as a form of pain management edgework" (2017, p. 50). Du Rose found in her studies that this kind of work is central to marginalised women who use drugs. Hanna is in many ways completely "off line": shoplifting, not having a home of her own, selling sexual services that she does not really want to be involved in, the absence of her children, and so on, are all parts of her life that she talks about with sadness and discomfort, and the line of drug use appears to be undesirable but her only viable path. She says: "I have to console myself all the time with the fact that soon I'm going to kick the habit". But what will be left if the heroin disappears? There is no guarantee that she will be able to get her children back.

The interviewees practise drug use in constant negotiation with how it relates to normative lines, with their promises of happiness, and conceptions of drugs as unhappy objects. Experiences of pleasure, tranquillity and adventure clash with non-acceptance, other people's notions of unhappiness and the risk of drug happiness becoming the only possible happiness through the work of pain management. Drugs are thus characterised by a dual emotional nature, as happy and at the same time unhappy objects.

If drug-related happiness can be contagious and entails the risk of being drawn to drugs, this presents an ethical problem for researchers who investigate drug use phenomenologically. The first-hand perspective of the interviewees may involve accounts of happy moments that can be neither completely omitted nor distorted if the research is to be based on the interviewees' experiences. However, in most cases, the women themselves did not describe happy experiences without weighing these against their own experiences and societal expectations of/about unhappiness. This meant that the reported drug use did not give the appearance of false happiness, but rather a happiness that is conditioned by various risks of unhappiness. However, for various reasons, the interviewees still thought it was worth the price, although sometimes with a certain degree of hesitation or, as in the cases of Carolina and Hanna, resignation.

Of course, there is still a risk that drug research that raises a topic such as happiness in relation to drugs may contribute to the contagion of drug happiness, but what is the alternative? Drugs are often portrayed in popular culture as attractive in various ways, and despite restrictive policies, criminality and the lack of scientific discussions on drug-related happiness, drug consumption in Sweden is currently at historically high levels. Perhaps, instead, discussions about negotiations of drug-related happiness in relation to unhappiness can provide a factual picture of a complex relationship between something that is actually common knowledge—the ability of drugs to induce feelings of happiness of various kinds—and how the risks of unhappiness entailed by the use of the same object look from the perspective of someone who uses them. If the relationship of drug use to happiness is not straightforward for people who use drugs, then their testimonies can serve as a counterweight to romantic portrayals of drugs.

References

Ahmed, Sara. 2010. *The Promise of Happiness*. Durham, NC: Duke University Press.

Ahmed, Sara. 2014. *Willful Subjects*. Durham, NC: Duke University Press.

Cvetkovich, Ann, and Karin Michalski. 2012. *The Alphabet of Feeling Bad* [Film/Art—Installation].

Du Rose, Natacha. 2017. Marginalised Drug-Using Women's Pleasure and Agency. *Social History of Alcohol & Drugs: An Interdisciplinary Journal* 31 (1): 42–64.

Ellervik, Ulf. 2011. *Ond kemi: berättelser om människor, mord och molekyler* [Evil Chemistry: Stories of People, Murder and Molecules]. Stockholm: Fri Tanke Förlag.

Ellervik, Ulf. 2013. *Njutning: Berättelser om kärlek, känslor och kemi* [Pleasure: Stories of Love, Emotions and Chemistry]. Stockholm: Fri tanke förlag.

Ellervik, Ulf. 2017. *Jubileumskurs: Konsten att njuta: Föredrag vid Lunds universitets 350-årsjubileum* [Jubilee Course: The Art of Enjoyment: Lectures at Lund University's 350th anniversary celebrations]. January 18

Ettorre, Elizabeth. 1992. *Women and Substance Use*. Basingstoke: Macmillan.

Jönsson, Håkan, and Richard Tellström. 2018. *Från krog till krog: svenskt uteätande under 700 år* [From Tavern to Tavern: Swedish Dining Out over 700 Years]. Stockholm: Natur & Kultur.

Malloch, Margaret. 1999. Drug Use, Prison, and the Social Construction of Femininity. *Women's Studies International Forum* 22 (3): 349–358.

Nehls, Eddy. 2009. *Kung alkohol och andra drogaktörer* [King Alcohol and Other Drug Actors]. Göteborg: Daidalos.

Preciado, Paul B. 2013. *Testo Junkie: Sex, Drugs and Biopolitics in the Pharmacopornographic Era*. New York, NY: Feminist Press.

Skeggs, Beverley. 2004. *Class, Self, Culture*. London: Routledge.

Wilk, Richard. 2014. Consumer Cultures Past, Present, and Future. In *Sustainable Consumption: Multi-disciplinary Perspectives in Honour of Professor Sir Partha Dasgupta*, ed. Alistair Ulph and Dale Southerton Oxford: Oxford University Press. Oxford Scholarship Online.

11

Is It Ok to Laugh?

Another aspect of happiness that is commonly described as contagious is laughter, which provides another entry point to ethical issues connected to drug research. There was a lot of laughter during most of the interviews included in this study. The interviewees laughed the most, but we also laughed together. Intoxicated people do hilarious things, it is an expected consequence that is not surprising (Waldén 2010). Nevertheless, the problem of the contagiousness of happiness and laughter is a chafing factor in research on potentially dangerous behaviour. To what extent does the researcher become part of the drug use through the interview situation? What role do interviewees' stories, including humour, play in the making of drug use?

Madelene lights up when I ask if drug use has led to any experiences that she would not otherwise have had. Her hitherto quiet and relatively brief way of answering the interview questions is replaced by a more eager, laughing way of talking. She says:

© The Author(s) 2024
E. Eleonorasdotter, *Women's Drug Use in Everyday Life*,
https://doi.org/10.1007/978-3-031-46057-9_11

> [Low-key laughter] But some of the absolute funniest experiences I've
> had, I've had when, when I or others have been under the influence of
> drugs. It would never have happened otherwise ...[1]

Then follows a story about a trip to Lisbon. There she used cocaine,
which she explains she had already experienced as a drug that makes her
paranoid, but she says that the quality was so high that she was tempted
to take it anyway (cf. Ahmed 2014, p. 80: sometimes proximity to the
wrong object can be perceived as the object insisting on being used, like
a cake that *wants* to be eaten).

> we lay down and took it [snorted cocaine] in my hotel room all night,
> instead of sleeping like the others because we had to catch a train at seven
> in the morning. But then we got stoned. So it ended up that a guard had
> to kick in the door to our hotel room. Because I had [laughter in the
> voice] I climbed out of the window and smoked, I used it as a door, so
> I didn't even realise there was a door any more. And I'd barricaded it.
> [Laughs] So... it was a rude awakening.

So Madelene becomes afraid of uninvited guests and barricades the door,
apparently with her friend's approval, and then climbs out of the window
to smoke instead. After being awake for a long time, they fall asleep.
When checkout time had passed, the hotel staff have to break through
the barricaded door to wake them up.

What is funny about this story? In and of themselves, the events—
barricading a hotel room door, the psychological reactions of paranoia
and sleeping so soundly that one only wakes up when a guard breaks
down the door—sound rather unpleasant and perhaps tragic. But this
stands in stark contrast to the way Madelene as a narrator recounts the
event as one of the funniest things that has ever happened to her.

The combination of desired mental states, (mentioned only between
the lines, in the judgement that the quality of the cocaine at the site
was good) and undesired ones, seems to imply a contradictory experience of terrifying pleasure. This is not an unusual account. This is how
many drug highs have been described throughout history: as experiences

---

[1] All quotes in Swedish have been translated by me.

of temporary madness where intense pleasure is interspersed with intense discomfort. The poet Mary "Perdita" Robinson, who lived from 1758 to 1800, is one of the people who use drugs who has described such experiences. Another is the dancer Anita Berber (1899–1928), known among other things for her "Cocaine Dance", which she performed in Berlin nightclubs during the 1920s, and which expressed euphoria, "freakout" and despair, according to the authors Palmer and Horowitz (2000, pp. 95f.), whose book on historical women's drug use also includes Berber's eerily dark poem "Cocaine" (Snow Poem) from 1923. The previously mentioned Birgitta Stenberg is another of those who has written about personal experiences of opium, cocaine and amphetamine intoxication in this way (see, e.g., Rapport 2017/1969). The respective drugs are portrayed in these works as evil and painful and their own behaviour as madness, but at the same time, the drug is described with love. Robinson, in her 1791 poem "The Maniac" (cited in Palmer and Horowitz 2000, p. 27), describes opium as a demon with a male pronoun:

> O'erwhelm'd with agonizing dreams, And bound in spells of fancied Night, I start, convulsive, wild, distraught! [...]
> The Form in silence I adore
> His magic smile, his murd'rous eye!

The anguished pleasure described in this more than 200-year-old poem resembles a destructive love affair. Despite anxiety and convulsions, Robinson admires the menacing demon and his "magic smile". In this type of experience, the horror does not detract from the pleasure, but becomes part of an intense experience.

In Madelene's story, the pleasure is implicit. Despite knowing that cocaine makes her paranoid, she cannot resist using it and, in retrospect, it is an experience that is narrated in a pleasurable and dramatic way, but also with laughter. Unlike the historical women, she perceives the drama as hilarious, including the strong emotions. What makes the drug story comical?

Madelene's story reveals the fundamental difference between life worlds that drugs can create. Her picture of reality clashes with that of her surroundings, where people act according to set plans: the train leaves, the hotel guard breaks in when Madelene does not leave the room. She is out of tune. From her starting point, her body, the world unfolds in a way that does not match the outside world. Ahmed discusses temporal non-attunement to the environment as being, sometimes, an adaptation to otherness (2014, p. 51). Madelene was temporarily out of tune, while in the interview situation she is back in tune. But she looks back on the out-of-tune experience as a wonderful otherness. This otherness contrasts with the impression of the physical and verbal Madelene sitting opposite me during the interview, who is a calm and serious person, but who lights up at the memory of what happened then. After discussing topics including her childhood, her social life and her career, the Lisbon tale stands out from the overall picture in a way that is rendered invisible here, where the story is presented by itself. Madelene finds what happened funny. As I interview her, I laugh at the tribulations she describes.

11.1 Laughter in Interviews

Interview responses in general, and laughter in particular, perhaps, can be misleading. They/it can reflect uncertainty, may be intended to cover up unsettling emotions, power structures and hierarchies, or mislead one in other ways (Billig 2005). Or, as folklorist Lena Marander-Eklund asks: "Are you able to say anything about emotions when analysing laughter? Is laughter a way of revealing emotions or a way of concealing them?" (2008, p. 96). Is there an ethical problem here? Is it ok to laugh at interviewees' stories about previous mentally unstable conditions? The question of the function of laughter comes into focus, how humour arises and why it is built into a story.

In his book *Laughter and Ridicule: Towards a Social Critique of Humour* (2005), sociologist and social psychologist Michael Billig posits that humour is a rhetorical question, that ridicule is essential for social interaction, and that this is universal. Laughter, in the case of ridicule, tells someone that a social convention has been violated, and it is expected that this will be met with feelings of embarrassment on the part of the offender. Examples of things that can lead to ridiculing laughter are deviant clothing, failures, falling and so on. These are deviations that need an audience in order to be funny, and they are, therefore, social phenomena (ibid., p. 121). Ridicule, Billig argues, functions as a basic type of reprimand that participates in the negotiation of social boundaries from early childhood. When adults laugh at children's behaviour, this also means that the child learns to expose others to laughter in similar situations. The task of the environment when someone laughs is either to participate in the laughter, and thus confirm the joker's judgement, or to refrain from laughing, to respond with "non-laughter", which is a sign that the joke and the laughter itself violated social boundaries.

Billig refers to such moments of laughingly recalling one's own shortcomings as "'laugh about it later' stories". Typical of these stories, he writes, is that the thing that happened was not funny to the narrator in the moment; it is only once it is recounted later on, accompanied by laughter, that it becomes funny. The person who experienced the situation has then, together with those listening to the story, become an observer of what happened and can be amused at the expense of the narrator's former self. Another typical feature of such a story, according to Billig, is that the narrator and the listeners laugh, but no one is described as having laughed in the actual situation. A story that includes the laughter of the contemporary environment is instead told to seek sympathy.

> In the "laugh about it later" story, the laughter must now belong to the teller and to their hearers, not to the witnesses of the original episode. In this respect, the story can become one about how "I/we disrupted the social interaction". [...] you, the hearers, are invited to laugh at the temporary disruption of social life. The teller, far from being a humiliated victim of embarrassment, becomes the unconventional hero/heroine, who can laugh at the surprise of others. (ibid., p. 233)

Billig highlights that a narrator who recounts a potentially embarrassing past event as a funny situation usually omits any third-party laughter from their story, in order to become (together with their audience) the laughing party. According to Billig, this means that storytelling provides a dual reward, where the person telling the story assumes the status-enhancing position of the laughing person, while the potentially embarrassing event in the past instead takes the form of a rebellious act, turning the former self of the narrator into a hero who breaks social rules. What was or could have been embarrassing in the past is thus renegotiated so that the narrator benefits from the embarrassment without suffering it in the present.

In Madelene's story, she behaves in a way that runs counter to expectations. However, the event is clearly depicted at a distance from her psychological state at the time, which makes the waywardness appear to stem from an alternative position, disconnected from her current person (cf. Lalander 2016, pp. 222f.). The story continues (with a chronological jump back in memory):

> I suddenly decided that I wanted to go out and have something to eat. But, like I said, I get pretty paranoid when I, you know, take things [breathes in through her nose]. So I clambered out of the room's window and just, "shit, the nearest place to eat." Then I found this place that did hamburgers [...] and *sat down on a bee.* [Laughs] And then I panicked like mad.

There is a pronounced vulnerability in this story: paranoia, shyness, physical pain and panic. Yet the sequence is part of what is presented as funny, and Madelene laughs at the memory of the bee. She is an observer who looks back with the power of laughter.

But, for this to work, the environment needs to recognise her, through laughter or some form of socially accepted compensation for laughter that lies between laughter and non-laughter. Billig states that such rewards can be acts such as groans or delayed, slow laughter (2005, p. 193). Here, a non-laugh or a laugh that "gets stuck in the throat" (cf. Jönsson and Nilsson 2014) could indicate that what happened was, for example, tragic, unethical, unsympathetic or, something I interpret as particularly relevant in relation to intoxication stories, that the distance between the narrator and their previous self is not credible and the temporality of the otherness is questioned.

I believe that the audience's assessment will largely depend upon the impression the narrator makes and the connection between the narrator and their norm-breaking former self. For the story to be funny, the narrator has to reenact their past self in a way that shows that they were a different person back then than the storytelling self they are now. If Madelene had appeared paranoid while narrating her story, it would have given a completely different impression. Here, I perceive that there must be a relationship of incongruence (see Billig 2005, pp. 57ff.) between the narrator and the narrator's former self, which can serve as a key to the humour that arises. But I also perceive a dimension that extends beyond what Billig describes, and that is the impression of solidarity with the former Madelene that her present self gives. There is a warmth in the way in which she looks back at her former self and embraces her. I interpret this as a bond that is usually hidden, a solidarity with another way of being.

Ethnologist Alf Arvidsson argues that the audience's reception of stories depends upon the authority that the storyteller manages to create. He suggests that this is why stories usually begin with the narrator attempting to establish authority, as a platform for the tale that is to follow (2014, p. 31). Such authority can be based, for example, on experience. I argue that this is also relevant for stories involving humour. A narrator can claim that something is funny, but whether or not their story will actually manage to make people laugh depends on the narrator's authority within that context (see, e.g., Billig 2005, pp. 177f.). Rhetorically, narratorial authority is tied to broader concepts such as ethos, character and the ability to understand and adjust one's message to one's audience (Johannesson 2013). Ethos can be criticised from a power-critical perspective as a factor that is influenced by class, gender, sexuality and so on (Ryan et al. 2016), which complicates the concept's relationship to experience as well as to the audience. Recounted experiences construct their narrator in different ways, depending upon who is listening.

When it comes to drug use, however, experience as a creator of authority can be a Catch-22. A person cannot talk about self-perceived drug use without experience, but that very experience can discredit the narrator because drug use is linked to untrustworthiness and low status, among other things (Lalander 2016). The experienced narrator as an authority, with the right to narrate, therefore, ends up in a peculiar grey area, where the very thing that grants them authority could simultaneously invalidate what they say. The distance between the temporary high and the narrator can be blurred by notions of the *knarkare*. In Madelene's story and those that follow, I perceive that the interviewees navigate performatively through the interview situation in a way that is intended to overcome this problem. Authority is built upon experience, but via a distanced narrator who marks that distance through laughter, and to this is added contributing ethos-strengthening factors, as Madelene does when her story continues.

In the midst of the scenario that Madelene paints, she describes a completely different aspect of herself than her mental vulnerability, namely her ability and interest in programming. She says that she "got into it" during her hotel stay and proudly recounts:

> I just sat there and built this fucking amazing system that's still in use, actually. One of Sweden's biggest – one of the world's biggest companies, actually – uses this system I built when I was out of my mind in a hotel room in, [laughs] in Lisbon. But they don't know that.

According to this quote, the mentally unstable person was also a person with great cognitive ability with links to "one of the worlds biggest companies". The drug story is no longer solely about vulnerability and mental queerness, and the hero of the story not only breaks societal rules but also acts as a cog in a high-tech wheel, someone who is central to the construction of the modern world. The laughter is now directed not only at Madelene's former self, but also at the unsuspecting company that uses a product created under such peculiar, drug-induced circumstances.

The ethos is thus built up in a conventional way, by referring to professional achievements, and at the same time by distancing the former self, in the way that Billig describes, which includes humour at the expense of the former, intoxicated self. If Madelene had not laughed at her story, the distance would be unclear and it would have become difficult to make out her current relationship to social norms, which would then affect her authority as a narrator. But the distance does not prevent the boundary-crossing heroine from being linked to Madelene's person through experience. She becomes someone who has experienced breaking social conventions and has the right to talk about it.

If I had not laughed at her story, it would have been a significant act (Billig 2005, pp. 75ff.), a non-laugh that would have signalled that her distanced approach to the previous events was not credible. Instead, I laughed (or made some kind of substitute-sound) and thereby confirmed her version of the story as boundary-pushing and heroic.

11.2 The Story as Part of Drug Use

Regardless of the response, the interviewer's actions are part of a dialogue that has consequences for the continuing narrative. Several researchers, including Sebastien Tutenges and Sveinung Sandberg (2013), have described how stories about self-experienced intoxication can constitute key aspects of the intoxication experience (see also Waldén 2010). From Tutenges and Sandberg's study of Danish young people on holiday in Bulgaria, they conclude that stories about events during intoxication are not only significant parts of the desired experiences, but also point forward, towards new intoxications that can mimic or trump the previous stories: "substance use generates stories, but stories also motivate substance use" (Tutenges and Sandberg 2013, p. 359).

Based on such an approach to the drug story, as a movement forward, orientated towards new drugs and new drug stories, the interviewer's response becomes part of an ongoing making of drug use.

The above researchers see a pattern in the events that the interviewees believe can form the basis of a good story.

Vomiting and sleeping in inappropriate places, for example, were recurrent themes. Other typical drinking stories involved individuals who hurt themselves, passed out, wrecked hotel rooms, shocked or annoyed strangers, climbed or jumped from balconies, got into fights, stripped, had public sex or encountered exotic individuals such as drug dealers and prostitutes. (ibid., p. 540)

Madelene's story fits well with several of these themes. She sleeps in an inappropriate place and time, injures herself, "passes out", the hotel room is vandalised, she annoys the hotel staff and climbs out of her window. But one difference I perceive is that the events that Madelene describes are largely attributed to her own psychological and mental states and abilities. I will return below to this way of linking the funny to the psyche and inner experiences.

The accounts from Bulgaria give a picture of unrestrained and largely carefree partying, which the interviewees justify by saying that they want to have fun memories to look back on and share with friends. They also want to be able to tell their children that they have had these experiences. One of the women interviewed, Birgitte, explains: "you've got to get out there and try stuff before you get old and grey. We don't want to find ourselves thinking back to an eventless life". And another interviewee, Kathrine, says: "Also, to be able to tell your children, 'listen, I was part of it, and I've tried it'. Then they will think, 'damn, my mother was really cool when she was young' [laughter]" (ibid., p. 542).

The theory that stories of intoxication lead people onwards thus assumes that there will be an ending, like old age or parenthood, when the momentum—intoxication, followed by stories, followed by repeated intoxication, and so on—eventually concludes with stories. Tutenges and Sandberg's interviewees exhibit a certain reflexivity, wondering whether they could have handled their intoxication differently. This reflexivity is even more evident in my material. The forward movements in the stories consist of ongoing orientations, with the stories largely pointing out directions away from the repetition of old mistakes. Laughter, which in Tutenges and Sandberg's interpretation is about a social reward for a successful story about intoxication and which is to be trumped next time, may in some stories rather have a function that is in line with Billig's analysis of ridicule as a correction mechanism.

Thea talks about an experience that she had in which the comical aspect of drug use is positioned entirely as an inner experience, which is an overall characteristic of most of the drug stories in my material. The intensity of this experience was conveyed wordlessly, through peals of laughter throughout the story.

Thea: I used a quarter of LSD I happened to have left, because I was bored. Then I went to the cinema. [Deep sigh] It... [sigh] Fuck, could have gone and watched something fluffy and nice [...] anything other than the latest Mad Max. [laughs] Which is what I did. That was stupid. But, I made it.

Emma: Why was it stupid?

Thea: The film. It's like, it's a dystopia. It takes less than a minute – and then it starts, the action. They just dive right in and... keep going and just "drrr", "pchh", and you can't miss these evil, evil characters in this, like, dystopian future. Skinhead types, mm, so it's like the opposite of what you...

Emma: Was it a poor choice of film, or...?

Thea: Yes, it was a poor choice of film. A really, really poor choice! [chokes with laughter] I still don't know what I was thinking. People had told me it was good but, I'd seen Mad Max films before, so... it was bad judgement on my part. I guess I was kind of bored... but it ended up being what I expected, everything with extra feelings, and I really got into the film. But I also repressed a lot of things. So when I walked out it was like, "right, open, air" and just "oh *god*", and I thought "What the hell. That was stupid." Cycled home.

Here, actually, and then things got pleasant and nice. I just kept thinking "God, what a waste, so stupid". And then I was here and enjoyed myself with music and headphones on for the rest of the evening.

Thea explains that this is something she should have understood and avoided: that watching a future dystopian action film while on LSD is an unpleasant experience that amplifies and distorts the impressions and emotions. The fact that the film she watched is of the type that tries to maximise the contemporary possibilities of creating strong sensory impressions made her exposed and vulnerable. She was holding back overwhelming emotions and describes great relief when she finally got out and could cycle home. "I made it", she comments.

To understand the intensity of Thea's experience, other stories of LSD intoxication can be helpful. These typically involve experiences of nature and quiet interactions with other people. Existential experiences of becoming one with large and small animals, plants, the universe and partners are common (see, e.g., Palmer and Horowitz 2000). People under the influence of LSD experience altered and heightened sensory impressions that can be overwhelming. Research conducted using LSD always includes some form of companion who can help when experiences become so overpowering that they risk leading to terrifying states, known as "a bad trip", which can pose health risks (Pollan 2018; Hofmann 2019). In one of her diaries, author Anaïs Nin recounts the first time she took LSD (*The Diary of Anais Nin: Volume 1947–1955, 1975*). It was an organised experiment. She was accompanied by her psychiatrist and it took place in his office. After taking it, she experiences some initial changes in the appearance of the room she is in, and then goes out into the back garden. With fascination, she describes the experience of a variety of sensory impressions:

> The dazzle of the sun was blinding, every speck of gold multiplied and magnified. Trees, clouds, lawns heaved and undulated too, the clouds flying at tremendous speed. [...] My senses were multiplied as if I had a hundred eyes, a hundred ears, a hundred fingertips. [...] The music vibrated through my body as if I were one of the instruments and I felt myself becoming a full percussion orchestra, becoming green, blue, orange. (1975, p. 256)

It is difficult to imagine having a hundred eyes, a hundred ears and so on, but the description can nevertheless give an indication of how LSD intoxication intensifies one's impressions from the environment. I interpret Thea as judging that a film about something "fuzzy and nice" might possibly have served as a companion through a pleasant experience. A violent film full of "evil" characters, loud noises and dystopian ideas, on the other hand, becomes almost unbearable for Thea to sit through with her heightened senses and experiences of dissolved boundaries between the self and the environment. Thea's comment "I made it" signals that it was not obvious that she would do so.

Thea repeats that the cinema visit and the choice of film were mistakes, and indicates this with laughter. As a contrast, she describes another direction for a pleasant high: being alone in her home and listening to music. The laughter here has the function of placing the cinema experience in a category of mistakes that have been experienced and should not be repeated. The social dimension is vague. Did anyone even notice that something unusual was going on in Thea's mind? That may have been the case, perhaps she looked terrified, but the social rule-breaking that Billig argues forms the basis for the humour of ridicule may have passed unobserved. From Thea's perspective, her breach is about poor judgement in terms of film choice, which is why she laughs at herself. But if the other cinemagoers had sensed Thea's state of mind, they would not necessarily have perceived the film choice as the socially norm-breaking component of the context. I would say that the situation points to an aspect that Billig does not address: that the social norm-breaking that is ridiculed in a "'laugh about it later' story" is based on the set of norms to which the narrator relates. It is in front of people who are expected to share her judgement that the choice of film was bad that Thea laughs at herself (Sandberg and Tutenges 2018). And it is also in front of them that her heroism can be appreciated. The humour is not linked to what the rest of the cinema audience is expected to think about her choice of film, or about women who experience LSD intoxication in public places in general.

Again, the role of the researcher comes into focus. In this case, I was expected to understand that the film choice was remarkable. Based on my prior knowledge of LSD, I did also perceive the situation as Thea exposing herself to an extreme psychological challenge because LSD in itself may involve mental challenges (Hofmann 2019). Thea's experience makes the LSD uses described above, with companions in calm environments, seem insipid in comparison.

In other words, I also perceived the choice of film as a remarkable component in this context. Depending on their point of departure, the researcher thus becomes a specific kind of audience, which has an effect on the interview.

If stories about intoxication are interpreted as a forward movement towards new intoxications, it seems inevitable that the interviewer's laughter can become part of such a movement. However, the direction that this movement takes is negotiated through laughter, rather than pointing straight towards repeated intoxication, as Thea's story shows. In both Thea's and Madelene's stories, laughter occurs mainly when less attractive parts of the high are recounted, such as Madelene sitting on a bee and Thea contemplating her poor choice of film.

But if (non-)laughter constructs the narrator through social interaction, then laughter itself is not the point here after all, Billig argues: instead, the point is what the story tells us about the narrator's ability to temporarily disrupt social norms. An instance of non-laughter on my part, during an interview with Pernilla, illustrates how non-laughter can also strengthen the story's ability to construct one's past self in this way.

Pernilla is telling an adventure story set during a holiday trip, and it shows how discomfort is intertwined with the qualities that make it fun for her. She begins, hesitantly in memory:

> a fucking, and it was also fun because it was mainly that, but it was awful, it was terrible... I remember – it was when I was in Bali, this is many years ago – then we slept in a hotel on a beach.

In a rather long-winded way, Pernilla recounts how she travelled to Bali, where she left her companions to go diving. Together with a group of young divers, she was welcomed by the hosts of the hotel, who set out various drugs on the terrace.

> Ah, there was a lot of pot [cannabis] in bamboo bongs [a kind of pipe for smoking cannabis]. And in a corner, there was a mat if you wanted to take opioids and so on. Yeah, yeah, yeah. Far out.

She says that she was smoking cannabis, enjoying the company and having fun at first, but then something happened. She began to worry that the situation had been set up as a trap by the Indonesian drug police. And then she saw a person whom she felt confirmed those fears:

> I start to notice how there are all these people sitting around, and just think "hang on, this is actually kind of a strange social situation". There's this short, thin man, who's wearing jeans and this kind of skin-tight leather jacket, if I recall correctly, and his hair was neatly combed, and he had these big bloody sunglasses. Right in the middle of the evening, mind. He looks like, you know, the epitome of a copper in a 1970s crime

series. So he becomes that for me. He becomes a civilian police officer. [laughter]

The sight of this man thus made Pernilla question the whole situation, which she imagined could have been set up as part of a drive to tackle drug tourism. She describes herself as paranoid but ambivalent about whether it was really as bad as she imagined, and says that she asked a Dutch man for his opinion. He laughed out loud at the idea and appeared completely unconcerned, giving her a sense of relief. As she recounts the incident, she sounds convinced that the man was simply right and that her fears were absurd. She says:

> it's the kind of situation that's just ridiculously funny in hindsight, because you look at it with sober eyes and go "my *god* you were cuckoo".

When I object that Indonesia, at least in recent years (the interview was conducted in 2018), is actually associated with police interventions against drug tourism,[2] unlike The Netherlands, where drug tourism is an established part of the nation's brand, she howls with laughter and comments that it was lucky I wasn't there. The unpleasant experience is funny when it is portrayed as completely crazy, with the image of the stereotypical 1970s cop at its centre, but it becomes funny all over again at the thought that her judgement at the time may have been reasonable and that she may have found herself in a strange situation that could have put her at risk of prosecution.

My reaction, not laughing, and the justification that risked killing the joy (cf. Ahmed 2010) in fact led to more laughter.

There is thus no choice of response on the part of the interviewer, which certainly constructs the narrator in a certain way. The interviewer's response becomes part of a living, and never entirely predictable, event that can lead to laughter, but also to silence or on to other paths.

---

[2] See, e.g., https://www.gov.uk/foreign-travel-advice/indonesia/safety-and-security [2023-08-10].

11.3 Women's Proud Madness

I perceive that there is a self-respect in this kind of laughing story, which does not tally with Billig's categorising into either funny stories that are told to become the laughing one who laughs, or stories that might include other laughers, told to seek sympathy in the latter audience. I perceive the differences as having to do with intoxication, but also with the making of gender. Billig's book lacks a gender perspective and a majority of the stories quoted are about men. Criticism of the lack of a gender perspective has previously been directed at classic humour research (cf. Jönsson and Nilsson 2014), but researchers in other fields have also had reason to question analyses of what is perceived and described as funny when they have not taken gender into account.

Criminologists Polly Radcliffe and Fiona Measham (2014) criticise Tutenges and Sandberg's study of young people partying in Bulgaria for lacking sensitivity to gender and other power differences. The events recounted by men include buying sex, groping, humiliating female sexual partners and degrading physical jokes with other men. The stories told by women include vomiting, karaoke in funny outfits and stripping at a club, but most of the space is taken up by reflections upon the men's and the young women's own behaviour, its significance and how it can be documented. Radcliffe and Measham write:

> We would suggest that the gendered organisation of these drinking stories/practices extends beyond the stories and context of their telling. [...] we suspect that the freedom that young women exercise within this reshaped post-feminist terrain may be insecure and contested. Our questions may point in part to the limitations of narrative research and in part to their wider contextualisation in fluid drinking cultures. We wonder too whether we may need to ask young women different sorts of questions in order to discover what scope they may have to do gendered drinking differently. (2014, pp. 346–347)

The stories I have quoted in this chapter do not include any sexual elements at all, but nevertheless I find Radcliffe and Measham's instruction to be sensitive to how the gendered meaning of the narrated events extends beyond the narrative situation useful. Madelene has talked about her mental illness in the form of constant anxiety since childhood, about a high-performance working life and a period of burnout. She can be perceived as a "good girl" who played sports, achieved high grades and was headhunted for demanding jobs. Against this background, her story about the Lisbon hotel room and her entire interest in drug use appears to be a way of creating her own space, despite being placed in a demanding life situation. The story describes a person who breaks with expectations, but also does not conform to a stereotypical representation of femininity.

The classical stereotype of women who use drugs is that they are mentally unstable, "mad, sad and bad" (Measham 2002, pp. 343f.; Du Rose 2017). Can the openness to and articulation of exceptional mental states be understood as a way of addressing this stereotype? The mental state is central to Pernilla's story, as it is to Thea's and Madelene's. Their attitude towards temporary mental vulnerability appears to be a significant part of their intoxication stories, including reactions of laughter when the events occurred, as in Pernilla's case. The funny story and the sympathy-seeking story do not appear to be separate types of stories for them, and the stories construct them as a particular kind of boundary-breaking heroes whose psyches have dealt with temporary vulnerable states. Thea's story is perhaps the clearest example in that it resembles the stories of extreme athletes or adventurers, who risk frozen fingers or other injuries but miraculously survive thanks to an extraordinary physique. The difference is that, instead of climbing a mountain or swimming through icy waters, Thea puts herself through extreme psychological stress. There was a pride in how these stories were told that includes pride in having experienced paranoia and other exceptional mental states.

I perceive this to be what makes the women's stories unusual. The laughter is related to experiences that include unpleasant delusions that could have been described as traumatic, dangerous and serious, and therefore cannot be comical. To tell these stories, the narrator is thus required to take a risk. The women who tell them explore and renegotiate their inner lives by exposing themselves to risks and then recounting them through new risks and laughing at them with pride.

In the conclusion to their article, Tutenges and Sandberg write that they too perceived that most of the stories they were told, whether by women or men, were recounted with pride and pleasure (2013, p. 543). In the quotes, the interviewees contrast their uneventful lives with a life that can be told as a "good story", which thus includes events that are usually perceived as negative, such as vomiting, abnormal sleep, injuries and violence (ibid., p. 540). But this does not necessarily mean that just anything can make a good story. The men are quoted when they talk about the abuse and humiliation of women, but no woman mentions herself as a victim. In my interview material, sexual abuse is also absent from the funny stories. Instead, they are mainly about experiences and thoughts induced by the drugs, the funny potential of which presupposes that there are other states and mindsets to fall back on. Bringing one's former, psychologically deviant self back to life by recalling events and laughing about them requires a space that is not always available. In that sense, there are parallels between my research and the stories in Trond Erik Grønnestad and Filip Lalander's study of individuals using drugs around a bench in a park in Norway (2015). Grønnestad and Lalander call some of these "decay stories":

> Within this frame, special kinds of stories are told that would appear odd in more "normal" settings. We call these types of Bench-sitter stories "decay stories" since they include central components of living on the edge, close to death and in misery. Such storytelling often contains black humour that includes topics and events otherwise regarded as taboo, such as death, serious illness and severe addiction. (ibid., p. 177)

Grønnestad and Lalander use Ervin Goffman and Mary Douglas to show how storytelling simultaneously creates a social community between survivors of extreme hardship, while also ritually recreating humiliating situations in an accepting context, thus "purifying" them. One example is a shared story, told to the other "bench-sitters" first by one of them before being continued by another, about how they started noticing vague symptoms that alerted them to the fact that something odd was happening to their bodies. They then went to the emergency ward, where they were told that they had a blood alcohol content of four and five per mil, respectively (2015, p. 178). Such a huge amount of alcohol would be lethal to most people, who have not been drinking extremely large amounts of alcohol for a long time. It almost killed the two narrators too, but they received emergency treatment and survived.

Most of the women I have interviewed are not part of social contexts in which they would approach a stigmatised place like the bench described in Grønnestad and Lalander's study. But there is an aspect of the men's stories described above that I perceive as having parallels to the women's stories, but which is omitted in the concept of "decay stories". This is about the boundary-breaking hero who is constructed through the response of the right audience. The clear sense of pride that Tutenges and Sandberg perceive in the young people's stories, and which also appears in my material, can be analysed in the same way on the basis of Billig's "laugh about it later" model, but with a modification in terms of the ridicule, which I perceive as partly relevant but insufficient to capture what the laughter is about. My interpretation of the purpose of this type of story, with narratives that revolve around a body that undergoes humiliating, dangerous, unpleasant or potentially fatal stresses but survives, is to look back from a distance but at the same time with a close connection to the past, and not only to be the one who laughs but also to have the space to examine that past experience while recognising it as a test of strength.

I perceive that this is about something more than cleansing oneself of dirt, which is only dirt in certain normative systems. The narrators in Grønnestad and Lalander's study, as well as those in mine, can take on something like action hero or superhero characters, i.e. in sharp contrast to the term "decay stories". The body undergoes dangers and discomforts but, in the end, can conclude that they "made it", in Thea's words. This is not to say that the structural conditions of the people studied at the bench (who are described as poor, constantly under the influence of alcohol or drugs, living in homelessness, etc.) are not blatantly defined as dirt in Mary Douglas' sense by large segments of society (2002/1966; see also the chapter **Avoiding the *Knarkare*)**. But the humorous action story of putting one's body through excruciating stresses and surviving them also constructs a hero (cf. Billig 2005, p. 233), whose body and/

or psyche has proven their strength. The narrative as a forward movement draws an alternative line (Ahmed 2006), along which the narrator describes special abilities and interests that, with the help of the audience's response, create a boundary-breaking person who is not intended to be judged within any other normative system than the one to which the narrator relates (cf. Sandberg and Tutenges 2018).

References

Ahmed, Sara. 2006. *Queer Phenomenology: Orientations, Objects, Others.* Durham, NC: Duke University Press.

Ahmed, Sara. 2010. *The Promise of Happiness.* Durham, NC: Duke University Press.

Ahmed, Sara. 2014. *Willful Subjects.* Durham, NC: Duke University Press.

Arvidsson, Alf. 2014. Berättelse, beskrivning, auktoritet [Narration, Description, Authority] *Kulturella perspektiv: Svensk etnologisk tidskrift* 23 (4): 30–38.

Billig, Michael. 2005. *Laughter and Ridicule: Towards a Social Critique of Humour.* London: Sage.

Douglas, Mary. 2002/1966. *Purity and Danger: An Analysis of Concepts of Pollution and Taboo.* London and New York: Routledge.

Du Rose, N. 2017. Marginalised Drug-Using Women's Pleasure and Agency. *Social History of Alcohol & Drugs: An Interdisciplinary Journal* 31 (1): 42–64.

Grønnestad, Trond Erik, and Philip Lalander. 2015. The Bench: An Open Drug Scene and Its People. *Nordic Studies on Alcohol and Drugs* 32: 165–182.

Hofmann, Albert. 2019. *LSD: My Problem Child and Insights/Outlooks.* Oxford: Beckley Foundation Press.

Johannesson, Kurt. 2013. *Retorik: Eller konsten att övertyga* [Rhetoric: Or the Art of Persuasion]. Stockholm: Norstedts.

Jönsson, Lars-Eric, and Fredrik Nilsson, eds. 2014. *Skratt som fastnar: kulturella perspektiv på skratt och humor* [Laughter That Sticks: Cultural Perspectives on Laughter and Humour] (Lund Studies in Arts and Cultural Sciences, 5). Lund: Department of Arts and Cultural Sciences, Lund University.

Lalander, Philip. 2016. *Människor behöver människor: Att lyssna till de misstänkliggjorda* [People Need People: Listening to the One's Made Suspicious]. Stockholm: Liber.

Marander-Eklund, Lena. 2008. Narratives and Emotions: Revealing and Concealing Laughter. *Folklore* (39): 95–108.

Measham, Fiona. 2002. "Doing Gender"—"Doing Drugs": Conceptualizing the Gendering of Drugs Cultures. *Contemporary Drug Problems* 29: 335–373.

Nin, Anaïs. 1975. *The Diary of Anais Nin: Volume 1947–1955*. New York: Harvest/HBJ.

Palmer, Cynthia, and Michael Horowitz. 2000. *Sisters of the Extreme: Women Writing on the Drug Experience*. Rochester, VT: Park Street Press.

Pollan, Michael. 2018. *How to Change Your Mind: What the New Science of Psychedelics Teaches Us About Consciousness, Dying, Addiction, Depression, and Transcendence*. London: Allen Lane.

Radcliffe, Polly, and Fiona Measham. 2014. Repositioning the Cultural: Intoxicating Stories in Social Context. *International Journal of Drug Policy* 25: 346–347.

Ryan, Kathleen J., Nancy Myers, and Rebecca Jones, eds. 2016. *Rethinking Ethos: A Feminist Ecological Approach to Rhetoric*. Carbondale, IL: Southern Illinois University Press.

Sandberg, Sveinung, and Sebastien Tutenges. 2018. Laughter in Stories of Crime and Tragedy: The Importance of Humor for Marginalized Populations. *Social Problems* 66: 564–579. https://doi.org/10.1093/socpro/spy019.

Stenberg, Birgitta. 2017/1969. *Rapport* [Report]. Stockholm: Norstedts.

Tutenges, Sebastien, and Sveinung Sandberg. 2013. Intoxicating Stories: The Characteristics, Contexts and Implications of Drinking Stories Among Danish Youth. *International Journal of Drug Policy* 24: 538–544.

Waldén, Susanne. 2010. Berättad berusning: kulturella föreställningar i berättelser om berusade personer [Narrated Drunkenness: Cultural Representations in Stories About Drunk People]. Diss., Uppsala universitet, Uppsala.

12

Conclusions

"They are *ordinary women*". This is how anthropologist Ulrika Dahl summarised her impression of the women in this study when she was the opponent of my thesis, on which this book is based. This is also how they appear to me, in the sense that they are, contradictory and diverse, cultural beings, rather than primarily being people who use drugs. Even Hanna, who feels crushed and imprisoned by her heroin use and life conditions, is above all a mother, a grieving mother whose attention is directed towards her lost children. The women also use ordinary drugs, substances that are in most cases widely available as legal medicines, but also objects of research and can be bought illegally. But drug use, whether it is prescribed, enabled by gifts or by buying drugs on an illegal market, is risky and uncertain. Drugs are morally charged objects with the ability to change the world of the mind, to make people healthy or sick, to numb or amplify emotions and experiences.

When drugs are used in everyday life, these aspects have multifaceted significance. They will affect situations like going to the movies, taking care of children and sharing secrets in the bath with a loved one, just as much as they affect everyday lives marked by classed drug use, where

© The Author(s) 2024
E. Eleonorasdotter, *Women's Drug Use in Everyday Life*,
https://doi.org/10.1007/978-3-031-46057-9_12

chasing cash for heroin or taking the morning bus to work after a sleep-less night in order to earn money for amphetamines is part of the daily routine. Some of the interviewed women link drug use to problems, while others describe how, with the help of various resources, careful planning and in relation to the rhythm of restraint and release that characterises modern consumer societies (Wilk 2014), their drug use is unproblematic. But these unproblematic aspects: happiness, legitimacy and propriety, are elusive and must be carefully balanced to avoid turning into their opposite—unhappiness, illegitimacy and impropriety.

In this book, I have followed twelve women along their paths. Through a queer phenomenological lens, I have explored how they oriented themselves towards illegal drugs in certain ways and ingested them into their bodies, starting from different class-related points that, regardless of what drugs they used and what fantasies about drug use they had, mattered for their further orientations. Along their paths, there lurk a whole range of risks that must be negotiated or avoided. The stigmatised *knarkare*, sober people, the syringe, the drug market, sunlight, children, prescribed medications and addiction, for example, are all described as having transformative power: a meeting with them can interrupt the path of drug use, making the drugs fail to extend the body in space and instead point towards the object of drugs—which means pointing towards the bodies that ingested them—and their failure or unwillingness to align with normative ideals (cf. Ahmed 2006). In the chapter **Avoiding the *Knarkare***, Pernilla narrates how she felt bad after using too much cannabis and therefore could not go out into town and use public transport. Her question: "How do you ask for help when you're under the influence of drugs?" illustrates how drug use can draw a line between the person who uses drugs and others, a line that can be difficult or impossible to cross. In Sweden, with its history of with-holding healthcare and life-saving treatment for drug-related problems, as discussed in the first part of this book, her question takes on an extended character that she probably did not intend. It is as though people who use drugs are considered to have walked out of the welfare state. And as they are no longer really here, how could they ask for help?

Drug use is thus a spatial matter, in several senses, rather than a practice. A place has been reached through an inner excursion together with a drug, a trip. But that journey commences from and in a certain time, a certain physical place, a certain body and a certain social and cultural context that allows a certain journey and certain conditions for the return. That starting point has a history of past actions that opens up opportunities for how a certain type of drug use can take place (cf. Ahmed 2010, p. 209). Oriented drug use is therefore about having access to resources and about being able to assess where a journey can take place in a desired way, and whether there are any paths from there that link the place to other places where the person who uses drugs wants to be. As we have seen, the perimeter of the drug-use location is less about the drug itself than the above factors, although the differences between drugs are vast and each one allows certain directions, but not others (see Appendix **Drugs and Medicines**).

In the right place, drug use can become an experience of intimacy, comfort and fun. However, a misjudgement about time and space can instead lead to disorientation and serious consequences, such as social exclusion and stigma. The key word is shame for middle-class people who use drugs, but for working-class women, shame is only one aspect of a whole package of repressive measures, a state-run stigma machine that is put to work if drug use is detected (Tyler 2021). Women can have their children taken away, lose their jobs and become one with the dirty drug swamp, *knarkträsket*, which is discussed in Chapter 3, where women are considered to be whores, whether they sell sex or not. The location of drug use can then turn out to be experienced as a prison, as Hanna has shown. It is a prison without walls, but nevertheless powerful in how it orients the body in repetitive loops and physically restrains her from moving in other ways.

Societal expectations about regulating oneself with drugs show that some drug use can occupy large, normative spaces. Women are expected to be in some mental states but not others, and are more likely than men to be prescribed medicines to align their inner worlds with the outside world, an alignment that can be aided by psychiatric medication (cf. Sandell and Bornäs 2017). Using psychoactive drugs in order to function as a well-oiled cog in the neoliberal market machine is something that several interviewees have resisted. Their drug use is rather an act of protest against such an adaptation and can instead be about creating bubbles and islands of illegal states of mind. Such drug use, which in the news, films and books is often linked to chaos, violence and crime, is on the contrary strikingly calm in these women's experiences.

12.1 Tacit Ways of Acting Out

In the previous chapter, Thea describes going to the cinema and then cycling home, Pernilla converses in her story about her trip to Bali when she stopped smoking cannabis for the evening. In Madelene's story, she barricades the door and goes out through the hotel room window, but above all she programmes and sleeps. When Boel describes herself using drugs, a paradox emerges between her rebellious perception of self and her drug-affected behaviour. She begins dramatically:

> I have some inner rock star, who likes to live out, sometimes, just "I'm a rock star and you suck", I'm harder than everyone else. So I have no barriers.[1]

She talks eagerly and mimes holding an imaginary tube to her nose, through which she pulls up imaginary cocaine. She says: "That's the point: letting go of control!" But this description of the "rock star" seems to be at odds with letting go of control. This is a highly conscious person who is orientated towards the drugs. Boel thinks about safety, chooses the variety, negotiates prices and quality and so on. She explains:

> I try to control it so that I can, at this end [holds out her hands and shows with her eyes how they represent two ends] just let myself go. So if I control so much here, maybe I can relax here.

Her explanation, where on the one hand the rock star lets go of control of certain parts (what can happen in the body after an intake) but at the same time appears to keep other controllable parts in an iron grip (environment, company and so on), is consistent with the concept

---

[1] All quotes in Swedish have been translated by me.

of "controlled loss of control" described earlier (Measham 2002). It is about women's ways of experiencing intoxication and at the same time performing femininity. Measham writes:

> The contradictions of conformity and social control, of "losing oneself" and "finding oneself" in drug use, of deviance and rebellion, of restrictions and independence, will be affected by the gender of the individual user and the gendered attitudes held toward these issues in the wider drugs setting. (ibid., p. 349)

Both conformity and rebellion in drug use, according to Measham, are thus affected by gender. So what does Boel do when she brings out her inner rock star and lets go of control? She says it is important for her to act out and not "have to behave" during her drug use, but she continues:

Boel: I'm probably much less outgoing than a lot of people I think. I'm very good at sitting in a corner and just being. [giggles].
Emma: So that's how you act out?
Boel: Yes, that's my, acting out, but being able to just sit and giggle. That freedom is really important, as well. I'm not one who likes to dance. I can, absolutely, do it but I'm not one who just [dramatises screaming:] "must dance!" So? No. I can sit in a swing for two hours and just "ah". Observe.
Emma: What happens then?
Boel: Yes, what happens? I don't know. I can't put it into words.

Boel's description of an outgoing state of intoxication thus ends up in a description of extremely quiet activities. Sitting in a corner, rocking, giggling and observing, she giggles both during the narration and in the story. What she emphasises as important is being able to "sit in a corner and just be". Her acting out is actually a refusal to act. Through using drugs, she withdraws from responsibility for the social and material context, from consuming the expected things and from working (Campbell 2000). This makes her feel like a rock star without barriers.

Paul B. Preciado in his book *Testo Junkie* (2013) provides a long list of examples of femininity codes in a list entitled "Some semiotechnical codes of white heterosexual femininity belonging to the postwar pharma-copornographic political ecology" (2013, p. 120). This list enumerates a set of white rules of conduct and signs for women in the modern West, which Preciado argues is characterised by being completely permeated by pharmacological technology and pornography. The codes of femininity include: "Little Women", "saying no when you want to say yes", "saying yes when you want to say no", "not leaving home", "not making any noise when you walk", "not making any noise when you eat", "not making any noise", "knowing how to wait" and "knowing how to restrain yourself". He also presents a corresponding list of masculinity codes, which includes: "knowing how to raise your voice", "knowing how to drink", "the city", "bars" and "bursts of laughter".

Those who follow the codes in one of these lists thus become either extroverted, loud and violent or withdrawn, quiet and cautious. The enactment of white femininity, which could also be expressed as the enactment of women's respectability (Skeggs 1998), is described as self-control and silence. Can Boel's account provide a nuanced perspective on these seemingly repressive feminine codes? Perhaps there is a variance between silences and states of self-control, where some women might in fact resist ideals of femininity, such as taking care of others, socialising and working? Illegal drug use and alcohol consumption are notorious ways to induce chaos and noise: sudden fits of laughter, a taste for loud music and impulsive behaviour. From Preciado's perspective, performing normative femininity seems to be about moving in the opposite direction, away from behaviours associated with drugs. Could an aversion to acting out and making noise even be a reason why women use fewer drugs than men?

However, not all drug use leads to extrovert behaviour, as we have seen throughout this book, as well as in the example given by Boel. Some substances are also known to help those who need to settle into a low-key existence, such as benzodiazepines (Metzl 2003). Preciado also gives examples of psychoactive substances in the femininity list, which consist of prescription anti-anxiety drugs and endogenous hormones (2013, p. 120; see also Ettorre 1992). The masculinity list, on the other hand, includes alcohol, Viagra and "speed", the last of which can be read as a synonym for street amphetamines and as a word depicting rapid movement. All three of these "masculine" substances are linked to agency and sex.

The behaviour of my interviewees occupies positions beyond these lists, but their calm and silent drug use is a consistent impression in the material. The silence is interrupted by laughter, as mentioned in Preciado's masculinity list, by conversation (Pernilla) and Thea's loud breathing when she comes out of the cinema. The most recent quotes, in this and the previous chapter, are about LSD, cocaine, MDMA and cannabis. The acting out that takes place appears to be very different from the violence and crime-ridden stories that appear in the media, books and films. I get the impression of an overlooked drug use that is neither seen nor heard, until it is told. But, as Boel's account shows, such passivity can be experienced as its opposite, as the acting-out of a rock star. The adventures occur mentally, inside the women's heads, which in turn are found in different locations—Bali, Lisbon, a cinema, somewhere where observation is possible. From there, the world unfolds.

As I have shown, contradictions, which Measham takes up as characterising drug use, have been a common (tangled) thread throughout the material. This also applies to stories about drug use, together with probable expectations of judgemental attitudes towards these stories, which complicates how they are presented. Swedish research on women's drug use has largely focused on women who have been positioned as sad, criminal and/or psychologically broken (Lander 2003; Rosengren 2003; Laanemets 2002; Lalander 2016), i.e. closely linked to the expression "mad, sad and bad". Therefore, I have not perceived that the change in research perspective described by Measham (2002), that I discussed in the introduction of this book, has yet occurred in Sweden. It might now be under way, as shown in Oriana Quaglietta's thesis in sociology, where pleasure and curiosity as motives for drug use are explored (2022). Through interviews with women who were not all gathered through institutions, but some through social media, Quaglietta provides a complex, yet more comprehensible picture of how drugs are used, in comparison with the previous repetitive stories of poor women's compulsive chronologies of a downward spiralling. The language of the academy was not developed to articulate working-class experiences (Skeggs 2004, 2011); thus, to understand drug use, middle-class interviewees can be key to deciphering the mysteries entailed in why someone would deliberately embark upon drug-use journeys. All anti-drug campaigns, policies and laws against drugs are seemingly directed against psychoactive substances. But as long as only certain groups of people are seen to represent the problem, drugs are sidetracked by these campaigns, policies and laws. Knowledge about drugs remains low and certain people, but not others, are targeted. Representations of drug use do not only have to do with class, however, but also with factors such as gender, race and age. Pernilla describes how she views herself (someone who uses drugs) in relation to the law and law enforcement:

> I feel like, in situations in which you've been out on the town and taken something, if you were stopped by the police, it really feels like… I just feel like it'd be easier for me to just, slip through the net, than for a man or a guy, depending on which age we're talking about. Like, it would have been easier for me to fly under the radar… the police are more likely to have an eye out for young men.

As a white, middle-class, forty-something woman, Pernilla does not regard herself as being on the police's radar when she is out on the town using drugs; she assumes that police officers will focus on young men instead. The idea of her as a person who uses drugs seems to be far removed from how people who use drugs are expected to appear. She comments on this by saying that a motive for her to participate in my study was to "crush stereotypes". What will happen to Swedish policies if such stereotypes are crushed? If a feminist perspective on drug policy was implemented? What would a campaign against drugs targeting middle-class women look like? Perhaps the work with such a campaign would lead to a revision and a nuancing of which drugs to target and why (cf. Edman 2019, and National Board of Health and Welfare 2022).

12.2 Psychoactive Effects

Wiklund and Damberg's book *As She Drank: Women, Alcohol and Liberation*[2] (2015), about women's drinking, highlights how women's intoxication in Sweden is not equivalent to men's. Wiklund and Damberg note that women do drink, despite being judged more harshly, and they show how alcohol can be a tool for liberation and pleasure, among other things. However, I perceive a need to deepen the scientific discussion on what alcohol, as well as illegal drugs, means and how psychoactive substances take their place in society and in people's bodies. Alcohol is hardly unproblematic, even when consumed on a gender-equal basis, but despite the problems associated with it, people who drink alcohol can experience intoxication as meaningful. These experiences do not disappear once they have passed, but remain as memories of intoxicating vantage points.

Madelene's comment that "[i]t would never have happened otherwise" in the previous chapter is made in connection with her reflection that drug use has led to some of the most enjoyable memories she has. The story is a sometimes chaotic, sometimes calm scenario that unfolds in a hotel room abroad where fun is mixed with horror, pain, sleep and a focus on work. In this case, what would not have happened otherwise is the absurd mixture of emotions, actions and experiences. In the midst of it, she created a computer programme that was disseminated throughout the world. To her, it is not strange that she programmes while intoxicated, it is just what she feels like doing when she uses cocaine. Merleau-Ponty's description of the dual belonging of the body in the world, of reciprocal insertion and intertwining of one in the other, has far-reaching implications through the extensions of the body that the computer represents. Where does it begin and end? Merleau-Ponty describes us as mixed up with the world (1968, pp. 137f.). This entanglement is affected in specific ways by drug use.

When the starting point, the body and where it is located, changes, the vantage point also changes. New directions become possible and others fade into the background. In my analysis, drug use is about precisely this:

---

[2] *Som hon drack* (2015).

how, for various reasons, the women's starting points have directed them towards drugs, and then in new directions under certain conditions, from drug-affected starting points.

People's starting points are affected in this way not only by illegal drugs, but also by pharmaceuticals and legal psychoactive substances, such as alcohol and coffee. The impact of psychoactive substances upon modern consumer societies is therefore difficult to overestimate. David T. Courtwright calls the economic interests behind the consumption of various addiction-related products "limbic capitalism" (2019, p. 6). This term brings into focus just how lucrative the market for mind-altering substances is. It is a market for what philosophers often claim is the goal of life: happiness, but also health, aesthetic experiences, alertness, well-being and sleep. Friends can become more entertaining, the desire to live can increase, self-confidence can grow to magnificent proportions, music can become better and monotonous work more bearable. From a perspective that focuses on the possibilities of drugs (and ignores the risks, stigma and illegality), it seems strange that anyone would turn them down. Above all, it is strange that people who experience major deficiencies in any of these areas say no, but, as we have seen through Skeggs' class analysis, these drug effects are in line with the compelling self-development demands of the middle class, while respectability is crucial for the working class (2004, pp. 135ff.). But the relationship of drug use to capitalism also highlights how vulnerability to addiction, the inability to stop using, relates to the socioeconomic conditions surrounding the body. The states of intoxication can lead, for example, to the creation of ingenious computer programmes or becoming trapped in cramped, repetitive spaces.

It is impossible to imagine what emotions, actions, experiences and directions would have been experienced and made possible without the enormous amounts of psychoactive substances that have been affecting people for many centuries, but increasingly so now. What would urban planning look like? Love life? The music industry? Academia? What research would have been conducted and how would healthcare have worked? We are not unaffected by drugs and the world is not drug-free (Buxton et al. 2020), not even in Sweden. On the contrary, it is steeped in intoxication and drug-induced disorientation and orientation throughout history in a way that means we would not be freed of their influence even if all drugs disappeared from the face of the earth right now, by magic. The directions that are indicated, based on our entanglement with the world, are thus drug-influenced regardless of what we take into our bodies. But the lines that are drawn are influenced not only by psychoactive drugs but also by the resources, capital, objects and bodies that are close by. Thus, when I asked Pernilla if she could tell me about an event that characterised drug use, she replied that, for her, drug use is not about doing crazy things:

> I'd done that kind of stuff anyway, or I've been to parties or raves, which last until the early morning, but I can also do it stone cold sober [...] those environments or situations and, fun stuff, I don't want to emphasise them as something I've been in because of the drugs, because I end up in them, anyway [...] it's not so much the external... environments that are different but rather my experience of them. [...] I don't take drugs because "yes, because then I'll freak out" and do a lot of crazy things, but because "then we'll... we'll relate to being in this situation together", and so on.

Pernilla thus says that "it would have happened anyway", to reverse Madelene's quote. The places and contexts that she seeks out would have been there, regardless of whether she used drugs or not. She follows the lines drawn in advance and does not deviate because of drugs. Instead, she explains that what is specific to her about drug use is a social experience of changing perspectives. She describes these experiences elsewhere in the same interview as experiences of intimacy, laughter, ethics and quietness in the form of "bubbles". The changes in how the world develops in relation to drugs are thus perhaps not so much about visible, drug-influenced acts but about a changed point of view and experiences of the extensions of the body. Pernilla's drug-use experience thus highlights a universal and collective concern that requires attention: How are people's starting points affected by psychoactive substances, what is made possible from there, and what is left behind?

References

Ahmed, Sara. 2006. *Queer Phenomenology: Orientations, Objects, Others.* Durham, NC: Duke University Press.

Ahmed, Sara. 2010. *The Promise of Happiness.* Durham, NC: Duke University Press.

Buxton, Julia, Lona Burger, and Giavana Margo. 2020. Introduction. In *The Impact of Global Drug Policy on Women: Shifting the Needle*, ed. Julia Buxton, Giavana Margo, and Lona Burger, 1–8. Bingley: Emerald Publishing.

Campbell, Nancy D. 2000. *Using Women: Gender, Drug Policy, and Social Justice.* Milton Park: Taylor & Francis.

Courtwright, David T. 2019. *The Age of Addiction: How Bad Habits Became Big Business.* Cambridge, MA: Harvard University Press.

Edman, Johan. 2019. Drogerna: Den nya berusningspolitiken [Drugs: The New Policy on Intoxication]. One of six booklets in the collection Det nya Sverige: Riksbankens Jubileumsfonds årsbok 2019, ed. Jenny Björkman and Patrik Hadenius. Göteborg and Stockholm: Makadam förlag.

Ettorre, Elizabeth. 1992. *Women and Substance Use.* Basingstoke: Macmillan.

Laanemets, Leili. 2002. Skapande av femininitet: Om kvinnor i missbrukarbehandling [The Creation of Femininity: About Women in Substance Abuse Treatment]. Diss., Lunds universitet, Lund.

Lalander, Philip. 2016. *Människor behöver människor: Att lyssna till de misstänkliggjorda* [People Need People: Listening to the One's Made Suspicious]. Stockholm: Liber.

Lander, Ingrid. 2003. *Den flygande maran: En studie om narkotikabrukande kvinnor i Stockholm* [The Flying Mara: A Study of Eight Drug-Using Women in Stockholm]. Diss., Stockholms universitet, Stockholm.

Measham, Fiona. 2002. "Doing Gender"—"Doing Drugs": Conceptualizing the Gendering of Drugs Cultures. *Contemporary Drug Problems* 29: 335–373.

Merleau-Ponty, Maurice. 1968. *The Visible and the Invisible: Followed by Working Notes.* Evanston, IL: Northwestern University Press.

Metzl, Jonathan. 2003. "Mother's Little Helper": The Crisis of Psychoanalysis and the Miltown Resolution. *Gender & History* 15 (2): 240–267.

National Board of Health and Welfare. 2022. *Dödsfall till följd av läkemedels- och narkotikaförgiftningar* [Deaths Due to Poisoning by Medicines and Narcotics]. Stockholm: Socialstyrelsen.

Preciado, Paul B. 2013. *Testo Junkie: Sex, Drugs and Biopolitics in the Pharmacopornographic Era.* New York, NY: Feminist Press.

Quaglietta, Oriana. 2022. In Her Words: Women's Accounts of Managing Drug-Related Risk, Pleasure, and Stigma in Sweden. Doctoral Thesis (monograph), Department of Sociology, Lund University.

Rosengren, Annette. 2003. *Mellan ilska och hopp: Om hemlöshet, droger och kvinnor* [Between Anger and Hope: On Homelessness, Drugs and Women]. Stockholm: Carlsson bokförlag.

Sandell, Kerstin, and Hanna Bornäs. 2017. Functioning Numbness Instead of Feelings as a Direction: Young Adults' Experiences of Antidepressant Use. *Sociology* 51 (3): 543–558.

Skeggs, Beverley. 1998. *Formations of Class & Gender*. London: Sage.

Skeggs, Beverley (2011). Imagining personhood differently: person value and autonomist working-class value practices. *The Sociological Review*, 59 (3).

Skeggs, Beverley. 2004. *Class, Self, Culture*. London: Routledge.

Tyler, Imogen. 2021. *Stigma: The Machinery of Inequality*. London: Zed Books.

Wiklund, Lisa, and Jenny Damberg. 2015. *Som hon drack: kvinnor, alkohol och frigörelse* [As She Drank: Women, Alcohol and Liberation]. Stockholm: Bokförlaget Atlas.

Wilk, Richard. 2014. Consumer Cultures Past, Present, and Future. In *Sustainable Consumption: Multi-disciplinary Perspectives in Honour of Professor Sir Partha Dasgupta*, ed. Alistair Ulph and Dale Southerton. Oxford: Oxford University Press. Oxford Scholarship Online.

Appendix: Drugs and Medicines

This chapter is intended to provide an overview of the objects included in this study, namely the drugs and medicines used by the participants. These preparations and substances are usually kept hidden by people who use them and the majority of these objects are unknown to most people. They therefore risk being interpreted as mysterious, through a filter of charged cultural beliefs. I have sought to avoid this and have therefore brought together different scientific descriptions of the drugs and medicines in this list.[1] Alcohol is omitted here even though it is a psychoactive substance that is often mentioned in the book, because the many alcoholic products are not hidden but, on the contrary, are visible and common.

In order to contextualise the objects and provide perspective on the perceptions surrounding them in the present, I have briefly outlined the history of each drug. Considering the controversial positions of various drugs in political debates, I have made trade-offs based on the purpose of this list and its comprehensiveness and have strived to reproduce information that I believe gives as accurate a scientific picture as possible. One

---

[1] The list is not complete, but includes all the drugs and medicines mentioned in the empirical chapters.

© The Editor(s) (if applicable) and The Author(s) 2024
E. Eleonorasdotter, *Women's Drug Use in Everyday Life*,
https://doi.org/10.1007/978-3-031-46057-9

aspect of drugs that I wanted to include for the purpose of demystification was their appearance, but such information is difficult to find in scientific texts. Therefore, for this type of data, I have used the police publication *Parent-school* (2020),[2] because I consider it reasonable to assume that the police testimony regarding the appearance of drugs is adequate, even though the data has not been reviewed as a scientific text.

A researcher who has strongly influenced the field of drug research is Norman E. Zinberg (1984), who showed how drugs are experienced differently and have different consequences depending on the mental state and expectations ("set") of the person who uses them, and the context in which the drug use takes place ("setting"). The effects of drugs are thus not only about their pharmacological properties. I see this as an important starting point, but it does not mean that the pharmacology of drugs is irrelevant. The interview material in this book indicates that the properties of drugs—as well as their cultural meanings, "set" and "setting"— are central to a drug-using experience. As the list shows, these characteristics are extremely varied, although the effects of psychoactive substances also vary greatly between individuals (Iversen 2012, Chapter 1, p. 11). Moreover, the effects are directly related to dosage and quality.

An important aspect that is often overlooked, according to Fiona Measham, is that illegal drugs are usually uncontrolled. This means that the drugs that people want to buy and use and subsequently are able to tell us about are named on the basis of what the person using the drug thought they had acquired (Measham 2017, 2019, p. 2). In reality, whole doses, such as tablets, may consist of completely different substances than what is stated (Measham 2017; see also Iversen 2012, chapter 8, p. 8).

---

[2] Föräldraskolan (2020).

Amphetamine, MDMA/Ecstasy and Amphetamine-Based Drugs

(One interviewee mentions the drug Elvanse [Lisdexamfetamine])

Appearance: Amphetamine is a white powder or white tablets. The powder can also be yellow, pink or grey (Police 2020, p. 9). MDMA/ ecstasy can consist of colourful tablets in various forms, white powder or crystals (ibid., p. 12). Elvanse is sold through pharmacies as colourful capsules (EMC 2023a).

Origin: Amphetamine was first synthesised in 1887, but its effects on the central nervous system were not discovered until the early 1930s (Fischman 2009a, p. 148). It quickly gained a number of uses: for example, to counteract fatigue, depression and pregnancy nausea and as a weight-loss drug (ibid.). During the 1940s and 1950s, amphetamine was used on a large scale in many parts of the world and was commonly used in the military (ibid.; Iversen 2012, Chapter 4).

In Sweden, there were around 200,000 people using amphetamine between 1942 and 1943, according to Sven-Åke Lindgren, which corresponds to 3% of the adult population (1993, p. 154). About 140,000 of these were estimated to be occasional users. The other 60,000 were estimated to use amphetamines with a frequency ranging from several times a year up to daily, of which the number of addicts was estimated at 200 people (ibid.). Use skyrocketed when the slimming drugs *Preludin* and *Ritalin*, then prescribed as antidepressants, were introduced in the late 1950s. By 1959, legal sales had risen to 33 million doses annually (Olsson 1994, p. 69). The above drugs were withdrawn from the market in 1965 and 1968, respectively, but in 1970 the number of people who were injecting and regarded dependent on amphetamine in Stockholm was estimated at 0.5% of the city's population (Rasmussen 2009, p. 157).

MDMA/ecstasy is an amphetamine derivative that was patented by the German pharmaceutical company Merck in 1914. It was initially not widely used, but in the late 1960s students began using the drug for its psychedelic effects (Iversen 2012, Chapter 8, p. 3).

Effects: In the case of amphetamines, use may lead to experiences of mood elevation, being able to stay awake and alert for longer, and monotonous tasks as easier to perform (Iversen 2012, Chapter 2, pp. 14f.). More specifically, elation, increased self-confidence, euphoric feelings and increased friendliness are reported as effects of amphetamines. A person who uses amphetamine may also perceive an improvement in performance, which has not been established through testing. The exception is cases where sleep deprivation is already present, when subjects are clearly positively affected compared to the control group (Fischman 2009a, pp. 151f.).

The effects of MDMA/ecstasy are somewhat different from those of other amphetamines. Like amphetamines, MDMA/ecstasy can induce euphoria, but psychological effects such as feelings of deep self-awareness and love for oneself and others are also typical (Iversen 2012, Chapter 8, p. 1).

Negative effects reported early on as a result of long-term use of high doses of amphetamine were psychoses with paranoid delusions (Rasmussen 2009, p. 156). Prolonged use can also cause jerky body movements (Police 2020, p. 9). Overdose can cause chest pain, loss of speech, coma, high fever and death (Iversen 2012, Chapter 7). The effects of smaller doses may include dry mouth, palpitations, headache, muscle weakness, disturbed sleep and reduced appetite (Iversen 2012).

Amphetamine usually does not cause physical withdrawal symptoms when use is halted, but can cause strong cravings and depression, especially after high intakes (Fischman 2009, p. 152).

The most common negative effects of MDMA/ecstasy are generally short term, according to Iversen. These may include rapid heart rate, jaw tension, loss of appetite, headaches and discomfort from bright light (2012, Chapter 8, p. 14). Body temperature may increase, which may pose health risks. However, Iversen argues that serious injuries and deaths are rare given the large amount of MDMA/ecstasy used (ibid., p. 15). Feelings of tiredness and depression are common after use, and it is unclear how long such effects may last (ibid., p. 17). Unlike amphetamines, MDMA/ecstasy does not appear to have a high addiction potential (ibid., pp. 15ff.).

Occurrence: According to chemist Leslie Iversen, the global illegal production of amphetamines is estimated at more than 500 tonnes per year (2012, chapter 1, p. 5). In Sweden, illegal amphetamine is a common drug (Lenke and Olsson 2002; Public Health Agency 2016). Amphetamine-based drugs are mainly prescribed to patients with a diagnosis of ADHD. MDMA/ecstasy is mainly used as a so-called club drug and in 2019 was estimated to account for 2% of the total drug market in Sweden (CAN 2020). In later years, studies on MDMA as a potential medication for psychiatric disorders such as post-traumatic stress disorder have spurred medical interest in the drug (e.g. Mitchell et al. 2021).

Possible ways of taking the drug: injection, sniffing, orally (Police 2020, p. 9).

Benzodiazepines

(One interviewee mentions Xanax and Klonopin)

Appearance: Tablets of various types. The police describe one often-seized kind of Xanax as "small blue" because these are small, light-blue tablets (Police 2020, p. 7).

Origin: Benzodiazepines first appeared on the market in 1955 under the name Miltown. They were developed by chemist Frank M. Berger, who was initially looking for an antibacterial substance that could work when penicillin was ineffective. When he discovered that mice became relaxed when he injected the substance mephenesin, he became interested in developing a drug that had such an effect. This interest led to the discovery of an even more potent compound, meprobamate, which is the basis for Miltown (named after his home town in New Jersey). The drug was a commercial success and was marketed as a miracle cure for worry and anxiety (Li 2006, p. 134). Later, a series of drugs with the same active ingredient, such as Valium (now deregistered in Sweden), were introduced.

Effects: Sedative and anti-anxiety. Together with opioids, benzodiazepines are the most common substance found in analyses of drug-related deaths, according to the National Board of Health and Welfare (2016). The Board's report states that the effects of high doses, which include respiratory depression and deep unconsciousness, can be life-threatening, especially when benzodiazepines are combined with opioids (p. 10). From another perspective, chemist Jie Jack Li writes in his book *Laughing Gas, Viagra and Lipitor: The Human Stories Behind the Drugs we Use* (2006) that benzodiazepines are remarkably safe drugs: "in fact, there is almost no known drug safer than benzodiazepines" (ibid., p. 135). The contradiction between these different sets of data highlights the difficulty of describing the potential dangers of a drug. Depending on the factors included in or excluded from an assessment, a substance may be considered safe or dangerous, curative or lethal. In the case of benzodiazepines, they are relatively difficult to overdose if no other drugs are taken at the same time (Ciraulo and Knapp 2009, p. 220). Furthermore, people without concurrent use or a history of problematic use of, for example, alcohol or opioids do not usually report experiences of euphoria. However, people who use benzodiazepines with such concurrent use of opioids and/or alcohol or historically problematic use do, and it is also primarily in such combinations that the drugs can be lethal (ibid., pp. 221f.). The very common side effects (of Xanax) include depression, dizziness, poor muscle control, impaired memory, speech difficulties, dizziness, headache, constipation and irritability (EMC 2023b).

Prevalence: Benzodiazepines are commonly used as medicines as well as street drugs. In 2017, 3.7 million tablets were seized by the Swedish police and benzodiazepines were more common than opioids (CAN 2019, p. 18).

Cannabis: Hashish, Marijuana and CBD Products

(One interviewee mentions CBD oil)

Cannabis sativa is a collective name for different parts of the cannabis plant. The resin from female plants, i.e. hashish, has been particularly well studied (Mills 2009, p. 277). Marijuana consists of the top leaves and flowers, also from female plants (Hollister 2009, p. 281). Cannabis contains a large number of cannabinoids. Tetrahydrocannabinol, THC, is the most important cannabinoid in terms of psychoactive effects (Hollister 2009, p. 281). The cannabinoid cannabidiol, CBD, has a similar chemical structure but does not produce a psychoactive effect (Lichtman 2009, p. 275).

Appearance: Hashish consists of lumps of brown or brown-black resin; marijuana is green flowers and leaves with five characteristic lobes (Police 2020, p. 10; Hollister 2009, p. 281).

Origin: Cannabis has been used for thousands of years in Africa and Asia for religious, recreational and medicinal purposes (Lichtman 2009, p. 275). Regulatory debates around the world have surrounded the use of cannabis in different ways throughout history (Mills 2009, p. 278). Cannabis was included in the International Opium Convention of 1925, but at that time it was used very little in Western countries (ibid., p. 279).

Prevalence: Cannabis spread in the USA and Europe during the twentieth century, and in the 1960s, it became a symbol of resistance culture (ibid., p. 279). It is now one of the most widespread and widely used drugs in the world (Hollister 2009, p. 280), including in Sweden (CAN 2019). Several countries have legalised the use of cannabis in the 2000s. For example, Canada and Uruguay have legalised use as such, while a large number of countries and states in the USA have legalised medical use. In Sweden, prohibitionism still has strong support (Månsson 2017). In December 2020, the United Nations changed the classification of cannabis so that the drug is no longer listed in the highest class. In the same month, the European Court of Justice ruled that CBD should not be classified as a narcotic drug.[3]

THC is used medically as an appetite stimulant for AIDS patients, to prevent nausea after chemotherapy and to reduce spasticity in patients with multiple sclerosis (Lichtman 2009, p. 275).

Effects of cannabis: THC can produce experiences of mild euphoria, intensified sensory experiences and increased appetite, among other effects. Negative effects may include increased heart rate, impaired short-term memory, and altered perception and time perception (Lichtman 2009, p. 275). Several studies show an increased risk of psychosis and schizophrenia (Allebeck 2007; Manrique-Garcia et al. 2012). However, when it comes to cannabis, particularly CBD, the research situation appears to be a battlefield. A large amount of research is underway, but different studies have produced contradictory or uncertain results.

---

[3] See "UN commission reclassifies cannabis, yet still considered harmful" at news.un.org, 2 December 2020, and "Cannabidiol (CBD) is not considered a 'narcotic drug' under European law" at emcdda.europa.eu, 16 December 2020.

A systematic analysis of empirical studies on the medical use of cannabis from the USA shows that patients commonly use it for pain, anxiety and depression (Kosiba et al. 2019). A high proportion of patients report that such use is helpful (ibid., p. 187), but these researchers point to ambiguities and question the reliability of a large proportion of the studies. As mentioned above, CBD does not produce a high, but is used medically for a number of conditions. In Sweden, CBD is approved as a drug for the treatment of epilepsy and multiple sclerosis (Läkemedelsverket 2020). In short, the state of research on the effects of cannabis is unclear, but, both as a recreational drug and as a medicine, it is used by many.

Possible ways of consuming these drugs: Cannabis can be eaten and smoked (Nyberg 2011, p. 170).

Cocaine and Crack Cocaine

Appearance: Cocaine is a white, crystalline powder. Crack can look like greyish-yellow lumps or flakes (Franck 2011, p. 184).

Origin: Cocaine is an alkaloid extracted from coca leaves, which grow on shrubs in tropical climates, mainly in the eastern Andes of South America. The historian David T. Courtwright writes that the earliest records of cocaine consumption date back to about 3000 BC, but that coca leaves were probably chewed much earlier (2002, p. 46). Coca leaves were shipped to Europe in small quantities by Spanish colonists as early as the sixteenth century, but they arrived in poor condition and did not attract any interest until 1860, when Albert Niemann in Göttingen wrote a paper on how to isolate cocaine from the leaves. In 1862, the Merck Company in Darmstadt started small-scale production, which was mainly sold to researchers (ibid.). Research interest later gained momentum due to the therapeutic properties of cocaine. It also began to be used as a local anaesthetic and Sigmund Freud, among others, was an enthusiast about its uses. It was tried as a treatment for a range of conditions, such as morphine addiction, impotence, alcoholism and indigestion (Karch 2009, p. 318; Freud and Byck 1974). Use skyrocketed and by the 1880s a variety of both pharmaceuticals and commercial products had been developed with cocaine in the ingredients list, such as drinks like Vin Mariani and Coca Cola (Courtwright 2002, pp. 46–48). As demand increased, coca leaves became scarce and cocaine began to be extracted locally in South America. Coca bushes were also planted in colonised Java, which quickly became a major producer. In 1912, Courtwright writes, 800 tonnes of coca leaves were produced in Java alone, and the largest producer was the Dutch Cocaine Factory, NCF, based in Amsterdam. The price went down from US$280 per ounce in 1885 to US$3 per ounce by 1914, making cocaine available to all classes of society. As a result, its use developed into what Courtwright calls a global epidemic (ibid., p. 50). An example of products from this time was Coca Bola chewing gum. Each stick of gum contained 710 milligrams of cocaine, equivalent to more than ten modern doses of cocaine or crack (Karch 2009, pp. 319f.). Coca leaves induce nausea if over-consumed, which discourages high consumption (ibid., p. 317). Cocaine, on the other hand, can be taken in much higher doses. Its use led to widespread addiction and poisoning, and thus, it began to be regulated, leading to a reduction in use. In the late 1960s, however, use began to pick up again in the USA (ibid., pp. 320f.), and by the 1980s, cocaine had become a popular but expensive drug for the rich—particularly in the USA, but also in some European countries such as the United Kingdom—and was written about in positive terms. In Sweden, however, writes Börje Olsson, cocaine had virtually ceased to be mentioned in medical journals during the 1960s (1994, pp. 37f., 125f.).

From 1986, crack began to spread in the USA. It has the same pharmacological properties as cocaine, but is smoked and thus produces a shorter and more intense high (Fischman 2009, p. 327). Cocaine is transformed into crack by adding ammonia or baking soda and water, after which it takes the form of a smokable rock. One gram of cocaine can be divided into 10–25 such rocks, making the price per rock relatively low, and therefore, crack is also used among economically underprivileged groups (Fischman 2009, pp. 423f.).

Effects: People who use cocaine/crack report experiences of euphoria, increased power, increased friendship and reduced fatigue, among other things. Repeated use can lead to impulsiveness and poor judgement

(Fischman 2009, p. 329). Major/long-term use can lead to anxiety, hallucinations, irritability, psychosis and various serious heart problems, such as stroke (ibid., p. 328).

Occurrence: Coca leaves are still used in the Andes where coca bushes have traditionally been grown, but are not associated with problems (Fischman 2009, p. 316). Cocaine is used medically as a local anaesthetic for surgery (ibid., p. 327). About ten tonnes are used annually for legal medical purposes. However, total production is around 1000 tonnes annually (2007) and the majority of the world's cocaine is thus used illegally (Karch 2009, p. 323). Especially in the USA, consumption remains high. In Sweden, consumption has recently risen sharply from low levels in the 2000s (CAN 2019, p. 16). In 2018, 0.9% of the population aged 17–84 reported using cocaine in the past year (ibid., p. 15).

Possible ways to ingest the drugs: Cocaine can be snorted, injected or rubbed against the mucous membranes. Crack is smoked or snorted (Franck 2011, p. 184).

LSD and Psilocybin

Appearance: LSD is one of the strongest known hallucinogens. A dose can consist of 10–300 micrograms. Therefore, LSD is usually mixed with liquid and dropped on paper (Freedman and Pechnick 2009, p. 374). Psilocybin is found in fungi. In Sweden, *Psilócybe semilanceáta* grow, for example, on pasture land. They are small in size and have a sticky cap (Ryman and Holmåsen 2006, p. 451).

Origin: LSD (lysergic acid diethylamide) was developed in the 1930s by chemist Albert Hofmann, who worked for the pharmaceutical company Sandoz in Basel, Switzerland. The substance was derived from a type of fungus, ergot, which grows on rye, but was not thought to have any interesting therapeutic properties. Nevertheless, Hofmann writes, he continued to take an interest in the substance (2019, pp. 18f.). Based only on a feeling that LSD could somehow be useful, he produced it again in 1943. He then began to feel dizzy and went home. In bed, with his eyes closed, he experienced an intense stream of colourful, kaleidoscopic images that went on for two hours. Without being sure that

LSD had actually caused the experience, he repeated the experiment, taking what he judged to be an extremely small amount, 0.25 milligrams, orally. This led to an overwhelming experience filled with anxiety. He lost control of himself and could neither write nor speak. His surroundings took on grotesque forms, people around him took on demonic shapes, and he had an out-of-body experience and mourned his imagined impending death. After a few hours, however, this state passed into experiences of happiness and beautiful, colourful hallucinations (ibid.).

Hofmann's description of his own intoxication can be seen in relation to the much-publicised LSD intoxications of the 1960s and 1970s in, for example, the hippie movement. On the one hand, advocates such as the psychologist Timothy Leary were convinced that LSD could reveal grand dimensions of human capabilities. On the other hand, many people panicked and ended up in psychiatric emergency rooms (Freedman and Pechnick 2009, p. 373). Hofmann himself was critical of Leary encouraging young people to use LSD and of Leary's own profligate use of the substance, which he felt had lost all connection with academic, potentially fruitful investigations (Hofmann 2019, pp. 61ff.).

The best-known psilocybin mushroom globally is the Mexican *Psilocybe mexicana*, which has a long history of being used in religious rites (Freedman and Pechnick, p. 308). In Sweden, the species *Psilócybe semilanceáta* grows (Ryman and Holmåsen 2006). These are classified as drugs.

After several decades of strict bans that basically prevented research, in the 2020s LSD has once again become a substance under investigation; for example, to alleviate anxiety in patients with life-threatening diseases (Liechti 2017) and to treat addiction (Kvam et al. 2018). All effects cease after three to four days if LSD is administered continuously (Freedman and Pechnick 2009, pp. 376f.). The substance is not associated with addiction and, despite being extremely potent, it is not toxic (Hofmann 2019, p. 53). However, LSD can lead to traumatic experiences and psychological difficulties, especially if the dose was high.

Effects: Feelings of happiness, insightfulness and closeness to others, colourful hallucinations, audiovisual synaesthesia, changes in the meaning of what is perceived, and enhanced emotions in relation to music, etc., have been reported (Liechti 2017, pp. 2116ff.).

Manic states and depression can occur and lead to life-threatening actions. In particular, high doses can lead to frightening visions, fear of death and fear of going mad (Hofmann 2019, p. 54). Within 10–24 hours after ingestion, various side effects have been reported, such as difficulty concentrating, headache, dizziness, lack of appetite, dry mouth, nausea, feelings of exhaustion, etc., which can last up to 72 hours (Liechti 2017, p. 2119).

Psilocybin produces similar effects to LSD, but milder (Freedman and Pechnick 2009, p. 307).

Prevalence: In Sweden, LSD is relatively uncommon, although police seizures of the drug have increased in recent years (CAN 2019, p. 17). EMCDDA states that overall use in Europe has been at a low, stable level for several years. In most countries, less than one percent of young adults, aged 15–34, report having used LSD during the past year (2019, p. 54). *Psilócybe semilanceáta* grow freely throughout the country, but I cannot find any data on how the use is spread.

Possible ways of ingesting the drugs: Both LSD and psilocybin mushrooms are usually ingested orally.

Opioids: Opium, Heroin, Morphine and Synthetic Opiates

(One interviewee mentions the painkiller Oxynorm)

Opioids are a group of substances with a morphine-like mechanism of action. The group includes opiates, which are based on alkaloids extracted from opium, as well as semi-synthetic and fully synthetic opioids (Pasternak 2009, p. 161).

Appearance: Opium may look like a brown, gum-like lump (Britannica 2017). Heroin is a white, greyish-white or brown powder or small stones (Police 2020, p. 13). Oxynorm is sold through pharmacies as capsules in different colours and as an oral solution (EMC 2022).

Origin: Opium is the plant juice of the poppy flower *Papaver somniferum*. The earliest indications of use date back 6000 years (Berridge 2013, p. 9). In particular, opium has been cultivated in Asia and the Balkans. It can be smoked, which has mainly been the tradition in East Asia (Berridge and Mars 2004, p. 749).

Opioids have made, and continue to make, a major impact around the world—politically, economically and in terms of health and disease. Twice, Britain launched wars against China, the so-called Opium Wars from 1839 to 1842 and from 1856 to 1858, in order to trade opium on the Chinese market. At the same time, Western governments wanted to restrict opium smoking at home (Schivelbusch 1993, p. 222). Historians Virginia Berridge and Sarah Mars write that opium smoking was not widespread in the West at the time. Efforts to restrict it, they argue, were more about the practice being considered foreign than about combating a problem. The practice of opium smoking, Berridge and Mars write, provoked the contemporary political preoccupation with social and racial purity (2004, p. 749).

Unlike smoking opium, various mixtures of opium, alcohol and water were common pharmacy products in colonial Europe (Olsson 1994, p. 43). They were used to treat a range of ailments, including as painkillers, cough suppressants and sedatives, for example under the name Laudanum (ibid., p. 179). Several preparations were specifically intended to calm young children. In Sweden, "rose poisoning drops", such as Tinctura dulcis Hartmanni, were used for this purpose (Olsson 1994, pp. 52f.). Historian Daniel Berg has tried to locate records that give a picture of the extent of medical opium use in Sweden before the 1923 regulations that banned non-prescription trade, but argues that the information he has found does not provide a complete picture. According to Berg (2016, p. 311), more than one tonne of opium per year was imported into Sweden during the years 1916–1920. Codeine and morphine are alkaloids derived from opium, and heroin is a semi-synthetic alkaloid, first produced in 1874 at St. Mary's Hospital in London by modifying morphine (Berridge and Mars 2004, p. 747).

In the USA and much of Europe, problems related to morphine and later heroin were already widespread at the beginning of the twentieth century (Schivelbusch 1993, p. 214). In Sweden, however, it was not until the 1970s that heroin seizure statistics increased (Lenke and Olsson 2002). Since the 1990s, heroin has been partially replaced by opioid drugs, which have become a more common cause of death (National Board of Health and Welfare 2016; CAN 2019, pp. 14f.).

Effects: Feelings of well-being, reduced anxiety and pain, cough suppressant and anti-anxiety effects, etc. (Pasternak 2009, p. 162; Olsson 1994, p. 44). If the use is repeated, the pleasant effects diminish (Martin 2009, p. 167). Very common side effects of Oxynorm include nausea, dizziness, constipation, itching and vomiting (EMC 2022), which is also consistent with other opioids. Respiratory depression is the most serious side effect and can lead to death (Martin 2009, p. 167). When frequent, repeated use ceases, the person who used opioids experiences withdrawal symptoms of varying degrees. The acute symptoms may include restlessness, chills, feelings of inefficiency, joint pain, muscle twitching and vomiting (Martin 2009, pp. 168f.). These subside after a few days or weeks depending on the substance. This may be followed by several weeks or months of prolonged withdrawal, which is somewhat similar to the acute phase. Individuals who previously used opioids frequently but stopped may again experience increased self-confidence, feelings of efficacy, euphoria and well-being if they return to using opioids (ibid.). Together, these effects mean that the drugs in this group are strongly associated with addiction.

Prevalence: Opioids are commonly used as painkillers and, through the long-acting drugs methadone and subutex, as treatment for opiate addiction. Just over 7% of the population of Sweden obtained prescription opioids in 2019 (see the National Board of Health and Welfare's statistics database at socialstyrelsen.se). As a street drug, opioid medicines are more common than heroin. In 2017, 3.7% of people aged 17–84 reported using non-prescribed opioid medicines, while only 0.2% reported using heroin. Among seized drugs, only benzodiazepines are more common (CAN 2019, p. 18).

Possible ways of taking the drugs: Opioids can be taken in many different ways depending on the substance, such as smoking, sniffing, injection or orally (Hoffman 2011, p. 201).

SSRIs and Tricyclic Antidepressants

(One interviewee mentions the tricyclic drug Clomipramine and another the SSRI drug Lustral [Sertraline])

Appearance: Tablets or capsules.

Origin: The most commonly prescribed antidepressants since 1988, when the drug Prozac was approved, are called SSRIs. The name means Selective Serotonin Reuptake Inhibitors. These replaced the tricyclic antidepressants (whose name refers to the appearance of the molecules, Li 2006, p. 146) developed in the 1950s. The older drugs have many side effects—such as sweating, low blood pressure and constipation—and are relatively easy to overdose (ibid., p. 149) which these newer drugs avoid to a certain extent. Both drugs work by inhibiting the reuptake of endogenous neurotransmitters, leading to an elevated level of these in the brain. The neurotransmitters that can be effective in depression include serotonin, noradrenaline and dopamine, and the selective reuptake inhibitors therefore mainly affect serotonin (ibid., p. 146).

Prozac, or fluoxetine as the active ingredient is known, was developed in the USA by chemists Bryan Molloy and David Wong by processing antihistamines. Subsequently, a number of other similar drugs have been developed and become sales successes, including Zoloft, which was worth $3.36 billion in 2003 (Li 2006, p. 149). Despite the lower number of side effects, there are still many side effects associated with this group of drugs, such as sleep disturbances, sexual dysfunction, nausea, dizziness and dry mouth (EMC 2023c), and they are no more effective against depression than the tricyclics (Li 2006, p. 149). They can also cause the life-threatening condition of serotonin syndrome. Children react differently from adults to the drugs and increased suicide rates have been reported among children as a result of SSRI medication, leading to precautionary measures being taken (ibid.). This also applies to young adults (see EMC 2023c).

Effects: In addition to the undesirable effects already mentioned, SSRIs are used to treat conditions such as anxiety, low mood and difficulty concentrating. These symptoms can be alleviated or resolved by treatment (Wallskär 2019). Treatment with SSRIs does not cause intoxication and does not lead to a "craving" for more medication (cf. Heilig

2015). They are therefore not described as addictive, although withdrawal, i.e. stopping the medication, can cause a number of unpleasant effects and take a long time (see EMC 2023c).

Prevalence: In Sweden, the use of SSRIs is common and consumption has increased throughout the 2000s. Use increased by 32% between 2010 and 2022. In 2022, SSRIs were used by about 9.4% of all women and 4.2% of all men (see the National Board of Health and Welfare's statistics database at socialstyrelsen.se). Consumption of antidepressants (of which SSRIs constitute a large proportion) is high in Sweden in international comparisons. In 2019, Sweden was ranked sixth in the world, with 97 daily doses of antidepressants per 1000 inhabitants (OECD 2019).

References

Allebeck, Peter. 2007. Cannabis och schizofreni: Finns ett orsakssamband? [Cannabis and Schizophrenia: Is There a Causal Link?] *Socialmedicinsk tidskrift* 84 (1): 27–31.

Berg, Daniel. 2016. *Giftets värde: Apotekarnas förståelse av opium i Sverige 1870–1925* [The Value of Poison: Pharmacists' Understanding of Opium in Sweden 1870–1925]. Göteborg and Stockholm: Makadam.

Berridge, Virginia. 2013. *Demons: Our Changing Attitudes to Alcohol, Tobacco & Drugs.* Oxford: Oxford University Press.

Berridge, Virginia, and Sarah Mars. 2004. History of Addictions. *Journal of Epidemiology and Community Health* 58 (9): 747–750.

Britannica. 2017. Opium. Britannica Academic, Encyclopædia Britannica. academic-eb-com.ludwig.lub.lu.se/levels/collegiate/article/opium/57209 [Online resource, accessed 2023-08-11].

CAN. 2019. *Drogutvecklingen i Sverige 2019 – med fokus på narkotika* [Drug Trends in Sweden in 2019—With a Focus on Narcotics] (Rapport 180). Stockholm: Centralförbundet för alkohol- och narkotikaupplysning.

CAN. 2020. *Narkotikaprisutvecklingen i Sverige 1988–2019* [Drug Price Development in Sweden 1988–2019] (Rapport 191). Stockholm: Centralförbundet för alkohol- och narkotikaupplysning.

Ciraulo, Domenic A., and Clifford Knapp. 2009. Benzodiazepines. In *Drugs, Alcohol & Addictive Behavior*, vol. 1, ed. Pamela Korsmeyer and Henry R. Kranzler, 217–223. Farmington Hills, MI: Gale.

Courtwright, David T. 2002. *Forces of Habit: Drugs and the Making of the Modern World*. Cambridge, MA: Harvard University Press.

EMC. 2022. *Oxynorm*. Healthcare Professionals (SmPC) leaflet. Last updated 06 May 2022.

EMC. 2023a. *Elvanse*. Healthcare Professionals (SmPC) leaflet. Last updated 22 May 2023.

EMC. 2023c. *Lustral*. Healthcare Professionals (SmPC) leaflet. Last updated 27 July 2023.

EMC. 2023b. *Xanax*. Healthcare Professionals (SmPC) leaflet. Last updated 28 July 2023.

EMCDDA. 2019. *Europeisk narkotikarapport: Trender och utveckling* [European Drug Report: Trends and Developments]. Luxemburg: Europeiska unionens publikationsbyrå.

Fischman, Marian W. 2009a. Amphetamine. In *Drugs, Alcohol & Addictive Behavior*, vol. 1, ed. Pamela Korsmeyer and Henry R. Kranzler, 148–153. Farmington Hills, MI: Gale.

Fischman, Marian W. 2009b. Coca Plant. In *Drugs, Alcohol & Addictive Behavior*, vol. 1, ed. Pamela Korsmeyer and Henry R. Kranzler, 315–316. Farmington Hills, MI: Gale.

Fischman, Marian W. 2009c. Cocaine. In *Drugs, Alcohol & Addictive Behavior*, vol. 1, ed. Pamela Korsmeyer and Henry R. Kranzler, 326–331. Farmington Hills, MI: Gale.

Fischman, Marian W. 2009d. Crack. In *Drugs, Alcohol & Addictive Behavior*, vol. 1, ed. Pamela Korsmeyer and Henry R. Kranzler, 423–424. Farmington Hills, MI: Gale.

Franck, Johan. 2011. Centralstimulantia [Central Nervous System Stimulants]. In *Beroendemedicin*, ed. Johan Franck and Ingrid Nylander. Lund: Studentlitteratur.

Freedman, Daniel X., and R.N. Pechnick. 2009. Lysergic Acid Diethylamide (LSD) and Psychedelics. In *Drugs, Alcohol & Addictive Behavior*, vol. 2, ed. Pamela Korsmeyer and Henry R. Kranzler, 372–378. Farmington Hills, MI: Gale.

Freud, Sigmund, and Robert Byck, eds. 1974. *Cocaine Papers by Sigmund Freud*. New York, NY: Stonehill.

Heilig, Markus. 2015. *Alkohol, droger och hjärnan: tro och vetande utifrån modern neurovetenskap*. Stockholm: Natur & Kultur.

Hoffman, Orsolya. 2011. Opiater och opioider. In *Beroendemedicin*, ed. Johan Franck and Ingrid Nylander. Lund: Studentlitteratur.

Hofmann, Albert. 2019. *LSD: My Problem Child and Insights/Outlooks*. Oxford: Beckley Foundation Press.

Hollister, Leo E. 2009. Cannabis Sativa. In *Drugs, Alcohol & Addictive Behavior*, vol. 1, ed. Pamela Korsmeyer and Henry R. Kranzler, 280–282. Farmington Hills, MI: Gale.

Iversen, Leslie. 2012. *Speed, Ecstasy, Ritalin: The Science of Amphetamines*. Oxford: Oxford University Press. Oxford Scholarship Online [ebook].

Karch, Steven B. 2009. Coca/Cocaine, International. In *Drugs, Alcohol & Addictive Behavior*, vol. 1, ed. Pamela Korsmeyer and Henry R. Kranzler, 317–324. Farmington Hills, MI: Gale.

Kosiba, Jesse D., Stephen A. Maisto, and Joseph W. Ditre. 2019. Patient-Reported Use of Medical Cannabis for Pain, Anxiety, and Depression Symptoms: Systematic Review and Meta-Analysis. *Social Science & Medicine* 233: 181–192.

Kvam, Tor-Morten, Lowan H. Stewart, and Ole A. Andreassen. 2018. Psykedeliske stoffer i behandling av angst, depresjon og avhengighet. *Tidsskriftet den Norske Legeforening* 138 (18): 1726–1731.

Läkemedelsverket. 2020. *Cannabidiol—CBD*. 28 February. Updated 8 June.

Lenke, Leif, and Börje Olsson. 2002. Swedish Drug Policy in the Twenty-First Century: A Policy Model Going Astray. *The Annals of the American Academy of Political and Social Science* 582: 64–79.

Li, Jie Jack. 2006. *Laughing Gas, Viagra and Lipitor: The Human Stories Behind the Drugs We Use*. Oxford: Oxford University Press.

Lichtman, Aron H. 2009. Cannabinoids. In *Drugs, Alcohol & Addictive Behavior*, vol. 1, ed. Pamela Korsmeyer and Henry R. Kranzler, 275–277. Farmington Hills, MI: Gale.

Liechti, Matthias E. 2017. Modern Clinical Research on LSD. *Neuropsychopharmacology* 42 (11): 2114–2127.

Lindgren, Sven-Åke. 1993. *Den hotfulla njutningen: att etablera drogbruk som samhällsproblem 1890–1970*. Stockholm: Brutus Östlings Bokförlag Symposion.

Manrique-Garcia, Edison, Stanley Zammit, Christina Dalman, Tomas Hemmingsson, Sven Andreasson, and Peter Allebeck. 2012. Cannabis, Schizophrenia and Other Non-affective Psychoses: 35 Years of Follow-Up of a Population-Based Cohort. *Psychological Medicine* 42 (6): 1321–1328.

Månsson, Josefin. 2017. *Cannabis Discourses in Contemporary Sweden: Continuity and Change*. Stockholm: Department of Social Work.

Martin, William R. 2009. Opioid Complications and Withdrawal. In *Drugs, Alcohol & Addictive Behavior*, vol. 3, ed. Pamela Korsmeyer and Henry R. Kranzler. Farmington Hills, MI: Gale.

Measham, Fiona. 2017. *Presentation, Parliamentary Drug Policy Symposium.* Wellington: New Zealand Drug Foundation. 5–6 July. [video] Published 17 August.

Measham, Fiona. 2019. Drug Safety Testing, Disposals and Dealing in an English Field: Exploring the Operational and Behavioural Outcomes of the UK's First Onsite "Drug Checking" Service. *International Journal of Drug Policy* 67: 102–107.

Mills, James. 2009. Cannabis, International Overview. In *Drugs, Alcohol & Addictive Behavior*, vol. 1, ed. Pamela Korsmeyer and Henry R. Kranzler, 277–280. Farmington Hills, MI: Gale.

Mitchell, Jennifer M., Michael Bogenschutz, Alia Lilienstein et al. 2021. MDMA-Assisted Therapy for severe PTSD: A Randomized, Double-Blind, Placebo-Controlled Phase 3 Study. *Nature Medicine* 27: 1025–1033.

National Board of Health and Welfare. 2016. *Narkotikarelaterade dödsfall: en analys av 2014 års dödsfall och utveckling av den officiella statistiken.* Stockholm: Socialstyrelsen.

Nyberg, Fred. 2011. Cannabis och cannabinoider. In *Beroendemedicin*, ed. Johan Franck and Ingrid Nylander. Lund: Studentlitteratur.

OECD. 2019. *Health at a Glance 2019*. Chapter 1. Figure 10.9. Anti-Depressant Drug Consumption, 2000 and 2017. Version 1. 3 November 2019.

Olsson, Börje. 1994. *Narkotikaproblemets bakgrund: Användning av och uppfattningar om narkotika inom svensk medicin 1839–1965* (CAN rapportserie, 39). Stockholm: CAN.

Pasternak, Gavril W. 2009. Opiates/Opioids. In *Drugs, Alcohol & Addictive Behavior*, vol. 3, ed. Pamela Korsmeyer and Henry R. Kranzler, 161–166. Farmington Hills, MI: Gale.

Police. 2020. *Föräldraskolan: Vad du som förälder behöver ha koll på när det gäller droger* [Parent School: What You Need to Know as a Parent When It Comes to Drugs]. Polisområde fyrbododal [Information Leaflet].

Public Health Agency. 2016. *Den svenska narkotikasituationen – en översikt över rapporteringen till EU:s narkotikabyrå* [The Swedish Drug Situation—An Overview of Reporting to the EU Drugs Agency]. Solna: Folkhälsomyndigheten.

Rasmussen, Nicolas. 2009. Amphetamine Epidemics, International. In *Drugs, Alcohol & Addictive Behavior*, vol. 1, ed. Pamela Korsmeyer and Henry R. Kranzler, 153–162. Farmington Hills, MI: Gale.

Ryman, Gunnar, and Ingmar Holmåsen. 2006. *Svampar: En fälthandbok* [Mushrooms: A Field Guide]. Stockholm: Interpublishing.

Schivelbusch, Wolfgang. 1993. *Tastes of Paradise: A Social History of Spices, Stimulants and Intoxicants*. New York, NY: Vintage Books.

Wallskär, Helene. 2019. SSRI hjälpte bättre mot ångest än mot depression [SSRIs Better at Treating Anxiety Than Depression]. *Läkemedelsvärlden*, 20 September.

Zinberg, Norman E. 1984. *Drug, Set, and Setting: The Basis for Controlled Intoxicant Use*. New Haven, CT: Yale University Press.

Index

© The Editor(s) (if applicable) and The Author(s) 2024
E. Eleonorasdotter, *Women's Drug Use in Everyday Life*,
https://doi.org/10.1007/978-3-031-46057-9